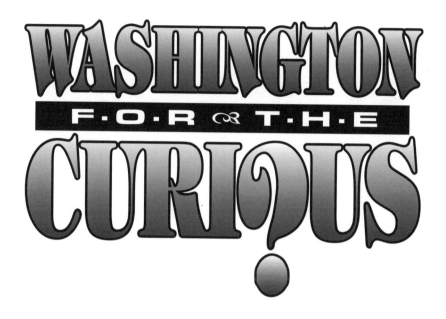

*A By-the-Highway Guide
to the Evergreen State*

by Rob McDonald
and Shawn Carkonen with Clarence Stilwill

Published by
The Curious Corporation
Mark Kashino - Clarence Stilwill

Distribution through
Peak Media, Inc
P.O. Box 925
418 North River Street
Hailey, ID 83333

Telephone: (208)788-4500
Fax: (209)788-5098
e-mail: peak@micron.net

Library of Congress Catalog Card Number 94-072411

Printing History: First published in 1996
ISBN #0-9639134-1-7
$21.95

10 9 8 7 6 5 4 3 2 1

Although the authors and publishers have tried to make
the information in this book as accurate as possible, they
accept no responsibility for any loss, injury or inconvenience
by any person using this book.

Printed in USA

Introduction

Prior to undertaking this project, we considered ourselves quite familiar with Washington, but thousands of miles later, after driving 186 highways and interstates — not to mention spending a disproportionate amount of hours aboard ferries in the Puget Sound and San Juan Islands (doing research, of course) — we now realize how little we actually knew about the state's incredible diversity and rich historical past.

The Evergreen State? Long stretches of U.S. Highway 101 and jaunts through the Willapa Hills or Mount Rainier National Park lend credence to the claim, but head east over the Cascades and suddenly the state's moniker will seem as appropriate as wearing a down parka to a Fourth of July Parade in the Tri-Cities. Highways that tour the tulip fields around Mount Vernon, the orchards of Wenatchee and Yakima, or the prolific Palouse wheat country prove Washington's agricultural richness. Travel to the coast to witness more variety as fishermen, beachcombers and surfers work and play along the rugged coastline, or spend time in downtown Seattle where aerospace engineers, computer programmers and university students stand in line for a cup of steaming espresso.

Written from an historical perspective and biased by our experiences on the road, *Washington for the Curious* is a compilation of our interpretations and observations of the state's past and present. We have attempted to describe how towns and cities have grown into what they are, or as in the case of Elberton on Highway 272, why they have disappeared. Read about Toppenish, a contraction of the Yakima Indian word *Xuupinish,* meaning "sloping hill," and learn how the city has rejuvenated itself by painting on the walls of its buildings.

The race to the elusive riches of the Klondike; the competitive strategies of the railways; and the tragic Indian wars of the 1850s, are a few of the episodes that have shaped our state and the people within it. Pick a highway and read about these events or plan a road trip that explores roads not previously traveled and be prepared to experience, as we did, your own sense of awe and wonder at this welcoming and truly wonderous state .

How Do I Get There From Here?

The book is organized by highway number and includes Interstates and all State and U.S. Highways. Roads are generally described south to north (Oregon to Canada) and west to east (Pacific to the interior). Branch roads that terminate are described from their origination to end regardless of direction taken.

Acknowledgments

Writers:
Rob McDonald
Shawn Carkonen
Clarence Stilwill

Editor:
Rob McDonald

Editor in Chief:
Clarence Stilwill

Creative Director:
Mark Kashino

Copy Editor:
Colleen Daly

Production:
Steve Sopkia
Tina LaVassar

Research:
Brad Popham
Brad Pearson
Amanda Angle

Marketing:
Brian Kotara
Michael Cord

Cover:
Design:
Mark Kashino

Photo:
Mt. Rainier
Courtesy of:
The National Parks Service

In a book with as wide a scope as *Washington for the Curious* it is difficult to properly recognize all who have contributed to its completion. The task is made even more challenging since a majority of the information obtained is the result of efforts of countless employees, volunteers, amateur historians and storytellers who work at Visitors Centers, Chamber of Commerces and Museums across the state. To these unsung heroes we give our gratitude. A special thank you is also extended to Cort Conley who paved the way with *Idaho for the Curious*.

This book would not be possible if not for the unwavering support, commitment to quality and friendship of the following individuals at Peak Media: Michael Cord, Mark Kashino, Brian Kotara, Tina LaVassar, Brad Pearson, Brad Popham and Steve Sopkia.

Also thank you to Bruce and Nancy McDonald, Paul and Paulette Carkonen, Bob and Carrie Crist, Jenise Carkonen, D.J. McDonald, Stacy Brown, Colleen Daly, Andrew Carras, Todd Sloan, Kevin Shapiro, Jamie Kripke, Aquila Kashino, Mariah Kashino, Michael Emerson, Dr. Jay Powell, Amanda Angle, Andrew McDougall, Bob White, Ted Borg, Harriet Fish, Carol Lichtenberg, Jim Quiring, Nick Hughes, Bea Raisanen, Mark Behler, Suzanne Lonn and Susan Gage Hageman.

In addition, county seat information and elevation and population statistics were obtained from the *1994 Washington State Yearbook*. The book is updated annually and is a great resource for local and state government. To obtain a copy contact Washington State Yearbook, Public Sector Information, Inc., PO Box 1422, Eugene, OR 97440-1422, Phone/FAX 503-689-0188.

Table of Contents

CB

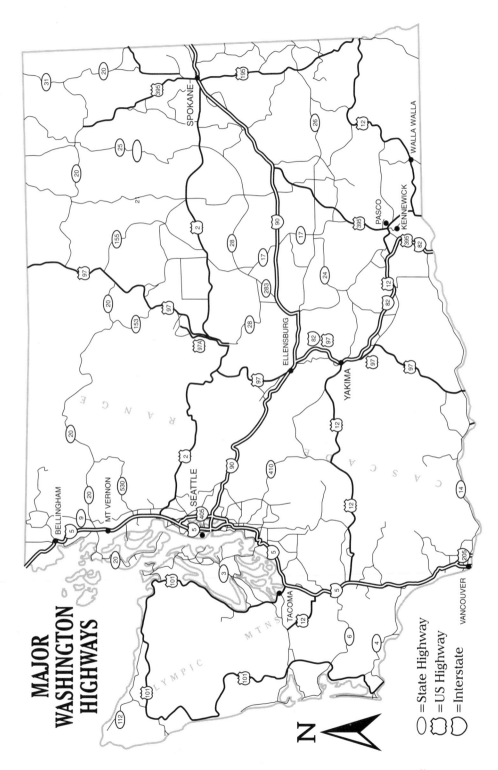

MAJOR WASHINGTON HIGHWAYS

○ = State Highway
⬡ = US Highway
▢ = Interstate

N

WASHINGTON HIGHWAYS
WEST OF THE CASCADES

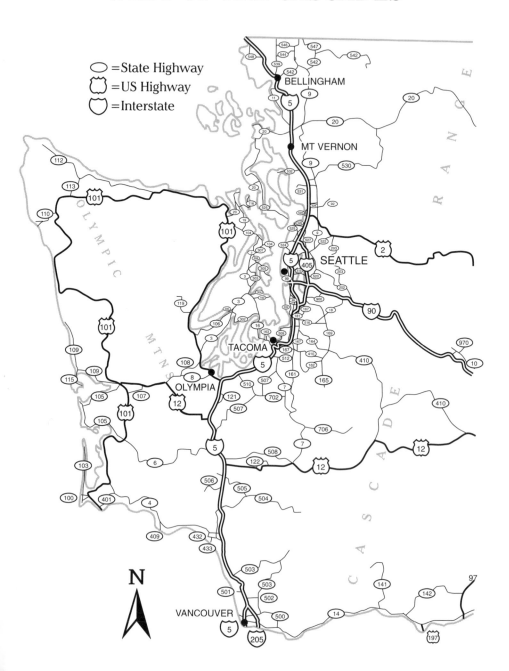

◯ =State Highway

⬡ =US Highway

🛡 =Interstate

N

WASHINGTON HIGHWAYS
EAST OF THE CASCADES

◯=State Highway   ⬭=US Highway   ⬭=Interstate

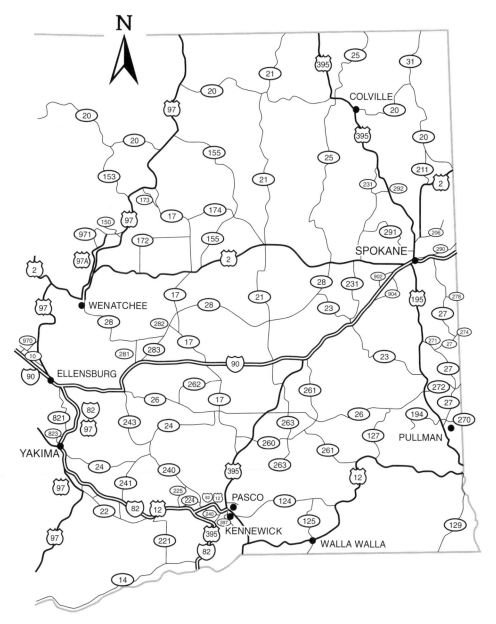

CLOSEUP OF I-5 CORRIDOR

◯=State Highway ⬡=US Highway ⬠=Interstate

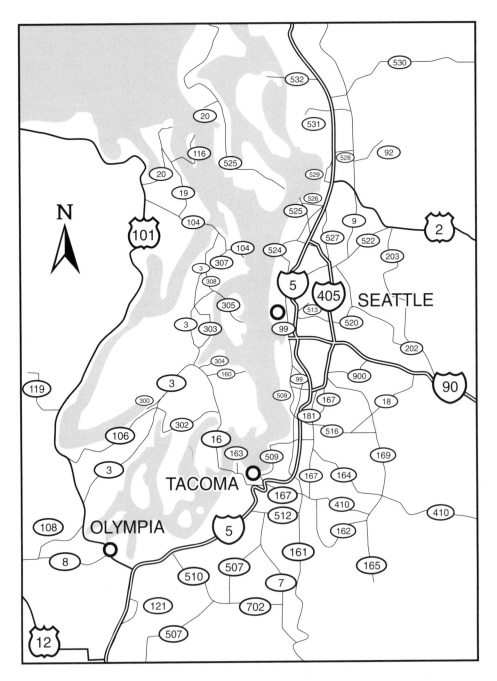

THE SAN JUAN ISLANDS

F = Ferry Landing

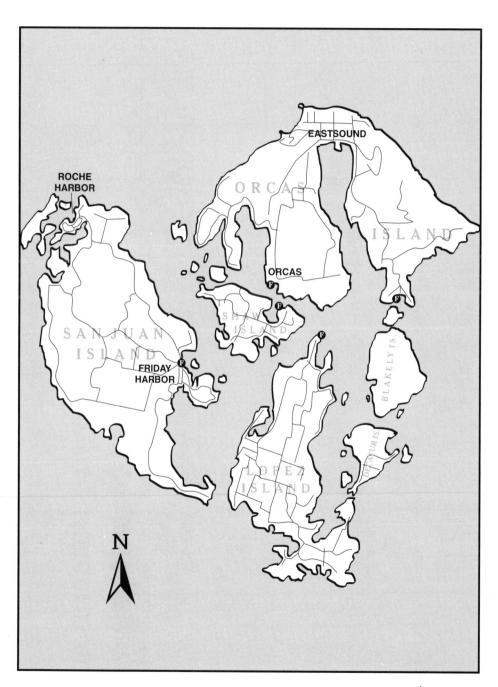

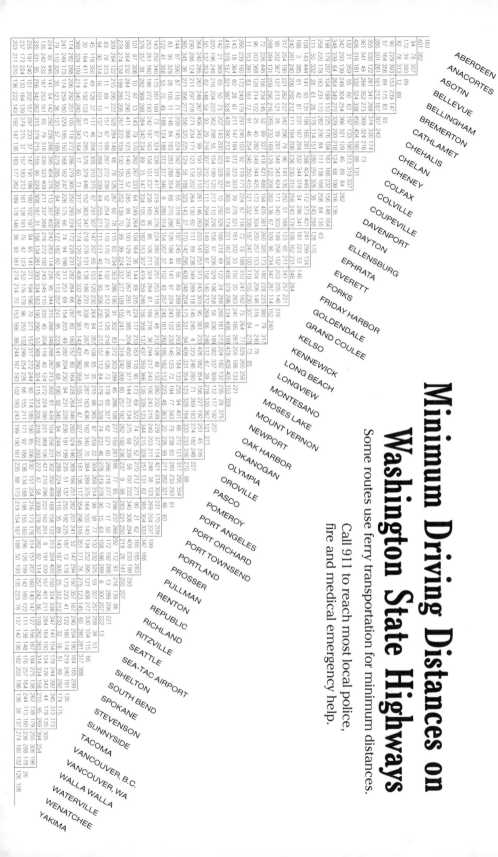

Minimum Driving Distances on Washington State Highways

Some routes use ferry transportation for minimum distances.

Call 911 to reach most local police, fire and medical emergency help.

US **Highway 2** from a junction with Interstate 5 in Everett, east via Snohomish, Monroe, Sultan, Gold Bar, Stevens Pass, Leavenworth and Cashmere, across the Columbia River at Wenatchee, north to Orondo, east through Waterville, Coulee City, Hartline, Almira, Wilbur, Creston, Davenport and Reardan to Spokane, then northeast to the Washington-Idaho border at Newport. (Overlaps U.S. Highway 97, Interstate 90, and U.S. Highway 395.) Route length: 323 miles.

Seven miles east of Everett, the inviting community of **Snohomish** (Elevation 26 to 220, Population 6,940) reclines at the confluence of the Snohomish and Pilchuck rivers. Its first resident and founder, E.C. Ferguson, staked a claim in 1857, threw up a prefabricated home and brought in goods to start a store. Hoping to capitalize on a proposed military road between Steilacoom and Bellingham, the enterprising Ferguson planned a ferry service across the Snohomish River.

Blackman Brothers Railway with wooden rails.

The road soon arrived, along with a bridge, thus rendering the ferry obsolete before it was even placed into service.

E.C. and another dreamer, one Ed Cady (the community was originally named Cadyville), turned their hands to roughing-in a trail over the Cascades to the new gold strikes on the Similkameen River north of Okanogan. When the trail was found to be impassable in winter and the mines never truly developed, that attempt to springboard their settlement failed also.

Undaunted, Ferguson settled down to saloon-keeping and politics, a well matched pair to pull any endeavor along. He succeeded in wrestling Snohomish County from what was then Island County, and in the process ended up holding most of the public appointments and titles. He wore many hats, including auditor, county commissioner, justice of the peace and probate judge. Of course, all official business was conducted from E.C.'s saloon, the "Blue Eagle."

Ferguson finally experienced his boom, or boomlet, around 1867 in the form of the burgeoning logging industry. When the innovative Blackman brothers built a mill in Snohomish in 1882, the town was finally put on the map. Farming, canneries and riverboat traffic all added to the town's prosperity.

1~

Today, the well-restored **Old Town** lends itself to a large trade in antiques that is a major contributor to the modern economy. Both small stores and large co-operative "emporiums" dot the town. And a good guess would be that a fair amount of business is still conducted in the saloons!

Further east, U.S. 2 edges through the small town of **Monroe** (Elevation 68, Population 5,120). Formerly a lumber shipping point on the Great Northern line and still the site of a state reformatory built in 1902, Monroe is fast becoming another bedroom community of the greater Seattle metropolitan area.

Up towards the Cascades, **Sultan** (Elevation 114, Population 2,395) was the site of promising placer strikes and vigorous mining attempts back in the mid-to-late 1800s that never really panned out. The town was named by miners to honor Tseul-tud, a chief of the Snohomish tribe. It boomed briefly as a construction camp for workers pounding survey stakes for the Great Northern Railroad over Stevens Pass in the 1890s. It has been claimed that the surrounding woods were so dense that the lamps had to be lit at three in the afternoon. At the height of its timber boom, colorful, high-spirited loggers in their "cork" boots and "stagged" high-water pants would hit town on payday, and the beer taps would flow like the surrounding rivers.

The little town of **Startup** is *not* named because you are starting to gain altitude into the mountains (although that's true), but for a mill manager, George G. Startup, who lived there when the Postal Service got tired of misdirecting mail between Wallace (the original name) and a town with the same name in Idaho. The first settler, F. M. Sparling, advertised for a bride in *Heart and Hand Magazine*, was answered by Eva Helmic of Ohio, and (supposedly) they lived happily ever after.

Head further east to the town of **Goldbar** (Elevation 169, Population 1,140). The name came from early miners following a placer strike, expressing more wishful thinking than reality. Goldbar's economy shares the history of most of these Western slope towns; easily summed up as mining, lumber, railroad construction and small farming. To access **Wallace Falls State Park**, turn left on First Street and follow the signs. At 265 feet, it is one of the highest and more spectacular waterfalls in the Cascades.

As you drive on, take a moment and turn into **Index**, one mile north of U.S. 2. Named for the jagged peak it sits under, this quaint community still has a **Red Men's Wigwam**, a fraternal hall built in 1903, and the **Bush House**, a hotel built by early residents to accommodate those doing business with the mines and railroads. The Sunset Mine that operated near here was known as a "man killer." A granite quarry and the inevitable sawmill were part of its early economic base.

Skykomish, or "Sky" as it is known locally, is next on U.S. 2. Hard to believe now, but it once housed over 8,000 people when the Cascade Tunnel was being built and logging was in its heyday. It later served as round-house for "helper" engines and a sub-station for the elec-trified section east

Bush House in the 1920s.

towards Appleyard. Skykomish is translated as "inland people."

Climbing out of Skykomish you will pass **Scenic**, the western portal of the Cascade Tunnel. Before Stevens Pass was open year-round, Scenic served as the snow-plow terminus. The hotel and spa were once a favorite among winter sports enthusiasts from both sides of the mountains, although those from the east had to ski down from the top across snow drifts to reach the entrance.

Above Scenic, the highway traverses **Stevens Pass** (Elevation 4,061), named for the Great Northern Survey engineer who chose this Northern Cascade route for the railroad. Now a popular ski resort, it also intersects the Pacific Crest Trail, once known as the Cascade Crest or the Skyline Trail before being incorporated into the National Scenic trail system.

From here you start your descent to the east, or the "dry side," of the Cascade Range. Towering peaks line the narrow Nason Creek drainage, as the road passes the east portal of the Cascade Tunnel at **Berne**. During construction of the first tunnel, the roaring camp of "Tunnel City" sprung up here. Famed for its saloons and dance halls (built without doors, since they never closed), one reporter from the *New York World* billed it as "the wickedest place in the world." The sinfulness ended in 1900 when fire flattened the camp, and now nothing but the mountain winds whisper of its former existence.

Leaving Berne, the road continues down to **Coles Corner** and a junction with State Highway 207, four miles from Wenatchee Lake. From Coles Corner, continue east to the entrance of **Tumwater Canyon**. This spectacular gorge between Icicle Ridge and Tumwater Mountain contains some of the wilder stretches of the Wenatchee River. In the spring, rock lilies bloom from crevices in the waterfall-polished rock; in autumn, the fall colors create a festival of their own.

Leavenworth's Bavarian Village and hills.

In 1950, a walk down **Leavenworth's** (Elevation 1,166, Population 1,825) Front Street would have revealed 24 empty store fronts, broken glass, rubble and citizens without much hope for the town's future. Ingenuity, luck and a million visitors a year has altered this picture. Fight through a horde of tour buses and RV's and immerse yourself in Leavenworth's Bavarian Village, set in the rugged North Cascades.

LIFE — Leavenworth Improvement For Everybody — formed in 1960. Ted Price, the head of the LIFE study, and Bob Rodgers bought Coles Corner (Squirrel Tree Inn) and remodeled the building in a Swiss Bavarian style, hoping that Bavarian architecture and Leavenworth's alpine setting would attract tourists to the town. The success of Solvang, a Danish community in Southern California, provided inspiration for the project. Initially, the town was divided as to whether the plan would work, but by the 1970s, after more Bavarian remodels and a German architect moved to town to help with the buildings' designs, tourists began streaming in.

Many factors led to Leavenworth's dilapidated state in the 1950s. Originally called Icicle, the gold mining town became a railroad town when the Great Northern Railroad appeared, replatted Icicle where Leavenworth is now located and named the town for Great Northern stockholder Charles Leavenworth. The future brightened as a sawmill was added and orchards were planted, but in the 1920s, Great Northern rerouted its tracks and the sawmill closed. The Great Depression arrived in the thirties and a short growing season never allowed for a fruitful crop.

Today, a description of the Bavarian Village is unnecessary and unjust, except to say that a visitor from Bavarian Germany would feel perfectly at home. In addition to the village, Leavenworth attracts tourists for its outdoor sports. Alpine peaks and the Wenatchee River provide mountain and rock climbing, skiing, rafting and fishing.

East of Leavenworth, a pipeline is visible along some stretches US 2 of Highway 2. The extensive irrigation system replaced 40 miles of open ditch and flumes built by the Icicle Canal Company in 1901. Before that, operators driving wagons mounted with wooden casks charged 25 cents to haul water from the Wenatchee River. Irrigation is essential; Chelan County only receives an average of nine inches of precipitation a year.

Orchards claim every available foot of valley land from Leavenworth to Cashmere, a distance of 11 miles. Along the way the road joins U.S. 97 and passes through **Peshastin** (peh-SHAS-tin), Indian for "broad bottom canyon," and **Dryden**, named for an eminent Canadian horticulturist who toured the area with James Hill, president of the Great Northern Railroad. Both towns exist solely to produce fruit. Take advantage of roadside fruit stands; the atmosphere is friendly and the fruit fresh and cheap.

"Tiny" the Cider King; his roadside fruit stand was the Northwest's largest.

When good Father Respari, **Cashmere's** (KASH-mir, Elevation 840, Population 2,585) first settler, started his mission along the Wenatchee River in 1863, he found his home to be a dry and dusty place. The snow-capped Cascade Mountains and the forest-covered foothills offered the promise of what could be, but transforming Cashmere into the cool, green oasis that it is today took generations of work and dedication. The solution was to transform Cashmere into "Tree City U.S.A." Besides orchards of apple, pears, cherries, peaches and apricots, the quaking aspen, a Russian olive or a Schewendler maple may be found along Cashmere's walking arboretum. Over 60 varieties of trees are seen on a one-hour walk through Cashmere's residential district (pick up a map at City Hall, 101 Woodring Street).

"And who has not heard of the Vale of Kashmir, With its roses, the brightest that ever gave?" Inspired by the words of Sir Thomas Moore, Judge James H. Chase suggested the name Cashmere when the town was incorporated on July 1, 1904. He believed the town's fertile valley setting emulated the beautiful Vale of Kashmir in India. Cashmere was originally known as *Old Mission* for early Catholic missions established by Oblate Fathers in the 1850s and by the Jesuits in 1873.

Pioneer Village is an authentic representation of a post Civil War Western community. Among the 21 buildings featured are a blacksmith shop, post office, doctor and dentist offices, saloon, hotel, homestead log cabins and an 1891 waterwheel, all set outside the **Chelan County Historical Museum** (Cottage Avenue). The museum contains Willis Carey's comprehensive collection of Indian artifacts and pioneer relics that date back 9,000 years. The collection is ranked among the top five in the nation.

Cashmere is also known for *Aplets & Cotlets,* a popular Pacific Northwest candy. Armen Tertsagian and Mark Balaban came to America to escape Turkish persecution in Armenia. The two young men became friends in Seattle but found the gray, wet winters difficult and so moved to eastern Washington. On the far side of Stevens Pass, nestled at the foot of the Cascade Mountains, they discovered a valley carpeted with fruit orchards. Struck by its resemblance to the old country — dry, rolling hills and an abundance of water and sunshine — the men bought an apple farm and named it "Liberty Orchards" in honor of their new homeland.

The men formed a business known as Northwest Evaporating and provided dehydrated food, especially apples, to the boys in Europe during World War I. Dehydrating extended the shelf life of food and saved local growers from dumping excess fruit in the river. Mark and Armen decided that the surplus of apples could also be used to make *Rahat Locum,* a popular candy they enjoyed as children. After some slight variations in the recipe, an apple and walnut candy known as Aplets was born. The fruit and nut confection was first sold at picnics and local fruit stands. Excited by the candy's success, Armen began traveling throughout the Northwest, selling the "Confection of the Fairies." Eventually people were sending boxes of the candy to faraway relatives as gifts from Washington and an extensive mail-order business began.

Aplets & Cotlets (apricots are used instead of apples) are Cashmere's answer to Seattle's Frangos, a chocolate delicacy made famous by upscale retail store Frederick & Nelson, once based in Seattle. If planning to buy Aplets & Cotlets or Frangos for friends or relatives in the state, consider which side of the Cascades they live on; regional loyalty can be fierce. Tours are available at the **Candy Kitchen** at Liberty Orchards (117 Mission Street).

Monitor lies between Cashmere and Wenatchee. The name commemorates the Civil War victory of the Union's iron-clad *Monitor* over the Confederate's armor-plated *Merrimac.*

At the confluence of the Wenatchee and Columbia Rivers, U.S. 2 and 97 head north. **Wenatchee** (Elevation 700, Population 23,000) is reached by way of State Highway 285. Wenatchee's history of success in the apple industry has earned it the title of "Apple Capital of the World." Although its southern neighbor, Yakima, produces more apples, the yield per acre in Wenatchee is higher than anywhere else in the world. High, treeless, yellow-brown hills surround the town, located almost exactly in the center of the state. The city's name is an adaptation of the Indian word *wenatchi,* meaning "river flowing from canyon." Depending on the season, the orchards are pink with blossom, green or bare.

Although 110 million bushels of Washington apples are now hand-picked by 50,000 workers during a six-week period each year (that's an average of nine apples per worker, per minute, for 42 straight 10-hour days) — enough apples to reach to the moon and halfway back if stacked side-by-side — the humble origins of the industry go back to the first orchards planted around Hudson's Bay Company forts in the early 1800s. Within two decades, perceptive settlers had noticed that the area's rich, lava-ash soil, plentiful sunshine, and cool nights created perfect growing conditions. They also noticed that apple trees planted along stream banks were healthier and more vigorous,

Spraying an orchard in the early 1930s. Only the tractor has an air filter.

prompting the pioneers to devote much effort and expense into developing irrigation systems.

The first exported apples went to California in 1849, when the boom associated with the gold rush created a strong demand for fresh produce. Today, millions of boxes reach destinations as far away as the Middle East and Pacific Rim.

The Red Delicious, America's favorite snacking apple, can trace its heritage directly back to one rogue seedling growing between rows in an Iowa orchard in the late 1800s. Mowed down three times, the tree just kept coming back. Finally, the owner decided to let the never-say-die sapling grow and, much to his surprise, ended up with one of the most widely praised apple varieties in history. Other popular (and profitable) varieties of Washington apples include: the winesap, the Rome beauty, the golden delicious, the criterion, the Granny Smith, the gala or royal gala, and the Newtown pippin.

Everyone is familiar with the old saw, "An apple a day keeps the doctor away," but few people realize that there is scientific documentation to back up that claim. Each apple contains five grams of water-soluble fiber (one-quarter of the recommended daily level), which has been proved successful in lowering blood cholesterol levels; 170 milligrams of potassium, a mineral that helps regulate the body's fluid balance as well as neuromuscular activity; yet has no sodium, no cholesterol, and virtually no fat — all in an 80-calorie package. Although not scientifically proven, many people claim that eating apples regularly can even reduce headaches.

Our ancestors thought a lot of the health properties of apples, as well. In England, it was believed that rubbing apple slices on one's warts would make them disappear. Early American colonists, fearing contaminated drinking water, solved the problem by drinking apple cider with every meal.

Growing apples is more labor-intensive than most people realize. The winter months are taken up with pruning and spraying for parasitic codling moths (whose larvae are those unpleasant "worms" that show up in the fruit of wild trees). Once April arrives and the trees have flowered, growers are busy protecting their trees from early frosts, as well as renting bee hives to help with pollination. A second round of spraying occurs in May, to help control insects, bacteria, and fungi, after which the trees are thinned to insure that the tree's energy goes to produce only the most select fruit. Irrigation is the name of the game all summer and by August another round of spraying speeds the ripening process while increasing sugar production.

Picking occupies September and October, while November is spent cleaning the orchard, baiting for mice, planting replacement trees, and spraying weeds. And December and January mean pruning time again.

At the end of each summer, producers must also decide what portion of the crop is going to be sold fresh and what portion kept in controlled-atmosphere storage. So-called CA storage involves keeping the bushels of apples in large, chilly (32-35 degrees), air-tight rooms in which the oxygen has been reduced from 21 percent to 2 percent, thereby retarding the ripening process. But without these advances in long-term storage, Washington apples wouldn't be the year-round treat they've come to be. The **Washington State Apple Commission Visitor Center** (2900 Euclid Avenue) provides a look at the state's largest agricultural industry.

Every spring, when a tidal wave of pink blossoms permeates the air of the town with its sweet fragrance, Wenatchee holds the

Washington State Apple Blossom Festival. This traditional Pacific Northwest event started in 1919 and includes the Queen's Pageant, an arts and crafts fair, parades and thousands of apple-crunching Washingtonians.

When trader David Thompson brought his cedar bateau to this area in 1811, he found old pithouse structures and a village of mat lodges. It is estimated that humans occupied the area up to 12,000 years ago. Excavations have uncovered Clovis points, a type of spear-head used by bison and mammoth hunters over 10,000 years ago.

In 1860 missionaries came, but the first permanent white settlers were Frank and David Freer and Samuel Miller. They took over operations in 1871 of a trading post whose previous owners were selling whiskey illegally to the Indians. The men had left the packtrain business in Walla Walla and come to Wenatchee for a new start. The post is preserved at the Chelan County Museum in Cashmere.

The next year, German immigrant Philip Miller (no relation to Samuel Miller), the "Johnny Appleseed of Wenatchee," brought the first apple trees to the valley from Walla Walla nurseries. Apparently, his apple crop was successful but he had trouble selling the fruit because there were no roads or railroads, and rapids restricted ships on the Columbia River. Miller's solution was to dig a hole on his property, which he used for making apple brandy. The brandy solved his marketing problems and made him a popular neighbor.

Significant growth did not occur until the Great Northern Railroad arrived in October of 1892. A population of 300 celebrated Wenatchee's link to the rest of the world. The town continued to grow but the problem of irrigating the land remained.

Small scale irrigation projects proved to newcomers that the volcanic soil was fertile and the sunny climate perfect for growing but they knew the lack of precipitation necessitated an extensive irrigation system. Until the construction of the **Highline Canal** in 1903, most of Wenatchee remained a desert. The canal was an extension of a smaller canal and stretched from one mile north of Dryden to Sunny-slope and then across the Wenatchee River by pipeline using a method called the inverted siphon, a technique long employed by plumbers.

Highline Canal being constructed across the Wenatchee River in 1904.

9~

The pipe takes water from an open trench, dips down 228 feet, raises the water and delivers it into an open trench again. The pipe is visible just west of the Wenatchee Avenue Bridge. In 1908, the Washington Bridge Company built a bridge across the Columbia River at Wenatchee. The bridge allowed for pedestrian and vehicular traffic and carried a pipeline that irrigated 4,000 acres in East Wenatchee. The bridge is now a bicycle and pedestrian crossing.

After exiting Highway 2, drive one mile through Wenatchee's unattractive commercial sprawl to **Riverfront Park** (between Fifth and Ninth streets along the Columbia River). Designed by Frank Lloyd Wright, the park offers miles of trails and athletic facilities. Enjoy a picnic and the Columbia's cool breezes on a hot Washington day.

The **North Central Washington Museum** (127 South Mission Street) is one of the most impressive museums in Washington. The region's historical society is extremely informed and the museum well maintained. Exhibits include a variety of local pioneer and Native American items, including petroglyphs from the Columbia River; an operating Great Northern Railroad diorama; a comprehensive Apple and Fruit Industry Exhibit, complete with actual apple sorting equipment; and the Clyde E. Pangborn Exhibit, which pays tribute to the aviation pioneer. The building occupies the former federal building, built in 1917; its annex was constructed in 1937 and once held the post office.

Despite the proliferation and importance of apples in the area, Wenatchee has contributed more to the world than the shiny Red Delicious. Overshadowed by Charles Lindbergh's Atlantic crossing, a little-known fact is that **Clyde Pangborn** and **Hugh Herndon** piloted the first nonstop flight across the Pacific Ocean, departing from Misawa, Japan on October 6, 1931 and landing in Wenatchee 41 hours later.

*Hugh Herndon, Jr., left; Clyde E. Pangborn, right.
First non-stop trans-Pacific flight in 1931.*

The trans-Pacific flight had a certain Kamikaze element to it. *Miss Veedol* was designed to hold 5,600 pounds but held an actual weight of 9,000 pounds. Excessive drag forced the pilots to drop their landing gear in the ocean, making a belly landing in Wenatchee necessary. There was no life raft, oxygen or radio aboard. Planes passing overhead were rare in those days and apparently Pangborn and Herndon's caught the attention of a short wave radio operator. He sent a message to the telephone company who relayed to a radio station that the plane was heading towards Wenatchee. By the time the aircraft arrived at the sandy airstrip, a crowd of people had gathered to see the rough landing.

Shortly before the plane's departure from Misawa, a young Japanese boy pushed through a crowd of onlookers and pulled out four red apples from his pant and jacket pockets and one from under his cap and presented them to the pilots. This act of goodwill was reciprocated about three months later when the mayor of Wenatchee sent a box of apples to Japan. At the time a problem with insect infestation in America prohibited sending fresh fruit so the customs inspectors sent the package back. Again three months passed and the mayor sent another package but this time the box contained five apple tree cuttings wrapped in moss and this letter:

> We, the people of Wenatchee, cannot forget the kindness you showed towards the two flyers Pangborn and Herndon. They told us again and again of your hospitality, especially about the five apples they received from a local boy.
>
> Our town is one of America's famous apple-growing areas. We sent you Richard Delicious apples that we recently improved as a token of our gratitude, but they were returned. So we mailed cuttings from that type of apple tree instead. They will surely pass through customs. Please take this token of our thanks and graft them onto your apple trees.

Three years after grafting the cuttings the native trees bore fruit. The new apple variety spread throughout Japan and today the country produces great quantities of Richard Delicious apples.

Another Wenatchee contribution was the passing of a national minimum wage law. Although legislation had been passed stating that woman and children could not be employed at wages that were below subsistence, employers generally paid whatever they wanted. This was especially true after the U.S. Supreme Court decision in *Adkins vs. Children's Hospital*, that a women's minimum wage was unconstitutional because it violated the freedom of contract.

At the end of a stint as a chambermaid for a Wenatchee hotel, **Elsie Parrish** presented a bill for $216.19, the amount the hotel owed her had they properly paid her, and claimed the hotel needed to "make things right." The hotel offered her $17 but Elsie said no and eventually the case was presented to the Supreme Court. The court was headed by the "Four Horsemen," a conservative group known for turning down many of President Franklin D. Roosevelt's New Deal programs. Surprisingly, the court overturned its previous ruling and decided that minimum wage laws were constitutional.

The court's decision had more repercussions than the legality of a minimum wage. Though not considered one of the "Four Horsemen," Justice Owen Roberts straddled the fence on many issues but usually voted with the "Horsemen" and against the liberal justices of the court. His swing vote accounted for many conservative five-to-four decisions. After the Parrish decision, the power of the "Four Horsemen" was gone.

The court went on to extend the minimum wage law to all workers, not just women and children. It then passed the Wagoner Labor Act, the right to collective bargaining, and after that, the Social Security Act. Elsie Parrish, a woman who has been long neglected by history, set the wheel in motion.

Chelan County: Wenatchee is the county seat of Chelan County, which was formed in 1899 from parts of Okanogan and Kittitas counties. The county is located in the north central part of the state and stretches from the eastern crest of the Cascade Mountains to the south-flowing Columbia River on the east. Fur traders first visited the county in 1811. Later, Catholic missionaries established themselves in the Wenatchee Valley. The development of the county in the nineteenth century was closely linked to the Northern Pacific and Great Northern railroads. In 1903, the construction of the Highline Canal opened up 20,000 acres of land for agricultural development in the Wenatchee Valley. Today the county is a major apple growing center while the wood products industry, mining and tourism also contribute to its economy.

Court House: Washington and Orondo Streets, Wenatchee 98801, SCAN 748-5215 (Commissioners), FAX 509-664-5246. Area: 2,925.8 square miles. State Ranking: 3rd. 1993 Population: 56,000. Unincorporated: 24,975. Incorporated: 31,025. Density: 19.1 persons per square mile. **Cities and Towns**: Cashmere, Chelan, Entiat, Leavenworth, Wenatchee. **Principal Economic Activities**: Agriculture, aluminum manufacturing, wood products, food processing. **Points of Interest**: Rocky Reach Dam, Lake Chelan, Site of Camp Chelan, Old Mining Arrastra, Ohme Gardens, Lake Wenatchee.

Climate: (Wenatchee - elevation 700)

	Jan	Apr	Jul	Oct
Max Temp. F°	32.9	65.2	87.4	63.1
Min Temp.	19.5	39.2	59.4	39.0
Mean Temp.	26.2	52.2	73.4	51.1
Precipitation	1.16"	.47"	.11"	.73"

Average Annual Maximum Temperature: 61.8
Average Annual Minimum Temperature: 39.5
Annual Mean Temperature: 50.6
Average Annual Precipitation: 9.00"

North of Wenatchee, U.S 2 and 97 cross the Columbia River and continue north on the east bank. Alternate Route 97 travels the west bank in the same direction.

Drive 12 miles through orchard-carpeted river terraces to **Orondo**. Founder J.B. Smith named the community for the chief of an ancient people who mined for copper in the Lake Superior region. Legend claims that the mythical miners escaped from Atlantis just prior to its sinking by way of an isthmus connected to North America.

Orondo's central location at the base of the Columbia Plateau and on the shores of the Columbia River made it an important transportation center. In 1902, an aerial tramway carried wheat from Waterville to Orondo, 1,700 feet below. A steamboat at Orondo then shipped the wheat to a railhead at Coulee City. This replaced the strenuous and time-consuming method of hauling the wheat the entire way by stagecoach. The tram became obsolete when tracks from the Great Northern reached the plateau. In 1914, a railroad on the west side of the Columbia made river travel unnecessary.

U.S. 97 continues north and U.S. 2 turns east entering picturesque Pine Canyon, also known as Corbaley Canyon. The road gains 2,000 feet in altitude in a short distance. Hairpin turns are cut into the steep, rocky slopes, covered with sage and yellow pine. The drive heightens one's respect for plateau farmers traveling to the river by horse to deliver grain and pick up supplies.

The change in scenery on top of the plateau is dramatic; as the terrain levels, basalt immediately succumbs to wheat. Like the pervasive orchards encircling Wenatchee, no fertile land is wasted. Ten miles

Historic downtown Waterville.

from Orondo, aficionados of early 1900s architecture should stop at historic **Waterville** (Elevation 2,600, Population 1,055); the entire downtown is listed as a National Historic District. Owners of the building on the corner of Chelan and Locust considered the construction of the block "the beginning of making our city compact and substantial." They agreed upon a uniform style, scale and material (brick), setting the tone for the entire downtown. The building holds the First National Bank, the Kincade Shops and the IOOF Block, the oldest fraternal organization in Douglas County.

In 1883, a bill creating the County of Douglas was approved by the governor of Washington. The town of Okanogan, once located about five miles east of Waterville, was platted for the sole purpose of becoming the county seat. It consisted of one tent and one inhabitant named Walter Mann. The problem with Okanogan, besides its scarce population, was that it was bone dry. A 285-foot well was dug but no water was found. Meanwhile, A.T. Greene, whose ambition in life was to someday own a town, moved from Davenport and located an extremely prosperous well.

A townsite was platted in 1886 and named for the excellent water drawn from the 30-foot well. Founding a town realized Greene's first dream, but success expanded his horizons. At a Democratic Convention held in Okanogan that year, supporters of Waterville made their first attempt to capture the county seat from their dry neighbors. They brought a barrel of water from Waterville showing that their vaunted water was a reality. A year later, Waterville was declared the new county seat and by 1892, the population was nearly 500.

"The Nifty" building in Waterville.

The two-story brick and stone county courthouse was built in 1905 and is topped by an impressive Queen Anne cupola. The original Douglas County courthouse, constructed by Greene at a cost of $3,000 and donated to the county for an affordable $1, was destroyed by fire.

Douglas County: Waterville is the county seat of Douglas County, which was created in 1883 and was once part of Lincoln County. It was named after Stephen A. Douglas. Situated in the north central portion of the state, it is bounded on the east by the spectacular Grand Coulee. Groups of settlers first entered the county in 1871 and by 1883 the lure of plentiful land for cattle raising brought ranchers into the county. The late 1880s were punctuated by range wars between cattlemen and sheep raisers. The disastrous winter of 1889-90 decimated the cattle herds and brought about a shift in the economy to grain raising. Today, agriculture still remains the county's main economic activity. Wheat and barley are primary crops with fruit production growing in importance.

Court House: 213 South Rainier, Waterville 98858, FAX 509-884-9401. Area: 1,839.3 square miles. State Ranking: 17th. 1993 Population: 28,500. Unincorporated: 20,702. Incorporated: 7,798. Density: 15.5 persons per square mile. **Cities and Towns**: Bridgeport, Coulee Dam (part), East Wenatchee, Mansfield, Rock Island, Waterville. **Principal Economic Activities**: Agriculture, metal industries. **Points of Interest**: Rocky Reach Dam, Rock Island Dam, Wells Dam, Chief Joseph Dam, Grand Coulee Dam, Banks Lake.

Climate: (Waterville- elevation 2,605)

	Jan	Apr	Jul	Oct
Max Temp. F°	29.7	57.4	80.8	58.4
Min Temp.	14.7	34.6	52.5	36.5
Mean Temp.	22.2	46.0	66.6	47.4
Precipitation	1.35"	.68"	.22"	.88"

Average Annual Maximum Temperature: 55.7
Average Annual Minimum Temperature: 34.5
Annual Mean Temperature: 45.1
Average Annual Precipitation: 11.57"

US 2

Waterville is a peaceful farming community with panoramic views. To the south of Waterville lies Badger Mountain (Elevation 4,000). The snow-capped Cascades fill the western skies and immediately east are miles of grain fields. Further away to the east are the rugged mountains of the Okanogan Valley. From Waterville the highway stretches across the vast Columbia Plateau farmland, occasionally diving into a deep canyon or coulee.

U.S. 2 crosses **Moses Coulee** about 12 miles west of Coulee City. Picture the deep channel filled to the top with raging ice-age floods. The water chiseled the gorge and left behind layers of basalt, stacked like logs. On the west end of the coulee, the highway crosses the north end of a giant gravel bar about 300 feet deep. The flat, sage-filled valley offered Chief Moses and his band protection from the cold, winter winds.

The Moses Coulee cuts a lengthy swath through the Columbia Plateau.

For a scenic side-trip, take Jameson Road north seven miles to **Jameson Lake**. The road rolls through Moses Coulee beneath crumbling basalt cliffs and arid sage fields. There are two campsites on the lake's west bank, which provide access to some of the state's best trout fishing (the public is already aware of this fact, and therefore, no secret has been revealed here).

After climbing out of Moses Coulee, notice the large boulders scattered randomly throughout the fields. Distributed by glaciers, the "haystack rocks" break the monotony a farmer faces while plowing his field.

Coulee City (KOO-lee, Elevation 1,585, Population 622), 40 miles from Waterville, divides Upper and Lower Grand Coulee. Both regions offer many attractions: Dry Falls; the Lake Lenore Caves; Soap Lake;

and Sun Lakes State Park (featuring an interpretive center of the area) are reached by way of State Highway 17. Banks Lake fills Upper Grand Coulee and is accessible via State Highway 155, which also leads to Grand Coulee Dam.

Guy Waring, in *My Pioneer Past* offers this fond recollection of Coulee City: "the branch train arrived too late for the stage which took you to Bridgeport on the Columbia River. Train and stage were scheduled to miss each other, and were invariably faithful to schedule. Had they connected the hotel would have died. So one waited in Coulee City till next day." His words make a stay in Coulee City sound like a prison term but local folk would disagree claiming that Coulee City is "the friendliest town in the West."

Once a junction point for railroad and stage travel, Coulee City attracted cattlemen who stayed and fed their herds on the miles of bunchgrass. Farmers eventually gobbled up the land, replacing the native grass with wheat, beans and potatoes and using Northern Pacific's lines to reach western markets. The tall grain elevators seen here are a familiar site in the small towns along this highway.

Until the Northern Pacific line was built, there was little reason to come to the area; economically it was not feasible. The railroad changed that, actively promoting settlement by distributing thousands of elaborate, multi-colored brochures in English, German, Russian, Norwegian and other languages. They ran specials, hauling immigrant families and their possessions at reduced rates. A pioneer scanning the passing countryside through his train window might find a bit of land resembling his homeland and decide to start a life there. The result are the small towns that line the tracks today.

Hartline (Elevation 1,911, Population 180) is the next such small town, 10 miles to the east. When the community of Parnell was by-passed by Northern Pacific, it packed its bags and replatted four miles south next to the railway. The new property was owned by John Hartline, hence the name.

Almira (al-MEYE-ruh, Elevation 1958, Population 316) is eight miles down the road. This wheat-shipping point was named for Almira Davis, wife of the area's first merchant and landowner. Originally called *Davisine,* Charles C. Davis sold his property to two men who wanted to establish a townsite. When Mrs. Davis signed the land deed the buyers noticed her name and applied it to the new town.

Leaving Almira, U.S. 2 follows an area eroded by the Spokane floods. The soil has been scrubbed away leaving scabrous fields of basalt and largely unproductive land.

Samuel Wilbur Condon (or Condit) came to the area in 1875 and engaged in several vocations typical of a frontiersman: stock raising, trading, freighting, and ferrying. Seeing the possibilities of the Canadian gold rush, Condon established a ferry and toll road into the Okanogan country claiming that his was the "Safest, Surest, Nearest and Best Route to and from Salmon River Mines, Conconully, Ruby City and Wannacut Lake."

While freighting supplies to the Okanogan, Condon shot into what he thought was a flock of Canadian geese. Instead he hit a Canadian priest's flock of tame gander, killing a poor honker and earning the nickname "Wild Goose Bill." The trading post he operated was sometimes called Goosetown but presently goes by **Wilbur** (Elevation 2,280, Population 875), Samuel's middle name and ten miles from Almira. Today, Wilbur is a farm-supply town, 14 miles south of the Columbia River. Every third week of May, Wilbur celebrates *Wild Goose Bill Days*, a typical small town celebration.

Eight miles further, **Creston** (Elevation 2,440, Population 255) lies in the heart of Big Bend Country, a large region south and east of the Columbia River where the water makes a swooping turn from west to south and southeast. Railroad officials named the town for the crest of a nearby butte, which represents the highest point on the Columbia Plateau at 2,462 feet.

Creston is a quiet, unassuming town with a notorious past. Occasional warfare between cattlemen and early settlers was common. Homesteaders would plant survey stakes into the ground, marking their claims. In retaliation, ranchers would rip out the stakes or drive cattle through settlers' property, often resulting in violent disputes.

Contributing to Creston's dubious notoriety was the fact that one of Washington's most celebrated outlaws, **Harry Tracy**, met his bloody end there on August 5, 1902.

Often compared to the infamous John Dillinger, the equally elusive Tracy proved to be an on-going nightmare for law enforcement officials in both Oregon

HARRY TRACY

Harry Tracy composite drawing.
Note the likeness to the photo on the following page.

and Washington. Although he was a cold-hearted murderer who personally accounted for the death of at least 20 men in his 27 years of life, a certain fascination about this contradictory character has grown since his death.

Born Harry Severns in 1875, Tracy had shot his first man (in Billings, Montana) by the time he was 18. Shortly thereafter, while a gambler in the rough-and-tumble mining town of Cripple Creek, Colorado, he killed a man who had insulted his girlfriend. Harry was subsequently apprehended by the local sheriff, but began what was to be one of his trademarks by escaping from jail two weeks later.

The reprobate spent some time hanging out with others of his ilk in Wyoming's Hole-in-the-Wall country. Eventually caught by a vigilante group, Harry narrowly escaped being hanged, prompting one of his captors to quip that it was a shame Tracy hadn't died of "an acute attack of suspended animation."

Harry eventually ran afoul of the law in Utah. Thrown into the Utah State Penitentiary, he managed a daring escape by whittling a gun out of wood, meticulously covering it with tinfoil to simulate the appearance of steel, then forcing a guard to relinquish his rifle and clothes before affecting his escape.

Bertillon-type photo of Harry Tracy.

After a bloody escape from the Salem, Oregon Penitentiary in June of 1902, which left three guards dead, Tracy and an accomplice, Dave Merrill, became the subjects of what was to be one of the largest manhunts in the Northwest. The escapees immediately outwitted the patrols in pursuit by hiding in a culvert in the woods just outside the prison walls, where they waited until dark — when the search parties had long since passed — to steal away. After "borrowing" a horse and buggy from a traveler in Salem, and being spotted by one of the posses, Tracy and Merrill managed to elude capture again by heading across a rough field. Just before he disappeared from sight, Tracy turned and doffed his cap, much to the chagrin of his slightly-out-of-range followers.

Contributing to Tracy's mystique was the fact that he inexplicably showed kindness to some of his hostages in the midst of this wild and woolly run. After forcing one farm wife at gunpoint to feed his cohort and him breakfast, he proceeded to help her milk the family cow. The two outlaws then enjoyed a glass of fresh milk, threatened the bewildered woman, and left.

Soon after Tracy and Merrill crossed the Columbia into Washington, Harry lightened his load. He confronted Merrill with the fact that he no longer trusted him, and challenged him to a "gentlemanly" duel to settle the matter. The two men were to stand back to back, walk ten paces, then turn and fire. At eight paces Harry spun and fired, later claiming that Merrill was in the process of doing the same — and, in any case, proving the old adage, "There is no honor among thieves." When Merrill's body was later found stashed behind a log, there were three bullet holes in his back.

After a series of close encounters with his pursuers, Tracy's final stand occurred at an out-of-the-way farm owned by the Eddy family, situated down in a small coulee near the town of Creston. As was his quirky custom, Harry was helping his captives hang a barn door when he noticed movement along the rim of the coulee. Sensing he was surrounded, he snapped off a quick shot in that direction and ducked into a field of tall, ripe grain. Police Commissioner Maurice Smith and a posse of local citizens began firing at any movement they noticed in the field. As the sun began to sink, they heard a muffled gunshot from the field. After slowly working their way into the area, they found that Harry Tracy had committed suicide by shooting himself in the eye. One of Smith's 30-30 slugs had broken Tracy's leg, severing an artery at the same time. Contemplating bleeding to death or capture, Harry chose to go out on his own terms, thus ending one of the most deadly and bizarre criminal careers in the history of the region.

Twenty miles further, the rocky soil succumbs to Palouse loess at **Davenport** (Elevation 2,450, Population 1,540), where "wheat is king." Davenport is the county seat of Lincoln County and the largest town on the Columbia Plateau. In the late 1800s, Davenport and Sprague contended for the county seat. In 1884, an election resulted in more votes being cast than the total population of the two towns. Tactics included enlisting children and people on passing trains to vote. Tombstone names were pirated from cemeteries.

Sensing that an election loss was imminent, Davenport posted guards around the courthouse to protect the results but when the guards tired, Sprague procured the records. Sprague won the election because of its ability to import voters by train while Davenport had to transport its outside vote by horseback.

Another election was held in 1896 and this time Davenport won. It was given the county seat and a block of land 215' by 250' where the **Lincoln County Courthouse** now stands (Fourth and Logan). Built of brick and limestone in a Classic Revival style, the courthouse holds a commanding position above Main Street, shaded by maple trees.

Prior to the invasion of white men, this area was one of the most popular Indian trails in eastern Washington. Up to 300 Indians at a time would camp by the springs beneath abundant cottonwood trees where Davenport is now located. Fur traders frequently traversed the area. David Douglas, the Scotch botanist after whom the Douglas fir is named, roamed *Cottonwood Springs* in 1826 and was known by

Lincoln County Courthouse built in a Classic Revival style.

local tribes as the Grass Man. Samuel Parker of Ithaca, New York, a missionary explorer, passed through in 1836 and Charles Wilkes' government expedition came in 1841.

A combination saloon and store was opened by John Harker in 1880. That same year, construction began on Fort Spokane, a U.S. Army outpost 23 miles north, bringing huge wagon trains full of supplies through Cottonwood Springs. With the army came the need to supply food to the soldiers, thus more farms were established. Businesses were opened to meet the demands of farmers and Cottonwood Springs began to grow.

A rival village closer to the Central Washington Railway line (a branch of Northern Pacific) was started by a group of businessmen and J.C. Davenport, a state legislator. In 1881 a fire destroyed the fledgling town but rather than rebuild the businessmen returned to the original site. A year later, people accepted the name of Davenport in honor of their friend and the town's major businessman.

Davenport's old residential district, on the hill south of Main Street, reveals several prominent homes. The 1899 McInnis house (1001 Morgan Street), a Queen Anne towered villa; the 1886 Hoople house, with its jigsawed front porch; and the Benson home (Sinclair and Sixth), fronted by tall colonnades, are just a few of the many interesting and charming homes in the neighborhood.

The **Lincoln County Historical Museum** (Seventh and Park) displays pioneer artifacts and an extensive history of Davenport and the county.

Lincoln County: Davenport is the county seat of Lincoln County, which was organized in 1883 and was once part of Spokane County. It is named after President Abraham Lincoln. It is located in the northeastern part of the state. It was first settled by former miners and government freighters who followed a spring on the trail to Walla Walla. In 1880, Fort Spokane was established on the northern edge of the county to protect the settlers from the Indians. Today the county is one of the major wheat growing areas of the state and the nation. Also of importance are cattle raising and barley and oat production.

Court House: 450 Logan Street, Davenport 99122, FAX 509-725-0820. Area: 2,305.5 square miles. State Ranking: 8th. 1993 Population: 9,200. Unincorporated: 3,822. Incorporated: 5,378. Density: 4.0 persons per square mile. **Cities and Towns**: Almira, Creston, Davenport, Harrington, Odessa, Reardan, Sprague, Wilbur. **Principal Economic Activities**: Agriculture, food products, mining. **Points of Interest**: Fort Spokane, Grand Coulee Dam, Roosevelt Lake.

Climate: (Davenport - elevation 2,450)

	Jan	Apr	Jul	Oct
Max Temp. F°	30.5	59.4	84.4	59.4
Min Temp.	18.1	34.0	50.4	35.8
Mean Temp.	24.3	46.7	67.4	47.6
Precipitation	2.11"	1.07"	.53"	1.42"

Average Annual Maximum Temperature: 57.6
Average Annual Minimum Temperature: 34.8
Annual Mean Temperature: 46.2
Average Annual Precipitation: 16.72"

The highway continues its cross-state journey 13 miles to **Reardan** (Elevation 1,630, Population 497), marked by a high-steepled church. Enterprising settlers hoping to land a Northern Pacific depot dug a well to prove to the railroad that water was available. Previous names included Capp's Place and Fairweather for early settlers of the same name. The town was named for a civil engineer on the Central Washington Railway.

Pine forests break the scenery and notify the traveler that Spokane is close. **Fairchild Air Base**, 12 miles from Spokane, was chosen over other cities in western Washington as the state's air base for several reasons. The War Department preferred Spokane's weather conditions, but more importantly a mountain range (the Cascades) and its position 300 miles inland served as natural barriers against a possible Japanese attack. Tours are available with advance reservations and show parts of the base and the B-52 and KC-135 aircraft. (Take Dover Road south 100 yards to the base entrance.)

On the north side of Dover Road is a plaque commemorating the Battle of Spokane Plains. The battle took place on September 5, 1858, and resulted in a decisive victory by Colonel George Wright's U.S. troops over the combined force of Coeur d'Alene, Spokane and Palouse Indian tribes. After the battle, which proved to be a turning point of the Indian Wars of the 1850s, Wright declared:

> I have met you in two bloody battles; you have been badly whipped... I have a large force, and you Spokanes, Coeur d'Alenes, Palouses and Pend O'Reilles may unite, and I can defeat you as badly as before... You must come to me with your arms, your women and children, and everything you have, and lay them at my feet; you must put your faith in me and trust in my mercy. If you do this I shall then dictate the terms upon which I will grant you peace. If you do not do this, war will be made on you this year and next, until your nation shall be exterminated.

The road joins U.S. 395 and I-90 at Spokane, travels briefly north with 395 to the city's outskirts and continues solo north and northeast into Pend Oreille County. The country between Spokane and Newport on Highway 2 is mostly mixed lodgepole pine forests and open farmland. The terrain is fairly gentle, interrupted occasionally by a small farm.

Diamond Lake, one mile long and covering 1,000 acres, sits in a shallow depression on a high plateau. The spring-fed lake was named by a party of hunters who found an ace of diamonds in the adjacent forest.

Squatting on the Washington-Idaho border in 1889, **Newport** (Elevation 2,100, Population 1,755), 41 miles northeast of Spokane, started life in Idaho on the east bank of the Pend Oreille River. When the Great Northern Railroad laid tracks past the old post office and set up a depot three blocks west, officially "Newport, Idaho moved 3,175 feet to Newport, Washington." The Idaho part of town is today called "Old Town."

A mining and lumber town, Newport owes much of its growth history to the coming and crossing of railroads built to ship ore and timber out of the area. At one time, the Washington legislature looked into constructing a "gravity flow" system of low dams to increase the size of Idaho's Flathead and Pend Oreille Lakes with a dam near Newport controlling a release of water through a network of natural lakes, siphons, tunnels and canals 130 miles long, turning the surrounding counties into productive farmland. Instead, the idea came to fruition with the Grand Coulee Dam.

Pend Oreille County: Newport is the county seat of Pend Oreille County, which was formed from Stevens County in 1911. It is named after an Indian tribe of the area and pronounced "pon-der-ray". The county is located in the far northeastern corner of the state and borders Canada to the north and Idaho on the east. It was first visited by Europeans in 1809 when David Thompson of the North-west Company passed through the county. The famous missionary, Father De Smet, was also active in the area. During the mid-nineteenth century, gold was discovered along the Pend Oreille River bringing in the first settlers. Steamboats brought the settlers supplies until 1909 when the first railroad arrived. Today the majority of the county is made up of national forest land. Its major economic activities are logging, agriculture, mining and tourism.

Court House: 625 West Fourth, Newport 99156, FAX 509-447-5890. Area: 1,402 square miles. State Ranking: 25th. 1993 Population: 10,100. Unincorporated: 7,185. Incorporated: 2,915. Density: 7.2 persons per square mile. **Cities and Towns**: Cusick, Ione, Metaline, Metaline Falls, Newport. **Principal Economic Activities**: Wood products, agriculture, mining. **Points of Interest**: Boundary Dam, Gardner Caves, Manresa Grotto.

Climate: (Newport - elevation 2,135)

	Jan	Apr	Jul	Oct
Max Temp. F°	31.4	60.0	86.0	59.0
Min Temp.	17.3	30.4	44.7	32.5
Mean Temp.	24.0	45.2	65.4	45.8
Precipitation	3.50"	1.71"	.61"	2.76"

Average Annual Maximum Temperature: 58.4
Average Annual Minimum Temperature: 31.3
Annual Mean Temperature: 44.9
Average Annual Precipitation: 27.16" ❧

State **Highway 3** from a junction with U.S. Highway 101 northeast through Shelton, Allyn, Belfair and Gorst to Bremerton, then north through Silverdale to a junction with State Highway 104. Route length: 60 miles.

Rarely does a viewpoint provide so much insight into a town's makeup as does the one found on Highway 3 overlooking **Shelton** (Elevation 12, Population 7,396). Facilities for the giant Simpson Logging Company comprise a good portion of town, extending from the shores of Oakland Harbor to Shelton's commercial district. Trains fastened with

Forest Festival parade on Main Street.

23~

giant metal prongs used to secure timber roll to and from the waterfront mills. Shelton has been called "Home of the Evergreen Forest" and "Christmastown USA" for the 2 million Christmas trees harvested here each year. The local high school's mascot is the Climbers.

The town's first settler, David Shelton, was a man of many talents. Part-time politician (he helped organize county boundaries and change the county name from Sawamish to Mason), gold prospector, fur trapper and farmer, Shelton also possessed a keen sense for real estate; upon arriving in 1853, he chose a prime spread of land that would later attract droves of settlers for its fertile and convenient location.

Years of successful logging endeavors, and for a while a thriving oyster industry, has given Shelton a sense of stability and prosperity best seen in the downtown built of brick. The imposing Mason County Courthouse (Alder and 5th) is also worth a visit.

Mason County: Shelton is the county seat of Mason County, which was organized in 1854 and originally part of Thurston County. It was first called Sawamish and later changed to Mason after C.W. Mason, the secretary of the first territorial governor. The county is located on the southwestern end of the Hood Canal and Puget Sound, and extends into the Olympic Mountains to the north. Much of the county's early history centered around road building as the early settlers were forced to cut through heavy stands of timber to gain access to trading centers. Today, Mason County's primary economic activity is in the production of wood products and logging.

Court House: 411 North Fifth, Shelton 98584, SCAN 576-6968, FAX 206-427-8425. Area: 962.3 square miles. State Ranking: 29th. 1993 Population: 42,900. Unincorporated: 35,504. Incorporated: 7,396. Density: 44.6 persons per square mile. **Cities and Towns**: Shelton. **Principal Economic Activities**: Wood products, food processing, manufacturing, agriculture. **Points of Interest**: Hood Canal, Lake Cushman.

Climate: (Shelton - elevation 12)

	Jan	Apr	Jul	Oct
Max Temp. F°	44.9	61n2	77.6	61.6
Min Temp.	31.7	38.0	50.8	42.1
Mean Temp.	38.4	49.7	64.3	51.9
Precipitation	10.37"	3.89"	.80"	6.09"

Average Annual Maximum Temperature: 61.2
Average Annual Minimum Temperature: 40.9
Annual Mean Temperature: 51.1
Average Annual Precipitation: 64.29"

From Shelton Highway 3 heads north through terrain in various stages of development. While some fields reveal acres of stumps, others are cluttered with young pine trees, uniform in height, and ready to reclaim the landscape.

Continue past the roadside driftwood art sometimes displayed in **Allyn** and then through the small but growing villages of **Belfair** and **Gorst**. A surprising number of real estate businesses and "For Sale" signs reveal the movement trend into the area.

Thirty-six miles northwest of Shelton, Highway 3 skirts the western boundaries of **Bremerton** (Elevation 30, Population 36,380), a well-established military city rising from a ship-filled harbor. Bremerton's present characteristics were shaped more than a century ago, when William Brenner facilitated the transfer of land between local farmers

Bracketed by water, timber and mountains, Bremerton is a scenic shipyard.

and loggers and a military commission in search of a site for a northwest naval station. Impressed by cheap land ($50.00 an acre) surrounded on three sides by water, the government bought 190 acres and the Puget Sound Naval Shipyard (PSNS) was born.

Through both world wars the PSNS built and repaired aircraft carriers, cruisers, destroyers, battleships and submarines. Except for a few active destroyers (the USS *Nimitz* is the most well-known) that occasionally make portage here, the majority of the vessels contained in the port are part of the "mothball fleet." Harbor boat tours and the Port Orchard Ferry provide great looks of the proud but dormant ships. One such boat, the USS *Missouri*, served in the Persian Gulf War and was the site of the Japanese surrender on September 2, 1945 to end World War II. Another ship of interest, the USS *Turner Joy*, was involved in the Gulf of Tonkin incident, an event which sparked an increased involvement by the United States in the Vietnam War. The ship's decks and various control rooms are open for tours.

Close to the waterfront the Bremerton Naval Museum (130 Washington Avenue) is joyfully cluttered with U.S. Navy and PSNS artifacts.

Highway 3 continues north up the Kitsap Peninsula, an irregular-shaped land mass that divides Hood Canal and the Puget Sound. **Silverdale**, five miles north of Bremerton, contains a large strip mall and a scenic waterfront location. In the 1880s the town was briefly called Goldendale, but when word was received of another Goldendale to the southeast in Klickitat County, a different prefix (and element) was chosen.

25~

Silverdale's first settler, William Littlefield, was paid $100 a year by the government to maintain a portion of the trail from Olympia between Manette Point (Bremerton) and Seabeck (on the east shore of Hood Canal); Silverdale lies approximately in the center of this former logging route.

Further north the road accesses the **Kitsap Memorial State Park**. In addition to overnight camping and expansive playing fields, the park offers impressive views of Puget Sound and the Olympics. Readerboards help differentiate between a wide variety of clams such as the Manilla, horse, butter or eastern soft-shell, oysters and the freakish but lovable geoduck.

Highway 3 continues three miles to a junction with Highway 104 and the Hood Canal Bridge. ∾

State Highway 4 from a junction with U.S. Highway 101 southeast via Skamokawa and Cathlamet to a junction with Interstate 5 in Longview. Route length: 57 miles.

Highway 4 offers a spectacular view of the **Naselle River** as it flows into Willapa Bay. Water is abundant in this wooded region; 111 inches of rainfall drench the area annually. The highway crosses several small creeks and sloughs that feed the Naselle, along with the Deep and Grays rivers. Among the hefty clear-cut areas that line the roadside, life quickly returns in the form of grasses, ferns and wildflowers.

Beach at Skamokawa Vista Park.

After weaving through the forest, the highway finds the Columbia River at the aged village of **Skamokawa** (Ska-MOCK-away), a Wahkiakum Indian word for "smoke on the water" and descriptive of the misty fog that lingers on most mornings. Located at the confluence of three creeks and a network of sloughs, settlers arriving in the 1860s built homes on the waters' edge, using canoes, riverboats and a series of connecting docks to get around. Farmers rode the creeks into lush valleys to work the soil, loggers floated timber back to the mills, and fishermen dragged their nets; all with much success. The settlement was also a busy landing spot for steamers running cargo and passengers traveling the Columbia. Skamokawa residents traveled to Astoria via boat to shop for goods and supplies. The emphasis on river travel earned the town the nickname "Little Venice."

In their journals, Lewis and Clark mention landing at Skamokawa in 1805, giving the chief a small gold medallion and some red ribbon for his hat in exchange for half a bushel of edible roots (what a trade!). In a considerably older historical reference, the remains of an ancient Skamokawa village dating back to 350 B.C. were discovered in 1977, leading to a two-year excavation of the area. Most of the Skamokawa tribe perished of fever in the 1830s, and only a few were scattered around the creeks when white settlement began.

The town was declared a National Historic District in 1976. Local history can be discovered at the **River Life Interpretive Center** at Redmen Hall, a building used as a school from 1894 until 1926. Greased logs, jacks and pulleys were used to raise the structure 30 feet up the hill to its present location to make room for the highway in 1930, effectively bringing an end to most river travel.

From Highway 4, follow Steamboat Slough Road along the Columbia River to the **Julia Butler Hansen National Wildlife Refuge**. Watch white-tailed deer, elk, swans, geese, hawks and the occasional bald eagle up close in your car or on foot. After crossing the sanctuary, the road again finds Highway 4 near Cathlamet.

A moody, fog-covered slough and gillnet off the Columbia River.

The crooked main street of **Cathlamet** (KATH-LA-muht, Elevation 340, Population 508) runs along the base of a steep hill where old homes overlook a collection of islands on the river. Named for the resident Indian tribe, the word translates as "stone" and refers to the rocky stretch of river on which it lies. James Birnie, a one-time employee of the Hudson's Bay Company, went into business for himself and started a trading post here in 1846, originally calling the spot "Birnie's Retreat." The house he built in 1857 still crowns the bluff.

At the urging of Birnie, other settlers began arriving in the late 1850s, and within a decade several salmon canneries were packed along the river's edge. Cutting down trees to make way for homes inspired folks to make logging a way of life. Timber was rolled downhill to the water where mills prepared them for loading onto steamers. In front of the **Wahkiakum County Historical Museum** (65 River Street) rests the Six-Spot Locomotive, one of 33 custom-built trains capable of negotiating steep grades and curves and used to haul timber from the backwoods after most trees close to the river had been cut. Begun in 1923, this fleet of rugged iron-horses dared to venture where no trains had gone before, climbing in and out of deep ravines and handling hair-pin turns like they were on rails (which, of course, they were). These machines helped clear the hard to reach Cathlamet Tree Farm from 1940 to 1958, adding significantly to the timber production of the region.

Wahkiakum County: Cathlamet is the county seat of Wahkiakum County, which was founded in 1854 from Lewis County. The county is located in the southwest portion of the state and borders the Columbia River on the south. The county was first settled in 1846, and from that time on settlers have found transportation to populated centers one of their foremost problems. Steamboat service on the Columbia River was always irregular so residents of the county volunteered their services over the years to build roads. In the 1930s, ferry services at Puget Island at last permitted county residents easy access to Portland. The county has depended on forest products and dairying as its primary economic pursuits.

Court House: 64 Main Street, Cathlamet 98612, FAX 206-795-3145. Area: 260.7 square miles. State Ranking: 37th. 1993 Population: 3,500. Unincorporated: 2,992. Incorporated: 508. Density: 13.4 persons per square mile. **Cities and Towns**: Cathlamet. **Principal Economic Activities**: Wood products, agriculture. **Points of Interest**: Columbia River, Puget Island.

Climate: (Grays River - elevation 50)

	Jan	Apr	Jul	Oct
Max Temp. F°	45	57	73	62
Min Temp.	33	38	49	42
Mean Temp.	39	48	61	52
Precipitation	20.54"	7.22"	1.77"	10.50"

Average Annual Maximum Temperature: 60
Average Annual Minimum Temperature: 41
Annual Mean Temperature: 51
Average Annual Precipitation: 111.32"

Past Cathlamet, Highway 4 hugs the Columbia where mammoth ships and fishing boats can be seen heading for the ocean. At the intersection of the Columbia and the Cowlitz rivers the highway finds **Longview** (Elevation 13, Population 32,650), the nation's largest planned city next to Washington, D.C. Pledging against building "just another sawmill town," timber mogul R. A. Long of Kansas City set his sights on the great forests of the Northwest to expand his Long-Bell Lumber Company. He purchased 70,000 acres of timberland in 1921 and a year later construction on the city began. Ambitious from the start, Long wanted to create an environment that would attract working men and their families, not troublesome I.W.W. members or transient workers accustomed to saloon-filled logging towns.

Architects from Kansas City were imported with instructions to quickly convert farmland into a modern residential area, all the while following carefully laid-out plans.

The first project was to construct several miles worth of dikes that would contain rising water that had

Longview and its trademark log stacks.

once doomed the area. (In 1866-67, a series of floods destroyed the settlement called Monticello — site of the 1852 Monticello Convention that proposed the creation of the Washington Territory — driving the people away and leaving a ghost town until Long moved in.) In terms of beautification, Long spared no expense in building his model city, donating two million dollars to help fund the public library, the high school that bears his name, a park, a railroad depot and the Community Church. A river slough was dammed and dredged to create the crescent-shaped **Lake Sacajawea** and surrounding park in the heart of downtown. Wide, tree-lined boulevards and the manicured R. A. Long Park, complete with sundial, were created to give a sense of rural warmth to the urban landscape. The wide streets were designed to prevent traffic congestion is an era of the encroaching automobile, and districts were created to separate industrial and residential areas. By 1924, the city was completed and prepared to thrive. All that was needed was a citizenry.

Clearly, Long was thinking of the long-term, but one element he could not control was population. According to estimates, 50,000 people were expected by the end of the first decade, but by 1940, less than half that number lived in Longview. The open spaces set aside for new businesses and growth never filled-out, resulting in a sprawling city with large vacant lots.

But if civic expectations fell short, the logging industry picked up the slack. By 1926, the Long-Bell Lumber Company was the biggest mill in the state, employing nearly 70% of the residents, while the port boomed and bustled with constant ship traffic. The mills continued to grow and prosper until the Great Depression brought the ax down on the economy. Though well past its heyday, the timber industry still reigns in Longview, producing large amounts of plywood, paperboard and various paper products. A chemical plant and pulp mill round out the economy.

Highway 4 crosses the Cowlitz River and connects with I-5 in Kelso, one mile further. ଔ

The lush country of Wahkiakum County.

Interstate 5 from the Washington-Oregon border in Vancouver north via La Center, Woodland, Kalama, Kelso, Castle Rock, Chehalis, Centralia, Tumwater, Olympia, Tacoma, Fife, Milton, Federal Way, Sea Tac, Seattle, Edmonds, Mountlake Terrace, Lynnwood, Everett, Marysville, Mt. Vernon, Burlington, Bellingham and Ferndale to the Canadian boundary at Blaine. (Overlaps U.S. Highway 12.) Route length: 274 miles.

Located on the state's southern border, **Vancouver** (Elevation 175, Population 55,450) is historically the most important city in the state, if not the entire Pacific Northwest. As the original springboard for the settlement of thousands of square miles of wilderness, Vancouver was the center of trade, authority and the first vestiges of European civilization on the western rim of the American continent.

Established as a Hudson's Bay Company trading post and fort on the banks of the Columbia River in 1824, the post flourished under the direction of **Dr. John McLoughlin**. McLoughlin (known to the natives as the White-Headed Eagle for his distinctive shock of hair) was considered ruthless by business competitors, but was always willing to aid new American or English settlers. Besides developing a profitable fur trade, farms, orchards and a sawmill, the company dominated the Northwest for 20 years, though technically it was neutral ground open to both the U.S. and England. Dr. McLoughlin wielded great power over business dealings in the region during this time, but was later dismissed by Hudson's Bay Company for being too sympathetic to American settlers, and even-

The Marshall House, Fort Vancouver.

tually faded into obscurity. In 1846 the entire area became the possession of the U.S. when the International Boundary was set at the 49th parallel.

Fort Vancouver, the first U.S. military base in the Northwest, was made part of the American Defense System in 1848. Many of the most recognized names in American military history did a tour of duty here at one time in their careers, including George Marshall, Omar Bradley, Nelson Miles, William Sherman, George McClellan, Philip Sheridan and Ulysses S. Grant.

Vancouver City was platted adjacent to the fort in 1850, and reflecting demand, its first commercial building was a saloon and

31~

bowling alley, which opened its doors on July 4, 1854. River traffic, gold mining, railroad construction and lumbering all stimulated the town's early growth and prosperity. Upriver dams, the aluminum industry, and Henry Kaiser's shipyards during World War II later helped the community to thrive.

After Fort Vancouver closed the National Park Service began restoring the remaining structures, including the Chief Factor's House (Dr. McLoughlin's one-time residence) and the famous Officers Row on East Evergreen Boulevard. Ten houses and eleven duplexes are now used as offices and living units or, as in the case of the Grant House, a restaurant. Other restored buildings are part of the Fort Vancouver National Historic Site (I-5, Exit 1-C).

The **Transpolar Flight Monument** is housed at the Pearson Air Park to commemorate the first nonstop flight over the North Pole, completed by three Russian pilots in 1937. Departing from Moscow, the trio flew for 63 straight hours before complications forced an unexpected landing here.

Today Vancouver is heavily influenced by Portland, Oregon's metropolitan expansion and its own creeping suburban sprawl. To combat the inner-city decay associated with rapid growth, ambitious urban renewal and historic reuse programs have been developed to preserve many reminders of the area's early prominence. One such living landmark is the Old Apple Tree in Waterfront Park, reputedly planted by Dr. McLoughlin, which continues to grow almost directly beneath an I-5 overpass. (If only that tree could speak.)

Clark County: Vancouver is the county seat for Clark County, one of the state's original counties. It was first organized in 1845 as the Vancouver District by the Oregon Provisional Legislature, then changed to Clark County in 1849 to honor explorer Captain William Clark. It included all territory north of the Columbia and east of the Cowlitz rivers. The county was first settled in 1825 when the Hudson's Bay Company established Fort Vancouver as its regional headquarters. American settlers arrived in the 1830s and 1840s and were well established when the Oregon country's boundary was set at the 49th parallel in 1846. In the early twentieth century lumbering and port facilities were developed along the Columbia River.

Courthouse: 1200 Franklin Street, PO Box 5000, Vancouver 98666-5000, 206-699-2000 (Information), SCAN 525-2000 (Information), FAX 206-737-6051. Area: 627.1 square miles. State Ranking: 35th. 1993 Population: 269,500. Unincorporated: 194,529. Incorporated: 74,971. Density: 429.8 persons per square mile. **Cities and Towns**: Battle Ground, Camas, La Center, Ridgefield, Vancouver, Washougal, Woodland, Yacolt. **Principal Economic Activities**: Wood and paper products, food processing, metal processing, textiles. **Points of Interest**: Fort Vancouver, Merwin Lake.

Climate: (Vancouver - elevation 175)

	Jan	Apr	Jul	Oct
Max Temp. F°	44.3	62.8	79.9	64.2
Min Temp.	33.2	42.4	55.1	46.1
Mean Temp.	38.8	52.6	67.5	55.2
Precipitation	5.63"	2.31"	.46"	3.58"

Average Annual Maximum Temperature: 62.7
Average Annual Minimum Temperature: 44.3
Annual Mean Temperature: 53.5
Average Annual Precipitation: 39.00"

Drive 15 miles north past countless creeks and green, undulating hills and take La Center Road to reach the quaint town of **La Center** (Elevation 150, Population 520), set about one mile east of I-5 on the banks of the East Fork of the Lewis River. Though now quiet, the town was a lively trading center and hub of both water and wagon traffic in the 1880s. Paddle-wheeled steamers would carry passengers, freight and livestock to and from Portland by way of the Lewis, Columbia and Willamette rivers until the railroad and the automobile rendered the route obsolete.

Back on I-5, cross the East Fork of the Lewis River and the Lewis River in succession, then a detached river bend now called Horseshoe Lake before rolling into **Woodland** (Elevation 33, Population 2,732). Enticed by the Donation Land Claim Act of 1850, Squire Bozarth wasted little time settling onto his free parcel which he called *Woodland Farm*. Within a few years he was joined by a small community of other farmers, mainly Finns, and the town grew into a bustling agricultural center by using the Lewis River to transport its goods.

While in town, visit the **Hulda Klager Lilac Gardens**, located near

Hulda Klager was known as the "Lilac Lady."

Horseshoe Lake on the southern edge of town. Through reading and a great deal of trial and error, Hulda succeeded in creating a hybrid apple she found to her liking. Thus inspired, she then focused her talents on a variety of flowers, granting special attention to her beloved lilacs. What began as a hobby blossomed into national fame for Hulda, who received admiring visitors year-round, sold seeds and offered gardening tips for free. The five-acre garden is now a museum run by volunteers who tend to the lilacs in memory of the "lilac lady."

33~

5 Continue north along the eastern shore of the Columbia to **Kalama** (kuh-LAM-uh, Elevation 100, Population 1,245), a variance on the Indian word *calama*, which means "pretty maiden" (or was it named for John Kalama, a Hawaiian trading agent for the Hudson's Bay Company)? The town was once the western terminus of Washington's first "transcontinental" railroad. In the 1800s the U.S. government offered land grants to railroad companies as incentive for building a line across the country. To acquire these grants the Northern Pacific was required to reach "salt water" by December 31, 1873, a task they completed 15 days ahead of schedule when workers reached

Reactor on the Columbia River near Kalama.

Commencement Bay in Tacoma on December 16. This amounted to a hollow victory though, since there was no track between Puget Sound and North Dakota. In a *minor* oversight Congress neglected to stipulate that the line must actually be connected coast to coast. Thus the transcontinental route was declared complete even though it was only 100 miles long; the lengthy middle portion was finished in 1887.

The interstate does not go though Kalama but rather over it, originally designed to keep out of the way of annual floods that used to interrupt traffic. In the unlikely event that a flood does occur, you may wile-away the time over a cool one at the Hart Brewing Company (west of the interstate), one of the Northwest's first and best microbreweries.

From Kalama travel north through rich bottomland to **Kelso** (Elevation 17, Population 11,850), two miles north of the confluence of the Cowlitz and Columbia rivers. If not for the Cowlitz, Kelso and Longview would probably be the same town; as it is, the two communities have grown together. Sitting on the east bank of the river, Kelso has been an important shipping and receiving port since its founding in 1847. Settlers moving north to Puget Sound used this water route extensively, and as the population swelled, it became an important logging center.

Cowlitz County: Kelso is the county seat for Cowlitz County, organized in 1854 from Lewis County and one of the first created by Washington's First Territorial Legislature. It is named after the river that Lewis and Clark called *Cow-e-liske* or "river of the shifting sand."

It is located in the southwestern part of the state and is bounded on the south by the Columbia River. The Cowlitz River was an early avenue of transportation to the Puget Sound region and on each end of the river there took place one of the two conventions that petitioned the U.S. government for Washington's territorial status, the Cowlitz Convention in 1851 and the Monticello Convention in 1852. Its port facilities on the Columbia River are continually growing in capacity.

Courthouse: County Administration Building, 207 Fourth Avenue North, Kelso 98626, SCAN 562-3020 (Commissioners), FAX 206-423-9987. Area: 1,143.9 square miles. State Ranking: 28th. 1993 Population: 86,100. Unincorporated: 35,670. Incorporated: 50,430. Density: 75.3 persons per square mile. **Cities and Towns**: Castle Rock, Kalama, Kelso, Longview, Woodland. **Principal Economic Activities**: Wood and paper products, metal production, shipping. **Points of Interest**: Mt. St. Helens Volcano Viewpoint, Silver Lake, Ariel Dam, Merwin Lake.

Climate: (Longview - elevation 13)

	Jan	Apr	Jul	Oct
Max Temp. F°	44.5	61.4	77.8	63.2
Min Temp.	31.8	38.6	50.4	43.0
Mean Temp.	38.1	50.0	64.1	53.1
Precipitation	5.81"	2.72"	.75"	4.40"

Average Annual Maximum Temperature: 61.6
Average Annual Minimum Temperature: 41.0
Annual Mean Temperature: 51.3
Average Annual Precipitation: 45.10"

Follow the Cowlitz 10 miles to **Castle Rock** (Elevation 54, Population 2,075). Named for a prominent, 150-foot river landmark, the little town is also identified by the large heaps of volcanic ash that the Army Corps of Engineers dredged and piled up after the 1980 Mt. St. Helens eruption choked the Toutle and Cowlitz rivers, drowning the town in the process. For more information on the eruption and some memorable views, travel east on State Highway 504 five miles to the Mt. St. Helens Visitor Center.

For the next 30 miles I-5 runs through fertile prairie lands spread at the base of Cascade foothills before reaching **Chehalis** (chuh-HAY-lis, Elevation 226, Population 6,710). Scattered among the town's quiet neighborhoods are several homes built between the 1850s and the 1880s that have been preserved and listed on the National Register of Historic Places. Another time-worn structure, the old Northern Pacific Railroad Depot (599 NW Front Street), houses the **Lewis County Historical Society Museum**, and serves as a testament to the gumption of early residents. Having originally been passed up as a depot site in 1873, the townsfolk built a warehouse and supply store beside the tracks, giving the railroad a reason to stop. The effort also brought the county seat to town in 1893. With transportation secured, dairy farms and a mill were able to sell their goods to Puget Sound markets, and a large manufacturing company transported ready-made houses across the country.

A "corner" building in Chehalis.

Lewis County: Chehalis is the county seat for Lewis County. In 1845 the Provisional Government of Oregon divided the District of Vancouver into two large counties; all land north of the Columbia and west of the Cowlitz Rivers was designated Lewis County and named after the explorer, Meriwether Lewis. It is located in the southwestern part of the state and stretches from the summit of the Cascade Mountains on the east to Pacific County on the west. Early settlers expended much effort and time in cutting and building roads through the vast forests that covered the land. Today, the county has a varied economy based on wood products, manufacturing, food processing and agriculture.

Court House: Courthouse, 351 NW North St, Chehalis 98532, 206-748-9121 (Switchboard), SCAN 621-1011 (Information), FAX 206-748-1639. Area: 2,449.1 square miles. State Ranking: 6th. 1993 Population: 62,900. Unincorporated: 38,588. Incorporated: 24,312. Density: 25.7 persons per square mile. **Cities and Towns:** Centralia, Chehalis, Morton, Mossyrock, Pe Ell, Toledo, Vader, Winlock. **Principal Economic Activities:** Wood products, food processing, publishing, metal industries, agriculture, manufacturing. **Points of Interest:** Borst Blockhouse, Claquato Church, Cowlitz Mission, Cowlitz Landing.

Climate: (Centralia - elevation 185)

	Jan	Apr	Jul	Oct
Max Temp. F°	45.6	62.8	79.1	62.8
Min Temp.	32.7	39.2	51.0	43.1
Mean Temp.	39.2	51.0	65.1	53.0
Precipitation	6.36"	2.68"	.73"	4.50"

Average Annual Maximum Temperature: 62.5
Average Annual Minimum Temperature: 41.5
Annual Mean Temperature: 52.0
Average Annual Precipitation: 45.53"

When you are about two miles north of Chehalis, keep an eye on the west side of I-5 for the Hamilton Farms billboard, a curious and often humorous roadside soapbox with political messages on both sides that usually spout unflattering, albeit witty, opinions regarding politics or simply clever observations on everyday life. Though the billboard is quickly resigned to the rearview mirror, the sentiments expressed are bound to spark a debate (or at least conversation) that lasts for miles.

Centralia (sen-TRAY-leeuh, Elevation 185, Population 12,380) is found four miles north of its sister city Chehalis. George Washington first settled in this area along the Chehalis River in 1852, and though he was among the first to arrive, he was initially prohibited by law to call the place his own. The son of a Virginia slave and a white woman, Washington was adopted by a white man named James Cochran when he was an infant. After encountering discrimination even in the so-called free states, Washington joined the Cochrans on a journey west hoping to start a farm and a new life, only to find that blacks were restricted from owning land in both the Oregon and Washington territories. Settling on a plot claimed by Cochran, Washington proceeded to build a home and till the soil as he had planned. When the law was overturned in 1857, Washington purchased the land from Cochran, divided it and sold parcels to other settlers and platted the town of *Centerville*. A park bearing his name is located in the center of town (corner of Main and Pearl streets).

Its location midway between Portland and Puget Sound made Centralia a bustling thoroughfare first for wagon trains and later for the railroad. After eyeing the thick surrounding forest and fertile land, many chose to stay here rather than continue on to uncertain destinations. A coal mine and logging operations became the first industries, but only the logging continues today.

On a tragic historical note, violence erupted here between American Legionnaires and members of the International Workers of the World (known as "Wobblies") during an Armistice Day parade in 1919. As the marching veterans approached the Wobblies' town (and regional) headquarters, a skirmish broke out in which four Legionnaires were shot and killed. Later that night a vigilante group stormed the jail where Wobblies were being held, grabbed one of the reputed killers, dragged him through town and lynched him. Eleven I.W.W. members were later sentenced to prison for the deaths of the Legionnaires; none of vigilantes were convicted of the lynching.

Continue pushing north past small farming communities to historic **Tumwater** (Elevation 150, Population 11,110), the site of the first permanent American settlement north of the Columbia River. After enduring the Oregon Trail, Colonel Michael T. Simmons, George Bush (on his second journey to the territory) and a rugged band of 30 pioneers arrived near the falls at the mouth of the Deschutes River in 1845. Though small, the mere presence of the settlement proved vital to American interests by providing at least a partial claim to a vast region dominated by the Hudson's Bay Company. Whether these nationalistic implications were important to the settlers is debatable; they presumably had other issues, such as survival and sustenance, to worry about.

Capitalizing on the hydro-power of the falls, they built a gristmill and water-generated sawmill within the first two years, while simultaneously breaking into the lucrative fur trading business already well established in the area. The success of these ventures and the seemingly unending supply of resources brought scores of new settlers to the site in the years to follow, beginning a migratory trend that has yet to cease.

A historic district is located on the east side of the freeway (take Exit 103 and follow the signs on Custer Way) though some structures were demolished in the 1950s to clear a path for I-5. Many current residents work for the state government in neighboring Olympia, while others are employed at the large Olympia Brewing Company in Tumwater, an enterprise that started with brewmeister Leopold Schmidt in the early 1900s. His original brewery was housed in the impressive brick building rising prominently on the east side of the highway.

Without a discernible break, I-5 rolls into adjacent **Olympia** (Elevation 114, Population 36,520). The story of Olympia begins with the adventurous Edmund Sylvester who traveled from his native Maine and sailed around Cape Horn to reach Portland, Oregon in 1846. There he met a newly-ordained Presbyterian minister named Levi Smith, and together they headed overland to the southernmost port on Puget Sound. Each selected a 320-acre land grant and combined their names to call the area Smithter. Eyeing the impressive timber supply, Sylvester saw the potential for a successful sawmill. Smith was more interested in the affairs of the newly created Territorial Government of Oregon, which in 1848 included all of present day Washington, and set out to be a legislator. When Smith suffered an epileptic attack in his canoe and drowned that same year, Sylvester became the legal recipient of Smith's claim, and the fate of the fledgling town was in his hands. One of the first decisions he made was to leave.

Like many other opportunistic ramblers, Sylvester followed the scent of gold to California in 1849, taking most of the other men in the tiny community with him. When the venture failed to pan out, he returned by ship with a handful of recruits who hoped to make a fortune running timber back to the recently burned down San Francisco. Among these imported settlers was Colonel Issac Ebey, who inspired Sylvester to name the town Olympia for the panoramic backdrop of the Olympic Mountains.

The first port of entry on Puget Sound was created in Olympia in 1851. Within a year a district court had convened, steady stage coach service brought new residents from the Columbia River region, two churches were constructed and the first edition of the *Columbian* newspaper was printed in September of 1852. The advent of the paper was to have a profound effect on not only the town, but the entire territory. With its original publication came an aggressive editorial campaign calling for the creation of two separate states to be divided at the Columbia River. Citizens rallied around this effort by sending a signed petition to Congress along with a steady stream of letters and memos. The outcry was soon answered. In March of 1853, the Washington Territory was created with Olympia as its capital, although it took several weeks before election results were returned from Washington D.C. (Originally the settlers wanted

A faded photo of a faded old brewery.

the territory named Columbia, but to avoid confusion with the District of Columbia it was named after the nation's first president.)

Isaac Ingalls Stevens of Massachusetts was appointed governor of the territory, and in a letter to his new constituents he listed his goals: the creation of a railroad from the Mississippi River to Puget Sound; a wagon road across the Rockies and Cascades to western Washington; reliable mail service; and solutions to problems with Indians and the Hudson's Bay Company. Clearly he had big plans. Such aspirations made Stevens a hero in the eyes of Northwesterners, and a celebration was scheduled for his arrival on November 25, 1853. When he reached Olympia he appeared so travel worn and ragged from his long journey that he had trouble convincing the assembled citizens who he was, finally pulling official documents from his bags to support his claim.

Stevens' new post was the result of many years of careful planning and political hobnobbing. After graduating first in his class at West Point, he went to work on the coastal defense network with the Army Corps of Engineers, which he quickly modernized, earning praise for his organizational skills and work ethic. Eager for action (and further recognition), he volunteered in 1846 for the war with Mexico, returning as a wounded hero and elevated to the rank of major. He then turned to politics and campaigned aggressively for Democrat Franklin Pierce in 1852, receiving favor when he won the presidency. Pierce rewarded him with the triple duty of Washington Territorial Governor, Superintendent of Indian Affairs and survey manager of the Northern Pacific Railroad in its effort to establish a route to the Northwest.

Ambitious, intelligent and inspired by previous successes, Stevens leapt headlong into establishing the government. As an administrator Stevens proved adept; he solved land disputes with the Hudson's Bay Company, organized militias, laid the foundation for a public education system and broke ground on new wagon roads — all within the first few months of his term. His enthusiasm and effectiveness gained him popularity with the citizenry, who dubbed him "Big Little Man," for his small stature (he was of dwarfish physique) and large accomplishments.

He experienced much less success in his dealings with the territory's Indian population, making poor diplomatic decisions that caused conflict and bloodshed on both sides. The task required sensitivity and tact, but he approached it with the same business-like and hasty manner used to establish the government bureaucracy, showing little respect for the tribes or the finesse necessary for subtle diplomacy. Four meetings were held west of the Cascades at Medicine Creek, Point Elliot, Point No Point and Neah Bay with the intention of assigning the tribes to reservations. The brief treaty sessions were conducted in Chinook jargon — a hybrid of English, French and Indian dialects used during trade relations and consisting of less than 400 simple words. Chiefs were required to sign treaties not written in their native tongue, causing obvious confusion and dispute.

Stevens employed the same hurried negotiating techniques in eastern Washington with equally disastrous results. When white settlers began to encroach on land reserved for or still belonging to the Indians (in violation of the treaties), violence erupted, leading to the Indian Wars of 1855-56. Unable to recognize that his own policies and actions had caused much of the conflict, Stevens turned vengeful, ordering attacks on tribes who would not comply with his wishes. After his illegal attempts to maneuver federal troops failed, he led local militias on brutal assaults against various tribes in retaliation for the deaths of whites.

The utter failure of his dealings with Indians ultimately undermined his authority in the eyes of both his constituents and the federal government, and he was forced out of office in 1860. With the advent of the Civil War, Stevens once again turned to the military. While leading troops at the Second Battle of Bull Run in 1861, he died from a gunshot wound to the head.

Meanwhile Olympia's status as the territorial capital was being challenged. In 1860, Vancouver attempted to obtain the territory's official seal by calling for a last minute legislative ballot when certain members were not present. They were nearly successful, losing the bid by a single vote. When Washington was declared the 42nd state on November 11, 1889, Ellensburg and Yakima vied for the capital designation, arguing that the state needed a more centrally-located capital. With strong support from Seattle (from whom Olympia had earlier received $500 for relief following the great fire of 1889), Olympia won handily over Ellensburg and Yakima. After the capital structure was erected in 1902, further calls for relocation fell on deaf ears.

Isaac I. Stevens, first Governor of Washington Territory.

For most early settlements, expansion and growth were clearly the goal, and few elements ensured success like the railroad. As the capital, Olympia warranted certain consideration for a depot, but its shallow harbor made it less desirable. When the Northern Pacific Railroad was deciding the best location for a main terminal in south Puget Sound in 1872, they hired Ira Thomas to purchase land for them. By buying parcels in his name they could avoid paying inflated prices normally reserved for the railroads. This money-saving plan may have fared well had not Thomas died when the tracks were just 15 miles from Olympia. Rather than waste time wrangling over ownership of his estate, the railroad simply chose Tacoma as the end of the line. This setback permanently stunted Olympia's growth. By the time the city was included on the line seven years later, Seattle and Tacoma had become the largest cities on Puget Sound.

To further complicate matters, a terrible earthquake leveled substantial parts of Olympia that same year, causing many citizens to relocate and the local economy to stagnate. But with statehood came excitement and much anticipated progress. Despite the economic depression of 1893, the 90s were truly gay for the capital town. Telephone and telegraph lines arrived, along with streetlights and a new water system. In 1894 the harbor was dredged, luring large shipping and trading companies to Olympia, and with them, jobs and new-found wealth. Steamboats, once operating on a periodic schedule, became the primary method of transportation along the Sound. Even electric streetcars buzzed along the once muddy downtown and waterfront areas. (The first cars had to be adjusted due to their tendency to shock riders holding brass handrails during heavy rains.) The Romanesque capital building, complete with rough-face stone arches and an octagonal clock tower, ushered in the new century when the congress met for the first time in their new home in 1905.

The growth of state government was so rapid at this time that within six years the new structure was deemed too small. Two young New York architects named Walter Wilder and Harry White submitted a revolutionary group concept rather than a single building to win a national architectural competition in 1911, and construction began on an enlarged site one year later. The entire campus is designed in a traditional classic Roman style, with immaculately maintained gardens and stone walkways connecting all the buildings. The Capital Group was fully completed in 1928, the same year a fire

State Capital Building.

destroyed the clock tower on the **Old Capital Building** (on the corner of Legion and Franklin).

The centerpiece of the capital cluster is the **Legislative Building**. The 287-foot edifice is the fourth largest, all masonry, domed structure in the world. Inside, marble steps and railings lead to balconies that look over the four-foot replica of the Washington State Seal in the middle of the floor near the entrance. The ceiling of the inner dome is 185 feet high and sports a five-ton brass chandelier. Huge busts of George Washington and George Bush, the first black settler in the area, sit on marble columns on the second floor. The original purple and gold flag of the state of Washington is hanging on the wall in the State Reception Room. The flag was changed to green and gold in 1923 when Washington became the Evergreen State. Solemn, experienced legislators and fast-walking, eager-to-please young aides climb the marble steps to second and third floor chambers, while outside, huddled meetings can be viewed along with handshakes, smiles and cellular phones. The atmosphere surrounding the capital is one of high energy and noticeable excitement, particularly when congress is in session. Legislators meet the second Monday in January each year and run for 60 days during even-numbered years, and 105 days during odd-numbered years. A full day can be spent exploring the Capital Campus grounds and the various buildings, including a five-block walk to the **State Capital Museum** (211 West 21st).

Another interesting site is the **Gold Bar Store and Restaurant** (222 North Capital). A room upstairs held the first legislative meetings, beginning in February of 1854. These early days of political wrangling often involved brawls and shouting matches in the conference room, and individual representatives debating with their fists in the street between meetings.

Many of Olympia's parks are located at the sites of some of the oldest settlements in the state. **Sylvester Park** (Capitol Way between Legion Way and 7th Street) was designed by founder Edmund Sylvester in 1850 with the intent of embodying the true spirit of a town square. He also donated land for a Masonic Temple, several schools and the 10 acres used for the Old Capital Building found east of the park. First used as a public pasture, the one-block plot was the site of a blockhouse large enough for the entire village during the Indian Wars of 1855-56. It later became a flimsy jailhouse in 1859, but was destroyed when an inmate set fire to it during an escape. Presidents Teddy Roosevelt, William Taft and Franklin D. Roosevelt as well as perennial candidate William Jennings Bryant all gave speeches here during visits to the capital. The shady trees and re-constructed gazebo make the park a popular gathering spot.

Take Eastbay Drive from the Olympia waterfront to **Priest's Point** on the east side of Budd Inlet. The site is named after Father Pascal Ricard, who started a mission on the bluff. Only minutes from downtown, the area offers isolation, campgrounds, hiking trails and access to the beach. The domed Legislative Building can be seen to the south, along with ships loaded with timber on the water and piles of sawdust from sawmills across the bay. Small fishing boats disappear around the wooded cape on their way to Puget Sound.

Outside the bustle of the state capital grounds, life moves at a comfortable pace, noticeably free of litter or noise pollution. For a panoramic view of Puget Sound, capital buildings and several bridges, take a walk around **Capital Lake** just below the Old Capital area. Bicyclists, joggers, picnickers and contemplative politicians take advantage of these parks and trails to find a little peace of mind.

Evergreen State College is located three miles west of the downtown area, and is regionally known for its unique curriculum.

Thurston County: Olympia is the county seat of Thurston County, organized in 1852 and named for Sam R. Thurston, the first Territorial delegate from Oregon. It is located at the southern end of Puget Sound. The first American settlement north of the Columbia River was established in the county in 1845 at Tumwater, along with the first industry, a gristmill established the next year. In 1853 Governor Isaac Stevens proclaimed Olympia the Territorial capital, and the first Washington Territorial legislature met here in 1854. Today, Thurston County, in addition to having the seat of government at Olympia, bases its economy on wood products, manufacturing, dairying and poultry raising. The Port of Olympia continues to grow in importance as an exporter of wood products.

Court House: 2000 Lakeridge Drive SW, Olympia 98502, SCAN 463-3800, FAX 206-786-5223. Area: 714.0 square miles. State Ranking: 32nd. 1993 Population: 180,500. Unincorporated: 105,535. Incorporated: 74,965. Density: 252.8 persons per square mile. **Cities and Towns**: Bucoda, Lacey, Olympia, Rainier, Tenino, Tumwater, Yelm. **Principal Economic Activities**: State government, wood products, food processing, agriculture. **Points of Interest**: State Capital Campus, State Capital Museum.

Climate: (Olympia - elevation 114)

	Jan	Apr	Jul	Oct
Max Temp. F°	43.1	59.2	77.5	60.8
Min Temp.	30.0	36.4	49.0	40.7
Mean Temp.	38.1	50.5	63.9	51.4
Precipitation	7.85"	2.96"	.76"	5.28"

Average Annual Maximum Temperature: 60.0
Average Annual Minimum Temperature: 39.4
Annual Mean Temperature: 50.8
Average Annual Precipitation: 52.37"

Passing the southernmost bend of Puget Sound and the mouth of the Nisqually River, I-5 runs by the Fort Lewis Military Reservation (State Highway 507) and into **Tacoma** (Elevation 150, Population 181,200). The "City of Destiny" envisioned by the optimistic founders of Tacoma was a long way off when British Captain George Vancouver landed at Brown's Point in May of 1792; the harbor did not receive a name until American Navy Lieutenant Charles Wilkes applied the title *Commencement Bay* in May of 1841. Eleven years later a small band of permanent residents settled around a lone sawmill built by Nicholas Delin of Sweden. As fascinated Indians looked on, Delin and a handful of workers toiled for months to send a shipment of timber to San Francisco, foreshadowing Commencement Bay's future prominence as an international port of call.

The Indian uprising in 1855 prompted settlers to seek refuge at Fort Steilacoom to the south, but hostilities did not squelch their enthusiasm. When the conflict cooled, the sawmill resumed its whirling and farmers moved in to till the logged land. New residents arrived by boat and wagon train to claim a piece of the rich resources and ample opportunity.

The most boisterous proponent for settlement came from General Morton Matthew McCarver, an aggressive land speculator, legislator and visionary who arrived in 1868. Having previously launched towns in Iowa, Oregon and California, McCarver knew a good location when he saw one, and wisely predicted that the Northern Pacific Railroad would build their western terminus here. After purchasing large tracts of property with a group of like-minded associates, McCarver sparked a massive advertising campaign to sell the location to businessmen, industrialists, homesteaders and, of course, the Northern Pacific. On advice from locals he changed the name from *Commencement City* to Tacoma, a slight variance on "tahoma," the Puyallup and Nisqually Indian word for Mt. Rainier.

Among the first to answer McCarver's call to prosperity were Charles Hanson and John Ackerson, timber moguls from San Francisco looking to expand. Encouraged by the available port and thick stands of virgin forest (and a deluxe sales pitch from McCarver), the giant Hanson and Ackerson Mill was constructed in 1869 to become the first large-scale operation in Tacoma. Along with attracting workers and their families, the mill enticed those anxious to open stores, saloons, hotels and other ventures. Business surged so suddenly that the local bank ran out of money, causing the Hanson and Ackerson Company to issue metal tokens that served as currency until traditional tender could be secured.

Years of speculation and anticipation reached a climax in 1873 when the Northern Pacific Railroad officially announced that Tacoma would serve as its Puget Sound headquarters. Though welcome news, it was not without the unexpected consequences typical of railroad expansion; the terminal was to be located two miles south of the existing town. This turn of events proved bittersweet for McCarver, for while he had succeeded in his energetic quest for the terminus, he had also accumulated over 2,000 acres of land he intended to sell to the railroad at a premium. Motivated by the same desire for profit, the N.P. bypassed McCarver's townsite and launched a real estate venture of their own by forming the Tacoma Land Development Company to sell land surrounding the chosen site.

The proposed terminal was a promissory note of sorts since at that time the westbound line did not even reach the Rocky Mountains. Nonetheless, the mere intention was enough to inspire a barrage of construction as homes, stores, churches, hotels, saloons and banks were erected and New Tacoma was born. As investments poured in, big industry took root, and in 1878 a spur line was completed to the productive coal mines in nearby Wilkeson and Carbonado. The port was then improved to accommodate larger vessels, opening new markets and boosting New Tacoma into the largest coaling station on the West Coast. Sawmills, salmon canneries and a flour mill also sprang up, along with several local newspapers, telephone service and two universities. Meanwhile, Old Tacoma did not dry up and blow away, it simply prospered at a slightly slower pace until the two towns consolidated in 1884 with a combined population of over 4,000.

A two year lull brought a rash of unemployment, but Tacoma again rallied when the Northern Pacific completed the Stampede Pass Tunnel and subsequently its direct transcontinental link to the Sound. Three days of jubilant celebration commenced with the arrival of the first train on July 3, 1887.

Riding the railroad to the big time, Tacoma relished its expanding importance in the region until the national financial crash of 1893 brought progress to a grinding halt and started a boom and bust trend that lasted until World War II. Four years of stagnation ended with the Klondike Gold Rush of 1897 as ships crowded Commencement Bay to transport supplies north. After an initial period of hope and excitement the revival fizzled as Seattle began to lure business away, determining once and for all the commercial pecking order on Puget Sound.

Presbyterian Church in Tacoma.

The logging industry received a welcome shot in the arm in 1900 when the giant Weyerhauser Timber Company established their home office in Tacoma to take advantage of the port facilities. World War I brought a thriving shipbuilding industry and the completion of the Port of Tacoma in 1918, along with the creation of the Army's Camp Lewis (later to become the Fort Lewis Military Reservation), which brought stability, continued growth and renewed confidence.

The trend repeated itself on a grander scale when the Great Depression claimed massive economic casualties, only to be born again when the second world war put the shipyards to work producing aircraft carriers, tankers and troop transports. Boeing also opened sub-assembly plants here for aircraft production. The shipbuilding industry sank with the end of the war, but was replaced by a naval station and expanded storage facilities which further elevated the importance of the harbor.

This deepwater port, prized since the beginning of white settlement around Puget Sound, is an entirely different place today, with its monstrous cranes, thousands of rectangular containers and constant kinetic activity, but the city's enduring economic link to the shipping trade continues. Huge barges bearing names of cities from around the globe negotiate the bay daily, making the Port of Tacoma one of the largest container ports in the world. The timber products industry remains huge as well, and the "aroma of Tacoma" provides a constant reminder of this fact. Pulp mills account for the distinctive scent hovering around the industrial area.

Downtown, impressive Victorian architecture abounds, though in places you may have to look carefully to find it among the less attractive by-products of rapid growth. A recent large-scale renovation of the downtown area has preserved old structures that represent Tacoma's history, such as the conversion of the ornate **Union Station** (Pacific Avenue and South 19th Street) to a federal courthouse, preventing shopping malls and subdivisions from sapping the city's soul. This urban renaissance has lured new businesses back into the heart of town, bringing with them more pedestrian traffic, vitality and a renewed sense of community.

Among the more relaxing locales is the charming waterfront district along Ruston Way, where a boardwalk lined with restaurants, fishing piers and Commencement Park begs for a casual stroll. In contrast to Tacoma's urban setting, Point Defiance occupies a large chunk of quiet land on the tip of the wedge-shaped Tacoma Peninsula, which separates the Narrows and Dalco Passage. The point contains an extensive park, a diverse zoo and aquarium and accesses a ferry to the southern end of Vashon Island.

Stadium High School, surely their mascot is a dragon.

Crowning a bluff overlooking the bay and the waterfront district, **Stadium High School** (North First and E Street) looks more like a home for royalty than a place for homeroom. Originally designed as a hotel in 1891, the panic of 1893 forced an end to the project and left a space later used as a glorified timber warehouse by the Northern Pacific Railroad. After ravaged by a fire in 1896, the building narrowly escaped the wrecking ball when the city school board purchased it in 1902, and four years later the first bell signaled the beginning of classes. The impressive amphitheater-styled stadium on the northwest side of the school was carved from a wooded gulch in 1910.

The high school is located near **Old Town**, the site of Nicholas Delin's sawmill and McCarver's townsite. Most of the original businesses are gone, but several venerable homes remain as reminders of the city's early days. The **Washington State Historical Society** (315 North Stadium Way) holds a wealth of facts and information on the entire state; a new museum is currently in the works next to the restored Union Station.

Pierce County: Tacoma is the county seat of Pierce County, organized in 1852 from a portion of Thurston County by the Oregon Territorial Legislature. It was named for President Franklin Pierce. It is located in the west central part of the state and stretches from Puget Sound on the west to Mt. Rainier. The first U.S. military base established on Puget Sound was Fort Steilacoom in 1849. The county achieved prominence in the late nineteenth century when two major transcontinental railroads made Tacoma their western terminus. Tacoma also became the headquarters for the Weyerhaeuser Company and a major Pacific shipping center. Today, Pierce County possesses a varied economy based on wood products, metal manufacturing, food processing and shipping. Its county seat, Tacoma, is the state's third largest city.

Court House: County City Building 930 Tacoma Avenue South, Tacoma 98402, SCAN 236-7272, FAX 206-596-6628 (Executive's office). Area: 1,675.9 square miles. State Ranking: 23rd. 1993 Population: 640,700. Unincorporated: 383,130. Incorporated: 257,570. Density: 382.3 persons per square mile. **Cities and Towns**: Bonney Lake, Buckley, Carbonado, Du Pont, Eatonville, Fife, Fircrest, Gig Harbor, Milton, Orting, Puyallup, Roy, Ruston, South Prairie, Steilacoom, Sumner, Tacoma, Wilkeson. **Principal Economic Activities**: Food processing, wood and paper products, metal industries, manufacturing, shipbuilding, chemicals and allied products, apparel and textiles, agriculture, tourism. **Points of Interest**: Mt. Rainier National Park, Fort Lewis, La Grande Dam, Brown's Point, Tacoma Narrows Bridge, Mud Mountain Dam.

Climate: (Tacoma - elevation 150)

	Jan	Apr	Jul	Oct
Max Temp. F°	44.2	57.8	74.3	59.8
Min Temp.	34.3	41.4	54.3	45.9
Mean Temp.	39.9	50.8	64.4	53.0
Precipitation	5.34"	2.37"	.74"	3.81"

Average Annual Maximum Temperature: 59.1
Average Annual Minimum Temperature: 44.3
Annual Mean Temperature: 52.1
Average Annual Precipitation: 37.06"

Unless its about 2:00 a.m. on a Sunday, expect to encounter plenty of traffic on I-5 as you drive north from Tacoma. Or, if it's between 8:00 a.m. and 5:00 p.m. on any weekday, look forward to a four-lane, slowly-moving parking lot jam-packed with commuters. From here to Seattle the highway passes a slew of cities with surging populations and a common history that can be summed up in two words: urban sprawl. Once beyond small communities such as **Fife** (Elevation 30, Population 4,455) and **Milton** (Elevation 40, Population 5,170), the cities get significantly larger, moving past the strip malls, housing developments and commercial complexes of **Federal Way** (Elevation 25, Population 75,320) and **Sea Tac** (Elevation 300, Population 22,840), and the maze of adjoining cities-in-waiting that fill in any gaps on both sides of I-5.

Approximately halfway up the length of Washington, I-5 skirts Boeing's spacious tarmac, rounds a bend and is warmly welcomed by the modern and graceful skyline of **Seattle** (Elevation 18, Population 527,700), Washington's largest city. Elliot Bay's sparkling waters, a ring of distinct hilltop neighborhoods and the distant ridgelines of the Cascade and Olympic ranges further bolster the Emerald City's image as an exceptionally hospitable place, yet paint a picture much different than that perceived by a witness to the landing party of Seattle's first white settlers:

> I can't never forget when the folks landed on Alki Point. I was sorry for Mrs. Denny with her baby and the rest of the women... I remember it rained awful hard that last day — and the starch got took out of our bonnets and the wind blew, and when the women got into the rowboat to go ashore they were crying, every one of them, and their sunbonnets with the starch took out of them went flip flap, flip flap, flip flap, as they rode off to shore. The last glimpse I had of them was the women standing under the trees with their wet sunbonnets all lapping down over their faces and their aprons to their eyes.

These words refer to the cold, rainy afternoon on November 13, 1851 when approximately two dozen men, women and children, pioneers from Cherry Grove, Illinois, disembarked from the schooner *Exact* and rowed ashore to join an advance team comprised of Captain Robert C. Faye, John Lowe, Leander Terry, and David Denny. The team had left their families and friends two months prior in Portland and headed north to build shelters and find land suitable for settlement.

Denny recalls:

> ... I went to look after the women and I found on my approach that their faces were concealed. On a closer inspection I found that they were in tears, having discovered the gravity of the situation... my wife and helpless children were exposed to the murderous attack of hostile savages [and] it dawned upon me that I made a desperate venture.

Denny's alarm was unjustified since the Duwamish Indians and their leader Chief Sealth were friendly and not "hostile." (Sealth probably realized that to resist the influx of white settlers into his people's territory would be an act of futility.) The settlers named the wind-swept beach they had landed on New York. *Alki*, a Chinook word for "by and by," was added to indicate that prosperity would come after a while.

Timber reaching to the horizon made lumbering the clear industry choice and in the winter of 1852, 35,000 board feet of logs were loaded onto the vessel *Leonesa* and shipped to San Francisco. Alki's shallow waters had made the transfer of logs to ship difficult, and recognizing a future in lumber and the importance of efficient transport of the product, the settlers ventured out with a crude 'sounding' contraption (Mary Denny's clothesline attached with horseshoes) to find a deepwater port. The following spring they picked the tide flats on the western shore of Elliot Bay and staked a claim, naming the land after the friendly Chief Sealth (pronounced *See-YAH-til*, and therefore Anglicized to its current spelling, *Seattle*).

Old downtown Seattle. The signs on the left offer mining supplies and beer.

Seattleites may recognize the names of some of the city's earliest pioneers as names of businesses or streets. Dr. David S. Maynard opened the first general store and attempted to ship salmon to San Francisco. This venture into the fish market — the fish arrived well past the "do not use after" date — proved to be a little before its time (and before the age of refrigerated boxcars). Thomas Mercer used the settlement's first horse to provide a milk delivery service.

Seattle's founding fathers, Albert and David Denny, the Borens, the Bells and "Doc" Maynard divided the waterfront into sections and donated a spread of land to Henry Yesler of Portland to build a steam-powered sawmill. Logs were dragged or "skidded" down timbered slopes to Yesler's mill. The route, today's Yesler Way, was known as "skid road" or "skid row" and became associated with the down-and-out people who frequented the area.

For the next two decades Seattle's growth was steady but not spectacular. Arthur Denny opened another store and his clerk, Dexter Horton, started a rudimentary bank. Money brought by loggers and trappers was labeled and "deposited" in the store's coffee grinds. Fraser River gold strikes in Canada led to the construction of a saloon, a blacksmith shop, a hardware store and a dance hall as miners passed through in their race to riches.

In 1861, Seattle managed to land the territorial university that governor Isaac Stevens had long campaigned for:

> And I feel confident that they will aim at nothing less than provide a system, which shall place within the means of all the full development of the capacities with which he has been endowed with every use, however limited his opportunities, can find his place in school, the college, the University, if God has given him the necessary gift.

When instruction began in November of 1861, the school's first pupils were apparently not "given the necessary gift;" of 37 pupils, 36 were below college level. Occupying a 10-acre tract (Fifth and University) downtown, the students were taught a curriculum "offering everything from ABC's to the classics." Asa Mercer, the school's president and lone instructor, was responsible for recruiting students — a difficult task considering the educational level of the rough-hewn community — and later for bringing females to the predominately male population. His first assignment was partly accomplished by allowing students to reduce their tuition fees in exchange for cords of split wood. The savvy 22-year-old educator traveled east twice to fulfill his second duty. His trips resulted in bringing back over 50 unwed and widowed ladies; "Mercer Girls," were a big hit with Seattle's sizable bachelor community.

In 1873 the fledgling city suffered a major setback when the Northern Pacific Railroad picked Tacoma as the terminus of its line. It was time for young Seattle to take charge of its destiny and so the locally-run Seattle and Walla Walla Railroad and Construction Company was formed. With Spokane's transcontinental connection far-off in their sights but close in their dreams, rails started the long march across the state. Four years later the line had reached the profitable coal mines of Newcastle, 12 miles east. The mines and the railroad were eventually purchased by railroad magnate Henry Villard of the Northern Pacific.

The combination of the timber, coal, and fishing industries, along with regular steamer service to San Francisco indicated a functioning economy and spurred significant growth. Its population grew from 3,500 in 1880 to 43,000 in 1890. Streets and sidewalks were graded, schools, churches, homes and offices erected, and electric street cars clammered up and down Seattle's many hills.

The area began to experience more ethnic diversity as Scandinavians, Englishmen, Finns, Germans and Irishmen came to check out the booming city on the Sound.

Tough jobs in mining camps and on rail lines attracted Chinese men who were willing, or forced out of necessity, to take menial, low-paying jobs. The white work force grew resentful (and racist) because they believed their own pay scale would decrease when others were willing to work for less. Several incidents occurred where mobs threatened or killed Chinese workers and in February of 1886 a sizable Chinese population was collected and herded onto ships for deportation. President Grover Cleveland declared martial law until tensions eased.

Another "hot" incident occurred on June 6, 1889 when a glue pot in a basement cabinet shop boiled over and sparked a fire that ignited the building. Before long Seattle's wooden downtown was ablaze. Alarms sounded but the volunteer fire department was of little help. One pumper attached a hose to a hydrant that had no water and the other made a futile attempt to draw water out of the Sound, but the tide was out. The department's chief was in San Francisco for a wedding. By next morning 64 acres of the business district and the entire system of wharves and piers were reduced to ash.

The fire, though devastating, was a blessing in disguise since it prompted the city to rebuild in aesthetically-pleasing brick and gave city planners an opportunity to build with future growth in mind, (although one stuck in today's traffic will question the scope of that planning). The city also was able to rectify a persistent plumbing problem where high tide would cause streets to flood. Downtown was raised one story and all former businesses formerly at street level were sealed, creating the underground city that exists today.

The city slowed after the depression of 1893 but any thoughts of stagnation were dismissed in 1897 when the steamer *Portland* dropped an anchor in the Seattle harbor with more than a ton of solid gold in its hull. Before too long — about the time it took to supply up and book a ride on a seaworthy ship — thousands of prospectors (and teachers, doctors, firemen, ministers and even Seattle's mayor) were heading for Alaska's Klondike. Seattle, the "Gateway to Gold," was the logical embarking point for the journey north, and as such the logical place to use your life savings to buy the recommended one-year's worth of food and equipment necessary to strike it rich. Most men returned with nothing; some of those who were lucky settled in the area or at least spent a week or so whooping it up in the accommodating saloons and so-called gentlemen's clubs.

Perhaps the culmination of Seattle's growth occurred in 1909 when the city hosted the Alaska-Yukon Pacific Exposition. The festive event celebrated trade between Washington, Alaska, Canada and the Pacific Rim countries and was seen by four million money-spending visitors. Some of those visitors never left.

The actions of men and women and the unpredictable dabblings of fate and fortune have certainly impacted modern-day Seattle, but perhaps it is the area's physical surroundings that have had a greater effect. Its position in the far northwest corner of the country allowed the city (and the state) to remain relatively anonymous for much of the modern century. Then in the 1980s, the prospect of clean air and of brilliant mountainous and aquatic surroundings prompted folks from other parts of the country to venture to the wet and wild Northwest.

These transplants discovered that the area was not exceedingly wet nor wild. Although Seattle is by no means a sunny place — gray skies with an intermittent drizzle is the standard forecast — it only receives 34 inches of rain per year. This is less rain than falls on New York, Chicago and Boston.

Hundreds of men poised to strike it rich; only a handful would fulfill their dreams.

In addition to being one of the nation's most educated and literate cities, Seattle has earned a reputation for its fine restaurants, microbrewed beer (high-quality beer brewed on a small scale), and gourmet coffee; espresso stands are found on nearly every corner. Seattle, usually ranked among the nation's "most livable cities," has become more well-known and subsequently a greater player in national and world affairs. Trade with the Pacific Rim has opened up and presidential nominees regularly make Seattle a stop.

Riddled with one-way streets, dead-ends and unmarked junctions, the "Queen City" can be difficult to negotiate. The following tour peruses the city's main neighborhoods and many of its interesting sites. Additional information is available at the Visitors Information office at the Washington State Convention and Trade Center (Union and 8th) and in numerous travel guides. Numbered streets in downtown's main core run north to south. The streets that flow east to west and form the core of downtown may be memorized by using the following mnemonic: "Jesus Christ Made Seattle Under Protest." The first letter of each word is the first letter of two corresponding pairs of street names. For example, Jesus stands for Jackson and James streets and Protest for Pike and Pine.

Pioneer Square, once occupied by Henry Yessler's sawmill, is found at the south end of downtown. One of the most architecturally-interesting districts in the city, a jumble of red-brick and cobble-stone plazas divide cockeyed streets originally platted by Arthur Denny and Doc Maynard. The two men disagreed on property lines and purposely saw to it that their streets did not match up. By day sidewalks bustle with those in search of a rare book or a strong cup of joe; when the sun sets, the bars and nightclubs open their doors and patrons stumble along in various stages of inebriation.

Pioneer Square also contains the **Klondike Gold Rush National Historical Park** (117 S. Main Street), and the **Underground Tour** (610 1st Avenue), two historically informative points of interest.

The massive gray form of the **Kingdome** (King County Stadium) dominates the space south of Pioneer Square. The stadium holds trade shows, concerts and professional football (Seahawks) and baseball (the mighty Mariners) games. The aesthetic value of the dome, which looks like a spaceship that has landed and has no intention of leaving, is an issue that generates much passionate conversation.

East of the Kingdome and the King Street Station (built in 1906), streets rise into the **International District**, home of Seattle's diverse Asian population. One way to become familiar with this hilly community is to visit the **Wing Luke Museum** (407 7th Avenue), which greatly details the International District and the relationship between Washington and immigrants from Pacific Asian countries. Another approach may be to spend hours walking its steep streets and soaking in the rich collection of sights, smells and sounds.

From the International District head north on 4th Avenue and as you approach the Westlake Shopping Center look west down Pike Street for the glowing **Pike Place Market** sign. The market was formed in 1907 to allow farmers to sell directly to the public. Not much has changed. Small-scale farmers bring their fruits, vegetables and freshly-cut flowers to peddle to a teeming mass of tourists and locals (a sign

Pike Place Market eliminated the middleman. Goods were sold directly from farmers to the public.

that the wares are considered high quality). In between booths of hand-made crafts and piles of 20-pound Chinook salmon, a street musician plays songs with amazing accuracy on a home-made instrument. Pike Place is the oldest continuously operating farmers market in the country.

A long flight of stairs leads from the market to the waterfront area (Alaskan Way). Gift shops and restaurants with ocean views and steaming piles of clams occupy several piers, while commercial fishing and transport vessels, the Seattle Aquarium and the Washington State Ferries occupy the rest.

Pike Street climbs the western slope of **Capitol Hill**, rising to a ridgeline dotted with fine homes and the stern but graceful Saint Mark's Episcopal Cathedral. The hill's name most likely came from the desire to secure the state capitol designation, but some literature claims it was named for a hill in Denver, Colorado. The district is a study in contrast. A few blocks from the cultural extravaganza that is Broadway Avenue are blocks of exclusive homes worthy of college architecture student tours.

The north end of Capitol Hill overlooks the **University of Washington**, the University District and parts of Lake Washington and Lake Union. Several roads drop from Capitol Hill and connect with Montlake Boulevard or Eastlake Way, both of which continue on to the university. The 45th Street exit is the most direct route from I-5. As you pass through the University District or walk up University Avenue, the "U-District" and "the Ave" respectively, a proliferation of coffee houses, theaters, frat boys, street punks, bookstores, chess-playing intellectuals and cheap, international cuisine reveal that a college is nearby.

INTERSTATE 5

The university has grown considerably since its days on Fifth and University. Land was purchased in the hills northeast of town and in 1895, classes began in spacious Denny Hall. In 1906 the expansive acreage around the campus was deemed suitable for the Alaska-Yukon-Pacific Exposition, funds were appropriated, and the Olmsted Brothers' firm went to work designing buildings, gardens

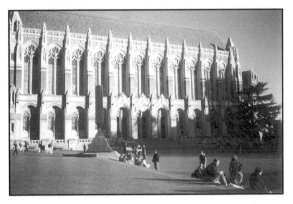

and parks that could accommodate the millions of visitors the fair would bring three years later.

The work done in the early 1900s by the prolific Olmsteds (City Beautiful proponents) has stood up to time; U.W.'s campus covers over 700 acres and is considered one of the most beautiful in the country. The main en-

"U-Dub" in the Emerald City is the place to find a brain.

trance to the campus is reached via 45th Avenue. A maple-lined avenue leads into the brick-laden Central Plaza, commonly referred to as "Red Square." The **Henry Suzzalo Memorial Library** (built in 1927) dominates the plaza in both size and detail. Its traditional appearance seems to be conducive to long hours of study (at least that is what tuition-paying parents hope).

Around the corner is **Rainier Vista**, which provides a look over Drumheller Fountain down a long line of campus buildings with a backdrop of Mt. Rainier. This stunning viewpoint is a testament to the greatness of the Olmsted's work.

From the U-District you may follow 45th or 50th street west over the hilltop community of Wallingford and down to **Green Lake**. Most Seattleites have walked, fished, skated, ran or at least driven by the lake, conveniently located between Interstate 5 and Highway 99 in a neighborhood of the same name. The 255-acre lake is a popular after-work and weekend destination for those looking to exercise or let the children run wild. The lake is encircled by a 2.8-mile long paved path. A three-mile gravel path forms a larger circle and runs adjacent to the streets that access the park. Grassy playfields fill in the gaps between the two paths. The nationally-recognized **Woodland Park Zoo** is found just south of the lake.

Fremont, located at the north end of Lake Union and spread along the banks of the ship canal, attracts an eclectic mix of restaurants, antique stores and art galleries. On weekends local craftspeople and other creative folk run a giant flea market and on special nights cult film classics are shown on the backside of a whitewashed building.

The sky-blue and pink **Fremont Bridge** is the most frequently drawn bridge in the world and a great spot to watch pleasure vessels negotiate the narrow canal. Also check out the **Fremont Troll** beneath the Aurora Bridge. The giant, with a life-size Volkswagen under its left hand, stares menacingly from beneath the bridge at the hordes of sightseers.

Beware when you walk under the Fremont Bridge.

Leary Way leaves Fremont and heads two miles to **Ballard**, platted in 1897 but not considered a part of Seattle until 1907. The town first attracted mill workers and was known as the "shingle capital of the world." Later, a large number of Scandinavians came to the area for the ready work and stayed because of the resemblance between the area and the waters, forests and mountains of their homeland. Ballard grew into a fishing enclave, an industry Norwegians were familiar with. A strong Scandinavian community continues today; the **Nordic Heritage Museum** (3014 67th Street) offers exhibits describing Nordic immigration to the Northwest and of their role in the fishing, logging and farming industries.

Continue west through town on Market Street to the **Hiram M. Chittenden Locks**, also called the Ballard Locks. Facilities include fish ladders, a botanical garden, a visitor center and two navigational locks. The locks allow vessels to travel between Seattle's inland lakes and Puget Sound by placing boats in chambers and either raising or lowering the level of water depending on the direction of travel. Visit the ladders in fall when the salmon are returning to spawn. Displays inside the fish-viewing room help differentiate between sockeye, chinook and coho salmon, as well as cutthroat trout and steelhead.

Fifteenth Avenue leaves Ballard and crosses over the ship canal. Below is a dense gathering of fishing trolleys and cargo ships. The hill to the west is called **Magnolia**, incorrectly named by a member of the U.S. coast survey when he mistook the area's native madrona trees for magnolia trees. The neighborhood supports an older populace and enjoys a relative quiet compared to the city's hustle and bustle.

Perched on a bluff overlooking Puget Sound, Magnolia's **Discovery Park** is the largest park in the city, covering 534 acres. The park serves as a wildlife sanctuary for nearly 200 species of birds and thriving populations of small mammals who flourish in dense forests of

Douglas Fir and western red cedar, freshwater ponds, meadows, beaches and even sand dunes. Trails explore the wooded interior of the park, intersecting others that venture to 300-foot cliffs peeking over into the Sound and down to a lighthouse and beach on West Point.

Several roads from 15th Avenue climb to **Queen Anne**, named for a common style of architecture used in early Queen Anne homes. The neighborhood has two main business districts: one at the base of

Cruising Seattle's ship canals.

Queen Anne Avenue and the other at the hill's summit. The steep hill was once negotiated by electric street cars that were helped along by an underground counterbalance. The subterranean truck weighed 16 tons and ran on narrow gauge tracks. When the passenger car, which weighed between 18 and 24 tons, ascended, the truck rolled downhill to help pull the passenger car uphill. The process was reversed on the passenger car's descent.

Streets on the edges of Queen Hill provide some of the best urban views of the region. Many postcards have been shot from the hill's south side which presents a bird's eye view of the Space Needle, downtown Seattle, and across Elliot Bay to West Seattle. The 605-foot high **Space Needle**, Washington's most recognizable structure, is to the state what the Eiffel Tower is to Paris. Erected for the 1962 World's Fair, the needle flies banners or decorations to celebrate important sporting, political or holiday events. Elevator rides are expensive but provide 360° views. The Space Needle is located within Seattle Center, a giant park that includes the Pacific Science Center, a food bazaar, concert facilities, a pro basketball arena for the Seattle Supersonics and an elevated monorail. If travel plans permit, take the monorail to end the tour at Westlake Center in downtown Seattle.

King County: Seattle is the county seat of King County, organized in 1852 from Thurston County. It was originally named after William R. King, Vice President under Franklin Pierce; it was renamed, in 1986, after civil rights leader Martin Luther King. Seattle grew and prospered during the late nineteenth and early twentieth centuries with the expansion of the shipping and lumber industries. It boomed again during and after World War II as an aircraft production and shipbuilding center. Today the county is the Pacific Northwest region's major manufacturing and shipping center.

~58

Court House: Courthouse 516 Third Avenue, Seattle 98104, County Administration Bldg 500 Fourth Avenue, Seattle 98104, 206-296-0135 (Information Desk). Area: 2,130.9 square miles. State Ranking: 11th. 1993 Population: 1,587,700. Unincorporated: 511,655. Incorporated: 1,076,045. Density: 745.1 persons per square mile. **Cities and Towns**: Algona, Auburn, Beaux Arts, Bellevue, Black Diamond, Bothell, Burien, Carnation, Clyde Hill, Des Moines, Duvall, Enumclaw, Federal Way, Hunts Point, Issaquah, Kent, Kirkland, Lake Forest Park, Medina, Mercer Island, Milton, Normandy Park, North Bend, Pacific, Redmond, Renton, Sea Tac, Seattle, Skykomish, Snoqualmie, Tukwila, Woodinville, Yarrow Point. **Principal Economic Activities**: Manufacturing, shipping and trade, agriculture, business services, shipbuilding, fishing, wood products, tourism. **Points of Interest**: Snoqualmie Falls, Seattle Area.

Modern day, downtown Seattle.

Climate: (Seattle - elevation 14)

	Jan	Apr	Jul	Oct
Max Temp. F°	45.6	59.4	75.1	60.4
Min Temp.	36.8	44.1	56.1	48.3
Mean Temp.	41.2	51.8	65.6	54.4
Precipitation	5.19"	1.97"	.63"	3.28"

Average Annual Maximum Temperature: 60.0
Average Annual Minimum Temperature: 46.4
Annual Mean Temperature: 53.2
Average Annual Precipitation: 34.10"

Driving north, I-5 passes Northgate Mall and then moves out of the Seattle city limits before venturing into more urban sprawl. Unlike the high population belt expanding south of the city, the housing developments and retail complexes are less obtrusive here due to the surrounding pockets of forest left standing. The cities of Edmonds

(State Highway 104), **Mountlake Terrace** (Elevation 400, Population 19,880), **Lynnwood** (Elevation 62, Population 29,580) and their growing environs spread to the southern extremities of **Everett** (EV-er-it, Elevation 36, Population 76,980), located about 30 miles from Seattle.

Occupying a high-bluff peninsula formed by the Snohomish River Delta and Puget Sound, in many ways Everett embodies the history of every community in the coastal Pacific Northwest. Pioneering spirit, entrepreneurship, land speculation, industrial and manufacturing phenomena, greed, labor violence, wildness giving way to a temperate and conservative society populated by a myriad of immigrants. Woven through all of this was the coming of the railroads, mining, fishing, "King Lumber" and the boom and bust cycles inherent to these industries.

Whaleback "C.W. Wetmore" unloading at Lowell dock.

Much of what was positive and negative about the settling of the Pacific Northwest can be read in the history of the settling of Everett. Captain George Vancouver landed here on June 4, 1792 and claimed the land for England. A century later the vast wealth of timber in the area drew those who created the city: the Ruckers, Colbys, Hewitts, Wetmores, Rockefellers; all names that are immortalized on the main streets of town. The combination of James J. Hills' Great Northern Railway and a deepwater port opened the world's markets to the nascent community. By the beginning of the century, Fredrick Weyerhauser had purchased almost one million acres of timberland and within a decade had built the largest sawmill in the world. This, along with shake mills, iron works and eventually great pulp and paper mills, placed Everett at its commercial pinnacle by mid-century.

Everett is once again revitalizing itself. Gone are the old-growth forests that choked the mill ponds with logs; gone are the huge bayside pulp mills that soiled the air and polluted the Sound, but the city spirit still lives. A downtown rebuilding program to combat the drain of shoppers and smaller businesses to suburban malls is nearly completed, and Boeing has one of its largest manufacturing facilities on the south edge of town. The bayside is thriving with a marina, a viable fishing fleet and the new Naval Station.

The **Chamber of Commerce Building** (formerly the Weyerhauser offices), the Naval Station, Marina and Fishing Fleet are all located on West Marine Drive on the waterfront. The Snohomish County Courthouse on Rockefeller is an adaptation of Spanish Mission architecture with white stucco walls and red tile roof complete with a cupola.

Forest Park, off of 41st Street, is most notable for displaying the type of work accomplished by the Works Progress Administration. The park once housed a good-sized zoo with bear caves, bison and elk parks, a monkey house and aviary. All of this has been reduced to a small animal petting zoo, but the grounds are still beautiful and the old floral hall built of peeled logs and the community swimming pool remain areas of community activity.

Grand Avenue Park offers spectacular high-bluff views of Puget Sound and the San Juan Islands and contains a small granite marker commemorating Captain George Vancouver's landing. Across the street the Georgian revival style house first built by city pioneer William C. Butler later belonged to Henry Jackson.

Murals inside the **Everett Public Library** (corner of Hoyt and Everett avenues), a wonderful building designed by Seattle architects Bebb and Gould in 1934, depict the city's history. Recently expanded, the library holds an enormous amount of material on lumbering history and a replica of Senator Henry M. Jackson's Washington office.

One of the city's beloved sons, **Henry M. Jackson** was born in Everett on May 31, 1912, and died in his home town on September 1, 1983. Nicknamed "Scoop" at the age of four by his sister, Jackson's public career spanned more than four decades and the terms of nine presidents. Scoop's motto was: "The vital unfinished work must be carried forward." He demonstrated an untiring commitment to that objective through his seven-day work week and in his many accomplishments.

After he graduated from the University of Washington, Jackson's national political career was prefaced by his career in Everett, including a three-year post as Snohomish County's prosecuting attorney. He served as a democrat in the House of Representatives from 1941 to 1952 and in the Senate from 1953 until his death in 1983. During Jackson's tenure, he served as Chairman of the Committee on Energy and Natural Resources. He was responsible for the creation of North Cascades National Park in 1968 and was instrumental in passing the 1978 National Environment Policy Act, which required federal agencies to submit environmental impact statements before they submitted a project. Jackson's friends and peers consistently describe him as possessing great character, and worthy of respect and trust. A close friend of John F. Kennedy, he narrowly missed being his running mate in the 1960 presidential election. He was described as a teacher, orator, statesman, peacemaker and friend. Items in the Everett Public Library Jackson Room have been donated to the city by Senator Jackson's wife, Helen. The desk and wooden armchair displayed in the library that were in Senator Jackson's office date back to 1909 when the Russell Senate Office Building opened. Red leather chairs and couch from the early 1950s were also in the senator's former office. The black leather chair was used in the Jackson's home on Grand Avenue in Everett.

Snohomish County: Everett is the county seat of Snohomish County, established in 1861 and once part of Island County. It is named after the tribe of Indians that once occupied the area. The county stretches from Puget Sound on the west to the crest of the Cascade Mountains on the east. The county was first explored in 1792 when Captain George Vancouver named the region New Georgia; he also named Port Susan and Port Gardner Bay. The vast stands of timber attracted settlers who set up mills and provided timber to build San Francisco and the transcontinental railroads in the mid-nineteenth century. Snohomish County enjoys a varied economy based on wood products, aircraft manufacturing and agriculture.

Court House: 3000 Rockefeller Avenue, Everett 98201, 206-388-3411 (Information), SCAN 649-3411, FAX 206-285-3472. Area: 2,098.2 square miles. State Ranking: 13th. 1993 Population: 507,900. Unincorporated: 265,254. Incorporated: 242,646. Density: 242.1 persons per square mile. **Cities and Towns**: Arlington, Bothell, Brier, Darrington, Edmonds, Everett, Gold Bar, Granite Falls, Index, Lake Stevens, Lynnwood, Marysville, Mill Creek, Monroe, Mountlake Terrace, Mukilteo, Snohomish, Stanwood, Sultan, Woodway. **Principal Economic Activities**: Transportation equipment manufacturing, wood products, food processing, electronic and electrical equipment. **Points of Interest**: Wallace Falls, Glacier Peak, Sunset Falls.

Climate: (Everett - elevation 36)

	Jan	Apr	Jul	Oct
Max Temp. F°	44.6	58.8	72.4	59.8
Min Temp.	32.6	40.4	52.3	43.8
Mean Temp.	38.6	49.6	62.4	51.8
Precipitation	4.45"	2.39"	.93"	3.54"

Average Annual Maximum Temperature: 58.8
Average Annual Minimum Temperature: 42.4
Annual Mean Temperature: 50.6
Average Annual Precipitation: 35.24"

From Everett, drive over the mouth of the Snohomish River and
Steamboat Slough and past the row of "U-Pick 'Em" strawberry fields
alongside I-5 leading to **Marysville** (Elevation 16, Population 14,570),
a farming community slowly being absorbed into suburbia. The neighborhoods are quietly reminiscent
of a small town, but streets bulge
with traffic in the mornings and
evenings with those commuting to
and from Everett and Seattle for
work. As surrounding rural land is
encroached by housing developments, Marysville marks the unofficial northern boundary for a
growing population center known
as "Pugetopolis" that stretches
through Seattle and south past
Tacoma.

Started as a trading post in
1877 to provide goods for the
neighboring Tulalip Indian Reservation, the town grew into a logging and ship building community.
One of the first logging locomotives
in the state ran along wooden

The Marysville water tower welcomes you.

tracks in Marysville, leading from the mills in town to the surrounding
forests. After plots of trees had been cleared, sloughs from the
Snohomish River were diked to make way for farms and to provide
irrigation, then periodically released to replenish the soil. Strawberries are such an essential part of the economy that the first day of
summer is celebrated with the Marysville Strawberry Festival.

The **Tulalip Indian Reservation** (Too-lay-lip) is one mile west of
Marysville, covering over 24,000 acres of Puget Sound waterfront and
timber land. Tulalip is an Indian word for "almost land-locked bay."
As a result of the 1855 Point Elliot Treaty with Governor Isaac Stevens,
this land was set aside for all of the coastal tribes, including the
Snohomish, Snoqualmie, Skykomish, Stillaguamish, Skagit and Samish
tribes. In exchange for their land, the U.S. government promised to
open schools and train the Indians in various trades, but it was nearly
50 years before any of these commitments were honored. Rather than
wait for the government to make good on their word, many tribal
members abandoned the reservation and scattered throughout the
western half of the state in order to adhere to their traditional fishing,
hunting and gathering lifestyle.

Each tribe included in the amalgamation is unique and has its
own language, but their origins, according to native legend, are the

same. The myth says that long ago the Great Spirit instructed the Rising Sun to take two cedar baskets with him on his east to west journey; one containing a collection of native peoples and the other a variety of languages. As Rising Sun followed his daily path, he picked the largest tribes from the basket and left each with a language of their own. As he approached the Pacific and was about to descend into the ocean, Sun realized that a few small tribes and dialects remained in the baskets, so he quickly sprinkled them along the coast, right up to the waters' edge, moments before stepping over the horizon.

When the government was slow in establishing schools for native children at Tulalip, missionaries arrived to fill the void, notably the Jesuit Eugene C. Chirouse in 1857. He became a beloved and re-spected member of the community, writing a dictionary and book of grammar on the Snohomish dialect that was used in teaching the children. Classes at the Jesuit school began in 1861, and seven years later the Catholic Sisters of Charity started a school for girls. The first contract Indian school in the U.S. was established at Tulalip in 1869, when the Federal Government agreed to finance the board and tuition of students in a Catholic boarding school.

Despite their presumably good intentions, the missionaries had a profoundly negative affect on the tribes by condemning or outlawing customs that had been part of their lives for untold generations. The ancient practice of extended families (including multiple wives) was declared unholy and illegal, as were the rituals of spirit healing and the potlatch ceremony designed to determine social status. At board-ing school, children were punished for speaking or singing in their native tongues. Federal Indian agents also required all native men to clear marshlands two days per year, or forfeit the equivalent of a day's pay if the work was not completed. The loss of traditions and language due to these restrictions strained relations and aroused deep resentment. The continuing growth of neighboring Marysville further deteriorated the tribes' condition, as contact spawned epidemics of white diseases, and although officially prohibited, a steady avail-ability of alcohol.

Not until 1914 were the Tulalip tribes legally allowed to gather together without government interference. Exercising this right, the reservation ushered in a renaissance period by rekindling old cus-toms and traditions. To cement economic self-sufficiency, they coop-erated in creating several logging camps, sawmills and expanded farms. Pollution and large-scale commercial fishing have decimated the once mighty salmon runs, but hatcheries on the reservation release up to 10 million fish a year with designs to provide for their people. Bingo, casino-style gambling and long-term commercial and private leases of Indian land now constitute the primary sources of in-come for the tribes. Money is constantly being raised to buy back reser-vation land that was sold to non-Indians and businesses over the years.

For a side-trip off of I-5 that will tickle the fancy of bird watchers, take Fir Island Road west to sparsely populated **Fir Island**, 17 miles north of the Tulalip reservation. The fan-shaped island is located between the North and South forks of the Skagit River, both of which create a series of sloughs before emptying into Skagit Bay. Farmhouses and barns sit on acres of potatoes and cabbage that thrive on the fertile soil and ample water supply.

The skeleton of **Skagit City** rests alone on the northern tip of the delta where the Skagit River divides in two. This forgotten shell of a town was the biggest "city" in the area between the 1870s and 1890s, when barge-size log jams fed hungry mills and steamers rushed to haul the timber to points along Puget Sound. A sizable community sprang up around the log booms, fishing the river for salmon and clearing areas for farming with the help of friendly coastal Indian tribes. The settlement ceased to exist in a hurry when the natural log jam cleared and the swiftly flowing river eroded away the banks, carrying most of the town with it. A dilapidated building and overgrown road are all that remain of Skagit City.

Besides a proliferation of water, the other constant feature of Fir Island are its birds. On the island's southern edge the **Skagit Wildlife Area** serves as a migratory stop for protected snow geese, and year-round habitat for trumpeter swans. Immense flocks of these graceful white birds can be seen hovering above fields of green. Large portions of land are devoted entirely to growing barley for the feathered friends to eat. Rotating seasonally, fields sing with multi-colored tulips in the spring, then make way for potatoes, corn and cucumbers in late summer and fall. In winter, swans and snow geese lay claim to the land.

From Moore Road on Fir Island, follow Chilberg Road three miles northwest past farmhouses and A-frames to the mouth of the Skagit River and quaint **La Conner** (Elevation 8, Population 713). Skagit Valley's oldest community and one-time county seat, La Conner served as a trading post and supply center as early as 1870 for settlers trying to dike the river and till the land. John Conner bought the post for $500 from his brother James in 1872 and named the new town for his wife, Louisa A. Conner. Soon a shipping port developed for timber and fish, and it became a regular stop for steamers delivering passengers and goods from Seattle. After showing early promise, the town's growth was permanently stunted at the turn of the century when the fishing industry sunk and the population of over 1,000 plummeted. But not all was lost. The boom era produced many large Victorian homes and a waterfront district that were never torn down or tampered with, leaving a legacy of yester-year that attracts the tourists in droves. Visit the **Skagit County Historical Museum** (501 4th Street) for a look at turn of the century life, along with a stunning view of farmlands, Skagit Bay, the Cascade Range and Mt. Baker.

65~

In the mid-1970s, tourism revived the streets of La Conner. Old homes and buildings now serve as bed and breakfasts and antique shops for weekend get-aways and day trips from Seattle and the surrounding areas. Over 75% of the businesses in town are in the retail, restaurant or hotel industry, making tourism the leading economic generator.

In the 1960s and 70s a community of artists inhabited the abandoned Indian village of Fishtown at the mouth of the North Fork of the Skagit River near La Conner. The dramatic scenery and isolation attracted painters, poets, musicians and craftsmen who set up a commune in the idyllic locale; Beat author Jack Kerouac (*On the Road, The Dharma Bums*) was known to have spent some time here, and more recently, popular novelist Tom Robbins (*Another Roadside Attraction, Even Cowgirls Get the Blues, Jitterbug Perfume*). The commune has since dispersed, but nationally-recognized artists still live and find inspiration in La Conner.

A tractor in a cloud of dust, a common sight from the interstate.

Back on the freeway, I-5 runs through the Skagit Valley and on to **Mt. Vernon** (Elevation 29, Population 20,450), named after George Washington's home on the Potomac. Settlers originally ventured into the valley in the 1860s, attracted to the Skagit River's capacity for transportation, irrigation and fishing. But these benefits were nearly counteracted by an impressive log-jam that held so much wood that navigation was impossible beyond it. The downed, water-logged timber had accumulated long enough for new trees and bushes to rise from the decaying bark and river sediment, forming unstable islands in the current. Unable to proceed further, pioneers platted Mt. Vernon at the beginning of this natural dam. After years of steady effort, the log-jam was finally cleared in 1879, opening up trade and commercial opportunities vital to early development.

The clearing of the Skagit coincided with the flow of hopeful miners following the scent of gold to the river's origin at Ruby Creek. Despite the hype, most returned with little more than gold dust on their trousers. Busted, many opted to settle in Mt. Vernon on the journey back downriver to become farmers and loggers. Timber was floated down the river to mills built along the banks where sternwheelers would carry them to markets around Puget Sound. Logging operations thinned out as the valley was cleared, making way for an agriculture industry that is now among the most productive in the state. In summer months, impromptu farmers' markets sprout up downtown, as fresh fruits and vegetables are sold from the back of pick-ups and out of the trunks of cars.

Of the countless different crops grown in the valley, perhaps the one that attracts the most attention is the tulip. Each April the town celebrates the end of winter with the Skagit Valley Tulip Festival. Bulbs were planted for years on a smaller scale, but the arrival of Dutch immigrants in the 1930s turned tulip planting into a major production. Bulbs from Mt. Vernon are now sold all over the world, including in Holland.

Skagit County: Mt. Vernon is the county seat of Skagit County, created in 1883 from Whatcom County and named after a local Indian tribe. It is located in the northwestern part of the state and stretches from Puget Sound on the west to the crest of the Cascade Mountains on the east. The county has been settled since 1859; however, gold strikes in the 1870s brought in miners who later took up logging and farming after the gold petered out. In 1889 the introduction of a railroad into the county helped increase its population. Today, Skagit County has a rich and diverse economic base. It is one of the state's most productive vegetable and berry growing areas. Dairying and poultry raising are important economic activities and the county is also a producer of cement, steel and wood products.

Court House: 205 Kincaid Street, Mt. Vernon 98273, 206-336-9313 (Information), FAX 206-336-9307 (Commissioners). Area: 1,734.6 square miles. State Ranking: 25th. 1993 Population: 88,500. Unincorporated: 42,213. Incorporated: 46,287. Density: 51.0 persons per square mile. **Cities and Towns**: Anacortes, Burlington, Concrete, Hamilton, La Conner, Lyman, Mt. Vernon, Sedro Woolley. **Principal Economic Activities**: Wood products, petroleum and coal processing, food processing, agriculture. **Points of Interest**: Upper and Lower Baker Dam, Skagit Valley tulip fields.

Climate: (Mt. Vernon - elevation 29)

	Jan	Apr	Jul	Oct
Max Temp. F°	45.1	58.2	75.1	60.3
Min Temp.	32.5	39.4	49.3	42.3
Mean Temp.	38.8	48.8	62.2	51.3
Precipitation	4.22"	2.40"	.81"	3.60"

Average Annual Maximum Temperature: 59.5
Average Annual Minimum Temperature: 41.0
Annual Mean Temperature: 50.3
Average Annual Precipitation: 32.15"

One mile north of Mt. Vernon the highway crosses the **Skagit River**, the source behind the valley's rich soil. Thousands of years of flooding and glacial runoff have nourished the earth and created a silt loam soil ideal for farming. Fourteen major floods have occurred since 1815, some leaving as much as eight feet of water on the valley floor. Early settlers built dikes, dams and levees to control the rising river, but each manipulation of the water supply created a greater risk of flooding. Dozens of settlements and would-be towns were violently washed away when dikes failed to hold. As technology progressed, hydroelectric power became the mainstay for the region; the Skagit River now supplies the juice for most of the greater Seattle area. At 125 miles long, the Skagit — "hidden from enemies" — is the second largest watershed in the state with over 2,900 tributaries contributing to the flow. One-third of all fresh water entering Puget Sound comes from the river.

Due to the high volumes of fish, the Skagit River Valley is home to one of the largest populations of bald eagles in the Pacific Northwest. Autumn is the best time to view the magnificent symbols of our nation, as they return to feed on the spawning salmon.

Blending into the outskirts of Mt. Vernon is **Burlington** (Elevation 34, Population 4,690). In 1890 Thomas W. Soules arrived in the newly organized state of Washington and staked a claim on a stump-covered lot in the center of a small, nameless logging community. No one in the sparse population lodged a complaint when he suggested the fledgling town be named Burlington after his native Burlington, Vermont, a similarly green place, so the name stayed. Though small, the town is an agricultural giant in the region, with soil fertile enough to make an old farmer stand back and let out a slow whistle. Expansive and well-manicured fields of tulips explode with color every spring.

Leaving the Skagit Valley, I-5 winds along wooded hillsides for 12 miles until Samish Lake makes brief appearances through the trees on the west side. The highway emerges from the forest and heads into **Bellingham** (Elevation 25, Population 55,480). Rich in resources, the area along the sheltered bay remained largely untouched for the first half of the nineteenth century due to territorial disputes between the U.S. and Great Britain. When the boundary was set at the 49th parallel in 1846, the northwest corner of the territory was deemed open for settlement.

The first to arrive were Captain Henry Roeder, a former skipper on a Great Lakes ship, and Russel V. Peabody, an adventurer prone to wandering. The two men first met on the Great Plains and decided to travel together to California, enduring Indian attacks, bandit raids and a harsh winter along the way. After several failed business ventures and a stint as luckless gold miners, they journeyed to the Pacific Northwest with plans to start a salmon cannery or timber mill. Finding  mills already whirling in Seattle, they continued to Port Townsend, then paddled a canoe to Bellingham Bay. Crowded stands of cedar, Douglas fir and hemlock all pointed to a future in the timber industry for Roeder and Peabody.

Since three nearby creeks — Padden, Whatcom and Squalicum — drain into Bellingham Bay, a water-powered mill seemed like a worthwhile endeavor. The Lummi Indian name for Whatcom Creek means "noisy all the time," so following the constant rumble, the two men discovered Whatcom Falls and an ideal spot for a mill. After obtaining the permission of Cha-wit-zit, the Lummi chief, they began construction. Early in 1853, Roeder sailed to San Francisco and returned by summer with supplies and a small party of workers and their families. The mill was soon cutting a profit, thanks in large part to the San Francisco fire that caused timber prices to soar. The town of Whatcom rose around the mill and soon became the seat of the newly established Whatcom County.

Later that year a second industry took root when William R. Pattle, an ex-Hudson's Bay Company man, uncovered a coal mine on his donation claim. Word of the rich deposits spread quickly, leading men northward with pick axes in hand. As the digs got bigger and the ore piled up, a need arose for more efficient transport. Capitalizing on the demand, Roeder built a schooner of local timber to ship coal to southern Puget Sound. On his northward return he brought mail, supplies and new residents.

A portion of Bellingham Bay.

Typical throughout the Washington Territory, Indian unrest seized Bellingham in 1855, sending settlers scurrying for the blockhouses. The greatest threat came from the warlike tribes of Alaska and British Columbia who regularly raided the bay, but even the friendly and non-aggressive Lummi and Nooksack tribes became resentful of increasing numbers of homesteaders. After urgent appeals for protection, the government sent Captain George E. Pickett (later a hero at the Battle of Gettysburg) to establish Fort Bellingham on a bluff overlooking the bay. The fort was manned for four uneventful years, granting the soldiers time to work on civic improvements such as buildings roads and a bridge spanning Whatcom Creek. This assurance of safety also encouraged further settlement along the bay.

A population boom echoed through the new settlements in 1857 when gold was discovered on the Fraser River in British Columbia. Bellingham Bay was a springboard to the northern mines, welcoming prospectors by the thousands. In a few short weeks, so many steamers had arrived that a wharf was constructed on the spot. Buildings, stores and saloons soon followed. Expansive tent cities covered the hillsides, and as land became scarce, lots were sold for as much as $500. But as was often the case, fortune turned quickly; it was soon declared that miners must report in Victoria before passing into Canada. Since Bellingham was no longer a convenient stopover, many left town as hurriedly as they had arrived. Despite the exodus, enough stayed to form the nucleus of new communities, and four towns were left in the wake of the retreating steamers: Whatcom, Fairhaven, Sehome and Bellingham.

The year 1880 brought both numbers and prosperity when nearly 600 new residents arrived from Kansas. Citing a inhospitable reception from existing land owners, they formed their own community across the creek from Whatcom and called it New Whatcom. Perhaps the size of the envoy was a bit intimidating for those already settled, but regardless of any perceived threat, the influx gave the area new life and a needed industrial boost. After building a wharf, the newcomers threw their energy into a cannery for salmon, herring and bottom fish. The first few years of the packing business were erratic at best, but served to take some pressure off of local timber and mining industries running in Whatcom. Consistent profits were still many years off, but the Kansans laid the foundation for what is still a primary industry.

In 1888, a millionaire named Nelson Bennett arrived in Fairhaven with 1,000 workers to build the Fairhaven and Southern Railroad and expand the existing town. With all the new activity, Fairhaven became a wild and violent place during the construction period. Saloons (28 in all) were among the first structures raised along the muddy streets, most equipped with adjoining brothels. Bennett had originally prohibited saloons, but when workers rioted and threatened to abandon their jobs, he dropped the dry status.

To counteract the debauchery, a team of Methodist Episcopalian missionaries assembled to save the lost souls, and a sort of religious martial law ensued to clean up the town. Discipline prescribed by the clergy council was severe. Public cursing was punishable by five days in the slammer (complete with daily visits from the preacher) and five days on the chain gang. Suffice to say, the sheriff was one busy man.

The separate towns may have considered themselves rivals, but prosperity, like adversity, spilled over from one to the other, making consolidation inevitable and more desirable. So, in 1890, Bellingham and Fairhaven joined to become Fairhaven. Less than a year later,

Whatcom, New Whatcom and Sehome combined to form the *new* New Whatcom. In 1905, Whatcom (which had since dropped the "New" from its name) fused with Fairhaven and by vote was called Bellingham. Sound confusing? Well, in many ways it was, but this helps to explain why the layout of the city seems a bit arbitrary. The streets of the old Fairhaven district are still lined with original cobble-stone, and though many century old homes and buildings received recent face lifts, the venerable complexion still peeks through.

Despite some bureaucratic complications, incorporation proved beneficial for Bellingham. The four hamlets in the wilderness fused to become the fourth largest city in the state. Three main railroad terminals were present by the turn of the century, bringing new inhabitants and expanded commerce. Electric street cars moved through town and two telephone and telegraph companies kept them well-connected to cities along Puget Sound. The Old City Hall, built in 1892, now houses the **Whatcom County Museum of History and Art** (121 Prospect Street).

Western Washington University.

Creatively organized, the museum re-creates life in Bellingham around 1900, accompanied by sound effects and recorded voices detailing early history.

Sitting atop Sehome Hill overlooking the bay and surrounding town is **Western Washington University**. Begun as the Northwest Normal School for teachers in 1893 when Governor McGraw approved its move from Lynden, it later achieved full university status in 1977. Sprawling and wooded, the grounds teem with friendly students and has a noticeably laid-back and casual atmosphere. Tucked among the campus' gardens and gracing its courtyards are 17 sculptures crafted by internationally-known artists, creating one of the world's largest outdoor collections.

Surrounded by wilderness just two miles east of downtown Bellingham is **Lake Whatcom**. For a scenic drive along the western shoreline of the curvy, 12-mile lake, take Lake Whatcom Boulevard east from downtown. **Whatcom Falls Park** (1401 Electric Avenue) is a popular student swimming hole and short hiking trail only minutes from downtown.

Whatcom County: Bellingham is the county seat of Whatcom County, organized in 1854 from Island County and named after a local

Indian chief. It is located in the northwest corner of the state. In the eighteenth century the county was visited by Spanish and British explorers; Bellingham Bay was named by Captain George Vancouver. The first settlers in the county arrived in 1852 and began cutting lumber for the San Francisco market. By the turn of the century Bellingham was an important salmon processing, lumber manufacturing and export center. Whatcom County has a varied economic base led by wood products, manufacturing, food processing, mining and dairying. Western Washington University is a center for higher education in northern Washington.

Court House: 311 Grand Avenue, Bellingham 98225, 206-676-6700, SCAN 769-6700, FAX 206-676-7727. Area: 2,126.2 square miles. State Ranking: 12th. 1993 Population: 140,900. Unincorporated: 66,461. Incorporated: 74,439. Density: 66.3 persons per square mile. **Cities and Towns**: Bellingham, Blaine, Everson, Ferndale, Lynden, Nooksack, Sumas. **Principal Economic Activities**: Food processing, wood products, petroleum refining, manufacturing, agriculture. **Points of Interest**: Mt. Baker, Fort Bellingham, Ross Lake.

Climate: (Bellingham - elevation 50)

	Jan	Apr	Jul	Oct
Max Temp. F°	43.2	56.9	72.9	59.3
Min Temp.	31.3	39.7	52.8	42.2
Mean Temp.	37.3	48.4	62.9	50.8
Precipitation	4.28"	2.56"	.93"	4.09"

Average Annual Maximum Temperature: 57.9
Average Annual Minimum Temperature: 41.6
Annual Mean Temperature: 49.8
Average Annual Precipitation: 35.12"

North of Bellingham on I-5 is **Ferndale** (Elevation 136, Population 6,420). The settlement was first known as *Jam* for the logjam on the Nooksack River that runs through town. The present title was coined by the town's first teacher, Alice Eldridge, because the school was located in a fern patch. Darius Rogers, an ambitious developer and businessman, established Ferndale in 1878 when he built a cedar building and set up the town's first post office. He encouraged and convinced many early businesses to set up shop in the community, and despite their small size, even led a charge to gain the county seat.

A botched attempt to secure a steamboat route between Ferndale and Seattle caused Rogers to lose his land holdings in town. Forced to relocate, he took the post office with him and moved to the west side of the Nooksack River, called it West Ferndale and succeeded in splitting the town into two factions. Despite years of protest, most businesses eventually followed and the West was dropped from the name.

Pioneer Park, located at the southern end of First Street, has one of the largest collections of vintage log homes in the state, with some

Pioneer Park in Ferndale dating back to the 1870s.

dating back to the early 1870s. Impressive in their design and dur-
ability, they were built with massive cedar planks up to two feet wide
that remain solid even after a century worth of weathering. The homes
were relocated here from around town and several scattered spots
in northwestern Washington.

Located on the U.S.-Canada border at the northern end of I-5 is
Blaine (Elevation 41, Population 2,860). Originally called Semiahmoo
for the local Indian tribe, the town began as the headquarters for the
American and British Boundary Survey Commission, a team created
to draw the official dividing line between the countries. Since that
time, the crossing has been a integral part of Blaine's economy. An
estimated 70,000 people pass through here daily, providing plenty of
opportunity for local service and retail businesses to thrive. When platted in 1884, the name was changed to honor James G. Blaine, the
unsuccessful Republican presidential candidate of that year, and later
U.S. Secretary of State.

Overlooking duty-free shops, the Customs and Immigration
Station and a steady stream of border traffic is the **International Peace
Arch**. Built in 1921 as an affirmation of peace between the U.S. and
Canada, the 67-foot white concrete monument straddles the border
on a long stretch of grass. Etched onto the U.S. side of the arch is the
motto "Children of a Common Mother;" the Canadian side reads
"Brethren Dwelling Together in Unity." Within the arch are caskets
containing portions of the Pilgrim ship *Mayflower* and the British
vessel *Beaver*, which in 1836 became the first steam vessel to cross
the Pacific Ocean. The passage between countries is controlled by a
gate that is hinged on both sides so that it cannot be closed without
mutual consent. Representing over 3,000 miles of undefended
border and over a century of peace, it is considered the only
monument of its kind in the world.

The Peace Arch was the inspiration of Sam Hill, an eccentric millionaire, visionary and proponent of good roads, who wished to create a legacy of amiable relations that would serve as an example to other nations. An estimated 10,000 people attended the dedication ceremony on September 6, 1921, years before Canada had even connected a road to the monument. At the dedication, a letter was read from President Warren Harding praising Hill's dedication to a worthy cause: "The fact that a boundary line over 3,000 miles long remains unfortified — these are the testimonies that the world grows wiser

Peace Arch State Park.

and better . . . I wish to convey to you personally my high appreciation of your patriotic service in providing a symbolic shrine to international peace." In 1931, land adjacent to the monument was purchased to create **Peace Arch State Park**. The 40-acre park and garden was partially funded by contributions from school children in Washington and British Columbia.

Long before the Peace Arch welcomed the flow of travelers, thick runs of salmon ran past Drayton Harbor and along the coastline. When the military arrived in 1856 to quell border disputes, settlers followed in their bootsteps, and most turned to fishing for their livelihood. So many boats began mooring permanently in the harbor that a salmon cannery opened in 1884 to process the mounting catches. The cannery also helped root a permanent population of workers. Stability brought new industries, and by the late 1880s several sawmills whirled in town. Present-day sport and commercial fishermen still base their operations out of Blaine's protected port. The piers are lined with an assortment of fishing and crabbing boats that work directly off the coast, along with larger commercial fleets sailing for the northern waters of Alaska. Peace Portal Drive, the town's main strip, skirts the edge of a bluff overlooking the harbor and moorage, with a clear view of Vancouver Island and the hills of Canada beyond.

Although I-5 concludes at the border, Blaine is not the last stop on the tour. That distinction belongs to a tiny severed tip of U.S. soil known as **Point Roberts**. To reach the estranged hamlet, you must first cross into Canada and travel 25 miles west through British Columbia towards Tsawwassen on Canadian Route 99 to reach the customs house. The result of a geographical oversight, the point was missed during the 1846 boundary talks between the United States and

Canada, when an impartial Kaiser Wilhelm I of Germany cited the
49th parallel as the international dividing line. When the line was
officially drawn in 1862, both countries were surprised to find this
five-square-mile peninsula to be on the American side.

Point Roberts has a long history of being overlooked. The Salish
Indians are the first known people to occupy the area, originally calling the peninsula *Tceltenum*, meaning "could not see it," when a group
of Indians crossing the Gulf of Georgia in canoes accidentally beached
during a dense fog that shrouded the shoreline. The chief then chose
the name to document their unexpected arrival. The discovery of a
large collection of buried artifacts helped date this landing back nearly
3,000 years.

A small salmon fishing operation worked off the point as early as
1853, and despite being declared a military reserve shortly after, other
fisherman arrived to claim land and make it their home port. Technically the land acquisition was illegal, but this seemed a minor issue
since the area was virtually ignored by the government. This vague
occupation led to conflict over property boundaries and a sense of
lawlessness ruled Point Roberts for many years. Land was taken and
held by force, and lives were lost defending disputed parcels and even
livestock. This free-for-all resumed until an act of Congress in 1884
awarded land to those already in place and public auction distributed the rest.

Isolation also turned Point Roberts into a notorious safe harbor
for smugglers and pirates who raided fish traps and menaced boats
around Birch Bay. Solo vessels were occasionally outnumbered and
forced to pay a "tax" for safe passage by the high-seas thieves. American moonshine was a hot item in Canada and was often exchanged
for cheap beef and other foodstuffs coming from the north. Illegal
activity slowed considerably after 1910 when the government built
the Point Roberts Lighthouse on the southwestern tip of the peninsula, signaling a greater attention to the customs operations on the
once-forgotten point. (An exception being during the Prohibition era
when intoxicating contraband trickled south across the watery boundary.)

Fishing, farming and logging were all pursued vigorously until
resources were exhausted, leaving the peninsula a quiet, rural community. The cape is now a popular summer vacation and retirement
spot for both Americans and Canadians.

State **Highway 6** from a junction with U.S. Highway 101 in
Raymond southeast via Menlo, east through Lebam and
Frances to Pe Ell, north to Doty, then east via Littell and Claquato
to a junction with Interstate 5 in Chehalis. Route length: 51 miles.

Highway 6 tours the rolling, verdant landscape of the **Willapa Hills**,
probably the least well known of the state's seven geographical

regions. Streams, marshes and ponds dot the lush terrain and form the headwaters for the Willapa and Chehalis rivers. Dairy farms and their healthy-looking cattle fill the valley floor and logging operations work the sporadically-placed, steeply-sloped foothills.

A few miles out of Raymond near the community of Menlo an historical sign marks the grave site of **Willie Keil**, the 19-year-old son of Dr. William Keil, leader of a communal group from Bethel, Missouri who settled in the area in November of 1855. Willie, who had shown a great interest in the wild frontier of the Northwest, died four days before the pioneers embarked on their journey. As a tribute to his son Dr. Keil converted the lead wagon into a hearse and enclosed Willie's body in a lead-lined, alcohol-filled casket, preserving him for a burial in the lands he had so desired to see. The grave is found a short distance up the hillside in the Fern Hill Cemetery.

The road heads south along the Willapa River, veers east at the Willapa Fish Hatchery and continues through small, sleepy communities with interesting names such as Nallpee, Lebam, Globe and Pluvius. In **Frances**, look for the beige-colored Catholic church (built in 1892) south of the highway. Most of these communities developed in the 1890s as the Northern Pacific laid tracks to transport lumber being processed at local mills. The area is lightly populated but is experiencing some growth as the scenic area becomes less of a secret.

Pe Ell (pee-EL, Elevation 411, Population 560) appears as the highway breaks clear of the forest about halfway between Raymond and Chehalis. The town's unusual name was the result of local Indians mispronouncing the name of a French-Canadian and Hudson's Bay Company employee named Pierre. A large Polish population, attracted to the area's endless logging opportunities, built an impressive Catholic church (Third Street) that is visible a few blocks off the highway.

The road continues, now along the Chehalis River, through a wide open valley and a marked increased in civilization as the I-5 corridor approaches. Two miles from Chehalis an historical marker describes the importance of **Claquato** (KLA-kwa-toh, an Indian word for "top of hill") and the Claquato Methodist Church. Founded in 1852 by Louis H. Davis, Claquato served as the seat for Lewis County from 1856 until 1873. When the Northern Pacific Railroad deemed the town's elevated location inconvenient, the county seat was lost to Chehalis and Claquato instantly quieted.

The solid Claquato Church was built in 1858 of hand-forged nails and a strong mortise frame. Its bronze bell was cast in Boston and shipped around Cape Horn to be placed in a steeple that is said to resemble Christ's crown of thorns.

Highway 6 crosses the Newaukum River and joins I-5 in Chehalis.∞

State Highway 7 from a junction with Interstate 5 south through Spanaway, La Grande and Elbe to a junction with U.S. Highway 12 in Morton. Route length: 57 miles.

Highway 7 could aptly be titled "the road to the road to Mt. Rainier." Occupying a large chunk of real estate to the southeast, views of the massive volcano improve with every mile gained. Travelers from south King County may take this highway 40 miles to a junction with State Highway 706, the indisputable "road to Mt. Rainier."

The first 10 miles of Highway 7 (Pacific Avenue) crawl through south Tacoma suburban sprawl, passing stoplights, strip malls, mini-marts and the entrance to **Pacific Lutheran University**, founded in 1890 and granted university status in 1960.

Modern condominium and apartment complexes and the Lake Spanaway Golf Course mask **Spanaway's** (SPAN-uh-way) history as one of the oldest settlements in Pierce County, but the Hudson's Bay Company operated here as early as the 1840s. The company's April 26, 1849 entry in the

Majestic Mt. Rainier.

Nisqually Journal of Occurrences lists "Two plows sent to Spannuch and one to Muck," a far cry from the bulldozers that have shaped the community in recent years. Spanaway somehow derived from the Indian word *Spannuch,* meaning "on the shore of the lake," a reference to Spanaway Lake.

Just past Spanaway, at an intersection with State Highway 507, thick forest draws an informal barrier against further development and the road continues as a two-laner. Twenty miles beyond the junction the highway meets the Nisqually River at La Grande, where in 1912 a hydroelectric plant was built to provide electricity for Tacoma. One of the earliest municipally-owned projects in the state, the plant had a generating capacity of up to 25,600 kilowatts.

The Nisqually River accompanies the road to **Alder Lake**. The shallow, seven-mile-long lake is noteworthy for its grayish-green hue, and for being the approximate location of the **Stratoliner Crash**. In March of 1939, the giant Boeing plane was on a test flight when it fell apart in mid-air; killing all 10 passengers instantly.

Firmly positioned at the southeast end of the lake beneath a circle of timbered ridges, **Elbe** (EL-bee) has long been a logging town (some of the state's earliest logging and mining railroads operated here), but has recently embraced tourism as its economic mainstay. Three retired railroad cars have been converted to a restaurant, a bar, and the Hobo Inn. During the summer and early fall you can ride aboard a steam train on the **Mt. Rainier Scenic Railroad**. The line chugs through tall forests and over bridges to Mineral Lake, offering broad, unobstructed views of Mt. Rainier.

Adjacent to the railroad siding is **E.V. Lutheran Kirche**. This small, quaint church was established in 1906 to serve a German-Lutheran population that began immigration in the 1880s. Primarily hailing from villages located along the banks of the Elbe River in Germany's Elbe Valley, the German contingency brought the namesake with them. The church is closed but maintained; a viewing stand outside allows you to peer into its cozy and charming interior.

Outside Elbe, you can either take Highway 706 to Mt. Rainier National Park or turn right across the Nisqually, climbing south over Summit Creek (Elevation 1,740). The remaining 17 miles are a glaring combination of thick forest and logged-off slopes; some mountains are completely bare. A large lumber mill signals the end of the road and your arrival in Morton. ∽

State Highway 8 from a junction with U.S. Highway 12 in Elma, east through McCleary to a junction with U.S. Highway 101. Route length: 21 miles.

McCleary (Elevation 320, Population 1,501), not visible from the highway, is enclosed by a circle of trees and logged-off hills. A cluster of uniform homes extend from a towering smokestack, an appendage of the McCleary Mill. What began as a small sawmill in 1898 expanded into the largest sash-and-door-producing factory in the country. (Some claim it was "the largest in the world," but who can keep track of such things?) By 1941, the depletion of timber resources forced Henry McCleary to sell his assets (he essentially owned the entire town) to the Simpson Logging Company of Shelton, and in an admirable act of fairness, that company allowed employees to purchase homes for 18 months rent. The mill shut down in 1985 but the Simpson Company continues to manufacture doors.

Located on the grounds of a small park in the center of town is an example of a tiny locomotive known as "dinky" or "the dink." First used to haul logs out of the woods on narrow gauge tracks for the

Puget Sound and Chehalis Railroad, the McCleary Timber Company bought the railroad and the dink in 1905 and rebuilt the workhorse to run on standard gauge tracks, hauling logs to the sawmill. Its weak braking system caused several accidents, so like an old racehorse turned out to pasture, the dink finished its distinguished career as a switch engine for the mills.

Highway 8 from McCleary offers more shades of green than a landscape artist could ever possibly use. The road tours the verdant landscape 15 miles to meet U.S. 101 six miles out of Olympia. ⋈

State Highway 9 from a junction with State Highway 522 north via Snohomish, Lake Stevens, Arlington, McMurray, Sedro Woolley, Deming, Nooksack and Sumas to the Canadian boundary. (Overlaps State Highway 542.) Route length: 96 miles.

Highway 9, more of a country road than a state highway, is a soothingly scenic, light-traffic alternative to the hectic Interstate 5. From its beginning north of Woodinville, it weaves lazily northward, generally avoiding population areas. The road's appeal lies with its geological diversity; thick forest, snow-capped peaks, open valleys and prairies, lakes, streams and rivers all make dramatic appearances along the route, set against a backdrop of green.

Fat and happy.

After skirting Snohomish (U.S. Highway 2), you'll roll past the west shoreline of Lake Stevens, named in honor of Isaac I. Stevens, first governor of the Washington Territory. The town of **Lake Stevens** (Elevation 220, Population 4,540), planted on the north edge of the lake, is a bedroom community of Everett.

A broken line of large farmsteads lead north to **Arlington** (Elevation 103, Population 4,690). A drive through the three-square-block town center reveals old Western-style wooden buildings that house feed and seed outlets, hardware stores, tractor maintenance and repair shops and friendly, down-home ma and pa restaurants. Cattle and sheep graze in yards just paces from the front doors of well-maintained homes.

Arlington was once divided into two small communities built at the confluence of the north and south forks of the Stillaguamish River. The older, platted in 1883, was a logging outfit called Haller City; the younger was constructed around a train depot in 1890 and named Arlington by railroad promoters for the national cemetery in Washington D.C. The adjoining towns were informally lumped together as Forks for a decade until a community vote made consolidation official in 1903.

For a postcard perfect view of the surrounding area, cross the bridge a half-mile east of town and take Arlington Heights Road north. At the top of a hill there is a turn-off in a clearing that looks over the rich, water-logged valley. Streams that roll out from the base of the Cascade Mountains create sloughs that turn the fields emerald green. The Stillaguamish River collects these streams while flowing east to Port Susan south of Stanwood. Clear-cut hills backed by the tops of snow-covered peaks dot the horizon. Logging trucks regularly roll down this road on their way through Arlington and on to I-5.

Back on Highway 9, continue winding through the woods and up to the shore of **Lake McMurray**, a small lake with an even smaller adjoining community called **McMurray**. The town is little more than a general store and a service station; a few homes surround the water. A shingle mill once sustained the town, but most folks around here have turned to more agrarian pursuits.

Gliding by Big Lake and Clear Lake and around Sedro Woolley (State Highway 20), the next 20 miles are pure pastoral pleasure. Wooded hills rise on both sides as the road dips and weaves through a long valley sprinkled with tiny communities, barns, grazing cattle and mechanical beasts of burden toiling in green fields. Friendly waves from passing farmers in pickups serve as mobile gestures of country hospitality. Crossing a bridge where the Nooksack and North Fork rivers merge, the highway meets Highway 542 in **Deming**, a logging community and tribal center for the Nooksack people.

After sharing five miles of pavement, Highway 9 branches off on its own again and proceeds north to the homey hinterland of **Nooksack** (Elevation 85, Population 675). The town was platted in anticipation of the arrival of the Northern Pacific Railroad in 1885, but the engines failed to materialize. Undaunted, the expectant settlers simply went ahead with their plans to build a farming community, using horses and riverboats to transport their produce. Though the name means "fern-eating people," most local folks prefer to snack on the raspberries that grow prolifically on the surrounding farms. Dairy farms add to the rustic setting.

The remainder of Highway 9 crosses a flat prairie of hayfields and silos before ending at the Canadian border in **Sumas** (Elevation 45,

Population 839). Sumas has long been a major thoroughfare, starting with wagons that carried hopeful miners to the Fraser River during the gold rush of 1858, and arriving at the current procession of motorized vehicles that line up to pass customs. Two main railroads built depots here prior to 1900, adding slightly to the population, but most stayed only long enough to catch the next train. Dairy farms, a minor lumber mill and services that cater to the flow of travelers add to the local economy. ↂ

Field, barn, and silo — American icons.

State Highway 10 from a junction with State Highway 970 southeast to a junction with U.S. Highway 97. Route length: 16 miles. Highway 10 can be reached by driving east from Cle Elum on Highway 970 for three miles.

If traveling to or from Ellensburg, take this highway as a scenic alternative to Interstate 90. The road passes through a rugged canyon and accompanies the Yakima River and Burlington Northern's tracks to U.S. 97. Ellensburg lies three miles further east. ↂ

State Highway 11 from a junction with Interstate 5 north to Bellingham. Route length: 22 miles.

Better known as **Chuckanut Drive**, this scenic highway covers two distinct landscapes characteristic of northwestern Washington: farmland and rugged coastline. The dividing line between the contrasting terrain is easy to recognize. Taking off from I-5 just past Burlington and rolling northward through the open greenbelt of the Skagit Valley, an abrupt hairpin turn leads to a wooded bluff overlooking Samish Bay. Twisting along a series of tight S-curves at the base of the 1,940-foot-high Chuckanut Mountain, the narrow roadway is canopied by thick trees growing only a few feet from the pavement. Simply negotiating the turns is exhilarating in itself, but the real thrill is the view. Aged madrona and evergreen trees grow to the extreme edge of the water, where waves break in a fury against the sawtooth rocks below. A handful of heavily wooded islands provide an impressive backdrop. Three viewpoints along the road allow room to park the car and soak it all in.

Built from 1916 to 1918, Chuckanut Drive is the state's oldest scenic highway, and portions appear to have not been re-paired since originally laid. The stretch along the jagged coast is prone to land-slides and falling rock and is riddled with potholes like some pre-asphalt throw-back. But the roughness gives the route character and seems appropriate consid-ering the location.

Highway 11 winding through the trees.

To reach the beach and conduct a firsthand exploration of the area, visit the 2,500-acre **Larrabee State Park**, seven miles south of Bellingham. Created in 1923, it is Washington's first state park and includes tide pools, two lakes and a net-work of trails. Just east of the highway, a five-mile hiking and biking trail leads from the park to the Fairhaven District in Bellingham. The path is an old roadbed for an electric railroad that connected Bellingham and Mt. Vernon from 1912 to 1930. Highway 11 ends its dramatic run at a connection with I-5 south of Bellingham. ℘

US Highway 12 from a junction with U.S. Highway 101 in Aberdeen, east through Montesano and Elma, south via Oakville, Centralia and Chehalis, east through Mossyrock, Morton, White Pass and Naches, southeast past Selah, Yakima, Union Gap, Zillah, Granger, Sunnyside, Grandview, Benton City, Burbank, Wallula and Walla Walla, then northeast via Waitsburg, Dayton and Pomeroy, to the Washington-Idaho border in Clarkston. (Overlaps Interstates 5, 82 and 182.) Route length: 429 miles.

From Aberdeen's (U.S. 101) timbered harbor, U.S. 12 extends 11 miles east to **Montesano** (Mahn-tuh-SAH-noh, Elevation 65, Popula-tion 3,510). The county seat of Grays Harbor (formerly Chehalis County) since 1886, historic Montesano lies at the confluence of the sluggish Wynoochee and the Chehalis rivers. The first settlement was made on the south bank of the Chehalis by Isaiah Scammon, who had come from Maine in 1852. Scammon's wife, a devoutly religious woman, proposed the town be named Mt. Zion, but instead it was called Scammon's, and later Wynooche, before receiving its present name; Spanish for "healthy mountain" and suggested by the large hill to the north.

As early as 1859 steamboats began to run the Chehalis River between Satsop and Grays Harbor. On February 9, 1860, the steamer *Enterprise,* built in Montesano and loaded with troops of Company A, Fourth Infantry, stopped at the harbor mouth to establish a fort at Point Chehalis (Westport). By 1880, Montesano was advertising steamer connections with San Francisco.

The timber industry, poised to explode, attracted droves of settlers. Many crossed to the north side of the river and began a second settlement. A town was platted and given the name of the old settlement, which then became known as South Montesano.

In February, 1883, upon hearing that the government was going to require applicants for timber claims to advertise legal notice, Joseph Calder and James Walsh hastily moved to Montesano and entered the news-paper business. The young but far sighted business-men brought with them a $400 roller press and eight fonts of type. When Calder retired after ten months, his pro-fits had reached 2,400 percent. More than anything else, this indicated the number of timber claims being stak-ed in the region,

Grays Harbor County Courthouse in Montesano.

particularly up the Wynoochee River. Mills sprang up along the Chehalis River, and in the early eighties a sawmill was built on Lake Sylvia, just north of the townsite. To compound the burgeoning city's prosperity, the Northern Pacific Railroad rolled into town in September of 1889 and one month later, Montesano turned on its first electric lights.

Montesano is a good town in which to park the car and walk around. Large, affluent homes are evidence of a successful past. Many buildings are fronted with reader boards offering descriptions of the structures and their historical significance. The **Grays Harbor County**

US 12 **Courthouse** (Broadway and First, built in 1910), a sandstone-faced building with a domed clock tower, overlooks the town below. Inside the courthouse are murals of Governor Stevens' treaty with the Indians at Cosmopolis, February 25, 1855 and Captain Robert Gray's discovery of Grays Harbor on May 7, 1792. There is also a plaque memorializing the lives of county deputy sheriffs, Collin McDenzie and A. V. Elmer, who were slain by **John Turnow**, known variously as the "Beast Man," "The Wild Man of the Olympics" and the "Human Gorilla."

Between 1910 and 1913, Turnow was a half-legendary figure of terror in the Grays Harbor and Olympic Wilderness country, a muscular giant, 6 feet 5 inches in height and weighing 250 pounds. A man of the woods, he clothed himself in skin and bark, and was a dead shot with a rifle. Turnow escaped in 1909 from an institution for the insane in Salem, Oregon, and a year later killed two young hunters in Grays Harbor County. Following a sighting of the "Beast Man" along the Satsop River, Sheriff McDenzie and Deputy Elmer went after him and were found shot to death 13 days later. A reward of $5,000 was posted and as many as one thousand men joined the manhunt, but Turnow continued to elude capture for several months. On April 16, 1913, his hideout was found by Giles Quimby, Louis Blair, and Charles Lathrop. In the rifle battle that followed, Blair and Lathrop were killed, but a bullet from Quimby ended the life of the bearded giant.

The courthouse was the site of the "Centralia Massacre" trials. Nine Industrial Workers of the World ("Wobblies") members were convicted of murder in the second degree for their role in the 1919 shootings of American Legionnaires at an Armistice Day parade in Centralia.

Grays Harbor County: Montesano is the county seat of Grays Harbor County, which was organized in 1854 from Thurston County. First named Chehalis County, its name was changed in 1915 to Grays Harbor County after Captain Robert Gray who discovered the harbor in 1792. The county was permanently settled in 1859 around Hoquiam, while Aberdeen was settled in 1861 by Scotsmen who set up a packing plant financed in part by investors from Aberdeen, Scotland. The great stands of timber in the county made logging, milling and timber exporting the main economic activities, and today wood products, fishing, agriculture and tourism are of primary importance.

Court House: 100 West Broadway, Montesano 98563, FAX 206-249-3783. Area: 1,909.8 square miles. State Ranking: 14th. 1993 Population: 66,500. Unincorporated: 26,246. Incorporated: 40,254. Density: 34.8 persons per square mile. **Cities and Towns**: Aberdeen, Cosmopolis, Elma, Hoquiam, McCleary, Montesano, Oakville, Ocean Shores, Westport. **Principal Economic Activities**: Wood and paper products, seafood processing, food processing, manufacturing. **Points of Interest**: Grays Harbor, Fort Chehalis, Quinault Indian Reservation.

Climate: (Aberdeen - elevation 12)

	Jan	Apr	Jul	Oct
Max Temp. F°	45.3	58.0	69.7	61.9
Min Temp.	34.0	39.5	50.4	43.5
Mean Temp.	39.7	48.7	60.1	52.7
Precipitation	12.70"	5.56"	1.51"	8.13"

Average Annual Maximum Temperature: 58.7
Average Annual Minimum Temperature: 41.9
Annual Mean Temperature: 50.3
Average Annual Precipitation: 84.54"

Back on U.S. 12, continue east over the Satsop River and pass a farming community of the same name. The Satsop moniker was taken from a local Indian tribe, the *Sats-a-pish*.

The Satsop Valley is a study in contrast. Expansive farms stretch across the open valley floor. A heavy rainfall irrigates fields and feeds numerous streams, keeping the valley exceptionally green. In spring-time, colorful bulb farms blossom. The idyllic scenery is broken by partially-timbered hillsides, clear-cut and looking worse than a bad mohawk haircut, and two massive atomic towers, a symbol of the ineptitude of the Washington Public Power Supply System.

The acronym **WPPSS** is pronounced "Whoops!" as in "big mis-take," a result of the project's notorious failure. The WPPSS began with hopes of satisfying future power needs but ended as a $24-billion municipal bond default, the greatest in American history.

In 1957, 17 public and private companies joined together to form WPPSS. Initially, the project looked promising. A few small hydroelec-tric plants and the Hanford steam plant were completed ahead of schedule and under cost, and within two years Hanford was produc-ing three times the energy of any other U.S. nuclear plant. Both the Atomic Energy Commission and the Bonneville Power Administration encouraged further construction by WPPSS, hailing nuclear energy as a safe, inexpensive and limitless power source.

In the 1970s, the decision was made to build three nuclear reac-tors in the Hanford vicinity and two on the Satsop River outside of Elma. The following years were filled with legal and contract disputes, cost overruns and delayed construction. Meanwhile, nuclear energy became a hot environmental topic. Concerns regarding harmful ef-fects began to creep into the national forum. Extremely high forecasts of future power consumption proved to be false and the Seattle city council voted to cancel its funding of the Satsop plants. After manage-ment problems and a new cost estimate of $23.8 billion instead of the original $4.1 billion, WPPSS announced its intention of a "work slow-down." Grass-roots organizations such as "Irate Ratepayers" denounced WPPSS and persuaded local utilities to abandon their participation. The final crash came in 1982 when WPPSS defaulted on its debt. Although one Hanford plant was completed in 1984, the pair of 500-foot-high cooling towers were never finished; they remain silhouetted against Satsop Valley's green hills as a non-functioning eyesore.

Like most regional towns, **Elma's** (Elevation 57, Population 3,011) lumber mill doesn't run with the same intensity as in years past. Some of Elma's residents now farm, while others commute to big city jobs in Olympia. Elma's two nicknames, the "Wild Blackberry Capital of the World," and the "Gateway to Grays Harbor," are reasonably accurate. Blackberry bushes grow rampant but the harbor's waters lie 20 miles west.

D. F. Byles and his family, Elma's first citizens, were members of the first party of immigrants to cross Naches Pass. It was suggested that the town be called Elmer, for Elmer E. Ellsworth, the first Union soldier killed in the Civil War, but postal authorities shortened the name to Elma. Downtown Elma is quiet and quaint. Large murals painted on the back of businesses portray pioneer life.

Just outside of Elma, the highway turns southeast, following the Chehalis River. Important sawmill and shingle towns that once existed along this stretch of road — Malone, Porter, and Cedarville — have disappeared as the industry has died. **Oakville** (Elevation 72, Population 632), 14 miles beyond Elma, hangs on, mostly due to highway traffic that U.S. 12 brings and the presence of the Chehalis Indian Reservation one mile south. An abundance of White Oak (*Guercus garryana*) led to Oakville's name.

Rochester, seven miles east, once lay at the junction of the Northern Pacific and Chicago, Milwaukee, St. Paul and Pacific railroads. The name honors a settler's hometown in England. Rochester is located just south of the Mima Mounds (State Highway 121), some of the most geographically unusual terrain in the state.

A signpost on the Oregon Trail.

Five miles east of Rochester, the community of **Grand Mound** is named for a tree-covered hillock nearby, a large earth mound rising from the prairie to a height of 125 feet. Pioneer travelers followed the open prairie through Grand Mound between Portland and the Puget Sound.

Joined by I-5, U.S. 12 turns south and then directly east, leaving the busy interstate ten miles south of Chehalis at a junction called **Mary's Corner**. The intersection is named after Mary Loftus,  who operated a store here in the 1920s, but significant for the **John R. Jackson House**, the first pioneer home north of the Columbia River. Jackson was a farmer from Illinois who arrived in 1844. His log cabin, a popular stopping point for travelers, was also used as a post office, a voting place, and after a remodel, a courtroom for the U.S. district court, the region's first federal tribunal. Army officers Ulysses S. Grant and George McClellan, passing between Fort Vancouver and Fort Steilacoom, and Washington's first governor, Isaac Stevens, all spent a night or two with Jackson and his wife, Matilda.

Running north-south through Mary's Corner is Old Highway 99 (the Jackson Highway). Drive south on the high-

The house of pioneer John R. Jackson.

way two miles to **Lewis and Clark State Park**. Although Washington is called the Evergreen State — a moniker it deserves but abuses — most of its forests are in their second or third growing stages. The park maintains one of the state's last stands of old-growth forest. As you walk the interpretive trails beneath towering Douglas firs, hemlocks and western red cedars, imagine how striking western Washington's old-growth forests must have appeared to pioneers, their thick canopy stretching for hundreds of miles.

Return to U.S. 12 and continue 17 miles past numerous tree-farms and flower nurseries to **Mossyrock** (Elevation 533, Population 495), a quiet farming and timber community named for a moss-covered rock rising 200 feet above the east end of Cowlitz Prairie. About every 125 years, something exciting occurs here. In 1855-6, the presence of the war-like Klickitats in the mountain passes to the east prompted the few settlers to temporarily abandon their homes. When Mt. St. Helens blew her top in 1980, Mossyrock was covered by a thick blanket of ash.

A rustic tavern in Mossyrock.

Morton (Elevation 945, Population 1,145) is 11 miles east of Mossyrock. Before reaching this lumber town, you'll cross the Cowlitz River and the northern tip of Riffe Lake. Farms alternate with sections of thick forest and denuded hillsides.

Morton wears its industry on its coat sleeves. Automobiles are outnumbered and outsized by logging trucks barreling to and from the large mill north of town. A giant mill wheel stands in front of a cafe/bar appropriately called the *Wheel*. Set at the base of Cutler Mountain in a wide, flat valley, Morton hosts the Loggers' Jubilee, where skilled lumberjacks from around the state gather every August to compete in logging contests.

The area's first white settler was Uncle Jimmy Fletcher, who came from Missouri in 1871. Twenty years later the town was incorporated and given the name Morton after the country's vice-president, Levi P. Morton. The town was firmly established in 1912 when the Tacoma Eastern Railroad arrived, bridging the gap between the region's rich forests and timber-hungry towns Tacoma and Seattle.

Leaving Morton, the highway passes through lush farmland, along the spacious Rainey Valley floor. This is "Big Bottom" country, a moniker adopted by a coalition of mountain people who immigrated to the fertile region in the late 1800s from southern states like Virginia, Kentucky and Tennessee. They occupied primitive shacks deep in the foothills, using their backwoods methods of hunting, trapping and collecting berries, giving the area a strong pioneer flavor.

The Cowlitz River meets the highway at **Randle**, 17 miles beyond Morton. In the 1820s, a French-Canadian by the name of Simon Plomondon built a home and established a farm for the Hudson's Bay Company on the nearby Cowlitz Prairie. On a previous trading mission, Plomondon was taken captive by the Upper Cowlitz Indians, who had grown leery of trading companies. They had good reason for their mistrust. In years past, Iroquois trappers sent to the region by Hudson's Bay Company's rival, the North West Company, had raped Cowlitz women and killed a Cowlitz chief.

After a few weeks of being held hostage, relations improved between Chief Schanewah and the Hudson's Bay delegation and Plomondon was released. The next year, Plomondon returned with gifts and the chief offered him one of his three daughters as a wife. As is a sad legacy in much of the West, disease brought by the white man would eventually wipe out the Cowlitz people.

Since Randle was established by James Randle of the Randle Lumber Company in 1886, a string of mills have come and gone. As forests have been cleared, dairying and agriculture have become necessary and productive diversions.

A lengthy but worthwhile excursion to Mt. St. Helens starts and ends at Randle; a round trip totaling 74 miles. This route is less crowded than State Highway 504 and passes several stunning viewpoints over-  looking the mountain, Spirit Lake and the devastation caused by the 1980 volcanic eruption. (Drive south on State Highway 131 to Forest Road 25 and continue to Forest Road 26, then follow Forest Road 99 to the Windy Ridge Viewpoint. For the return trip take Forest Road 99 to Forest Road 2560, then Forest Road 25 back to Randle. There is a shuttle bus available to viewpoints along Forest Road 99. The loop is closed in the winter.)

U.S. 12 continues to climb the western slopes of the Cascades, reaching **Packwood**, 14 miles beyond Randle. The town takes its name from William Packwood, a guide and explorer who came to the area in 1844 from Virginia. In 1853, as part of James Longmire's wagon train team, Packwood made a difficult but successful crossing of Naches Pass. The next year, the two explorers discovered Cowlitz Pass (originally Packwood Pass; located north of White Pass), an easier route to the Puget Sound. Packwood was a familiar figure on mountain trails with his string of pack horses. For $2.50 he would guide a party anywhere in the region.

Defined by a lumber mill, Packwood also caters to recreationists who use the town as a starting point to the surrounding bounty of mountain lakes, trails and campgrounds in the Cascades and the **Goat Rocks Wilderness Area**. This is rugged terrain, where snowfields, glaciers and pinnacle rocks are blunted and beautified by fields of flowering meadows. Over 120 miles of hiking trails crisscross the region. The area was used by Yakima Indians for foraging and religious rituals.

The wilderness lies in the northern part of the **Gifford Pinchot National Forest**, which encompasses one and a half million acres of the southern Cascades. The forest was established as the *Columbia National Forest* in 1908 and changed in 1949 to honor Gifford Pinchot, a conservationist and the first chief of the United States National Forest Service.

Rugged country.

The highway continues winding and climbing. Breaks in the thick timber offer great views of Mt. Rainier. Two miles past the State Highway 123 Exit, a road sign directs you to a scenic view of the **Palisades**, a 486-foot canyon wall comprised of basalt that appears as if someone has run an extremely large and sharp comb up its length. This rock formation is a striking example of columnar jointing, which resulted from rapid cooling of a basalt lava flow. During the millions of years since molten rock spread over the area, the slow erosive action of the Clear Fork River has gradually exposed this formation. There is also a view of Mt. Rainier's Backbone Ridge.

White Pass (Elevation 4,500) was discovered by Charles W. White, a civil engineer for the Northern Pacific Railroad Company. Construction of the road was a lengthy process. The National Forest Service began their attempt to cross the pass in 1922, starting from Randle, and didn't finish until 1951. The road's completion was a healthy boost to eastern Washington farmers and loggers who sought an easier route to western markets.

In addition to being a car passage through the southern Cascades, White Pass is a popular destination ski resort. Also, the Pacific Crest Trail covers this ground, crossing the highway and continuing both north and south along the length of the Cascades.

Another viewpoint worth stopping at is **Clear Creek Overlook**, two miles east of the pass. A 300-foot waterfall interrupts a series of clear tranquil pools. Clear Creek follows the highway and empties into **Rimrock Lake** (Tieton Reservoir). The lake is contained by Tieton Dam and serves as a reservoir for Yakima Valley irrigation. When the dam was built in 1925, it was the largest earthen dam in the world.

At the east end of the lake, the community of Rimrock was comprised of people who worked on the dam: engineers, loggers, muleskinners, miners who excavated tons of earth and rock, and laborers who did a little of everything — poured concrete, raised scaffolding, carved timbers and built railroads.

Goose Egg Mountain, an important Indian landmark, rises above Rimrock. Legend claims the mountain was once the chaste bachelor chief Me-oh-wah, whose people lived in the Yakima Valley. Chiefs far and near sent their fairest daughters to dance before Chief Me-ow-wah, believing that he would succumb to their charms. Me-ow-wah consulted with Speel-yia, the crafty, who counseled him to sacrifice the maidens and himself in order to preserve the chastity of the tribe. Seeing the maidens coming up the valley, Me-ow-wah shouted in a voice of thunder, "Mit-whit" (stop). The astounded maidens were turned to stone. Several Washington mountains — are named for these frozen maidens.

The Tieton (TEYE-uh-tuhn) River flows from Rimrock Lake, through the narrow Tieton Canyon. By now, forested slopes have conceded to bronze-colored hills of cheatgrass, a sign that you have entered the eastern portion of the state. Similar to finding shapes and objects in puffy cumulus clouds, you can spend hours staring at the jagged volcanic rock spires that project from the acres of sagebrush. When the sun is shining, which is often, the light strikes the volcanic rock revealing many shades of red and brown.

The highway continues east, following the Tieton River. During draw-down periods when water is released from the reservoir, the river runs high and hard, attracting rafters and kayakers and white water outfitters from Yakima. *Tieton* is an Indian word meaning "roaring water."

Twenty miles past Rimrock, the Tieton empties into the Naches River and U.S. 12 turns southeast to **Naches** (NA-CHEEZ, Elevation 1,460, Population 689), five miles further. Orchard groves dominate the Naches Valley floor, stretching from the highway to the lower portions of the foothills. Like grain elevators in Washington's wheat country, fruit-packing warehouses wait beside railroad tracks (and now the highway) for a connection to distant markets. The word Naches derives from *naugh chez*, meaning "rough water." Naches began in 1908 with the advent of a federally-supported irrigation system.

Just south of Naches, across the Naches River above what is now Eschbach Park, is the former location of Colonel Wright's **Basket Fort** (Fort Naches). During the 1850s, when tensions between whites and the natives were high, Wright's troops located a large Indian band camped near the trail junction. A hastily constructed fort made of earth and topped by baskets full of rocks became known as the Basket Fort. The fort could protect a company or two of soldiers and hold their supplies. Fort Naches was abandoned in the summer of 1856 when Wright moved his troops out to establish Fort Simcoe.

After crossing the Naches River, four miles south of Yakima, take a right on Achle Road to the **Indian Painted Rocks**. These pictographs depict religious experiences, records of hunts and meetings with other tribes. A trail that passed through here connected an old Ahtanum band of the Yakimas with the Wenas Mountains. In the 1850s, miners traveling to British Columbia gold fields used this same trail. The rocks were partially destroyed by an

Indian painted rocks.

irrigation flume that was built across the face of the cliff and have been further damaged by graffiti. There is a trail and interpretive signs along the way.

The **Yakima Valley** was not settled until 1858, primarily because of clashes between native and white cultures, which crystallized in the Yakima Indian War of 1855-7. With the Yakima defeated and forcibly relocated to reservation lands by the U.S. Army, cattlemen drove their herds into the valley. Until irrigation became prevalent, settlement lagged, for despite the extreme fertility of the volcanic ash soil, the low precipitation was insufficient for farming.

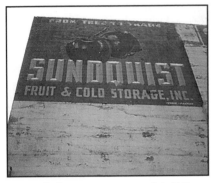
Backwall advertising is a common sight in Yakima.

In 1870, John W. Beck planted 50 peach and 50 apple trees. Two years later the first irrigation system was established when Sebastian Lauber and Joseph and Charles Schanno constructed a canal from the river to their string of fields. Before long, where cattlemen had fought over range and water rights, irrigation became the major interest. These early water systems marked the end of cattle-raising in the valley and the beginning of its prosperity as a diversified farming and fruit-growing area.

An 1870 census showed 432 pioneers residing in Yakima County, established in 1865. Ten years later word escaped of the area's rich volcanic soil, 300 days of sunshine and a nearby river. Three thousand people inhabited the county and a settlement called Yakima City was incorporated. Sensing potential profits, in 1884 the Northern Pacific Railroad extended their tracks into the Yakima Valley and attempted to buy land in Yakima City. When some of the residents refused to sell, the railroad retaliated by laying out a new townsite named North Yakima four miles north and rerouting its tracks to the new terminal site.

The railroad then offered to move any of Yakima City's existing buildings to the newly established community. More than 50 buildings made the strange migration. The court-

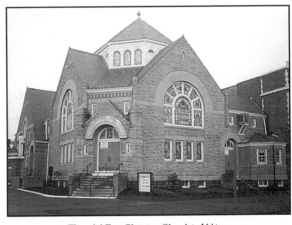
The solid First Christian Church in Yakima.

house, banks, general store, blacksmith shops, saloons, hotels, and several homes were dragged by horse and oxen teams on rollers and skids along the trail. Business continued as the buildings straggled along the route. The new city retained the name North Yakima until 1918, when the "North" was dropped. Yakima City became today's Union Gap.

Yakima (YAK-i-maw, Elevation 1,068, Population 59,580) lies in one of the most important fruit producing and diversified agricultural regions in the world. Of the 3,072 counties in the United States, Yakima County ranks first in the number of all fruit trees; first in the production of apples, mint, winter pears and hops; and fourth in the value of all fruits. Over 9,000 acres of vineyards in the Yakima Valley help make Washington State the second largest producer of fine wine grapes in America behind California.

Solid downtown buildings, wide city streets and the sweet smell of orchards give the "Palm Springs of Washington" a sense of permanence, having found a niche in the desert climate. West Yakima Avenue accesses Yakima's downtown and leads to the city's first stone building, **Saint Michael's Episcopal Church** (Yakima and Naches), built of native lava rock. First services were held on January 6, 1889. A portico, added in 1923-4, was copied from the English church described by the poet Gray in his "Elegy Written in a Country Churchyard."

Continue on Yakima Avenue and turn left on Third Street. When the **Capitol Theater** (19 South Third Street) opened on April 5, 1920, it offered performers the largest stage on the West Coast and was capable of seating 1,500 people. The theater, known as

The Renaissance Revival architecture of the Capitol Theater.

Yakima's "little jewel box," was the largest in the United States for playing a combination of vaudeville and various performing road shows.

The theater fell into disuse after vaudeville's popularity diminished and the motion picture industry developed. In 1975, the theater's interior was destroyed in a fire caused by faulty wiring. Three years later, 85-year-old theater designer Tony Heinsbergen, the executor of the original murals and ceiling paintings, returned with his brush and paint and recreated the images he had painted so long ago. Mr. Vaudeville, Bob Hope, inaugurated the second life of the Capitol Theater. The theater is home to the Yakima Symphony Orchestra, and presents a variety of theatrical entertainment and concerts.

US 12 Next door, the **William O. Douglas Federal Building** was named in honor of Yakima's first and only Supreme Court justice. By the time **Chief Justice William O. Douglas** (1898-1980) had concluded his 36-year stint on the U.S. Supreme Court, he had become known as both an outspoken proponent of environmental protections and a champion of civil rights. Born in Minnesota to a very poor family, young Douglas' formative years were spent mingling with Yakima's so-called undesirables. In his book *Go East, Young Man; The Early Years*, the justice remembers one episode from those early days that would give him a life-long resentment of hypocrites and a feeling of compassion for the underprivileged:

> A prominent churchman in town, the father of one of my friends, was bent on ridding Yakima of prostitutes and bootleggers. The prostitutes were scattered in brothels along South Front Street. . . . At that time Yakima, having the benefit of local option, allowed beer to be sold but no hard liquor. The bootleggers, however, brought the whiskey to everyone, including the high churchmen and other members of the elite.
>
> This particular reformer had several sons, my age and older, and he and they would have made an admirable vice squad. But as he told me, he would have none of that; he wanted to "save" his sons from being polluted by these evil people. That is why he approached me. Would I, for one dollar an hour, spend Saturday and Sunday nights "working Front Street?" My instructions were, "See if you can buy a drink from someone. When the night is done, check in at the office, execute an affidavit, and the police will move in."
>
> And so a teenage boy became a stool pigeon in a red-light district. Never did I have such a shabby feeling, and in the end, never did I feel sorrier for people than I did for those I was supposed to entrap. . . . In time I came to feel warmth for all these miserable people, something I never felt for the high churchman who hired me. As much as my family needed the money, a few weeks of this job were all I could endure.
>
> I never quite got rid of that resentment against hypocrites in church clothes who raise their denunciations against petty criminals, while their own sins mount high. This feeling somehow aligned me emotionally with the miserable people who make up the chaff of society. . . . I have always been quicker to defend them than I would have been but for the high churchman of Yakima.

Any justice who writes over 1,300 legal opinions is bound to anger a number of adversaries, which might account for the fact that twice during his years on the bench Douglas' enemies tried, yet failed, to impeach him. In spite of the controversy he generated in those days, William O. Douglas is now regarded as one of the most sensi-  tive and influential jurists in the Supreme Court's history.

The **Yakima Valley Museum** (2105 Tieton) features a replica of the late Chief Douglas' Supreme Court office. The museum is also known for its collection of over 50 horse-drawn vehicles. Included are authentic originals of classics such as the Conestoga covered wagon, Concord stage and mail coaches and the Overland Express wagon.

Yakima's visual landmark is the **A. E. Larson Building** (Second Street and Yakima), named for one of the area's wealthy pioneers and built in 1931. The building makes a striking impression, even to one not concerned with architecture. Built in an Art-Deco style, the 11-story reinforced-concrete structure is faced with 13 shades of brick. The lobby contains bronze elevator doors and terrazzo floors.

Another place of interest is North Front Street, once the center of activity for North Yakima. Built of rough hewn local rock, and void of frills, the **Lund Building** (Yakima and Front) exemplifies Yakima's pioneer spirit. In 1899, a Chinese Restaurant, *Sam's Cafe*, was housed here. Upstairs was a "hotel" catering to gentlemen callers. Other colorful establishments on Front Street included the *Alfalfa Saloon*, the *Chicago Clothing Company*, the *Longbranch Saloon*, and *Switzer's Opera House*.

Opera was not the music of choice in the small "cowboy and Indian" town of Yakima. At the turn of the century, the Opera House folded and became the *North Yakima Brewing and Malting Company*. The passage of the 18th Amendment closed the brewery, but in 1981, Bert Grant opened the *Yakima Brewing and Malting Company*. Today, **Grant's Brewery Pub**, America's oldest brew pub, occupies the old *Northern Pacific Depot Building* (Front and East Avenue).

Hops and Washington are synonymous.

Yakima County: Yakima is the county seat of Yakima County, which was founded in 1865 from Ferguson County, no longer in existence. It was named after a local Indian tribe and is located in the south central part of the state. The county was first settled in 1858 after the Indian wars of 1855-57 resulted in the formation of the Yakima Indian Reservation. In the 1870s, cattlemen and farmers began constructing irrigation systems. Growth continued into the 1880s, when the coming of the Northern Pacific Railroad created a boom in the county. In 1950, the federal government began a major series of irrigation projects in the county that had profound results. Its economy is based on fruit production, wood products and food processing industries.

Court House: 128 North Second Street, Yakima 98901, SCAN 665-4000, FAX 509-575-4131. Area: 4,271.1 square miles. State Ranking: 2nd. 1993 Population: 197,000. Unincorporated: 90,328. Incorporated: 106,672. Density: 46.1 persons per square mile. **Cities and Towns**: Grandview, Granger, Harrah, Mabton, Moxee, Naches, Selah, Sunnyside, Tieton, Toppenish, Union Gap, Wapato, Yakima, Zillah. **Principal Economic Activities**: Agriculture, food processing, wood products, manufacturing. **Points of Interest**: Fort Simcoe, Priest Rapids Dam, White Pass Ski Area, Yakima Indian Agency, Sundome, Greenway.

Climate: (Yakima - elevation 1,061)

	Jan	Apr	Jul	Oct
Max Temp. Fº	36.0	63.9	88.3	64.2
Min Temp.	19.3	35.4	53.5	35.6
Mean Temp.	28.1	49.7	70.9	50.0
Precipitation	1.22"	.62"	.16"	.47"

Average Annual Maximum Temperature: 62.8
Average Annual Minimum Temperature: 36.3
Annual Mean Temperature: 49.6
Average Annual Precipitation: 8.03"

The Indians called **Union Gap** (Elevation 980, Population 3,170), five miles from Yakima, *Pahoticute* — "the place where two mountain heads come together." White settlers called it "Two Buttes." Also known as Yakima City, Union Gap's present name derives from its location near the gap in the Ahtanum Ridge that connects the central and lower portions of the Yakima Valley. Formed by prehistoric Yakima River water flows, the gap is best seen from a distance where the power of erosion is fully appreciated.

After the Northern Pacific spurned Yakima City (Union Gap) and relocated the commercial district four miles north to North Yakima (now Yakima), Union Gap became a quiet agricultural community.

Highway 12 continues east, following the meandering Yakima River upstream. Lined by a fertile wall of green, the river is the valley's lifeline, indicated by the scattered towns that rest on its banks. The valley floor is packed with vineyards, orchards and fields of hops, all of which climb the sage-covered hills as far as possible. Running parallel to the river are the Burlington Northern and Northern Pacific rail lines and the Yakima Valley Highway, which accesses the region's towns.

Zillah (ZIL-uh, Elevation 1,000, Population 2,060) is perched on a plateau above the Yakima River, eight miles from Union Gap. At a christening party for the Yakima irrigation canal in 1892, 16-year old Zillah Oakes, daughter of the president of the Northern Pacific Railroad, caught the eye of Walter Granger, engineer and president of the Sunnyside Canal Company. Granger had engineered the extensive irrigation system under the employ of Zillah's father and was surveying a location for a townsite. Impressed by Miss Zillah's artistic talents and beauty, Granger received permission from Mr. Oakes to name the townsite after his daughter.

An orchard in Zillah's "Fruit Loop."

The fields north of Zillah are littered with wineries, usually open for tours and wine-tasting. Zillah's **Fruit Loop** is a circular route through several area wineries, orchards and farms. Maps of the drive are available at the Chamber of Commerce (Fifth Street and First Avenue) and offer descriptions of wineries and the types of fruits and vegetables visible from the road. Expect to see a variety of crops including: cherries, pears, grapes, apples, alfalfa, tomatoes, corn, peppers, apricots, peaches, nectarines, plums, corn, spearmint and hops.

Throughout the orchards are tall stands attached with propellers. The machines, a common sight in Washington's orchard regions, are diesel-powered and circulate warmer upper air with the lower cooler air, preventing freezing of fruit during spring frost and cold nights.

Four miles beyond Zillah, **Granger** (Elevation 731, Population 2,081), was named for Walter Granger, the "irrigation king." The first and only non-profit Spanish language radio station in the state broadcasts here, evidence of Granger's large Hispanic population. Summertime Mexican fiestas are common, and Cinco de Mayo, commemorating Mexico's independence from France, is a widely-celebrated event. Plans for an Hispanic Cultural Center are underway.

Granger achieved notoriety in 1936, when an enterprising justice of the peace charged only 39 cents for performing weddings. Love birds from miles around came for the frugal ceremonies.

Continue 11 miles to **Sunnyside** (Elevation 700, Population 11,420) where Yakima Valley's first white settler, Ben Snipes, homesteaded in 1859. His log cabin, and other local history, is preserved at the **Sunnyside Museum** (Fourth and East Grant). Snipes and his brother-in-law gained prominence and profit from the large herds of cattle they drove between the Columbia River and the Okanogan.

Sunnyside was platted in 1893 and named because of a track of irrigated land that sloped toward the midday sun. Walter Granger had made irrigation possible, buying 90,000 acres of cheap land from Thomas Oakes, president of the Northern Pacific Railroad, and starting the Sunnyside Canal, bringing precious water to the fertile but arid land.

In 1898, the Christian Cooperative Colony, a branch of the German Baptist or "Dunkard" church, settled and essentially took over the town. They built a community that "had no fear to express their convictions against saloons, Sunday desecration, dancing, horse racing, gambling, and other vices." Those who committed these transgressions could lose their property to the powerful CCC. Hundreds of like-minded citizens moved to the area; at one point the "Holy City" had 22 churches.

Besides the temperate environment, Sunnyside's main attraction, and Yakima Valley's as well, was the region's extensive irrigation system, which until Grand Coulee's completion (Columbia irrigation) was the largest reclamation system in the Pacific Northwest. By 1904, the Sunnyside project included 700 miles of canals and laterals irrigating 36,000 acres.

The reclamation movement began at the end of the century, when observers noticed that the frontier was rapidly disappearing. The goal was to create a new frontier by reclaiming the vast, arid, barren lands of the West. Reclamation was considered social reform; it would provide new farmland, jobs for the unemployed, food and ultimately, "homes for the homeless." This was misleading since reclaimed land was too expensive for the impoverished to afford.

The Reclamation Act of 1902 authorized federal irrigation projects and selling reclaimed land to settlers. In 1905, the Yakima Project began a program which, according to a Yakima newspaper, would reclaim "from the desert. . . every acre of which is available for cultivation." By 1910, over 200,000 acres were under irrigation in the Yakima Valley, two-thirds of the state's irrigated land. With proficient irrigation, railroads, fertile land and a steady influx of settlers, the Yakima Valley was on the map for good.

Grandview (Elevation 811, Population 7,590), six miles further down the road, was named for its vistas of Mt. Rainier and Mt. Adams. No significant growth occurred here until 1906, when both irrigation canals and Northern Pacific lines were completed and the town was platted. Grandview is distinct for several buildings that are listed as National and State Historic Places.

The **Grandview Herald Building**, built in 1922, remains essentially unchanged since its original construction. The interior of the two-story, 1911 **Iowa Building** features an intricate tin pressed ceiling. It has been used as a billiard hall, restaurant and public library. A large

Hart, Shaffner and Marx advertisement is painted on the south exterior wall of the **Keck Building**. Such advertisements are usually faded, but in small towns, a common sight on the backs and sides of buildings. These historic buildings and several others are found on Division Street.

Around the corner is the **First National Bank** (Second and Division), built of ornate sandstone. Raised in 1918, the building still contains its original black bank vault.

Washington State's oldest bonded winery, **Chateau Ste. Michelle** (West Fifth and Avenue B), is internationally renowned for its red wines. Grandview's appreciation for wine culminates in the **Grandview Grape Stomp**. Based on age-old traditions of squeezing the juice from the grape by foot, competitors from all over the Northwest compete in this annual fall event. The team that stomps the most juice out of their grapes in the allotted time is declared the winner.

A Chateau Ste. Michelle vineyard.

Highway 12 rejoins and crosses the Yakima River at Prosser (State Highway 22) and continues east 14 miles to **Benton City** (Elevation 514, Population 1,950). Situated on a platform above the Yakima River, Benton City marks the end of terrain dominated by orchards and vineyards, and the entrance to Benton County, the driest region in the state with an average annual precipitation of only seven inches. To give that statistic some perspective, Seattle, located in King County, receives 34 inches of precipitation a year. Wahkiakum County, situated in the southwest corner of the state, gets soaked by 111 inches annually! Wahkiakum generally receives as much rain in April as Benton County does in a year.

How Benton City received its name has many possibilities. The railroad station was platted by and originally called Giezentanner, after J. G. Giezentanner, postmaster of Kiona, a small settlement across the Yakima River. Some say it was then named for Benton C. Grosscup, who had helped separate Benton County from Yakima and Klickitat counties. Others believe it derived from Benton County, named after Senator Thomas Hart Benton of Missouri, a proponent for Western expansion who helped pass the Donation Land Act in 1850, which gave land to pioneer settlers. Regardless, Benton City is easier on the ear than Giezentanner.

US 12 Benton City mushroomed when the Hanford Atomic Site was raised during World War II. The population grew from a few hundred to nearly 1,000. The Hanford Reservation is reached by taking State Highway 225 along the Yakima River 10 miles to State Highway 240.

Six miles past Benton City, I-82 leaves U.S. 12 and heads southeast to a junction with U.S. 395. U.S. 12 continues past Richland (Highway 240), Kennewick and Pasco (U.S. 395), and then heads solo southeast across the Snake River. The boggy marshlands that extend from both sides of the highway are part of the **McNary National Wildlife Refuge**, a 3,629-acre plot frequented by up to 100,000 migrating waterfowl. The Columbia River runs west of the road.

A little further, giant fruit orchards and expansive farms take over the land and roadside produce stands invite the traveler to stop. Groves of fruit trees are surrounded by tall rows of poplars. This tree fence protects the orchards from severe side winds that whip off the Columbia and erode precious topsoil.

Wallula (wuh-LOO-luh), a collection of homes on the banks above the Columbia River, means the same in the Walla Walla Indian language as the word Walla Walla does in the Nez Perce tongue — "place of many waters" — a reference to the nearby Columbia and Walla Walla rivers. Wallula's small size belies its historical importance. In 1818, Donald McKenzie and Alexander Ross of the North West Fur Company, hoping to capitalize on the well-traveled and easily accessible spot near the confluence of the two rivers, built a fort and trading post called Fort Nez Perce (later renamed **Fort Walla Walla**).

Covering one hundred square feet, the fort was surrounded by an outer wall of whip-sawed planks 30 inches wide, six inches thick and 20 feet long. A balustrade, four feet high, was provided with loopholes and slide doors. A gallery inside enabled a guard to pace the wall and keep an eye on the surrounding territory. The houses, one of stone, the others of driftwood, were inside this wall. At the corners were 200-gallon water tanks to be used in case of fire. Indians were relegated to conduct their transactions from outside an 18-inch-square window. When rebuilt in 1843 after a fire, adobe took the place of timber. (A sign on the highway near Wallula marks where the fort once stood.)

From this post, eventually taken over by the Hudson's Bay Company, traders and trappers pushed into the rich Snake River basin. The fort was abandoned at the start of the Indian war in 1855, but soon after, a steady stream of river boats, under control of the Oregon Steam Navigation Company, began to drop off miners headed for gold country and *Wallula Landing* was established. Wallula Landing (later shortened to Wallula and moved one mile east) was a rough and primitive town, its hotel and string of saloons offered gold diggers one last

~100

night of makeshift civilization — and an ample supply of spirits and wild entertainment — before heading off into desolation.

Miners, teamsters, crews cutting wood for the boilers of steamboats and cattlemen, stopped to satisfy their thirst, but rarely their eyes. Author Frances Fuller Victor describes the landscape: "Sand ... insinuates itself everywhere. You find it scattered over the plate on which you are to dine; piled up in little hillocks in the corner of your wash-stand; dredged over the pillows on which you thoughtlessly sink your weary head."

Wallula's greatest surge of prosperity came in 1874, with the arrival of Dr. Dorsey S. Baker's railroad, which transported wheat from Walla Walla to Wallula, replacing the outdated stagecoach method. Eventually the Oregon Steam Navigation Company assumed operations, reorganized as the Oregon Railway and Navigation Company, and extended tracks to The Dalles, superseding steamboat travel and further opening the country.

Past Wallula, the Columbia River narrows as it passes through **Wallula Gap**. The high, U-shaped cliffs once retained a 1,000-foot deep lake that formed as ice-age floods filled the Pasco Basin. When the water broke through, 40 cubic miles a day raged through the gap, more than the current combined discharge of all the rivers in the world, draining the whole lake in a few days.

At the confluence of the Columbia and Walla Walla rivers, the highway turns east and follows the Walla Walla through a sage- and rock-filled canyon. The river's meager flow and the deep cut of the canyon indicates how the river's volume has changed. As farms in the Walla Walla Valley expanded and irrigation needs increased, overuse has reduced the river to a trickle.

The Touchet (TOO-shee) River descends from the north to empty its contents into the Walla Walla River at **Touchet**, a few square blocks of homes on the edge of farmland. Early French-Canadian settlers applied the French verb *toucher*, meaning "to drive or strike with a whip," to the settlement by the river whose people raised horses and cattle near the banks of the rivers.

Seven miles out of Walla Walla you'll come to the site of the **Whitman Mission**, a Protestant outpost founded in 1836 by medical missionaries Dr. Marcus and Narcissa Whitman among the Cayuse tribe in Waiilatpu, "place of the people of the rye grass."

As early as the 1820s, missionary groups from the east looked to the Oregon Territory to spread their word, but the remote location made access nearly impossible. Following a surveillance journey in 1835, Dr. Whitman set out west a year later with his new bride and fellow missionaries Henry and Eliza Spalding. Hastily constructed by unskilled workmen, the mission held few luxuries. A visiting missionary described the setting in 1838:

> It was built of adobe, mud dried in the form of bricks, only larger — there are doors and windows of the roughest material, the boards being sawed by hand and put together by no carpenter, but by one who knows nothing about the work. There are no fences, there being no timber with which to make them. The furniture is very primitive; the bedsteads are boards nailed to the sides of the house, sink fashion; then some blankets and husks make the bed.

Shortly after the Whitman's arrival, "Oregon Fever" gripped the nation when the first sizable caravan completed the 2,000 mile journey from Missouri to the mouth of the Columbia River in 1842. The following year brought the "Great Migration" as the Oregon Trail beckoned the adventurous to "Go West." Deep ruts developed in the trail as families packed up their belongings and pointed their horses in the direction of promise and prosperity. The rise in traffic made the trail more navigable, but the trip was always treacherous and often deadly. One pioneer recalls the difficulties in entering the Walla Walla Valley:

> The trail that led down to the plateau was very steep with numerous spiral turns. Those people that were on foot sometimes took a short cut, a little path that was extremely steep and therefore very dangerous. I had already reached the prairie, when I could not help admire the courage of an American lady. In order to get down the hill this lady would get hold of a plank from an abandoned wagon and after placing her child at one end of it, she positioned herself at the other end and by making a little movement she sent the plank in motion and slid straight down to the floor of the prairie without the slightest mishap.

The rise in migration was noticeable to the Cayuse, who saw trouble with each passing covered wagon. In 1841, 25 people rolled through the mission and by 1847, the number ballooned to 5,000. The trail was re-routed away from the mission after 1844, but many continued to use the old route to receive shelter and medical assistance from the Whitmans. Orphaned children or those unable to complete the journey were left in the care of Narcissa.

The Whitman's objective was to "minister to the Indians spiritual and physical needs" and to create an island of civilization in a wild land. Satisfied that their needs were already met, the Cayuse people did not readily embrace the teachings of the white intruders, and converts were few and usually fickle. They attempted to turn nomadic hunters and fisherman into farmers, but the natives saw no reason to change techniques that had been successful for centuries. The concept of organized worship and an English education held no value to the Cayuse, arousing little more than indifference among the tribe.

The Whitmans never established a strong rapport with the Cayuse, often showing little respect for Indian customs and treating them like young, naive children in need of parenting. Feelings of hostility and distrust reached a climax in 1847 when emigrants brought a measles epidemic to the mission. Dr. Whitman worked to save the Indians, but the medicine and care he provided proved no match for their lack of resistance to the disease and nearly half of the tribe died. In contrast, no one from the mission perished, and the tribe believed that the doctor had inflicted a deadly curse upon them in order to make room for incoming settlers. Cayuse elders concluded that the "evil spirit" must be killed to save what remained of their people.

On November 29, 1847, after 11 years of strained coexistence with the Indians, a swift attack was waged on the mission. Tomahas, the Cayuse chief, nearly decapitated Dr. Whitman with a blow from his tomahawk, while Narcissa was shot through the heart at close range. Eleven others were killed in the uprising and

The Whitman Mission in 1846.

buildings and fields were torched. A few managed to escape, but the remaining 50, mostly women and children, were taken captive. Three of the children would soon die of the measles, and the rest were exchanged for supplies a month later. The massacre ended Protestant missions in the area and led to a vigilante war between the Cayuse and white settlers. In 1850, five Cayuse members allegedly responsible for the murders were captured, tried, convicted and hanged.

A visit to the Whitman Mission is a well-documented journey back in time. An interpretive trail runs through waist-high native rye grass, a 100-yard stretch of the well-worn Oregon Trail, and reader and soundboards that detail the history of the mission. On top of a high hill stands the 27-foot-tall Whitman Monument, built in 1897 on the 50th anniversary of the missionaries' death. From this vantage point you can see the treeless slopes of the Blue Mountains to the southeast, as well as rolling wheat-covered hills to the north. At the base of the hill is the "Great Grave," where the remains of the 13 murdered at the mission are buried.

US 12 One mile out of Walla Walla, **College Place** (Elevation 949, Population 6,530) grew up around **Walla Walla College** after a donation of 40 acres was made to the Seventh-day Adventist Church on the condition that a school be operated for 25 years. Founded in 1892, the school is a coeducational, four-year liberal arts college with an enrollment of about 1,800.

Folks from other parts of the country may recognize the name **Walla Walla** (WAH-luh-WAH-luh, Elevation 949, Population 28,820) as a question from Jeopardy — "Where is Walla Walla?" — but any serious student of Washington state history would be wise to study this important city.

House and sign painting, paints and oils, wallpaper and window shades.

The Indian uprising at the Whitman Mission and the following years of sporadic fighting caught the attention of the Washington Territory Governor and Superintendent of Indian Affairs Isaac Stevens, who in 1855 called for a great council at the spot where Walla Walla now sits. Invited were Kamiakin and Owhi of the Yakima, Peopeo Moxmox of the Walla Walla, representatives of the Cayuse, Nez Perce and Umatilla tribes, and a smattering of others. The number of Indians present — the Nez Perce brought over 2,000 of their people — compared to about 100 white men, may indicate how important each side considered the meeting. Waiting in the wings across Mill Creek were 50 soldiers; 3,000 horses pastured in the surrounding grasslands.

Governor Stevens spent the week promoting the benefits of schools, stores, mills, and supervised husbandry for the tribes accepting the reservation lands. The Indians found some parts of the treaty attractive but still had not reached an agreement when Looking Glass, chief of the Nez Perce, rode in, was apprised of events, and without bothering to dismount cried out: "My people, what have you done? While I was gone you have sold my country. I have come home, and there is not left for me a place on which to pitch my lodge. Go home to your lodges, I will talk with you." Despite his objections, Stevens was able to obtain signatures for the treaty within a month.

The next year Colonel Edward Steptoe established Fort Walla Walla to give the area a military presence, and settlers, already drawn by the land's fertile soil and plentiful irrigation (Walla Walla is an Indian word for "place of many waters"), formed a community around the fort.

Growth of the village, aided by the completion of the Mullan Road, was steady but not spectacular until the discovery of the Clearwater River gold-fields in Idaho in 1860. The next decade would see Walla Walla become the largest city in the Washington Territory, with a population of 3,500. A few days travel from gold country, Walla Walla became a certified boom town as thousands of transients supplied-up before heading off to stake their claim. During the winter, those who had struck it rich returned to Walla Walla to spend their fortune. Men with pockets full of gold who have been in far away places usually return to civiliza-

The imposing Baker Boyer Bank.

tion with more on their mind than a Sunday stroll down Main Street. Lawlessness reigned. The usual businesses thrived; hotels, stores, livery stables, saloons and dance halls. Beer and wine flowed freely and "ladies of the night" made a lucrative living.

But all good things must come to an end. Fortunately, when the gold petered out, the wheat industry was there to take its place. By 1867, mills in Walla Walla, which had been supplying grain for Idaho mining camps, faced a surplus as the gold boom declined and harvesting methods became more efficient. In order to reach Portland markets, grain was hauled via stagecoach to Wallula and then shipped on the Columbia, a necessary but time-consuming endeavor.

In 1874, Walla Walla businessman Dr. Dorsey S. Baker funded the primitive Walla Walla & Columbia Railroad, the first railway in eastern Washington. Connecting Walla Walla and Wallula, the "rawhide railroad" ran on wooden rails covered with half-inch strap iron. A steam engine, a "crude-looking monster," was brought around Cape Horn from Pittsburgh to push the "hearse" as the passenger car was called. Part of Baker's train crew was a collie dog that ran ahead of the train to drive cattle from the right-of-way. In 1878, Baker was able to ship, via the railroad, river barge, and a schooner, 66,000 bushels of wheat to England.

Although the first transcontinental railroad passed north of Walla Walla through Spokane in 1883, slowing development and establishing that city as the leader of the eastern half of the state, years of prosperity and a strong agricultural foundation guaranteed Walla Walla's success. The city retains a quiet dignity. Wide streets and sidewalks and large Victorian homes are shaded by fully developed maple and oak trees. Several fine old brick buildings comprise Main Street's restored nineteenth-century business district. The **Baker-Boyer Building** (Second and Main) began in 1861 as a General Merchandise store, operated by brother-in-laws Dr. Dorsey Baker and John F. Boyer. It was converted to a bank in 1869, making it the oldest in the state.

A few blocks from Main Street, **Whitman College** (Boyer Avenue) began in 1859 as the Whitman Seminary, established by missionary Cushing Eells in memory of Marcus and Narcissa Whitman. It is the oldest chartered institution of higher learning in the state and nationally, a highly-rated liberal arts college. Of architectural interest is the Memorial Building, fronted by a grand clock tower and built in 1899 in a Romanesque Revival style.

Fort Walla Walla Guard Mount in the 1880s.

Another point of interest is **Fort Walla Walla Museum** (Dalles-Military Road). The fort was moved from its original location, where Mill Creek meets downtown Walla Walla, and has been converted into a Veterans Hospital and an historical museum. A pioneer village and five buildings full of local artifacts are more than enough for any history buff. In the third building is a replica of a 33-mule-team Harris combine from 1919. The "Shandoney" hitch allowed one man to drive the entire team. The harness is also called the "equalizer" — a device that distributed weight evenly among the horses and mules. Prior to this, overworked animals that died in mid-toil were dragged along by the "dead hitches."

The area's commitment to agriculture is evidenced by encroaching wheat fields and apple trees, which seem to grow like weeds. Almost every home on the outskirts of Walla Walla has a garden, their plots large enough that residents could consider themselves mini-farmers. The city is also home to the **Walla Walla Sweet Onion**, a large onion that supposedly can be eaten like an apple. In the late 1800s, a soldier from France, Peter Pieri, brought with him seeds to grow an Italian-type of onion. In the 1920s, a local farmer, while developing his own strain of a Spanish-type onion, grafted the two strains and the Walla Walla Sweet was born. The mildness of the onion is due to a low sulfur and high water content, factors which lessen the globe's bite and tear-evoking qualities.

There are 28 mules pulling the front wagon in this 1906 photo on the Geourge Drumheller Ranch.

Walla Walla County: Walla Walla is the county seat of Walla Walla County, which was established in 1854 and is named after an Indian tribe that once lived in the area. The name means "running water." The county is located in the southeastern part of the state and is bounded on the north by the Snake River and Oregon on the south. The establishment of the Mullan Road through the county in 1858 brought permanent settlers, and many more arrived when gold was discovered in Idaho and the town of Walla Walla became a supply center for the mines. The transcontinental railroad arrived in 1875 and began an era of great prosperity in agriculture and related industries. Today the county, with its rich soil and lengthy growing season, produces and ships grain, and is also a major vegetable growing and food processing center. Three colleges and a number of state and federal facilities contribute to the county's economy.

Court House: 315 West Main Street, Walla Walla 99362, FAX 509-527-3214. Area: 1,267.3 square miles. State Ranking: 26th. 1993 Population: 51,800. Unincorporated: 15,154. Incorporated: 36,646. Density: 40.9 persons per square mile. **Cities and Towns**: College Place, Prescott, Waitsburg, Walla Walla. **Principal Economic Activities**: Food processing, agriculture, wood and paper products, manufacturing. **Points of Interest**: Whitman Mission, Fort Walla Walla, Lower Monumental Dam.

Climate: (Walla Walla - elevation 949)

	Jan	Apr	Jul	Oct
Max Temp. F°	39.0	63.8	89.2	64.6
Min Temp.	27.4	43.7	62.7	45.6
Mean Temp.	33.2	53.8	76.0	55.1
Precipitation	1.89"	1.40"	.21"	1.53"

Average Annual Maximum Temperature: 63.6
Average Annual Minimum Temperature: 44.7
Annual Mean Temperature: 54.2
Average Annual Precipitation: 15.50"

The drive east of Walla Walla rises up to the southern boundaries of the Palouse, prolific and rich wheat country that extends north to the Spokane Valley. Expect stretches of monotonous and idyllic wheat fields interrupted by small, well-preserved towns including county seats in Dayton and Pomeroy.

Herman C. Actor settled **Dixie** in the 1860s but was overshadowed by the Kershaw brothers, a trio of Southerners who arrived after the Civil War and were quick to sing to anyone that would listen to their rousing rendition of "Dixie."

Lying in flats of the Touchet Valley 10 miles north of Dixie, **Waitsburg** (Elevation 1,272, Population 1,016) is a model of stability; it continues to operate under the terms of its original territorial charter. Main Street retains a turn-of-the-century charm. Way back in 1865, Sylvester M. Wait erected a flour mill along the banks of the Touchet River, where land had already proven to yield strong wheat crops and flour was selling for $44 a barrel. Farmers donated land for the mill and agreed to hold their grain until spring, at which time Wait was to pay $1.50 a bushel. The arrangement worked for both parties, saving farmers a trip to Walla Walla, and by 1869 Waitsburg was platted.

Cross a small concrete bridge that leads out of town and continue four miles to **Lewis and Clark Trail State Park**. During the month of May in 1806, 33 members of Lewis and Clark's expedition survived on parsnips, dog meat and a single duck. A small cottonwood forest here provides a shady oasis in the middle of the vast prairie.

The road follows the Touchet River past lush fields four miles to **Dayton** (Elevation 1,612, Population 2,490). A massive block of grain elevators on the east edge of town show how citizens here earn their keep. Dayton is wonderful town to explore. Pick an alley and drink in the wealth of advertisements painted on back walls. Residential streets are lined with comfortable bungalows and modest mansions.

Also of interest is the **Dayton Depot** (Second and Main). Built in 1881, it is the oldest existing depot in the state. The two-story building has been restored with railroad memorabilia and local antique furnishings. The station master once lived on the second floor.

Dayton has always been well-traveled. An early Indian cross-roads, Dayton was also the site of a Lewis and Clark campground in 1806. Captain Benjamin de Bonneville stopped by 30 years later and

hundreds of men passed through in the 1860s on their way to Idaho gold country. Platted in 1871 by Jesse Day, Dayton captured the seat of Columbia County four years later. Despite devastating fires in the early 1880s and the deflation of mining booms, the area's extreme agricultural pro-

Columbia Grain Growers storage.

ductivity and the service of both the Oregon Railroad and Navigation Company and the Northern Pacific by 1890 assured Dayton's success.

Columbia County: Dayton is the county seat of Columbia County, which was created in 1875 from part of Walla Walla County. It derives its name from the Columbia River. Situated in the southeastern part of the state, it is bordered by Oregon on the south and the Snake River on the north. The Blue Mountains occupy the southern part of the county. In 1806 the Lewis and Clark expedition crossed the county and later in the century, in 1860, the residents of the county witnessed

the first steam navigation of the Snake River. Today Columbia County bases its economy on agriculture, with wheat and vegetable production leading its output.

Court House: 341 East Main Street, Dayton 99328, FAX 509-382-4830. Area: 859.5 square miles. State Ranking: 31st. 1993 Pop-ulation: 4,100. Unincorporated: 1,445. Incorporated: 2,655. Density: 4.8 persons per square mile. **Cities and Towns**: Dayton, Starbuck. **Principal Economic Activities**:

Dayton County Court House.

Agriculture, food processing, wood products. **Points of Interest**: Snake River, Blue Mountains.

Climate: (Dayton - elevation 1,612)

	Jan	Apr	Jul	Oct
Max Temp. F°	39.2	62.2	87.5	64.6
Min Temp.	24.0	38.5	53.8	39.4
Mean Temp.	31.6	50.3	70.7	52.0
Precipitation	2.43"	1.56"	.40"	1.89"

Average Annual Maximum Temperature: 62.6
Average Annual Minimum Temperature: 39.2
Annual Mean Temperature: 50.9
Average Annual Precipitation: 19.53"

U.S. 12 makes a detour north into the Pataha Valley, then intersects with State Highway 127 and drops into **Pomeroy** (Elevation 1,856, Population 1,435), platted on May 28, 1878 by Joseph P. Pomeroy. A civil war veteran and a mechanic for Wells, Fargo and Company, the young man migrated from Ohio to Illinois in 1850 at the age of 20. He moved to Oregon two years later and in 1862 came to Dayton where he opened a blooded-stock farm on Pataha Creek to meet the demands of stagecoach operators on their way to Lewiston, Idaho.

Joseph wasn't lonely in those early days. Pomeroy's Main Street (U.S. 12) was reportedly lined with 20 saloons. Recalling the boom days, an old timer said: "Main Street had twenty saloons and things were poppin'. The town ain't bigger now an' nothin' is poppin'." While things may not be "poppin'," Main Street, comprised of a vintage nineteenth century business district, is worth the long haul through the wheat fields. The **Garfield County Courthouse** (Eighth and Main) is in excellent condition. A rounded tower topped by a statue of blind justice graces the whitewashed frontside.

Garfield County: Pomeroy is the county seat of Garfield County, which was organized in 1881. It was created from part of Columbia County and was named after President James A. Garfield. It is located in the southwestern corner of the state and is bounded by the Snake River on the north and the state of Oregon on the south. In the nineteenth century, many of the region's major explorers passed through the county —Lewis and Clark in 1806 and Captain James Bonneville in 1834. Today Garfield County is the state's least populous county and has the lowest crime rate. Its economy is based primarily on growing grain, livestock raising and the processing of food.

Court House: County Courthouse, Pomeroy 99347, FAX 509-843-1224. Area: 712.8 square miles. State Ranking: 33rd. 1993 Population: 2,300. Unincorporated: 865. Incorporated: 1,435. Density: 3.2 persons per square mile. **Cities and Towns**: Pomeroy. **Principal Economic Activities**: Agriculture. **Points of Interest**: Snake River Canyon, Blue Mountains.

Climate: (Pomeroy - elevation 1,856)

	Jan	Apr	Jul	Oct
Max Temp. F°	39.1	61.4	86.9	65.0
Min Temp.	23.8	37.6	52.5	37.8
Mean Temp.	31.4	49.5	69.7	51.4
Precipitation	2.02"	1.27"	.32"	1.50"

Average Annual Maximum Temperature: 62.4
Average Annual Minimum Temperature: 38.0
Annual Mean Temperature: 50.2
Average Annual Precipitation: 16.58"

The county seat changed so often between Pomeroy and **Pataha**, two miles east, that until an act of the U.S. Congress solidified the political situation, the courthouse should have been placed on wheels. Now Pataha is an abandoned community with only a few residents.

U.S. 12 drops down a series of long, rolling hills to meet the Snake River at **Chief Timothy State Park**. The park is located on an island formed in 1975 by flood waters from the newly built Lower Granite Dam. Rugged basalt cliffs rise from the shore, offering shelter and revealing why Chief Timothy of the Nez Perce farmed and lived here. Located near the park's entrance, the **Alpowai Interpretive Center** makes this more than an aimless day in the sun, sharing the history of the local Nez Perce Indians and of the pioneer community of Silcott which took their place.

Continue along the river into **Clarkston** (Elevation 825, Population 6,725), sandwiched by the Snake and Clearwater rivers. In 1863, William Craig established a small ferry system and for the next several years transported thousands of prospectors from Jawbone Flats — as Clarkston was first known — to the Clearwater gold fields.

Still, it wasn't until 1896, when the Lewiston Water and Power Company platted the community of Vineland — as Clarkston was second known — that the area began to grow in earnest. Backed by eastern capital, an extensive irrigation system developed and soon property sold for $1,000 an acre.

By 1899, the population of Concord — as Clarkston was third known — had reached 1,500. The city was renamed the next year for William Clark, who passed through with fellow explorer Meriwether Lewis in 1805. As in their traveling days, Lewiston is always close by, across the river in Idaho.

Clarkston marks the end of the highway's run in Washington. The city functions as a "bedroom community" to Lewiston, which is more of the region's center of commerce. But as much as that implies about the docile nature of Clarkston, its nickname, the "Gateway to Hells Canyon," is deserving. Tours and white water rafting trips launch from here and head up the river into what is, at 7,900 feet, the deepest river gorge in the world. ∾

State Highway 14 from Vancouver east through Elsworth, Camas, Washougal, Skamania, Stevenson, Carson, Underwood, Bingen, Lyle, Maryhill and Roosevelt to a junction with U.S. Highway 395 and Interstate 82. Route length: 184 miles.

It was the mid-1800s when Indian problems near Walla Walla prompted the federal government to consider creating a highway on the north side of the Columbia River Gorge. (Troops out of Fort Vancouver needed a quicker way to get to the upriver trouble spot.) The advent of steamboat travel, however, soon relegated road construction to the back burner, where it remained for the next five decades.

By the early 1900s, with more and more settlers pouring into the region and the touchy situation with the Indians around Walla Walla much improved, the state legislature decided to put plans for construction of Highway 14 (sometimes called the Lewis and Clark Highway) back on the drawing board — with the new eastern terminus to be Pasco in the Tri-Cities area. Although not much more than a narrow, rocky cow-path when "completed" in 1907, the new road was heralded as a major link between the southwestern and southeastern portions of the state.

A tribute to Lewis and Clark.

In addition to linking southern Washington, Highway 14 peruses some of the state's most scenic landscape, closely following the mighty **Columbia River**'s north shore. When explorer Meriwether Lewis first saw the river he proclaimed, "We to our inexpressable joy discovered a large tract through prairie country lying to the SW and widening as it appeared to extend to the W. Through that plain the Indian informed us that the Columbia River (in which we were in surch) run [sic]."

In 1792, Captain Robert Gray discovered the river, a feat that greatly extended America's claims to the land that would eventually encompass the state of Washington. Moving south from Nootka Sound on Vancouver Island, it was in the midst of stormy weather and southerly currents that Gray noticed the presence of what he thought was a large river. Kept at bay by an overpowering current, exploration of the mouth was delayed for a full week before conditions finally allowed them to cross. In his official log he describes the moment with a scientific terseness:

> At four A.M., saw the entrance of our desired port bearing east-south-east, distance six leagues; in steering sails, and hauled our wind in shore. At eight A.M., being a little to windward of the entrance of the Harbor, bore away, and run in east-north-east between the breakers, having from five to seven fathoms of water [sic].

Not exactly an exuberant reaction to finally penetrating the "great river of the West" which had been desperately sought by Spain, Great Britain and America for so long. It is evident that Gray's emphasis was on trade and commerce rather than political exploration since he paid relatively little attention to the Columbia River and recorded nothing of

Captain Gray's ship entering the Columbia River.

"the thrill of discovery." A short, 10-mile run upriver satisfied Gray's curiosity about the river's course, and after just a week of trading with the natives, he sailed out the Columbia River for the first and last time. Later the river was named after his ship, the *Columbia Rediviva*.

Only a few years after the Lewis and Clark expedition had arrived in 1805, a fur trading company was established at Oak Point, 40 miles upriver from today's Astoria. Business grew rapidly and the Columbia River became the headquarters of a trading empire that stretched as far as Alaska. By the 1880s, fish-trap operations on the lower Columbia sustained the economy, producing annual salmon catches of about 35 million pounds.

By turning deserts into green lush farmland, providing lighting for homes, and transforming towns into cities through industry, the importance of the river to all of the small towns along Highway 14 can't be overstated. From its Canadian ice field beginnings in British Columbia, the four-mile-wide river flows 1,243 miles south and west before finally coming to rest in the Pacific Ocean. With over 125 dams in the Columbia River Basin, including the Grand Coulee Dam, the river is the greatest power generator on this planet, generating millions of kilowatts of electricity and a third of all the hydroelectric power in the country.

The high concentration of dams (there are seven) have eliminated rapids that once made river travel difficult and all but eliminated the salmon runs that used to fill the river. Slow-moving and smooth, the Columbia flows beneath steep basalt cliffs, forming the boundary between Washington and Oregon. The river is also a major water highway. Barges, their movement nearly imperceptible, crawl along the placid river, transporting wheat and produce to western markets. Waterskiers, fishermen and windsurfers add to the congestion.

Six miles east of Vancouver lies the small community of **Elsworth**, originally homesteaded by emigrants from the Twin Cities of Minneapolis and St. Paul, as well as from Omaha, Nebraska. Unfortunately, the man who had sold these hardy folk on the benefits of life on the north shore of the Columbia — and for whom the hamlet is named — Elmer Elsworth, died before the first settler had moved to what would later be south central Clark County.

Eight miles further along the highway are the back-to-back towns of **Camas** (Elevation 59, Population 7,220) and **Washougal** (waw-SHOO-guhl, Elevation 250, Population 5,190). The term "Twin Cities" is once again bantered about, not because these towns were settled by Minnesotians, but rather because there have been some unsuccessful efforts to wed the cities, thereby creating a larger municipality.

As is often the case when Native American words are involved, the city of Camas owes its name to mispronunciation. The local Indian populace was especially fond of an edible root they called *quamash*. By the time early botanists had translated it into English, the word had become *Camassia*, which was eventually shortened to *Camas*.

The Lewis and Clark expedition chose the present townsite as a camp in 1806. While Clark crossed the Columbia in search of the Willamette Valley, Lewis stayed put, hunting and drying meat for what they knew would be a long return trip.

Thirty-eight years later, in 1844, the Michael T. Simmons party — consisting of people of color — also camped on the present site of Camas. They were hoping to avoid persecution by settling in the Willamette Valley, but abandoned that plan when they learned that Oregon's provisional government had recently decided that "all Negroes and mulattos would be flogged once every six months until he or she shall quit the territory." The group eventually settled near Puget Sound.

Present-day travelers, unsure about whether or not they've actually made it to the town of Camas, need only roll down their windows, stick their head out, and take a whiff. Odors from Crown-Zellerbach's giant pulp and paper mill — maker of shopping bags, paper towels, tissue wraps for fruit, etc. — will leave little doubt as to the location.

Paper production, regardless of its olfactory implications, does  have a long history in the area, dating back to 1883 when Portland investors, with the help of Chinese laborers, built the first mill to convert cottonwood, fir, and straw into newsprint for a paper called the *Vancouver Independent*.

A mere three-mile drive past Camas one enters Washougal, the residents of whom tried out the names *Parker's Landing*, *Point Vancouver*, and *Washoughally Camp* before settling on the present moniker. There is some discrepancy about the meaning of the Indian word from which *Washougal* was derived. According to one opinion, it meant "rushing water," and referred to the Washougal River that enters town from the north. A second assertion is that it's a Chinook word meaning "a pleasant land of plenty." Considering that archeological evidence indicates that there have been villages in the area for over 3,000 years, the latter meaning makes most sense.

Washougal has always been known for its woolen mill. The original mill was purchased shortly after opening in 1912 by Clarence Bishop, whose family had also taken over the Pendleton Mill in

Columbia River Gorge National Scenic Area.

Oregon. In spite of its reputation for producing fine twill-weave called cassimere, the Washougal mill also produced blankets for World War I soldiers and — perhaps anticipating the environmental concerns of the late 20th century — so-called "smelter bags" used as smokestack filters.

Although on the grid, the small, former logging community of **Skamania** (skuh-MAY-nee-uh), 16 miles down the two-laner from Washougal, is certainly anything but a big electric consumer. Before early settlers decided to rename their wooded town after an Indian term, *skamania*, meaning "swift water" or "swift river," it had been called *Butler*. Today, Skamania is considered the western gateway to the 75-mile-long Columbia Gorge.

Timeprints of the millennia are boldly etched on the walls of the **Columbia River Gorge**, recording a 40-million-year-long story of geological change, endurance, and majesty. The Gorge as we know it today, is a chronicle of ancient volcanic eruptions and gigantic lava flows, mudslides and ashfalls, but is actually the comparatively recent result of catastrophic flooding that took place 13,000 years ago. Those torrents, which were the greatest floods ever to occur in North America, scoured out the canyon walls, creating in the process more than 71 spectacular waterfalls.

Early Indian culture flourished for thousands of years in villages commonly located at creek mouths throughout the Gorge. Native Americans considered this beautiful and bountiful area to be a great source of both spiritual and physical strength.

According to Indian lore, a princess named Wahatpolitan attempted to draw on the spiritual powers of 848-foot-high **Beacon Rock** — located just three miles east of present-day Skamania — using it as sanctuary from her vengeful father, who disapproved of her marriage and had threatened to take out his anger on her infant son. Legend has it that mother and son both died on the small, flat summit of Beacon Rock, and that eerie echoes of her death song can still be heard when Chinook winds whistle over the promontory.

The Lewis and Clark expedition camped underneath the monolith on their way to and from the coast, and were the first to call the landmark *Beacon Rock*. Over time, more and more people began calling it *Castle Rock*, but a decision was made in 1916 to return it to its original name.

On a more scientific note, Beacon Rock is actually an andesite plug, meaning that it is all that is left of the basalt heart of a volcano that has long since eroded from around it. Next to the famous Rock of Gibraltar, Beacon Rock is the second largest monolith in the world.

Were it not for a group of conservationists who purchased the landmark in the early 1900s, this geological treasure might have ended up as nothing but fodder for a local quarrying operation, who intended to sell stone blocks for jetties on the coast. Concerned citizens managed to purchase the land, however, and later offered it to the state for a park.

For a spectacular view of Hamilton Mountain to the north, and the Gorge's waterfalls and basaltic cliffs to the east and west, head into **Beacon Rock State Park** and take the 4,000-foot trail, with its 53 switchbacks, to the top of Beacon Rock. The trail owes its existence to a man named Henry Biddle, who owned property in 1915 that included the rock, and who took three long years to construct a navigable route to the top. The 4,482-acre park covers almost 10,000 feet of Columbia River shoreline, including the sheer, lower south face of Beacon Rock, which provides some of the most challenging rock climbing in the Northwest.

Four miles further is the mammoth **Bonneville Dam** project. It includes a 48-mile-long reservoir impounded by the dam. The project was named for Army Captain Benjamin Bonneville, an early-day visionary who led an exploration to the Oregon Country and charted extensive sections of what later became the Oregon Trail.

Construction of the dam began in 1933 by the U.S. Army Corps of Engineers, with completion (and a dedication by President Franklin D. Roosevelt) four years later. The Bonneville Dam, which cost $88.4 million to build, was the first of eight federal lock and dam projects on the Columbia/Snake River. As the Northwest grew, additional hydropower projects were built upstream. Construction of a second Bonneville powerhouse, begun in 1974, more than doubled the project's power-producing capability.

Bonneville Dam from the highway.

Twelve years later, the Bonneville Lock and Dam project was placed on the National Register of Historic Places, primarily because of its unique engineering design, the project's contribution to the region's industrial development, the lock's role in transportation, and the part that the project played in the government's effort to combat the Great Depression of the 1930s. Over 100 people are currently employed to operate and maintain the Bonneville project.

About three miles up the road from the dam you'll reach an impressive steel bridge perched atop tall concrete footings. The **Bridge of the Gods**, as it is called, got its name from an Indian myth that, it turns out, was grounded in geological fact. According to Klickitat legend, two young chiefs, vying for the affections of a svelte Indian princess, met to do battle on a land bridge across the Columbia River. An old woman named Loowit attempted to stop the love-blind warriors, but to no avail. The boulders that the combatants were hurling at each other eventually destroyed the bridge, permanently separating the people who lived on opposite banks of the river. The principals in this mythical drama

Northern approach to the Bridge of the Gods.

then transformed into mountains: the young chiefs turned into Mt. Hood and Mt. Adams, the well-intentioned crone into Mt. St. Helens, and the beautiful princess into Squaw Mountain.

It's interesting to note that the land bridge mentioned in this fable was once a geological reality. In 1260, gigantic mudslides, probably triggered by earthquakes from a Mt. St. Helens eruption, came roaring down from Table Mountain and Greenleaf Peak, cutting a devastating swath two miles wide and seven miles long before slamming to a halt against the far wall of the Columbia Gorge. A reservoir was formed behind the slide, backing up to a depth of 270 feet — a process that took over two years — and eventually spilling over the natural dam. It was only then that the water could begin to erode the millions of tons of earth that blocked its original channel.

The Bridge of the Gods is also Washington's southern trailhead to the 2,550-mile **Pacific Crest Trail**, which stretches between the frontier of Canada and the Mexican border. While within Washington's boundaries, the trail runs the length of the Cascades, passing through four national forests, nine wilderness areas and two national parks.

Three miles further east along Highway 14, hunkered down on a low bluff above the river, is the town of **Stevenson** (Elevation 486, Population 1,155). It was founded by a man named George Stevenson who came from Missouri in 1880 to take up residence in what was then the low-lying town of Cascades. Flooded out 14 years later, he moved to higher ground where he platted the new community.

One of George's consuming passions was the fish wheel, an ingenious device for harvesting salmon that were returning upriver to spawn. Fish wheels, as the name might suggest, were large waterwheels (40 feet in diameter) with three or more mesh fish baskets attached. As water turned the wheel, the baskets would scoop up spawning salmon that had crowded near the shore to avoid the swifter, mid-river current, then dump them in waiting barges.

By the beginning of the twentieth century, over 75 fish wheels were operating on the Columbia, primarily at The Dalles and on the rapids that then boiled through the Gorge. By 1935, Washington had joined Oregon in banning fish wheels, gill nets, and seine nets, all of which, by virtue of their efficiency, were contributing to the decimation of the area's salmon population.

Although the days when millions of migrating salmon roiled the waters of the Columbia may be a thing of the past, windsurfing enthusiasts, with their multi-colored sails, keep the breezy Gorge jumping from late spring to early fall. A sailboard park that borders Stevenson to the southwest is reputed to be one of the best windsurfing spots in the country.

Overlooking the river on a 10-acre site, also at the west end of Stevenson, is the **Columbia Gorge Interpretive Center**, a must visit for anyone interested in the geological and archeological history of the mid-Columbia region. The 15,000-square-foot center features dramatic exhibits that bring to life scenes from the natural and cultural history of the area.

Skamania County: Stevenson is the county seat of Skamania County, which was founded in 1854 from Clark County. Its name means "swift water." It is located in the southern part of the state and is bordered on the south by the Columbia River. The county is bisected north and south by the Cascade Mountains and contains Mt. St. Helens, the most active volcano in

The Columbia Gorge Interpretive Center has the answers.

the continental United States. The county is heavily forested and its economy depends primarily on logging and the wood products industry. Bonneville Dam on the Columbia River touches Skamania County and gave impetus to the county's economy. Fishing on the river has also provided a source of income.

Court House: County Courthouse, 240 NW Vancouver, PO Box 790, Stevenson 98648-0790, FAX 509-427-4165. Area: 1,672.3 square miles. State Ranking: 24th. 1993 Population: 9,000. Unincorporated: 7,387. Incorporated: 1,613. Density: 5.4 persons per square mile. **Cities and Towns**: North Bonneville, Stevenson. **Principal Economic Activities**: Wood products, agriculture, tourism. **Points of Interest**: Mt. St. Helens, Ice Caves, Government Mineral Springs, Bonneville Dam.

Climate: (Wind River - elevation 1,150)

	Jan	Apr	Jul	Oct
Max Temp. F°	38.4	59.7	80.0	61.4
Min Temp.	25.6	33.6	46.9	37.4
Mean Temp.	32.0	46.6	63.5	49.4
Precipitation	16.05"	6.26"	1.01"	8.74"

Average Annual Maximum Temperature: 59.5
Average Annual Minimum Temperature: 36.2
Annual Mean Temperature: 47.8
Average Annual Precipitation: 99.51"

Road-weary travelers whose historical curiosity is still alive and well might want to plan enough time for a visit to **Carson Hot**

14 WASHINGTON

Mineral Springs Resort. To get to this area landmark, head north on Wind River Road, three miles east of Stevenson. Another mile and a half or so east on Hot Springs Avenue and you're there. It won't take long to understand why folks flocked to these healing, steamy waters as early as 1876.

The hotel and general store were built just before the turn of the century, making the springs a little town unto itself. Cabins were built in the 1920s to accommodate the growing number of visitors. The Carson Hot Springs general store has since been destroyed, but all other buildings still remain in active use, adding flavor and history to what is sure to be a relaxing soak in the hot mineral baths.

Ironically, the man who originally developed the health resort, Isadore St. Martin, died in a quarrel with a visitor who dared to doubt the curative properties of the hot baths.

Proof of the state's geographical diversity is found northeast of the Carson Hot Springs at the **Big Lava Bed**. (Drive seven miles east of Carson and head north on the Cook-Underwood Road. After five miles turn left on Willard Road, continue another two miles and turn left on South Prairie Road. There are several access points along this road to park and explore.) This early lava flow, the largest exposed lava flow in the state, covers over 12,000 acres.

After returning to the Lewis and Clark Highway and traveling six miles east past the tiny settlements of Home Valley, Dog Mountain, Cook, and Hood, curious travelers will find themselves at **Underwood**, a small burg situated at the mouth of the White Salmon River. Beginning in the early 1920s, Underwood was the destination point for the **Broughton Flume**, a nine-mile long, water-filled, wooden trough used until 1989 to carry rough lumber from Willard to the Columbia, where it was floated to a finishing mill. The trestle that supported what would turn out to be Washington's last operational flume is still visible on the cliffs to the west of town.

The Gorge is a world-renowned windsurfing location.

Four more miles of two-lane brings travelers to the town of **Bingen** (BIN-jin, Elevation 101, Population 650), one of the Gorge's prime windsurfing locales. Winds blowing through the Bingen Gap in the opposite direction of the Columbia's current make for dramatic swells and whitecaps. Windsurfing enthusiasts launch their surfboards-with-sails up to 30 mph in this region.

Bingen was originally named by German settlers after a town in their homeland, *Bingen-on-the-Rhine.* According to a Ripley's "Believe it or Not" newspaper column, the town can claim to be the only community in the U.S. whose railroad-depot sign lists the names of two towns. Apparently, a legal battle between the citizens of **White Salmon** (Elevation 700, Population 1,910) and Bingen over whose name would appear on the sign could only be resolved by this unprecedented compromise.

You don't have to be a graduate student in geology to appreciate the interesting rock formations just east of **Lyle**, a town that garnered its original name, *Klickitat Landing,* because steamboats used to ease their bows onto a nearby sandbar while loading or unloading live-stock. Make sure to notice the well-defined basalt flows that comprise these steep, textured bluffs. Thanks to the scouring effect of an ice-age flood that occurred about 12,000 years ago, the dirt that once hid the different lava flows from view has been washed away.

A dry, eastern stretch of the river.

Proceed east through the Rowena Gap portion of the Gorge two miles past the small town of Murdock to **Horsethief Lake State Park**, which earned a listing on the National Register of Historic Places as a result of its Indian petroglyphs and paintings. The park sits on the site of an ancient Indian village by the name of Wakemap (WAH-kuh-map), once a major crossroads for both north-south and east-west travelers. Explorer William Clark confirmed this by noting in his journal that Wakemap was ". . . a great emporium . . . where all the neighboring nations assemble."

If, as Emerson once wrote, "An institution is the lengthened shadow of one man," then the stately grandeur of **Maryhill Museum** — sprawling pretentiously atop a ledge of the barren Klickitat Hills, overlooking a scenic bend in the Columbia River — would suggest that the man responsible for its creation, Sam Hill, was at the very least a mover and shaker, if not somewhat larger than life.

As usual, reality is never quite that black and white. The enormously energetic Hill, the bulk of whose fortune was made speculating on the pre-Depression stock market, had earned a reputation nationally as an outspoken advocate of this country's Good-Roads Movement. He is credited for almost single-handedly masterminding construction of the Columbia River Highway, for a long time one of the most scenic byways in the Northwest. "Good roads are more than my hobby," he once declared, "they are my religion."

But it was Hill's decision to build an imposing Flemish-style chateau at Maryhill that forever linked his name with a perplexed or confused state of mind — as in the folksy exclamation, "What the Sam Hill are they doing over there?"

Who in the Sam Hill was Sam Hill? This is his eighteenth century palace.

Writer Edmond S. Ellerby, apparently no fan of Mr. Hill's, described him as, "a raving American eccentric . . . a giant aging sheepdog of a man with a cherubic, Santa-Claus face, a shock of white hair, and a penchant for building ramshackle monuments to pipe dreams."

Although those words might seem a bit harsh, and possibly an unfair assessment of the man, it did take 26 years from the time the construction of the chateau was begun until an eclectic art museum became its final reality. In fairness, however, much of why the mansion remained in half-completed disarray for so many years was attributable to Hill's obstinate refusal to continue the project until the state of Washington would provide the site with a finished and suitably-paved highway. Not a surprising stance considering Sam's obsession with roads in general.

Hill was first attracted to the "castle's" building site, which was a mile or so northeast of the existing burg of Columbus and about 400 feet higher in elevation, when he realized that it met an important criterion: He had been looking for "a land where the rain meets the sun;" in other words, a locale in a climate zone between Washington's dry country to the east and its rainy country to the west.

After failing to interest Quakers in participating in what he hoped would be a 7,000-acre, idyllic agricultural community, Hill next decided to operate a cattle ranch on the land. The 60x140-foot, 50-foot-high, cement and steel chateau was originally conceived as a "comfortable and substantial *farmhouse*, [where] a few friends drop in and take potluck with me."

In 1917, with money tight because one of Sam's largest business ventures was in receivership, and there was no improved access road on the horizon, he decided to discontinue construction of the building. During the next nine years, while the hulking, partially-constructed edifice became a home for rats and nesting swallows, Hill, at the urgings of exotic dancer Loie Fuller and sugar heiress Alma Spreckles, made the decision to turn it into an international art gallery. To demonstrate to the world the seriousness of his intentions, he invited Queen Marie of Rumania to formally dedicate the building. From the moment that the Queen disembarked at the railroad station and the red carpet was rolled out, the event threatened to be an embarrassment of international proportion. John Tuhy writes in his book *Sam Hill — The Prince of Castle Nowhere*: They then proceeded to the chateau . . . where they were again welcomed by a red carpet which had been obtained after a frantic search by removing it from a hotel back stairway in Portland. The same carpet was used at each site, then . . . quickly rolled up and rushed to the next location.

Marie must have been dismayed by the sight of the half-finished 'Museum of Fine Arts,' built on what was then a by-road. She had brought with her, as a gift, over two million dollars worth of paintings and statuary that were ear-marked for specially designated rooms in Hill's museum, but when she got there, the rooms in question were not even close to being finished. One witness commented, "It was perfectly ridiculous and I never was so embarrassed in my life. I thought, 'What in the world are we going to do?'"

The Queen, however, speaking from a tacky and hastily improvised wooden throne, proved that her unflappable royal countenance ran deep by delivering a speech at the dedication ceremony that was equally touching, euphemistic, and for Hill, face-saving:

> As I stand here today in this curious and interesting building, I would like to explain why I came. There is much more than concrete in this structure. There is a dream built into this place — a dream for today and especially for tomorrow. There are great dreamers and there are great workers in the world. When a dreamer is also a worker, he is working for today and for tomorrow as well. For he is building for those who come after us.
>
> Sam Hill is my friend. He is not only a dreamer but he is a worker. Samuel Hill once gave me his hand and said if there were anything on earth that I needed, I had only to ask. Some may even scoff, for they do not understand. But I have understood. So when Samuel Hill asked me to come overseas to this house built in the wilderness, I came with love and understanding. Samuel Hill knows why I came, and I am not going to have any other explanation. Sometimes the things

dreamers do seem incomprehensible to others, and the world wonders why dreamers do not see the way others do. . . .

Maryhill Museum finally opened on May 13, 1940 — Sam's birthday. Unfortunately, its visionary if eccentric founder had died nine years earlier. In spite of the fact that *Time* magazine called it "The world's most isolated art museum," over 49,000 visitors were admitted in its first year of operation.

No, this isn't England. This is Stonehenge three miles east of Maryhill.

On a wind-swept bluff above the Columbia River Gorge, three miles east of the Mary-hill Museum, sits **Stonehenge**, the first life-size repro-duction of Britain's Stonehenge ever created, and the first memorial built in the country to honor servicemen who had died in World War I. Some see this 108-foot-in-diameter stone monument as another testament to financier Sam Hill's generosity and vision, while his detractors prob-ably see it as one more example of the folly of a grandiose eccentric.

Writer Leverett Richards claims that Hill's inspiration for creating an American version of the ancient monument came to him when he was touring the Salisbury Plain with his British host, Lord Earl Kitchener. Although Lord Kitchener's assertions are now believed to be apocryphal, he piqued Sam's imagination by claiming that the original Stonehenge was the location for bloody Druid rituals. Prisoners of war were thought to have been sacrificed on the Stonehenge altar to appease the Druids' heathen war gods.

Sam is said to have replied that, in his opinion, humanity apparently hadn't learned much in the almost 4,000 years since the original Stonehenge was built: "We are still sacrificing the blood of our youth to the gods of war," he noted. Hill believed that it would be appropriate to build a reproduction of the famous monument to "remind my fellow man of [that] incredible folly."

Considering the pacifistic quality of Sam's initial sentiments, it's interesting to note the jingoistic tone of the Memorial's final inscrip-tion: *To the memory of the soldiers and sailors of Klickitat County who gave their lives in defense of their country . . . in the hope that others inspired by the example of their valor and their heroism may share in that love of liberty and burn with that fire of patriotism which death alone can quench.*

One ironic note about Hill's choice of location for his memorial: The ancient Stonehenge was laid out so that, on the Summer solstice, the rising sun would strike the tall obelisk that stands outside the double circle of massive stones and cast its shadow on the central altar. In Sam's reproduction, the Klickitat hills block the rays of the sun at sunrise on June 21, eliminating a significant and probably meaningful characteristic of the original.

Unfortunately, a present-day visit to the Sam Hill's Stonehenge Memorial is unsettling if not depressing. Apparently Hill lacked the means to endow money for ongoing maintenance, an obligation which the state has not assumed. As a result, visitors find the memorial covered with graffiti and littered with trash and broken glass. As John Tuey put it so aptly in his book *Sam Hill,* "Like an untended grave, America's Stonehenge seems a more fitting reminder of our indifference to our war dead than of their sacrifices."

Just five miles east of Stonehenge is another monument — albeit more utilitarian — to human endeavor: the John Day Dam. In the eastern portion of Lake Umatilla, the 76-mile-long portion of the Columbia that backed up behind the massive dam, is an island containing both the **Umatilla National Wildlife Refuge** and **Crow Butte State Park**.

Before the construction of the dam, this portion of the Columbia contained numerous islands, with plentiful habitat for waterfowl. The wildlife refuge was established to replace some of that lost habitat. White pelicans and long-billed curlews nest on the island over the winter, and ducks and geese use it as a way station during their spring and fall migrations.

Crow Butte State Park, in spite of signs warning visitors to stay on designated trails for fear of encountering rattlesnakes, is a shady, green oasis — a respite from the dry, sagebrush country that otherwise characterizes this portion of the state. Interestingly, the 671-foot-high butte is merely the top portion of a small mountain that was surrounded by water when the dam created Lake Umatilla.

Approximately 15 miles east of the John Day Dam and only one mile past the blink-and-you-miss-it community of Blalock, is another tiny community, **Roosevelt**, notable only because its founder, T.B. Montgomery, devised a rather unique plan to lure potential merchants and residents to his newly platted municipality. The creative Montgomery built stores, hotels, and a smattering of other structures, which he then proceeded to offer, rent-free, to anyone who would settle there. Judging by the size of the hamlet today (and in spite of the fact that the community was named after this country's popular 26th president, Teddy Roosevelt), Montgomery's come-on apparently failed to attract many passersby.

125~

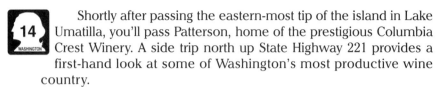

Shortly after passing the eastern-most tip of the island in Lake Umatilla, you'll pass Patterson, home of the prestigious Columbia Crest Winery. A side trip north up State Highway 221 provides a first-hand look at some of Washington's most productive wine country.

If it weren't for the irrigation water provided by **McNary Dam** (one mile east of the conclusion of Highway 14, at the junction of Plymouth and U.S. 395), the mid-Columbia agricultural region's productivity would be significantly smaller. The practice of irrigating crops was first introduced to this area in the late 1800s, but was limited to small orchards and vegetable gardens near farmsteads.

By the 1960s, six years after Senator Charles McNary had helped convince the federal government to construct the dam that would later bear his name, irrigation water from the upstream impoundment of 62-mile-long Lake Wallula had further extended the agricultural potential of the region. The average size of farms, number and types of crops produced, and labor practices all changed as irrigated farming became more practical in an area where the annual rainfall is a measly 9 to 12 inches. Much of this precipitation happens to fall in winter and early spring, leaving the summer growing season hot and dry.

In addition to grapes, irrigated crops such as wheat, potatoes, barley, alfalfa, apples, melons, onions, and asparagus account for more than $200 million in annual revenues. Reliable barge transportation — another major benefit that has resulted from the construction of dams along the Columbia — carries a variety of these products to downstream ports, opening new markets for the region. ∞

McNary Dam construction circa 1953.

State Highway 16 from a junction with Interstate 5 in Tacoma northwest over the Narrows and through Gig Harbor to a junction with State Highway 3. Route length: 44 miles.

16 WASHINGTON

Working slowly through Tacoma's urban spread, Cheney Stadium, home of the Tacoma Rainiers — a Triple A baseball team — appears to the north. While debate continues regarding the plausibility of an outdoor baseball stadium (and a retractable roof) in Seattle, the Rainiers endure under grey but playable skies.

Highway 16 ties Tacoma to the Kitsap Peninsula by way of the **Narrows Bridge,** a towering, mile-long span with an unstable history

The sturdier Narrows Bridge has replaced "Galloping Gertie."

(don't worry, it's safe now). Following its opening in July, 1940, the long-awaited bridge was used by two sets of people: those traveling from one side to the other, and thrill-seekers who enjoyed the "roller coaster" sensation the bridge presented when the winds picked up. "Galloping Gertie" lasted four months, collapsing on November 7 under the duress of 42 mph winds. "Gertie's" solid slab sides caught the wind full force causing the bridge deck to rock and the cables to snap. Once the first cable broke, the rocking motion increased and the ill-fated bridge was doomed. The dramatic scene was captured on film and is sometimes used in commercials contrasting the stability of one's product to the instability of the bridge. Fortunately, no humans were injured but one frightened dog refused to leave his vessel (the back seat of a car) as the ship went down. The bridge remains on the channel floor.

The town of **Gig Harbor** (Elevation 175, Population 3,660), 10 miles east of I-5, rises from a narrow, crowded harbor of the same name. Encircled by a wooded hillside, the cove offers a windbreak for a multitude of fishing and pleasure vessels, an attraction that led to its discovery in 1841 by members

Gig Harbor's protected waters.

127~

of explorer Charles Wilkes' expedition team who were seeking refuge from a storm in the ship's gig (rowboat).

For years the lake-like harbor was the launching point for purse seiners following fish runs up the West Coast. Manned predominately by fisherman of Scandinavian and Croatian descent, Gig Harbor retains its nautical-European charm.

The highway concludes at a junction with Highway 3, two miles south of Bremerton. ଔ

State Highway 17 from a junction with U.S. Highway 395, northwest through Moses Lake to Soap Lake, then north through Dry Falls to Bridgeport and a junction with U.S. Highway 97. Route length: 137 miles.

The first 50 miles of Highway 17 are neither curious nor significant in terms of human history, but do convey a feel for the wide open spaces that dominate much of eastern Washington. From Mesa to Soap Lake, endless acres of dryland farms leave no doubt as to the state's agricultural bounty.

Starting at the intersection with State Highway 28, a sequence of lakes extend for 21 miles, each connected by a stream. The lakes receive their water from the much larger Banks Lake, which is fed by the Grand Coulee Dam and the Columbia River. Both the Grand Coulee and the lakes scattered within were formed as a result of several million years of geological rearrangements, most notably, the great Spokane Flood.

Soap Lake is the southernmost lake in the Grand Coulee aqua chain. Over 20 high-alkaline minerals cause the water to lather and collect on the shore during heavy winds, giving it the appearance of a colossal bubble bath. Tsincayuse Indians migrated annually to the lake to set up a type of primitive health spa and camping spot. They poured water over hot stones to create steam baths, held horse races on the beach and took long baths in the lake, often spreading bottom mud over their bodies. The Indians called the lake *Smokiam,* which means "healing waters."

Trappers for the Hudson's Bay Company stumbled across the salty lake in 1811 and witnessed the Indians refreshing ritual. Deciding the natives were onto something,

Lather up and get well in Soap Lake's healing waters.

early hunters and explorers made the lake a resting spot, often leading livestock into the water to heal travel wounds and kill ticks and lice.

Confirming what Indians have known for centuries, scientists have proven the water's medicinal qualities. A high alkaline content kills bacteria and viruses and can help soothe a variety of skin ailments. During the summer months, the water temperature often reaches 100° Fahrenheit, creating the equivalent of a natural communal bathtub. When ingested, the sodium-filled liquid has been known to relieve some stomach and intestinal ulcers. (It works as a powerful laxative as well, so be warned.) While hardly a cure-all or miracle elixir, the lake is unique for its rich mineral composition.

The town of **Soap Lake** (Elevation 1,189, Population 1,260) was platted in 1908, a result of the lake's growing popularity and the arrival of a westbound railroad. Bombarded by tourists eager to break the healing waves, local entrepreneurs built a string of hotels along "Sanitarium Lake." Sprawling tent cities served as shelter when there was no more room at the inns. This tourism boom continued until the Great Depression tempered summer vacations.

In 1933, the federal government began the massive Grand Coulee Dam project and the construction of highways, signaling the resurgence of people and money to the area. Soap Lake again thrived as a tourist town. During the Depression, agriculture was introduced to the valley to offset dependence on the unpredictable tourist trade. Farms in the area harvest wheat, corn, potatoes, onions and carrots.

A small outlet stream leads from Soap Lake to **Lake Lenore**. A succession of caves along

Caves in the rocky bluffs at Lake Lenore.

the water's eastern rim were used as hiding places and housing by prehistoric people. The caves, now filled with thousands of nesting swallows, were created when the great floods roared through eastern Washington and snatched loose basalt from the walls of the coulee. They can be explored on a hiking trail or seen from the small parking area near the **Lake Lenore Caves Historical Area**.

Winding through the coulee, past **Alkali Lake**, named for the high degree of alkaline in its water, is **Blue Lake**. The lake is famous for the mold of an ancient rhinoceros that was found in a cavity here in 1935. The mold is preserved in pillow basalt and a thin bed of sand and is referred to as the "Blue Lake Rhino." Researchers estimate that the rhinoceros was dead and lying bloated in a shallow pond when molten lava flowed into the pond and chilled, causing a mold to form around the rhino like a tomb, perfectly fossilizing the teeth and bones.

Shadows creeping across the Sun Lakes.

Continue north past Park Lake into **Sun Lakes State Park**. A series of small lakes and ponds lead to **Dry Falls**, arguably one of the most fascinating natural sites in the state and the country. Three and a half miles wide and 400 feet high, the world's largest waterfall once roared over this cliff. In comparison, Niagara Falls is one mile wide and 165 feet deep, with only one-tenth of the total water output. The falls were left high and dry when flood water retracted almost 20 miles to the Columbia River channel. An interpretive center offers lectures and tours of the falls.

Thirty-five miles northwest of Dry Falls on the Columbia River is **Chief Joseph Dam**, named for the famous Nez Perce chief. Originally built to provide inexpensive energy and irrigation for farmers in the area, Chief Joseph Dam and its 16 original turbine generators were constructed between 1949 and 1958. In 1980, the Army Corps of Engineers raised the dam water 10 feet and installed 11 additional turbines, making Chief Joseph Dam the second-most productive hydroelectric facility in the country, behind only the neighboring Grand Coulee Dam.

Rufus Woods Lake backs up behind the dam, stretching for 51 miles and giving a good idea as to the amount of water being contained. The dam was named for the former publisher of the Wenatchee *Daily World* newspaper, Rufus Woods, a strong supporter of development on the Columbia River. Through his editorials and persistence, Woods helped gain approval for several Columbia River projects, including Grand Coulee Dam and Chief Joseph Dam.

Cross the Columbia River north from Chief Joseph Dam to **Bridgeport** (Elevation 835, Population 1,640). In the late 1800s, the heart and soul of Bridgeport was a large, three-story flour mill that employed nearly everyone not at work in the surrounding wheat fields. Soon after the turn of the century, the Bridgeport Warehouse and Milling Company built a steamer landing to fill a need for cheaper, more efficient transportation from the local wheat crop to market. Continuing their progress, the company then built a mill and a wheat elevator in Bridgeport, and a

Dry Falls' lofty viewpoint.

Ponds at the base of (nearly) Dry Falls.

warehouse and two steamboats in nearby Brewster. Shuttling wheat by riverboat helped the town to thrive for several years, but when trucking revolutionized the transportation industry, apple harvesting became the core of the town's economy. ෬

S **tate Highway 18** from a junction with Interstate 5 in Federal Way east to Auburn, then northeast to a junction with Interstate 90. Route length: 28 miles.

Attention botany lovers: just north of the I-5/Highway 18 interchange you can find the **Rhododendron Species Foundation** (2525 South 336th), home of the world's largest rhododendron collection. Over 17,000 starts from 475 species of Washington's state flower are grown here in the greenhouse and expansive gardens.

A few miles east Highway 18 rolls into **Auburn** (Elevation 90, Population 34,550). Platted in 1887 as *Slaughter* to honor Lieutenant W.A. Slaughter who was slain by Indians here in 1855, townsfolk objected to the inhospitable name and changed it six years later. (The original name did inspire some humor though: the hotel was called the Slaughter House.) After aphids foiled an attempt to cultivate hops, the land was converted into dairy and berry farms, which proved profitable and more stable. In 1913 both the economy and the population were boosted when the Northern Pacific established a freight terminal in Auburn and built branch lines to connect with Seattle, Tacoma and other cities along Puget Sound. Products were sent to Auburn in box cars via the spur lines, then rerouted to points across the country. This lean towards industry continues to this day, as giant manufacturing and defense plants sit where farms once flourished. On the retail front, the colossal Supermall of the Great Northwest (the largest in the Northwest) serves as a consumers paradise on the outskirts of town.

From Auburn the highway moves through the small farms and subdivisions of Maple Valley and past a meeting with State Highway 169 before slipping between Tiger Mountain (Elevation 3,004) to the west and Rattlesnake Mountain (Elevation 3,517) to the east. Tiger Mountain is managed by the State Department of Natural Resources and offers a developed hiking and biking trail system. From there it's a straight shot past privately held timber tracts to the road's end at a junction with I-90 west of North Bend. ∝

 S **tate Highway 19** from a junction with State Highway 104 north via Chimacum and Irondale to a junction with State Highway 20. Route length: 14 miles.

Highway 19 runs the length of the Quimper Peninsula by way of the Beaver and Chimacum valleys, a pastoral basin made lush by streams, ponds and a shelter of pine. Beginning adjacent to the **Olympic Peninsula Gateway Visitor Center**, the highway runs four miles north past the Egg and I Road. Writer Betty MacDonald lived on a chicken ranch here from 1927 to 1931, and described her exploits in the 1945 novel, *The Egg and I.* Her country-bumpkin characters,

Port Ludlow occupies prime real estate across from Admiralty Inlet.

Ma and Pa Kettle, were later used in several movies, perpetuating Washington's backwoods image.

Up the road a piece, Highway 19 skirts the neighboring communities of Chimacum, Irondale and Port Hadlock (Highway 116), collectively referred to as the Tri-Area. **Chimacum**, home to a large school complex, takes its name from the Chimacum Indians, a small, now-extinct tribe who once inhabited the area.

A collection of neat, prosperous homes mark **Irondale**, a residential center for several outlying farms. Iron and steel production brought a mini-boom to the area into the early 1900s.

From the highway's end four miles south of Port Townsend, it is possible to loop back by returning south on Highway 19 and taking State Highway 116 east to Oak Bay Road. This route follows the coast along Admiralty Inlet and accesses **Port Ludlow**, a resort community built up around the shores of Ludlow Bay. Long before land was cleared for a 27-hole golf course and tennis courts, lumbermills and shipyards dominated the scene. A large mill established in 1852 enjoyed moments of prosperity, bringing about many of the small settlements along the Puget Sound and a fleet of sailing schooners and steamers. Unfortunately, the mill was better known for its rash of mechanical difficulties than for its productivity, often operating for a day, then spending the remaining week repairing what had broken.

In 1877, the deep-pocketed Pope and Talbot Company from Port Gamble bought the sawmill and successfully ran it for the next 20 years. Market fluctuations, depletion of the region's timber, and a shift towards rail rather than water transport foreshadowed the mill's demise. When the mill closed for good in 1935, company homes were loaded onto barges and shipped to Port Gamble.

In 1968, Pope and Talbot returned, not to cut down trees, but to start a resort town. The idea soon caught on, and Port Ludlow now seems at ease with its role as a vacation hot-spot. Lulled into relaxation by the spectacular views, mainland escapists saunter casually en route to the links or a game of tennis. A hillside full of condos overlooks the harbor brimming with pleasure vessels, a far cry from the days of industry.

Oak Bay Road turns west and rejoins Highway 19 two miles further. ∽

State Highway 20 from a junction with U.S. Highway 101, north through Port Townsend and across Admiralty Inlet via ferry to Keystone, continue through Coupeville, Oak Harbor, Deception Pass and Anacortes, east via Sedro Woolley, Lyman, Hamilton and Concrete, over Rainy and Washington passes, then east through Winthrop and Twisp to Okanogan, north to Tonasket, east via Republic, Sherman Pass, Kettle Falls and Colville to Tiger, then southeast past Cusick to a junction with U.S. Highway 2 in Newport. (Overlaps U.S. Highway 97.) Route length: 376 miles.

Highway 20 is a fascinating road that tours five of Washington's seven geographic regions, beginning in the west on the Olympic Peninsula. It traverses the Puget Sound Basin, the Cascade Mountain Range and the Okanogan Highlands, and stops at the northern tip of the Columbia Basin. The highway is a vast historical and scenically divergent feast for the curious traveler.

The first few miles of Highway 20 offer a thumbnail sketch of the natural wonders of the **Quimper Peninsula**, named by Captain George Davidson in honor of Sub-Lieutenant Manuel Quimper, who explored the Strait of Juan de Fuca in 1790. Quickly winding upward, the road levels out for five miles along the top of a densely wooded hill overlooking the sheltered Discovery Bay. Only the occasional towering evergreen obstructs the view of waves breaking against steep rocky cliffs on the opposite side of the water. Separating from the coastline, the road runs through patches of thick old-growth forest, punctuated by intersecting logging roads and near perfect clear-cut squares that serve as reminders of the region's dependence on timber. At mile 12 it again finds the sea at Port Townsend.

With its ideal location at the entrance to Puget Sound and a springboard to the Pacific, **Port Townsend** (Elevation 10, Population 7,740) once reigned as the Northwest capital for sailing vessels from around the world, culminating in 1854 when a U.S. Customs Office moved here, just two years after the first permanent settlements were laid. Consistently favorable winds and just 18 inches of annual rainfall brought hordes of sea-faring folks to this promising town to seek fortune among the waves — whether they intended to or not. Heavy rumors shroud the area concerning the comatose capture of needed (and cheap) deck laborers. Seamen would locate some wet-behind-

~134

the-ears logger in a local watering hole, offer him a pint, then slip him a mickey and remove the sleeping lad by way of tunnels and trapdoors beneath certain taverns and brothels. Rowboats were used to silently complete the shuttle to departing ships waiting in the harbor. Many an unlucky landlubber is reputed to have awoken not to the shouts of "Timber!," but to the sound of crashing waves and screaming sails.

It's almost lunch time in Old Port Townsend. The Delmonico Hotel offered steam-heated rooms.

Despite the importance of the shipping and timber trades, it was the unconfirmed promise of the railroad — the life line of the early West — which sparked the largest speculative explosions. In the late 1800s, Port Townsend built itself into a Victorian city waiting for the country to knock on its door. The Uptown District, with its ornate homes and churches covering the bluff overlooking the water, appears today as it did over a century ago, including 70 buildings that are National Historic Sites. Preparation for a boom included detailed, far-reaching plans for city growth and ambitious population predictions designed to create a "western New York." Although Port Townsend claimed only 7,000 residents in the mid-1880s, its housing and streetcar systems could accommodate 20,000. Clearly this small town held big expectations. Such aspirations proved a bit much, however, when the Union Pacific Railroad elected to sell the land rather than extend its lines. The 20 miles of track that waited for a connection ran a shuttle for a brief five years before it was abandoned, along with the hopes and dreams of the town. Economic stability did not return until 1927, when a major pulp mill opened.

Port Townsend was discovered by Captain George Vancouver and his men in May of 1792, and recognizing its importance, was named after the English Marquis Townsend. **Fort Townsend** was established in 1856 (one mile south of town on a spur off Highway 20), but today the buildings are gone and a state park has taken its place. In 1896, **Fort Worden**, named for the famous Civil War officer Admiral John L. Worden, occupied the northwestern tip of the town. Along with forts Flagler and Casey on the nearby islands of Marrowstone and Whidbey, the three formed a "Defense Triangle" or "Triangle of Fire" to protect the entrances to Puget Sound and ports in Seattle, Tacoma and the Puget Sound Naval Shipyard in Bremerton.

Ships docked at the Hadlock sawmill.

After much preparation for an attack that never came, the fort became a state park in 1972.

Although neither fort ever fired a shot at an enemy, the sea floor surrounding Port Townsend must look like a battlefield. A documented 364 shipwrecks occurred here, often within view of the town's red brick and cobblestone Water Street. An ancient-looking document encased in a glass frame in the **Jefferson County Historical Museum** (210 Madison Street) lists every lost vessel and the year she went down.

Jefferson County: Port Townsend is the county seat of Jefferson County, one of the first counties organized by the Washington Territorial Legislature in 1852. It was named after President Thomas Jefferson. The county is located in the northwestern corner of the state and is bordered by the Pacific Ocean on the west and Puget Sound on the east. It has one of the most colorful county histories in the state. During the mid-nineteenth century the city experienced a building boom resulting from its status as a major Puget Sound port of entry and is now a showpiece of Victorian architecture. Today the county bases its economy on wood products and agriculture while the Olympic National Park, occupying over half of the county, and the unique character of Port Townsend make tourism a major industry.

Court House: 1820 Jefferson Street, PO Box 1220, Port Townsend 98368, FAX 206-385-9195. Area: 1805.2 square miles. State Ranking: 18th. 1993 Population: 23,500. Unincorporated: 15,760. Incorporated:

7,740. Density: 13.0 persons per square mile. **Cities and Towns**: Port Townsend. **Principal Economic Activities**: Tourism, wood products, agriculture and fishing. **Points of Interest**: Olympic National Park, Historic Port Townsend.

Climate: (Port Townsend - elevation 10)

	Jan	Apr	Jul	Oct
Max Temp. F°	44.0	57.3	71.4	58.6
Min Temp.	34.9	41.4	51.2	44.7
Mean Temp.	39.4	49.4	61.3	51.6
Precipitation	2.20"	1.12"	.68"	1.68"

Average Annual Maximum Temperature: 57.9
Average Annual Minimum Temperature: 43.2
Annual Mean Temperature: 50.5
Average Annual Precipitation: 18.34"

From Port Townsend, catch the ferry for a 30-minute ride across the **Admiralty Inlet** to Keystone on Whidbey Island. Manuel Quimper navigated these waters in 1790 and named it Ensenada de Caamano. A year later Juan Francisco de Elize arrived and changed the name to its present form to honor the British Board of Admiralty.

Fort Casey State Park is directly off of the ferry landing. Gun and mortar batteries still aim at imaginary enemies attempting to penetrate Puget Sound, but are now strictly for show and open to exploration. Mysterious corridors and ammunition holding rooms beckon the curious; all you will need is a flashlight. The view from the fort and the surrounding bluff give a good impression as to why this point was considered so strategically important during the days when England's maritime might was a force to reckon with.

The longest island in the continental U.S. at over 45 miles from tip to tip (New York's Long Island was officially declared a peninsula), the 210-square mile **Whidbey Island** was named by Captain George Vancouver for Master Joseph Whidbey, who proved it was an island by charting through Deception Pass on June 2, 1792. Upon landing, Whidbey was met by some 200 mystified Indians who had gathered to gawk at the first white man they had ever seen. To disprove their belief that he was covered in ash, he opened his shirt to display his true colors.

Known for its fertile valley in the midst of evergreen forest, the island's rich soil has been preserved due to mild cultivation methods of cultivation, land management and a good long dose of limited use. Cattle grazed and fields of grain rolled over central Whidbey's prairie as early as the 1830s, while just a few miles away on the coastline, trading ships came and went with timber and supplies for the British Columbia Goldrush (1858) and the Klondike Goldrush (1897). Hudson's Bay Company held a fur-trading post here for a short time before moving elsewhere, further boosting the island's notoriety.

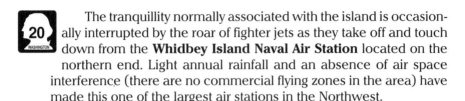

The tranquillity normally associated with the island is occasionally interrupted by the roar of fighter jets as they take off and touch down from the **Whidbey Island Naval Air Station** located on the northern end. Light annual rainfall and an absence of air space interference (there are no commercial flying zones in the area) have made this one of the largest air stations in the Northwest.

Six miles from the ferry landing Highway 20 connects with **Coupeville** (KOOP-vil, Elevation 73, Population 1,510), the oldest town on the island and the second oldest in the state. Named for its founder, Captain Thomas Coupe, who took a Donation Land Claim in 1852, farmers had lived in the area for two decades prior. Early on it acquired the nickname "Port of Sea Captains" because it was a popular resting spot for retired salty dogs and career military men with an eye for fine detail and worldly sophistication, evident in the immaculately maintained Victorian architecture. Since no one *had* to work, Coupeville became the island's social center, hosting community activities centered around the restoration and preservation of their historic past.

Island County: Coupeville, a preserved historic town, is the county seat of Island County; now the state's second smallest in area, it once encompassed Snohomish, Skagit, Whatcom and San Juan counties. It was created from Thurston County in 1853, is located in the east central portion of Puget Sound and consists primarily of Whidbey and Camano Islands. The county was first settled by Isaac N. Ebey in 1850 and later by Captain Thomas Coupe in 1852. The U.S. Naval Air Station on Whidbey Island created an economic revival in the county when it was founded in 1942. Today the main economic activities are government, farming, fishing and tourism.

Court House: Sixth and Main Streets, PO Box 5000, Coupeville 98239, 206-679-7300 (Information), SCAN 592-7300 (Information), FAX 206-678-3449. Area: 211.6 square miles. State Ranking: 38th. 1993 Population: 66,500. Unincorporated: 45,125. Incorporated: 21,375. Density: 314.3 persons per square mile. **Cities and Towns**: Coupeville, Langley, Oak Harbor. **Principal Economic Activities**: Manufacturing, agriculture, fishing, tourism and wood products. **Points of Interest**: Historic Coupeville, Whidbey Island, Camano Island.

Climate: (Coupeville - elevation 73)

	Jan	Apr	Jul	Oct
Max Temp. F°	43.3	57.2	71.3	57.9
Min Temp.	33.3	40.2	50.5	43.0
Mean Temp.	38.5	48.7	60.9	50.5
Precipitation	2.01"	1.12"	.67"	1.73"

Average Annual Maximum Temperature: 57.4
Average Annual Minimum Temperature: 41.9
Annual Mean Temperature: 49.7
Average Annual Precipitation: 17.73"

Due south of Coupeville, on the narrow strip between Penn Cove and Admiralty Inlet lies **Ebey's Landing**, the first National Historic Reserve in the country. The idea behind the reserve is to introduce and maintain a land ethic that combines traditional farming methods with the efficiency of modern machinery, while remaining economically productive. Fearful that the land would fall under the control of developers itching to build condos or resorts, local conservation groups enlisted the financial assistance of the federal government to preserve the integrity and character of the rural history. Sold on the idea, the government purchased conservation easements that left the farmers to care for the land. As a result, the 1,000-acre prairie which makes up Ebey's Landing remains lush and unspoiled. The entire town of Coupeville, a 22-mile district that includes 48 historic buildings, is part of the reserve.

The prairie is named for its civic-minded founder, Colonel Isaac Neff Ebey, who arrived and claimed his plot in 1851 under the Donation Land Law of 1850, which granted free parcels to anyone willing to homestead the Oregon Territory for four years. Active in everything from politics to law to military service, Ebey devoted much effort to establishing and maintaining the settlement before meeting a tragic fate on the same piece of land which first rooted him to the area. In retaliation for the loss of their chief in a showdown with the U.S. military, members of the Tlingit tribe of Alaska attacked the town leader's home in 1857, shooting and customarily decapitating him on his front porch.

The road continues north along **Penn Cove**, explored by Captain George Vancouver in 1792 and named in honor of a "certain friend," believed to be statesman and patriot William Penn. Penn Cove is an inlet for Saratoga Passage between Camano and Whidbey Islands. West of the cove and one mile off of Highway 20 is **Fort Ebey State Park**. A World War II defense bunker stands guard over history, while the arid climate hosts a unique collection of several species of cacti. Bald eagles can often be seen soaring overhead.

Nine miles from Coupeville you will find **Oak Harbor** (Elevation 15, Population 18,930). Founded in 1849, early settlers named the area for the unusually ample number of oak trees which characterized the landscape. The strong presence of the Whidbey Island Naval Air Station has aided in making Oak Harbor the largest town on Whidbey Island. A steady stream of Irish settlers began arriving in the late 1860s, followed by a wave of Dutch immigrants and a sizable population of Chinese tenant farmers in the 1890s. This colorful combination gave the town a rich heritage still seen in hand-painted signs in Dutch that dot various buildings.

Continue north for a high and scenic bridge crossing of **Deception Pass** and the home of Washington's most popular state park,

Deception Pass State Park. This waterway separates Whidbey Island from Fidalgo Island and is known for its forceful tides and aversion to navigation. During strong ebb tides, two and a half billion gallons of water funnel through the channel each hour. The pass was named by Captain Vancouver who originally though it was a port after being tricked by foggy conditions. The quarter-mile Deception Pass Bridge connects the neighboring islands and offers a straight-shot view of the Strait of Juan de Fuca and a dizzying gaze of the rough water below, slowly eating away at the rocks.

The Deception Pass Bridge is visible at the top of this photo.

Fidalgo Island was explored by Lieutenant Juan Francisco de Eliza in 1791 and named for Salvador Fidalgo of the Spanish Navy. A telling myth printed on a totem pole at Rosario Head on the southwest corner of the island adds to the aqua mystique of the area. The story is the Samish tribe legend of the Maiden of Deception Pass, known as Ko-Kwal-Alwoot. While on the shore gathering shellfish one day, she was encountered by the sea spirit who rose from the depths to admire her beauty and poetically express his love for her. A long court-ship began, and the young woman often visited the beaches in order to hear his passionate proclamations. One day the spirit approached the girl's father to ask for her hand in marriage, and although he promised eternal life for his bride-in-waiting, her father refused the offer. Angered, the sea spirit brought famine and drought to the land until the father was forced to concede. His agreement carried only one condition: that his daughter be allowed to visit her village once a year. Thus agreed, the sea spirit and Ko-Kwal-Alwoot were married and headed to their home beneath the waves. For four years she faithfully returned, but each time more reluctantly than before and with noticeably more barnacles attached to her skin. Recognizing the change, the village dismissed her obligation to return and she never left the sea again. She did not forget about her beloved village though, for she continues to look after its descendants by supplying plenty of salmon and shellfish and keeping the water clean and pure. And if you squint just right you can see her seaweed hair floating to the rhythm of the tide.

The port town of **Anacortes** (A-nuh-KOR-tez, Elevation 18, Population 12,260) fills the northern tip of Fidalgo Island. Like Port Townsend, the excitement of the distant sound of the railroad helped bounce the population of Anacortes from dozens to thousands in the opening months of 1890 alone. One man delighted to see the eager crowds arrive was town founder Amos Bowman. He settled his claim in 1876 and began building a town which he named for his wife, Anna Curtis (the current spelling was adopted by the post office and it eventually stuck). Furiously lobbying to bring the revered tracks into town, he opened a post office and started a newspaper to convince railroad prospectors of the town's vitality and importance. Considered the "Father of Anacortes," Bowman never saw his dream of railroad pay-dirt materialize, but many settlers stayed put and became part of a stable fishing industry and timber trade. Cod became king here in the first few years of 1900, bringing about the largest cod processing plants on the West Coast. Today, oil refineries have risen as large employers and strong contributors to the local economy.

An international ferry system runs out of Anacortes, connecting Sydney and Victoria, British Columbia, as well as the San Juan Islands.

From Anacortes, head briefly south along Fidalgo Bay, then east 16 miles across I-5 to **Sedro Woolley** (SEE-droh WOO-lee, Elevation 50, Population 6,920). In 1884, when town founder Mortimer Cook suggested the name "Bug" for the proliferation of insects that swarmed the small lumber community, his fellow settlers threatened to add the prefix "hum." A compromise was reached by using — but misspelling — the Spanish word cedro, meaning "cedar," as a more appropriate name, deriving from nearby Cedar Mountain and the surrounding landscape of western red cedar.

A few years later the Great Northern and Northern Pacific railroads established a junction slightly north of Sedro and P.A. Woolley platted a townsite around the depot and named it after himself. To reduce the costs of dual governments, the adjacent towns were combined (with a now-forgotten hyphen) as Sedro-Woolley in 1890.

After significant forest depletion, industry shifted to farming. The town's prosperity reached a zenith at the height of the gold rush due to its strategic location on the Skagit River and accessibility to the Mt. Baker "pot of gold" region. Except for the presence of the interstate, Sedro Woolley is a quiet agricultural community.

The road continues five miles up the Skagit River Valley through **Lyman** (LEYE-muhn, Elevation 100, Population 290) and **Hamilton** (Elevation 95, Population 234), former logging and mining towns that have since embraced agriculture as their mainstay.

Welcome to Concrete.

The solid cement buildings of **Concrete** (Elevation 260, Population, 730) are found two miles upriver from Hamilton. The discovery of clay and limestone by Amasa Everett led to the formation of the Washington Portland Cement Company, and well into the 1900s, Concrete's cement was used in projects throughout the state. In addition to the majority of public buildings that are comprised of cement (the obvious choice of material after a fire leveled the town in 1921), a conveyor belt carrying limestone between the company plant and the quarry hovered 100 feet over the streets of Concrete. The bridge that spans the Baker River, listed in the National Historic Register, was built of concrete and used as a model for other long-span concrete bridges across the country.

Cross the bridge and turn north on East Lake Shannon Road for a birds-eye view of **Baker Dam**. Built by the Puget Power and Light Company in 1924, the dam supplies electricity for much of northern Washington. Lake Shannon, an artificial lake impounded for hydroelectricity, extends over seven miles from the lower stretch of Baker River to the northern limits of Concrete. At the north tip of Lake Shannon is Upper Baker Dam and the 10-mile-long Baker Lake.

Back on Highway 20, towering peaks with daunting names like Mt. Despair, Mt. Fury, Damnation Peak, Phantom Pass and Mt. Terror serve notice that you are entering north Cascade country. **Rockport**, little more than a highway junction, lies at the confluence of the Sauk and Skagit rivers. The community's mellow appearance belies its former bustle and significance. Once the main supply and shipping point for mining and logging operations in the mountains, Rockport received a shot in the arm while the Seattle City Light dams were under construction, but now rests in quiet repose at the foot of the Cascades.

Sauk City (SAWK), Rockport's former incarnation, was a couple of miles downstream and across the river. The town was used mainly as a landing for river boats on their way to the heavily mineralized

Monte Cristo region (a comparison to the fabled wealth of the Count of Monte Cristo) in the 1890s. The Sauk City Hotel and a shingle mill provided the community with even greater economic stability, but a fire in 1889 ravaged the entire settlement and forced residents to move to the opposite bank and upriver, where Rockport now lies.

Beyond the junction with Highway 530 the road encounters the **Skagit River Bald Eagle Sanctuary**, a seven-mile stretch of river where hundreds of eagles congregate each fall to clean the water and banks of spawning and dying chum salmon.

Marblemount, a cluster of neat buildings and immaculate gardens, is the oldest settlement along this stretch of road. Prospectors and miners stocked-up here before heading upriver for riches. William Barrett built a hotel in 1891 and also operated a cable ferry. Barrett's hotel-keeper, Mrs. Buller, gave Marblemount its name for a mountain of marble across the river.

Lichen-covered canyons and broken cliffs loom above as the highway climbs to the village of **Newhalem**. Built as headquarters for Seattle City Light construction projects, its houses sheltered hundreds of workers for the years that the Gorge, Diablo and Ross dams took to complete; some employees remain. In the 1930s tourists who were shipped by train were greeted by music from loudspeakers concealed on Mt. Ross. After an ample meal in the huge community dining hall, they would stroll over behind the power plant and view the tropical gardens developed by John D. Ross, superintendent of Seattle City Light, who brought in exotic plants and shrubs from all over the world. Pathways ran alongside Ladder Creek Falls, lit at night with multi-colored submarine lights, while inspirational music drifted from loudspeakers in the surrounding gardens. The next day, via the combination of open-air electric train, incline railcar lift, and a tour boat, all the construction sites were visited and the surrounding grandeur of the north Cascades enjoyed.

Northeast of Gorge Dam are the **Diablo** and **Ross** dams; both have man-made lakes for hydroelectric power production. Ross Lake extends 24 miles up Ruby and Beaver creeks, stretching into Canada. The only launch facilities on Ross Lake are at its north end, at Hozomeen, reached by a 39-mile gravel road from Canada. It was John Ross who first realized the power potential of the area and filed on the site in 1917. Ross' name became synonymous with northwest power generation; in later years he was summoned to the White House to advise President Roosevelt on power development and appointed to a position on the Securities and Exchange Commission.

As the highway edges Diablo Lake, State Highway 20 officially becomes the North Cascades Highway, the most scenic automobile crossing of the range. Completed in 1972, the highway marked the first accessible route across the north Cascades, sometimes called the "American Alps." Several snow-capped peaks (Sourdough Mountain, Mt. Triumph, Jack Mountain and Liberty Bell Mountain) are visible in the reflection of the blue-green water; its vibrant hue is caused by glacial silt suspended in the water reacting to light.

The highway climbs and winds its way across the **North Cascades National Park**, which combined with adjacent wilderness areas creates one of the wildest, most pristine segments of untouched land in the nation, occupying over half of the entire Cascade Range in

Dramatic peaks of the north Cascades.

Washington. Wild peaks and trench-like canyons mark **Rainy Pass** (Elevation 4,860) and **Washington Pass** (Elevation 5,477) and the approximate point at which the highway closes during the winter. In the spring deciduous trees are bright green with new leaves and an abundance of water tumbles over cliffs patched with snow.

From these lofty heights, the high range gives way to the wide open meadows and scattered ponderosa pine forests of the upper Methow (met-how) Valley. Continue through the rustic village of Mazama into **Winthrop** (Elevation 1,765, Population 335), one of the first 'civilizing attempts' of the Methow Valley. Miners in the 1890s brought the valley its first boom, and then fruit-raising, farming and dairying became the chief sources of income. At present tourism and real estate may be added to the mix.

Winthrop's commercial district.

Located at the junction of the Methow and Chewack Rivers, Winthrop began as a trading post for cattle ranchers and miners. Congressman John L. Wilson named the town after Theodore Winthrop, the young author of *Canoe and the Saddle*. Originally entitled *Klallam and Klickitat: Nature and*

Natives of the Northwest, the book describes the New Englander's impressions of the rugged Cascade country. Admiral Winthrop also earned an unfortunate distinction as the first Union officer killed in the Civil War.

Today's Winthrop has been converted into a stage-set western town (where tourists now elbow one another off the boardwalks, much like miners and ranchers of old). Winthrop stops most travelers going either east or west on the North Cascades Scenic Highway three seasons of the year and is the hub of some of Washington's best cross-country skiing and snowmobiling in the winter.

East of Winthrop is the birthplace and the home of the **North Cascades Smokejumpers Base**. Operated by the U.S. Forest Service, experiments with "smokejumping" began in 1939 and have proven to be a fast and successful method of combating wildfires.

The road turns from Winthrop and heads 11 miles south to **Twisp** (Elevation 1,500, Population 900) and the confluence of the Methow and Twisp rivers. After a stint at mining proved unprofitable, settlers focused their efforts above ground, harvesting the surrounding forest and then farming and grazing cattle on the cleared land. These activities continue on a small scale, with tourism serving as a seasonal economic supplement. The Twisp namesake evolved from the Indian word *T-wapsp*, meaning "yellow jackets," and a reference to the insects that pestered native women as they dried salmon.

The road journeys east over Loup Loup Pass and then down a long grade into the southern end of the Okanogan Valley and a junction with U.S. 97 in Okanogan. The two roads head north for 23 miles to Tonasket and then Highway 20 breaks east via another long grade, exiting the lowlands amidst arid surroundings and basaltic formations.

Passing the entrance to the Aeneas Valley, a recommended side trip into the Okanogan Highlands, drive another 10 miles to the former site of **Wauconda**, a gathering of scattered buildings and a mere speck

It's pie auction time at the Town Hall.

against the plateau of gently rolling hills. The townsite moved to a location near the head of Toroda Creek after the Wauconda mine was exhausted. Named for the mine, the Indian word translates as "master of life." Settlers reported that local tribes worshipped this "master of life" as a religious entity who inhabited nearby mountains. The less colorful origin of the town's name stems from the three Hedge brothers, hailing from Wauconda, Illinois, who discovered gold in the area in 1898.

20 Highway 20 passes over Wauconda Summit (Elevation 4,310) and down the west fork of Granite Creek to join Highway 21 in the community of Republic before heading east again on its own. Carefully drive along the sharp bends of the misnamed **Sherman Pass** (Elevation 5,575), 12 miles east of Republic. Although General T. Sherman of the U.S. Army and Civil War fame is credited with the route's discovery, it was Henry H. Pierce who first crossed the pass in 1882. Nearby Sherman Creek and Sherman Peak are also unfairly titled, since the general arrived a year after Pierce and recorded that he "viewed out the road enroute" after finding the creek. The pass traverses through the central mountain range of Ferry County and is the highest highway pass in the state (some of the most panoramic views as well).

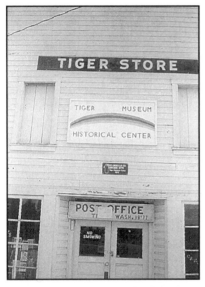

The sign says "No longer a Post Office."

Roosevelt Lake, the upper expanse of a dammed section of the Columbia River, offers a break in the forested and rugged terrain. The road briefly joins U.S. 395 at Kettle Falls, on the east bank of the river, for another 10 miles to Colville. After temporary respite, you will again be surrounded by steep mountains and towering trees as you jog 36 miles northeast through the Colville National Forest before winding steeply down through the timber to **Tiger**. Originally established as a trading post by a fellow named Yoder, the town was named for its first pioneer settler, George Tiger. There are no tigers disturbing the quiet of Tiger, and usually nothing nearly so exotic happens here. In fact, the sign above the general store which boasts, 'No Longer A Post Office, Tiger, Washington.' says it all. The town has been superseded by the larger Ione, four miles north, and is basically a crossroads settlement where State Highway 31 heads north to Canada and Highway 20 turns west.

Highway 20 completes its cross-state trek by heading roughly 47 miles directly south, edging the Pend Oreille River, and running through the old sawmill settlements of Cusick, Usk and Dalkena. The highway traverses the wide valley rimmed by hills, where forested areas alternate with fenced pastures.

The Diamond Match Company bought a mill in **Cusick** (KYOO-sik, Elevation 2,000, Population 247) in 1920 and felled massive amounts of virgin forests to make their matchsticks. Today the mile-long river stretch of rotting moorings reveals that the days of bustling, lumber-filled steamboats are long gone. The town is named for Captain Cusick, who skippered steamboats on the river, and established the town in 1902.

One mile downriver, the tiny town of **Usk** (UHSK) sits quiet as a church mouse. Logging operations burst out of the gate at the turn of the century, chopping and hauling at such a clip that precious little remained to cut just three decades later. Left with acres of rotting stumps and unyielding, gravelly soil, most settlers abandoned Usk to search out new employment and resources elsewhere.

To visit **Manressa Grotto**, cross the bridge at Usk and drive north on LeClerc Road for six miles. This glacially-formed cave on the Kalispel Indian Reservation was used for religious ceremonies by Indians and early missionaries since the 1800s. The Kalispel tribe holds 4,629 acres (talk about the diversity of necessity, the tribe keeps a bison herd as a meat source and owns an aluminum processing plant at Cusick). The natural rock shelter is basically a cave with two entrances and a simple stone alter inside. Today the cave's cool hush of natural sanctity is belittled by name carvings and graffiti stains left by thoughtless visitors.

The four-mile path of decayed mooring piles stretching from Usk to **Dalkena** anticipates the status of the town, which is little more than a memory. The enormous mill that ate lumber at terrific speeds 24 hours a day is now reduced to a handful of burnt-out foundations along the quiet river like the ghost of a crumbling, heroic Greek ruin. The combination of timber depletion and a destructive fire in 1935 damaged the economy to a point from which it has never recovered. Lumbermen Henry Dalton and Hugh Kennedy established the mill operation in 1902, and called it Dalkena, a combination of their names.

Beyond this point Highway 20 extends another dozen miles along the placid Pend Oreille River and ceases at Newport. ⊗

Although no state highways service the **San Juan Islands**, there are several fine county roads available on the four main islands: San Juan, Orcas, Lopez and Shaw. A sampling of these roads are included in this section.

SJ

Scattered amongst the waters north of the Strait of Juan de Fuca, hard against the floating Canadian boundary that runs up the Straits of Georgia and Haro, the San Juan Islands are last in terms of geographical accessibility but not least in the hearts of many Washingtonians. Their strong feelings are bound to pine-covered islands, white sand and rocky beaches, lush farmland, and the countless bays, harbors and channels that define the place.

SJ The archipelago consists of 172 habitable islands and hundreds of mostly-submerged rocks that make an appearance at low tide, requiring that sailors study their charts. Bridging the gap between Vancouver Island and the North Cascades, the islands are the peaks of a flooded, low-lying mountain range that is topped by Orcas Island's Mt. Constitution (Elevation 2,454).

Orcas Island is the chain's largest island, but San Juan Island, the second largest, is a more common destination and site of the infamous **Pig War**, an event that nearly led the United States and England to battle. Discovered in 1791 by Spanish explorers Lopez Gonzalez de Haro and his commander Francisco Eliza, the territory was named Isla y Archipelago de San Juan. Later George Vancouver (circa 1792) and Charles Wilkes (1841) came sailing through and applied and renamed geographic features. The territory (with its Spanish-English-American place names intact) was claimed by both America and Britain as their own.

At first glance the Oregon Treaty of 1846 seemed sufficient to end past territory disputes. The treaty granted the United States possession of land south of the 49th parallel, defining the new boundary as the "channel which separates the continent from Vancouver's Island; and thence southerly through the middle of the said channel, and of Fuca's straits to the Pacific Ocean." The vagueness of this declaration led Americans to interpret the "channel" as Haro Strait; the British claimed it meant Rosario Straight. In between lay San Juan Island, which by the 1850s was occupied by a Hudson's Bay Company sheep ranch and salmon-curing station, and a growing number of American farmers.

On June 15th, 1859 a pig owned by a British farmer rooted in Lyman Cutler's potato garden. Cutler, who was known for his hot temper and marksmanship, shot the pig and when British officials sought to arrest him, fellow Americans on the island wrote a petition requesting government protection. Captain George E. Pickett's (leader of the famous Confederate charge at Gettysburg) 66-man 9th U.S. Infantry answered the call and hunkered down on a narrow spit of land between Haro Strait and Griffin Bay. The governor of Vancouver Island, James Douglas, responded by sending three British warships.

Forces and tensions grew throughout the summer and by August 31, 461 Americans and their 14 cannons faced 5 British warships armed to the gills with 167 guns and carrying 2,140 troops. Fortunately, before the outbreak of war, higher ups from both sides realized the folly of a "Pig War" and negotiated a truce, agreeing to leave only small token forces until the boundary dispute could be resolved. Pickett's Camp became American Camp and England established British Camp on the shores above Garrison Bay.

For the next 12 years the two sides lived in peace, even sharing holidays together. After the Civil War, America found time to tidy up unresolved national affairs such as boundary lines. Acting as arbiter,

Kaiser Wilhelm I of Germany spent one year consulting with geographers and lawyers before ruling that the boundary ran through Haro Straight, a decision which gave America sole possession of San Juan Island. The pig's death remains unvindicated to this day. **SJ**

A trip to the San Juans usually starts from the ferry terminal on Fidalgo Island in Anacortes, although private vessels able to negotiate the open sea and small planes also make the journey. Ferries sail west across Rosario Strait towards Thatcher Pass, which is separated by Blakely Island to the north and Decatur Island to the south. After clearing these small islands the common route is north around the tip of Lopez Island (a ferry stop), and then either southwest through Upright Channel directly to San Juan Island or west via the narrow sea lane that divides Orcas and Shaw islands (both have ferry terminals), and then on to San Juan Island. Ferries from Seattle continue west to British Columbia's Sidney on Vancouver Island.

The ferry to San Juan Island docks at **Friday Harbor**, a heavily-touristed but charming island port. A full day may be spent viewing the wide variety of boats that moor in the harbor or perusing the town's cluster of knick-knack shops, artisan galleries and restaurants that specialize in fresh seafood. The ship-filled harbor takes its name from a Hawaiian sheep herder by the name of John Friday who was imported to tend sheep for the Hudson's Bay Company.

A short distance from the ferry terminal, in a 100-year-old building overlooking the harbor, **The Whale Museum** (1st and Court) reveals the natural history of whales and dolphins through biological

"What bay is it?" "Friday." Some say that's how Friday Harbor got its name.

and artistic displays. The museum, "a center for environmental education and marine research," is a must-stop for anyone interested in the massive mammals or for those planning on doing any whale watching. Three pods of orca whales make their home within a 200-mile radius of San Juan Island.

SJ There are numerous two-lane country roads to explore on San Juan Island. The following suggested route leads through tidy island farms and along miles of windy coastline accessing several of the island's historical and scenic sites. From Friday Harbor follow

Bucolic San Juan Island.

Spring Street to Mullis Road and continue south on Cattle Point Road to **American Camp**. Maps of the expansive grounds and historical literature may be obtained from the interpretive center at the park's entrance. A one-mile trail leads past historical markers and land that once sheltered Captain Pickett's troops (a thriving rabbit population has taken its place). Panoramic views of Haro Strait and Griffin Bay and of Mt. Baker and the Olympic Range add to the park's appeal.

North of American Camp via Cattle Point and Bailer Hill roads is **Lime Kiln State Park**, one of the island's best locations to spot killer

English Camp above Garrison Bay.

whale pods. Picnic tables line a rocky cliff that functions as a natural amphitheater for the graceful mammals. The compact lighthouse has guided boats into Haro Strait since 1919.

Continue on Westside Road to **English Camp**, which occupies grassy fields on a rise above Garrison Bay. Four historic buildings remain including the Guardhouse and Barracks building. Trails climb from the camp through the British cemetery en route to Mt. Young (Elevation 650) and 360° views of the aquatic surroundings and British Columbia.

The next stop on the San Juan Island tour is **Roche Harbor**, a postcard-perfect cove a few miles up the road from British Camp. (Continue north on West Side Road and turn left on Roche Harbor Road.) Less frequented than Friday Harbor but by no means desolate, the harbor's gentle waters support a multitude of Canadian and

American pleasure crafts. Long a resort community (Presidents Teddy Roosevelt and William Howard Taft stayed at the Hotel de Haro), Roche Harbor was also an industry town. In the 1880s the Roche Harbor Lime and Cement Company was the largest producer of lime west of the Mississippi. The old quarry and abandoned kilns are found in the hills sheltering the harbor. **SJ**

Roche Harbor Road returns south past scattered homesteads and llama-raising farms to Friday Harbor. While driving on the islands keep an eye out for slow-moving vehicles such as mopeds and bicycles. Adopting "island time," the laid-back, watch-dipped-in-molasses-attitude, is also recommended.

Like the gaping maw of a killer whale the Orcas Island Ferry landing awaits.

The ferry to **Orcas Island** docks at the community of Orcas, in sight of the white-washed Orcas Hotel (built in 1904) and a handful of restaurants and shops.

Similar to the roads on San Juan Island, there are many driving and exploring options but the main route, the aptly-named Horseshoe Highway, is a scenic stretch worthy of hours of idle driving. The road rolls north and east around East Sound, which nearly divides the island in two, and then heads south to **Moran State Park**.

The bountiful park, filled with over 35 miles of trails, multiple campgrounds and lakes, the Environmental Learning Center, and Mt. Constitution, would be considered impressive no matter where in the state it was located, but the fact that it occupies a large chunk of land in the middle of the northern Pacific waters makes it spectacular. The mountain is accessible by car or bike (for strong riders); bring a camera and hope for clear skies.

Shaw and Lopez islands are also accessed by ferry but are more appropriate for two-wheel forms of transportation than by car. Citizens on both islands eye development with a good dose of skepticism but will gladly stop to help fix a flat tire or offer directions to the nearest ferry terminal.

SJ **San Juan County**: Friday Harbor is the county seat for San Juan County, which was organized in 1873 from Whatcom County. The county is the state's smallest in area and is made up of a small cluster of islands located east of Vancouver Island in Puget Sound. The county's most significant historical event was the dispute between Great Britain and the United States over the islands' sovereignty known as "The Pig War." Today, the primary economic pursuits are produce, farming and tourism.

Court House: 350 Court Street, Friday Harbor 98250, FAX 206-378-6256. Area: 179.3 square miles. State Ranking: 39th. 1993 Population: 11,900. Unincorporated: 10,170. Incorporated: 1,730. Density: 66.4 persons per square mile. **Cities and Towns**: Friday Harbor. **Principal Economic Activities**: Agriculture, fishing, tourism. **Points of Interest**: American Camp, English Camp.

Climate: (Olga - elevation 80)

	Jan	Apr	Jul	Oct
Max Temp. F°	43.6	57.0	70.1	58.0
Min Temp.	33.6	40.2	48.9	43.7
Mean Temp.	38.6	48.6	59.6	50.9
Precipitation	4.04"	1.65"	.88"	3.04"

Average Annual Maximum Temperature: 57.2
Average Annual Minimum Temperature: 41.7
Annual Mean Temperature: 49.5
Average Annual Precipitation: 28.78" ☞

One of countless land forms comprising the San Juan Islands.

S tate Highway 21 from a junction with State Highway 260 in Kahlotus, north through Lind, Odessa and Wilbur, across the Columbia River through Republic and Danville to the Canadian boundary. (Overlaps State Highway 20.) Route length: 191 miles.

The highway increases in both beauty and interest as it heads north. Its origin, at a junction with Highways 260 and 263 at Kahlotus, is somewhat remote, but it is possible to join the highway at U.S. Highway 395, Interstate 90 or U.S. Highway 2 and not miss much.

One mile west of U.S. 395, **Lind** (Elevation 1,300, Population 470) is spread out in a hollow on both sides of a small coulee. Two brothers from Iceland named Nielson platted the town in 1888, established a store and developed a well from a natural spring. They used the letters from their name as the initial letters for the town's street names. There are several possible origins for the town's name: Lind is the Icelandic word for spring or small waterway; a woman cook on a passing railroad crew was named Lind; or in honor of Jenny Lind, the Swedish nightingale. Take your pick.

The highway continues north across the Columbia Plateau. Spotted occasionally in the endless wheat fields are farmhouses, which appear as islands in a vast green or yellow sea (depending on the season). Sometimes farmers will plant a few trees for windbreak, but they hate to surrender even a yard of their precious plowed ground. The farmhouses and farmsteads look like model toy communities, as if a child were given little barns, houses, corrals, windmills and silos to place upon a barren canvas of wheat.

A few miles before Odessa (Highway 28) is a small Bohemian cemetery, established in 1903, with maybe 25 graves. There are no standing headstones, just small flat monuments out in the middle of an idyllic prairie. Little moves out here but the wind, and by the information on the markers, the slow march of generations.

North of Odessa, the road winds through several dry coulees, but eventually the rolling hills of grain return. On some of the giant wheat farms it seems possible to pull a disk plow for half a day in one direction before turning around, coming back to the start, and calling it a day's work.

Ten miles past Wilbur (U.S. 2) the road begins to

Keller Ferry has crossed the river in the same manner for 100 years.

twist and turn, dropping 1,300 feet from the plateau to the Columbia River. Along the way there are spectacular views of the middle reaches of Roosevelt Lake, a man-made reservoir comprising 151 miles of the Columbia. To cross the lake you must take **Keller Ferry**, a two-man ferry operation that holds a dozen vehicles. The ferry has crossed the river in virtually the same manner for the last 100 years.

Franklin D. Roosevelt Lake comprises 151 miles of the Columbia.

Highway 21 resumes on land encompassed by the **Colville Indian Reservation**, which at 1.3 million acres, covers an area larger than the state of Rhode Island. The Colvilles were first visited by Lewis and Clark in 1806, and later by traders from the Pacific Fur Company and the Hudson Bay Company, which founded Fort Colville in 1825. By the mid-1800s, increasing amounts of whites in the area brought conflict and disease, including a major smallpox epidemic.

President Ulysses S. Grant established the reservation in 1872, a treaty not signed by the Colville people. The early years of the reservation were filled with friction. Within a short time, borders began to shrink as white settlers inhabited land east of the Columbia River and miners came in droves to stake claims in the northern half. There was also intertribal friction over land rights as rival tribes were brought together. Remnants of at least 11 bands comprise today's Confederated Colville Tribe.

The road follows the Sanpoil River through a gorge of serrated, basaltic outcroppings. It is curvy but not difficult. Cattle graze open

An empty old house once full of young hopes.

sections of the valley floor and coniferous forests dot the hillside. As you approach Republic, the canyon narrows, and then opens up to broad meadows and lower, rounded hills. The river, deeper and quieter, meanders in a gooseneck fashion through these meadows.

Discovery of gold on Granite Creek by John Welty in 1896 opened the northern section of the Colville Indian Reservation and brought an influx of prospectors to **Republic** (Elevation 2,503, Population 1,055), a mining community perched on a steep hillside, 53 miles from the Keller Ferry crossing. Named for the Republic Gold Mine, it was originally called *Eureka,* the name of a creek on which a rich gold strike was made. Before that, Indians called the area *Kleopus,* "valley of the cliffs."

The Republic area has yielded more gold than any other region in the state. Several miles north of Republic, the High Knob Mine, Washington's most productive gold and silver mine, works an ore body composed of large quartz veins.

Episcapal Church made of stone-like cement.

An extinct Stonrose Fossil flower.

Republic's soil yields more than precious metals. The **Stonerose Interpretive Center** (15 N. Kean Street) contains a fossil site that provides pictures of the plants, animals, and climate of the area from nearly 50 million years ago, a period of great volcanic activity known as the Eocene Epoch. At that time, the area now occupied by Republic was part of the bottom of an ancient lake. Over many years, volcanic ash and other sediment materials settled on the lake bottom covering leaves, twigs, insects and fish which had also collected there. The volcanic ash hardened into a fine-grained stone called tuff, a substance which breaks easily into many layers revealing exact fossil remains. More varieties of plant fossils have been found at Stonerose than in any other paleobotanical dig in the world. Scientists have used the fossils to trace many of today's common plants,

such as the alder, birch, and horsetail, to their ancestors. Stonerose received its name from the oldest known ancestor of the rose family, also found at the site. The rose plants are so old that they are thought to be the ancestors of all the distant "cousins" of the rose: apples, plums, and other fruit trees.

Amyzon fish fossil, catch and release only.

Stonerose offers fossil digging tours to the public. The tours start at the interpretive center across from the park in Republic.

Ferry County: Republic is the county seat of Ferry County, which was established in 1899 from part of Stevens County. It was named after Washington's first governor, Elisha P. Ferry. Located in the eastern part of the state, it is bounded on the north by Canada. The region was first visited by Canadian trappers in the early nineteenth century. The Colville Indian Reservation, established in 1872, now encompasses over half of the county. The gold rush of the 1890s brought permanent settlers to the region. Today, lumber, mining and agriculture are the county's major economic activities.

Courthouse: 390 East Delaware, Republic 99166, FAX 509-775-2492. Area: 2,202 square miles. State Ranking: 9th. 1993 Population: 6,900. Unincorporated: 5,845. Incorporated: 1,055. Density: 3.1 persons per square mile. **Cities and Towns**: Republic. **Principal Economic Activities**: Mining, wood products, agriculture. **Points of Interest**: Colville Indian Reservation, Roosevelt Lake.

Climate: (Republic - elevation 2,503)

	Jan	Apr	Jul	Oct
Max Temp. F°	30.0	58.4	83.5	58.6
Min Temp.	14.0	29.5	44.4	30.6
Mean Temp.	21.6	44.1	64.1	44.5
Precipitation	1.79"	1.13"	.78"	1.27"

Average Annual Maximum Temperature: 56.9
Average Annual Minimum Temperature: 29.4
Annual Mean Temperature: 43.2
Average Annual Precipitation: 14.89"

Five miles past Republic, **Lake Curlew** is surrounded by glacial deposits and sparsely timbered hills. The deep, five-mile-long lake, Curlew Creek and the community of Curlew all carry the name of the snipe-like bird that once nested in abundance on the banks of the lake. Curlew is the English version of the Indian karanips.

Hayfields lead right to **Malo's** (Mah-loh) backdoor, a weathered village among mountain peaks. Built in 1903, the **Malo Store** was once the town's center of activity. The present front porch of the store was previously the back door and a freight loading area for the Kettle Valley Railroad. The back of the store was formerly the front and faced the tracks of the Great Northern Railroad.

Between Curlew and Malo is the **Antique Car & Truck Museum**, an unlikely location for several rare automobiles. The museum features: a 1925 Howard Cooper, one of four ever built; a 1926 Yellow Knight, built by the Yellow Cab Company and one of three in America; a 1928 Ford Phaeton owned by actor Walter Brennen of the Real

McCoys and used in some of his early movies; and the Orange Peel, the smallest street-legal car in the world.

The Orange Peel, so named because of its bright orange paint job, was manufactured on the Isle of Man, off the west coast of Wales, from 1960 to 1964. On a trip to London to finance production, the 12 owners of the car manufacturing plant were killed in an airplane crash. They were preparing for world-wide production and had 11 years of back orders based on three cars per day.

From an environmental standpoint, the loss of the Orange Peel's brain trust was significant since the car was the ideal commuter, traveling 40 mph and going 100 miles on a tank

Antique car and truck museum.

of gas. It weighs a mere 130 pounds with a full tank of gas, but its size is deceiving, as it will hold a 6'8" man weighing 300 pounds.

Curlew, six miles beyond Malo, was built on an old fur trading site. Prospectors stopped here on their way between Republic's mines and a smelter near Grand Forks, British Columbia. To accommodate railway travelers the **Ansorge Hotel** was erected, bringing elegance to an otherwise unrefined place. Built in 1906, the hotel has a board-walk front, cornered entrance doors, and sheet-metal sidings with a rock-like appearance. Henry Ford stayed here in 1917. Also of note, famous world-wide traveler and adventurer Ranald McDonald was buried 10 miles west of here in Toroda.

The Kettle River dominates the landscape from Curlew 10 miles north to **Danville**, just south of the Canadian Border. Danville began in 1889 as a general store that straddled the border. Customs officers suspected that the store's merchant was selling goods bought in one country to customers of the other country without applying a duty tax and forced the store to relocate south of the border.

The valley opens wide, offering a long look into Canada. It is not necessary to backtrack at this point; instead drive three miles on High-

The Hotel Ansorge. Tickets please.

way 3 into Grand Forks, British Columbia, a Canadian mining town that shares an historical heritage with Washington's mining districts. Continue east briefly before turning off the scenic highway and heading back to the American border. U.S. 395 begins, or ends, at Laurier, Washington. ⌀

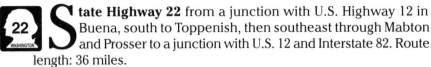

State **Highway 22** from a junction with U.S. Highway 12 in Buena, south to Toppenish, then southeast through Mabton and Prosser to a junction with U.S. 12 and Interstate 82. Route length: 36 miles.

Highway 22 leaves U.S. 12, crosses the Yakima River and travels three miles to Toppenish (U.S. Highway 97). The road then angles southeast through irrigated fields of alfalfa and hops and the eastern edge of the Yakima Indian Reservation, reaching **Mabton** (Elevation 700, Population 1,495) 20 miles further. Mabton was named for Mabel Baker, daughter of Dr. Dorsey S. Baker, the founder of a primitive railroad between Walla Walla and Wallula. Known as the "rawhide railroad," the line was bought out by the Northern Pacific Railroad, which established a station in Mabton in 1885.

The Mabton-Bickleton Road leads southwest 26 miles to Bickleton (U.S. 97), the "Bluebird Capitol of the World." Thirteen miles further on Highway 22, a sign notifies visitors that **Prosser** (Elevation 680, Population 4,540) is a "pleasant place with pleasant people." Wide, shady streets, an abundance of scenic vineyards, and its position on the banks of the Yakima River lend credence to this claim.

During salmon runs, Native Americans camped here at "Tap Tap Falls," descriptive of the sound the river made as it plunged over the nine-foot falls. James Kinney homesteaded near the falls in 1880 and two years later was joined by Colonel William Prosser, who opened a trading post for the scattered ranchmen and railroad crews of the area. In 1883, the site was renamed Prosser Falls; "Falls" was later dropped from the name.

Besides the arrival of the Northern Pacific Railroad in 1885, the most significant addition to the town was William Heinzerling's gristmill, also located at Prosser Falls. Started in 1887, the Prosser Flouring Mill was powered by the Yakima River, processing wheat for farmers from the surrounding country. Flour from the mill was sent as far as San Francisco to aid victims of the 1906 earthquake.

Prosser's venerable downtown, built of brick and plastered with neon signs, deserves a visit, as do several other sites. The **Benton County Historical Museum** (Paterson and Seventh) offers detailed exhibits including: a turn-of-the-century general store; a school house; a lady's shop; a 1900 homestead shack; and a Victorian parlor.

The three-story brick county courthouse (Market and Dudley, built in 1926) dominates the downtown. A plaque explains how the courthouse represents "a turning point in the county seat controversy" with Kennewick; a battle that raged for years. Close to downtown are several houses built between 1899 and 1907. A walking tour reveals a variety of architectural styles: Queen Anne, Stick Eastlake, Dutch and Colonial Revival, as well as craftsman bungalows. The tour starts at the Chamber of Commerce (1230 Bennett Avenue; maps are available).

Benton County: Prosser is the county seat of Benton County, which was founded in 1905 and was formerly part of Yakima and Klickitat counties. It is located in the southeastern part of the state and is bordered on the south and east by the Columbia River. In the past many famous explorers of the Northwest passed through the county, among them Lewis and Clark and Captain Bonneville. Early wagon roads from Walla Walla to Puget Sound also traversed the county. In the 1880s the coming of railroads brought settlers to the region and the irrigation projects of the 1890s created a rich agricultural economy. The establishment of the Hanford Atomic Energy Center has made the county the nation's major atomic research center. Today the county enjoys a diversified economy based on agriculture, wood products, food production and government installations.

Courthouse: 620 Market Street, Prosser 99350, FAX 509-786-5601. Area: 1,722.1 square miles. State Ranking: 22nd. 1993 Population: 122,800. Unincorporated: 32,610. Incorporated: 90,190. Density: 71.3 persons per square mile. **Cities and Towns**: Benton City, Kennewick, Prosser, Richland, West Richland. **Principal Economic Activities**: Food processing, chemicals, metal products, nuclear products. **Points of Interest**: Hanford Science Center, McNary Dam.

Climate: (Prosser - elevation 680)

	Jan	Apr	Jul	Oct
Max Temp. F°	38.7	68.0	90.3	66.6
Min Temp.	23.7	38.2	55.6	38.9
Mean Temp.	31.2	53.2	72.9	52.8
Precipitation	.94"	.55"	.17"	.92"

Average Annual Maximum Temperature: 65.6
Average Annual Minimum Temperature: 39.3
Annual Mean Temperature: 52.4
Average Annual Precipitation: 7.77" ∞

Scablands near Sprague.

State **Highway 23** from a junction with U.S. Highway 195 in Steptoe northwest via St. John and Sprague to a junction with State Highway 28 in Harrington. Route length: 65 miles.

Highway 23 is notable for touching three distinct geographical regions. It begins in the Palouse, samples the Channeled Scablands near Sprague and meets the eastern edge of the Columbia Plateau around Harrington.

St. John (Elevation 1,945, Population 512), a small wheat town 14 miles northwest of Steptoe, has not been blessed by saints. Instead, the fertile Palouse soil and the adjacent Union Pacific Railroad have determined its prosperity. The town was settled by Edward St. John in 1881.

About 10 miles further, stop in **Ewan**, a 1911 depot for the transcontinental Chicago, Milwaukee and St. Paul Railroad, and head north on Rock Lake Road two miles to **Rock Lake**. The narrow, 10-mile-

Max Steinke barn on the Charles Dechenne Ranch, St. John.

long lake is hemmed in by steep basalt cliffs, which are cut with numerous caves. As you approach the lake, imagine the proud but beaten Yakima Indian Chief Kamiakin seeing his final home for the first time. Kamiakin held a leading role in the resistance to white settlers in the 1850s. After a self-imposed exile from his camp near Yakima, he came to Rock Lake to farm until his death in 1877.

An entrepreneur brought a motor boat to the lake in 1903, giving rides to wide-eyed tourists and eventually building a hotel to accommodate them. A small community named Rock Lake existed until the railroad established their stop at Ewan.

From Ewan the road continues 21 miles and makes a perpendicular crossing with the Burlington Northern Railroad at Lamont, skirts the waters of Folsom, Crooked Knee and Sheep Lakes (small finger lakes formed by the Spokane Flood), and passes through Sprague (U.S. 395) en route to Harrington (Highway 28).

"And those fields of wheat they sure smell sweet . . ."

The 20 miles between Sprague and Harrington covers mostly wheat and graze land and marks the entrance to the Columbia Plateau. Actually, most of southeastern Washington is covered by the massive lava flow that provides the base for the Columbia

Plateau, but specific regions have developed within this area. A high concentration of wind-blown sediment formed the Palouse, and massive floods and flowing rivers have carved coulees and rocky ravines creating the Channeled Scablands. The region now known as the Columbia Plateau has elements of both the Palouse and the Scablands, but is drier and mostly covered by glacial sediment. Despite the arid climate and more rocky soil, the region is strong agriculturally and has crops more varied than that of the Palouse. ∞

State Highway 24 from a junction with Interstate 82 in Yakima, east through Moxee City, north across the Columbia River, then east to a junction with State Highway 26 in Othello. Route length: 80 miles.

A drive through **Moxee City** (Mock-see) reveals this region's contribution to the beer industry. Supported by 18-foot tall poles and wire trellises, rows of hop vines stretch from the road thick as jungle. Harvest occurs in late summer when the hops become crisp and their color changes from a light silvery green to a deep yellow. The value of the hop is contained in the lupulin, a yellow substance that provides beer with its distinctive bitter flavor and pleasant aroma.

Before hops were planted, the Moxee Valley floor was covered in ryegrass. Protected by the Yakima Ridge to the north, and the Rattlesnake Hills to the south, Moxee Valley was the ideal home for settler Mortimer Thorp and his large herd of Durham cattle. Thorp arrived in 1867 and was joined shortly after by a contingent of French-Canadians who recognized the value of the soil and its suitability for growing hops. The French influence was seen in print on street signs and above shops, as well as in Catholic services where sermons were given in the native tongue.

Moxee is an Indian word with conflicting interpretations. One definition is "whirlwinds," possibly for the dust tornadoes that predominated in the area. The word is also said to mean "smoke on the water," a reference to a hot spring on Thorpe's property that emitted steam.

As the highway continues east through Moxee Valley, hop fields give way to family-owned orchards and sporadic herds of grazing cattle. Occasionally, a cropduster will buzz overhead and dump a load of fertilizer. Substantial farm homes indicate the quality of the area's rich, dark brown soil. There is plenty of available land out here, and what has not already been utilized for agricultural purposes needs only irrigation to be made productive.

Further east, 31 miles from Moxee City, the road passes a junction with State Highway 241, which runs south to Sunnyside, and enters the United States Department of Energy Hanford Site. By now,

24 farmland has succumbed to sage and scrubgrass. Washington is not known as a state that contains desert land, but this remote stretch of road — the sort where if you hit seek on the radio, no station will come in — certainly disproves that myth. Such desolation provided the privacy needed by the government in the 1940s to operate their atomic research and production facilities.

Hanford's B-Reactor operated until February of 1968.

Eight miles past Highway 241, the highway arrives at a junction with State Highway 240 and turns north, crossing the Columbia River five miles further. The road again heads east, providing views of cleanup facilities and inactive atomic reactors including Hanford's B-Reactor, the world's first large-scale reactor. The facility produced the plutonium used in the World War II Nagasaki bomb.

The last 36 miles of Highway 24 travels through the Saddle Mountain National Wildlife Refuge beneath the southern slopes of the Saddle Mountains before coming to a junction with Highway 26 at Othello. ❧

25 State Highway 25 from a junction with U.S. Highway 2 in Davenport, north across the Columbia River and continuing adjacent to the river through Fruitland, Hunters, Marcus and Northport, then recrossing the river to the Canadian boundary. Route length: 121 miles.

Leaving Davenport, Highway 25 runs north through hills of wheat, scarred occasionally by patches of scrub pine, sagebrush and scablands before arriving at **Fort Spokane**, 24 miles later. Located on a bluff above the confluence of the Spokane and Columbia rivers, Fort Spokane was founded by the U.S. Army in response to a large shift in migration from the Colville area to the vast wheat fields south of the Columbia River. When the fort at Colville closed on February 11, 1882, the transplanted soldiers moved south to their new barracks.

In its heyday, the fort consisted of about 50 buildings and was modern enough that one could place a long distance telephone call to Chicago. A giant howitzer is still perched on the mountainside as testimony of the fort's one-time military might. Despite the preparation, Fort Spokane's soldiers never experienced an actual battle, spending their on-duty time in drills and training, and off-duty hours socializing, playing baseball and, in the words of Major V.B. Hubbard, enjoying "the great beauty of the natural scenery and the healthfulness and salubrity of the climate." In 1895, soldiers in the D, G, and H Foot Infantry made up a garrison of about 205 men.

The army played the role of policeman and sometime mediator in the region, relying on its sheer presence to maintain the peace. Their first priority was to enforce reservation boundaries; keeping whites off of native land and vice versa. By no accident, the fort was located near the campgrounds of the Sanpoil and Nespelem people, whose leader, Chief Skolaskin, was of the volatile Dreamer faith. Due to this affiliation, the chief was considered a potential threat to the hair-trigger stability, and kept under close observation in case an uprising was in the works. Troops also served as security aboard trains during labor disputes in the early 1890s. The men monitored the rails in case striking miners decided to dig up a little trouble.

The fort was eventually abandoned in 1899 when it no longer served any practical purpose. Now it is a sprawling park with floating docks, picnic tables, boat ramps, campgrounds and a large area for houseboats. The fort also contains a museum and walking tour that features trailside history markers.

The highway crosses the Spokane River and follows the Columbia north across the western edge of the **Spokane Indian Reservation**. When the Colville Reservation was established in 1872, the Spokane tribe was expected to move across the Columbia River to join the confederation. Few members recognized that a reser-vation had been organized, and even fewer moved. When the tribe was assigned to its own area in 1881, most continued to ignore the official boundaries and stayed where they were since the reservation fell primarily on ancestral land. The relatively small size of the tribe allowed them anonymity, even when they refused to move.

Highway 25 continues through **Fruitland**, a former mining and orchard area that once carried the name *Robber's Roost* for the rakish element it attracted. Formed in 1886, Fruitland was said to be one of the toughest hell holes around and a known rendezvous for desperadoes and cattle thieves.

When the Columbia River was dammed in 1939, towns along the river were forced to move above the 1,310-foot level. One of those towns was **Hunters**, about 16 miles from Fort Spokane. Rising water forced citizens to leave behind rows of apple orchards, the town's primary source of industry, and a water-powered sawmill and feed-mill, located at the mouth of Hunter's Creek. A ferry service ran from the creek across the Columbia River. Hunters was also a distri- bution center for miners who frequented its three stores, church, hotel and cheese factory for supplies, solace and rest.

Grand Coulee Dam was finished in 1941 and Franklin D. Roosevelt Lake was formed.

Most orchards and several towns north of Hunters were lost or forced to relocate when the Grand Coulee Dam was finished in 1941 and **Franklin D. Roosevelt Lake** was formed. The lake (also correctly referred to as a river) comprises 151 miles of the Columbia River and is used extensively for irrigation. It extends northeast from Grand Coulee to Canada and is encompassed by Okanogan, Lincoln, Ferry and Stevens counties. The Works Progress Administration began planning the reservoir in 1936, clearing away all timber and man-made structures below the 1,310-foot mark. It is named for the 32nd president of the U.S. who, unlike his predecessors, supported the power and irrigation movement in eastern Washington.

Highway 25 parallels the water, threading its way northward. The Huckleberry Mountains are a blue-green line in the east; gaps in the trees allow the western slopes of the Kettle River Range to peek through.

It is possible to cross the river on the Gifford-Inchelium car ferry two miles south of the Gifford store. The ferry is free and takes about five minutes. Gifford was a trading point for poultry and various fruits until dust storms, cloudbursts and low prices drove farmers away.

Sandy, loam beaches follow the miles and miles of Roosevelt Lake shoreline. Old and new farms, equally handsome, fill in the spaces between coniferous mountain slopes and sweeping, rolling hillsides.

This route along the east bank of the Columbia was followed by John McLeod, superintendent of the Hudson's Bay Thompson River District. In 1826 he drove the first herd of cattle to the Northwest region through hundreds of miles of Indian country to Fort Colville.

Marcus (Elevation 1,400, Population 144), five miles north of Kettle Falls (U.S. 395), is the oldest town in Stevens County. In 1860 a team from the British Boundary Survey Commission built 12 comfortable barracks and occupied them until 1862. The next year Marcus Oppenheimer moved into the vacated buildings, opened a trading center and platted a townsite.

For years Marcus thrived as a pit stop for miners heading to the north half of the recently-opened Colville Indian Reservation. Prospectors also caught stern-wheelers from Marcus with hopes of striking it rich in British Columbia. Trains eventually replaced steamboats as the main mode of travel, connecting Canadian mines and major transportation centers to northeastern Washington, bringing more people to the already booming town.

Logging brought additional jobs to Marcus, pumping its population to 3,000, but in its prime the town was forced to move one and a half miles northeast to its present locale to avoid being submerged. Today its quiet demeanor masks its prosperous past. The community rests on a plateau above the old town site, enclosed by a pine forest.

The next 40 miles of road passes apple orchards and depleted rock quarries, and is wedged between the river and steep wooded hillsides, most of which are named: Lookout, Grande, Staghorn, O'Toole, Alice Mae, Black Hawk and Silver Crown Mountains.

In 1892, the Spokane Falls and Northern Railroad connected to **Northport** (Elevation 1,330, Population 353), then a year later continued on to the Canadian border. Its destination was ore mines in Nelson, British Columbia. Northport continued its industrial ways when railroad owner D.C. Corbin built a smelter in town that once employed as

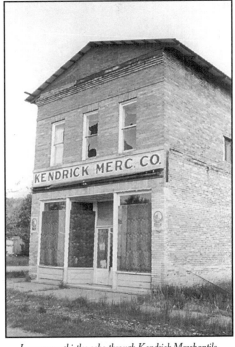

Lonesome whistles echo through Kendrick Merchantile.

many as 500 laborers. A towering smokestack lingers as part of an unhealthy legacy of toxic fumes and 12-hour work days. A U.S. Customs and Immigration office once operated out of Northport, but has since moved six miles further north to the U.S.-Canadian border and the end of Highway 25. ∝

26

WASHINGTON

State **Highway 26** from a junction with Interstate 90, east through Royal City, Othello, Hatton, Washtucna, Hooper, La Crosse and Dusty to a junction with U.S. Highway 195 in Colfax. Route length: 134 miles.

The highway departs the heavily-traveled interstate and sets off on its own venture first south along the Columbia River and then east into the Sand Hollow foothills. Geography buffs will notice hills comprised of pillow basalt (cylindrical shaped masses of basalt formed when lava flows into water) and palagonite (a yellowish, clay substance created by the mixture of steam and basalt).

The road winds alongside Sand Hollow Creek and straightens as it approaches **Royal City** (Elevation 1,000, Population 1,145), 18 miles from its beginning. History reveals no traces of kings or queens or

Deer, fish and waterfowl flourish in the Columbia National Wildlife refuge.

other visiting dignitaries; the town's founders probably thought that a high-sounding name would bring good fortune.

South of the highway lie the Saddle Mountains; the Frenchman Hills are in the north. Portions of the **Columbia National Wildlife Refuge** occupy both sides of the road. Deer, fish and waterfowl flourish in lakes, streams, cattailed-filled marshes and sage-covered fields. The refuge covers approximately 25,000 acres and extends north to the Potholes Reservoir.

As the Saddle Mountains fade and the valley opens wide, the land becomes more suitable for farming. Although the area is not a hotbed for theater, **Othello** (Elevation 1,039, Population 4,690), 24 miles east of Royal City, was named for Shakespeare's tragic character. H.R. Williams served as Vice President of the Chicago, Milwaukee and St. Paul Railroad and spent his free time naming Washington towns.

Nearby stations on the Chicago line include: *Corfu,* for the Greek island; *Smyrna,* after the ancient Turkish port on the Aegean Sea; and *Jericho,* biblical name for the town in Palestine.

To the weary traveler, Othello appears as an oasis in a desert. Before the **Columbia Basin Irrigation Project** brought precious water to the area, Othello was a desert. The project was known as the "country's most ambitious agricultural reclamation." This massive landscaping job uses Columbia River water to irrigate a half million acres of land. Eventually, an additional half million acres will receive water. Irrigation has allowed Othello to harvest a wide variety of crops including: sugar beets, corn, alfalfa, pears, plums, peaches, cherries, grapes, and potatoes.

In the late 1800s and early 1900s, three railroads were completed across the Columbia Basin. These transportation systems, which provided an efficient means to deliver farm products to markets, prompted a burst of settlement and agricultural development.

Dryland farmers experienced successful crops in years of above-average precipitation but scarce rainfall often resulted in widespread crop failure. Though the growing season in the Columbia Basin is ample — about 165 days annually — and the soil well-suited for crops, precipitation is unpredictable. Eyeing the Columbia River as a potential water supply, the Washington State Legislature funded a study for large-scale irrigation in the basin. Proposals were made and then studied by the State Legislature, individuals and private organizations, and the U.S. Congress. Finally, with the recommendation of the U.S. Army Corps of Engineers, a plan to dam the Columbia and pump water up to the Grand Coulee was deemed most economical and feasible. Initially, Congress withheld approval of the project due to the national Depression, but in 1933, President Franklin D. Roosevelt included the Columbia Basin Project in his Public Works Administration Program. Its construction, including Grand Coulee Dam, was assigned to the Bureau of Reclamation. Work began the following year.

Six of the world's largest pumps draw water from Franklin D. Roosevelt Lake to Banks Lake, formed by damming both ends of upper Grand Coulee. From the lake, the water flows through a main siphon, tunnel, and canal to an area that begins about 50 miles south of Grand Coulee Dam. About 2,300 miles of canals and laterals distribute the water to nearly 6,000 farms, transforming sections of central and eastern Washington into productive farmlands with more than 60 different crops.

The road continues perfectly straight through sprinkler-irrigated farmland for 20 miles to **Hatton** (Elevation 939, Population 90). The first postmaster and postmistress, J.D. *Ha*ckett and Miss Ida Belle S*utton,* married and combined their last names. Talk about commitment, or at least, political correctness. The railroad established a land

26
WASHINGTON

office where prospective settlers could study the surrounding acreage and negotiate prices for land. Besides vast, arid fields, research would have shown numerous coulees; the numbers and size increase as you head east.

The Washtucna and Staley Coulees collide at **Washtucna** (wawsh-TUHK-nuh, Elevation 600, Population 266), 23 miles from Hatton. The Indian name for the town "many waters," is misleading, for although settlers were first attracted to the natural springs in the area, the inability to irrigate the region defines Washtucna's history. The *Palouse Irrigation Ditch Company*, the *Palouse Irrigation and Power Company* and the *McGregor Land and Livestock Company* all attempted to bring water and people to the arid site but economics and the dry land proved unfriendly. About four miles east, an abandoned irrigation ditch whose funding expired runs parallel to the highway.

Head another nine miles to **Hooper**, set on the east bank of the Palouse River. Hooper's most famous residents, the McGregors, escaped Scotland at a time of English persecution and came to eastern Washington to work as sheepherders. The family is a great example of the Scottish work ethic and of immigrants making their mark.

The McGregors took advantage of a payment system which allotted them a small amount of sheep every spring in addition to their wages. With careful planning, a lifetime of experience with sheep, and the ability to be frugal, another Scottish trait, their flock soon grew to over 15,000. Besides raising sheep, the McGregors left other marks on Hooper: they sold cars, insurance and fruit; opened a chemical fertilizer company still present in the Palouse; and developed the McGregor Land and Livestock Company, the largest landowner in the area.

Take a good look at the landscape before it suddenly changes. Flat-topped buttes overlook the Palouse River flowing lazily through the fertile valley. The highway has cut through a few of these buttes, exposing long columns of crumbling basalt. Graffiti from near by Washington State University serve notice that you are entering "Cougar Country," the school's mascot and domain.

Having reached **La Crosse** (Elevation 1,400, Population 350), one mile north on Scott Road, wheat fields marching to the horizon mark a new geographical region, the Palouse. A construction engineer for the Union Pacific line hailed from La Crosse, Wisconsin, which, in turn, was named for the Native American racquet and ball sport.

Ten miles down the road, the early residents of **Dusty** looked around, rubbed the dust out of their eyes, and decided that their town's name would describe the quality of air. This name could apply to any number of towns in the Palouse. In the fall, at the end of harvest when the fields are bare, wind raises the dry soil to such an extent that roads sometimes close due to poor visibility. The hills of the Palouse were formed by such wind-blown dust, known as loess, which lies 200 feet deep in some places.

The Dusty Cafe, a grain elevator, and a chemical spraying co-op are Dusty's predominant structures. The Dusty Cemetery, established in 1901, is absolutely immaculate, yet Dusty is only a half a handful of houses. A higher population exists in the Dusty graveyard than does in town.

Seventeen miles later, Highway 26 meets U.S. 195 at the north end of Colfax. ෬

State Highway 27 from a junction with U.S. Highway 195 north via Palouse, Garfield, Oakesdale, Tekoa, Latah, Fairfield, Rockford and Opportunity to a junction with State Highway 290 in Spokane. Route length: 88 miles.

The highway explores the same country as the more popular Highway 195, but the desolation of the two-lane road heightens the value of the scenery. A massive, red barn among rows of verdant, springtime wheat sprouts is best appreciated when one is able to stand on the

Kamiak Butte from below.

side of the road without the roar of a passing semi. The towns are linked by the railroad and the requisite grain elevator, common at railroad sidings.

The first stop out of Pullman is **Kamiak Butte**, 10 miles away. Kamiakin, the mighty Yakima Indian chief, might have found it ironic that his white enemies would name a geographical landmark in his honor. After all, he had been extremely effective in numerous skirmishes with the whites and had humiliated Colonel Steptoe in their historic battle. Obviously some time and racial acceptance occurred before a white man could honor a successful Indian. Perhaps even more ironic is that Steptoe, a man whose great military failure would haunt him until his death, had the adjacent Steptoe Butte named in his honor. Time does strange things for one's image.

About one billion years ago, quartzite rock lying at the bottom of an ancient sea was raised by powerful forces into a mountain range.

A few of the peaks (Kamiak may have been the highest) rose far above the surrounding crests. Much later, lava poured from fissures in the earth, slowly burying all but the highest portions of these mountains. Eventually a fine silt covered the lava, forming the Palouse and leaving Kamiak Butte at its present height of 3,360 feet.

The views along Highway 27 are great, but Kamiak Butte allows for a broader perspective of the Palouse. With a little imagination you can picture the Palouse as sand dunes covered with wheat. In fact, the soil (wind-blown dust called loess) was collected by wind, in the same way that sand dunes are formed. The main difference is that loess is exceptionally fertile.

Take Fugate Road to reach the parking lot and picnic area. There are 170 kinds of vegetation on the butte, including ponderosa pine, Douglas fir, and western larch. In the spring, the hillside is covered with buttercups and violets. Hikes of one-half mile and two miles reach a vista point and the summit overlooking waving seascapes of grain.

The gently, rolling road continues to **Palouse** (puh-LOOS, Elevation 2,200 Population 925). Before wheat's monopoly on the countryside there was bunchgrass, thus the French-Canadian term for the area *La Pelouse*, or "grassland country," was accurate. The small town of Palouse, not to be confused with the Palouse region in which it is centered, or the adjacent Palouse River, has a jack-of-all-trades sort of employment history. Livestock, gold mining, logging and now farming have all kept Palouse's citizens busy. Large, quaint homes grace the bluff above the river and the brick downtown, an historic district.

Nine miles north you'll pull into **Garfield** (Elevation 2,485, Population 597), named after the nation's twentieth president. Platted by Samuel J. Tant in 1882, numerous, shade trees keep the town cool.

Pass the grain elevator named **Belmont** and arrive in **Oakesdale** (Elevation 2,500, Population 410), 11 miles from Garfield. Flour production was the town's major industry until Joseph Barron converted his four-story flour mill (still standing) into a grain-storage facility. The town celebrates Old Mill Days every May.

Oakesdale was named for the general manager of the Northern Pacific Railway Company. Originally called McCoy, it lent that name to a smaller area four miles away on State Highway 271.

Impress the locals by pronouncing **Tekoa** (TEE-koh, Elevation 2,506, Population 861) correctly. Lying in the southern foothills of Mount Tekoa (Elevation 4,006), Tekoa was settled by F. P. Connell who came to the area in 1875. Connell established a trading post and was so respected among the Coeur d'Alene Indians that he acted as their counselor and peacemaker in times of trouble. Connell also raised stock; the first smoked meat shipped to Spokane came from his farm.

Connell's first neighbor, Daniel Truax, wisely started a sawmill and officially platted a town when he learned that the Washington and Idaho Railroad was building a line through the area. His efforts paid off as that line became the main artery to Spokane; two branch lines also ran through the town. Truax's wife suggested the town's name from the bible; Tekoah, a town near Jerusalem and Bethlehem, meaning "sound of trumpet."

In 1908, the Milwaukee Railroad laid its transcontinental tracks through Tekoa, building the steel trestle visible at the north end of town. Tracks laid by the Milwaukee across the state have been converted into the John Wayne Memorial Trail. The trail is a 213-mile-long gravel path stretching from Tekoa to Easton near Snoqualmie Pass.

Hangman Creek joins the highway and meanders along the road six miles to **Latah** (Elevation 2,000, Population 219). The creek was the site of the hanging of Qualchan, a Yakima chief, by Colonel George Wright in 1858. After the Walla Walla council of 1855, Kamiakin and other Yakima chiefs warned the intruding white men to stay out of the Yakima country or be killed. Shortly thereafter, a war party led by Qualchan, a nephew of Kamiakin, encountered and killed a number of white men on the Yakima River. For this act Qualchan became a marked man.

During the guerrilla warfare of the next three years, both Qualchan and his father, Owhi, took leading

Chief Kamaiakin warned, "Stay out or be killed."

parts. As the Indian wars were winding to a close, Colonel Wright encamped on Latah Creek and summoned those Indian chiefs who had not yet made satisfactory treaties. In response, Owhi rode alone into the camp to discuss the possibility of peace and was promptly seized and placed in irons. Wright then sent a message to Qualchan that unless he surrendered his father would be hanged. The faithful son, Qualchan, arrived and in his report for September 24, Wright would state: "Qualchan came to see me at 9 o'clock, and at 9:15 he was hung." Several Palouse Indians were hung later that day. Legislature eventually changed the stream's name to Latah Creek, but some maps and locals still use Hangman.

In 1878, the remains of a mastodon *(Elephas Columbi)* were found in the vicinity of Latah and later displayed at the Chicago Field of Natural History. This important discovery brought recognition to Latah and helped promote immigration. More settlers came when the Oregon Railway and Navigation Company extended their lines from Tekoa to Spokane through Latah in 1888.

Signs at Latah's entrance read "Centennial Town, 1892-1992." Latah's patriotism is slightly bested by **Fairfield's** (Elevation 2,558, Population 590), lying eight miles to the north. "The Town that Celebrates Flag Day" draws hundreds every June 14th for an annual celebration of our nation's colors. Fairfield was first known as *Truax* and then *Regis* before being renamed a final time to describe the quality of the fields surrounding the town. Once a bank and a post office, a mission-style structure painted in pastels is found on Main Street (turn east from the highway). The architect presumably was disoriented and forgot what part of the country he was in (actually famed Spokane architect Kirtland Cutter drew the designs).

The road rolls through the whistle-stop villages of **Rockford** and **Freeman** and drops into the Spokane Valley reaching **Opportunity**, a hopeful settlement known for its truck farming, 23 miles later. A public contest by real estate promoters for a suitable name for the community was won by Miss Laura Kelsey; the prize was $10.00.

The highway enters Spokane's suburban sprawl, crosses I-90 and terminates at a junction with Highway 290. ∞

State Highway 28 from a junction with U.S. Highways 2 and 97, south to East Wenatchee, east through Rock Island, Quincy, Ephrata, Stratford, Wilson Creek, Odessa, Lamona and Harrington to a junction with U.S. 2 in Davenport. Route length: 131 miles.

Take the high, steel bridge across the Columbia River to **East Wenatchee** (wuh-NACH-ee, Elevation 630, Population 3,970), a suburb of Wenatchee that houses most of that city's employees. Muscle cars from around the state congregate at the Wenatchee Valley Raceway every summer, burning rubber and attracting crowds for weekend races. Air transportation has made its mark as well. Clyde Pangborn and Hugh Herndon, Jr. made aviation history when they belly-flopped here in 1931 to complete the first nonstop flight over the Pacific Ocean. At the airstrip just east of town the Pangborn-Herndon Memorial commemorates the event.

Eight miles southeast on Highway 28 is tiny **Rock Island** (Elevation 615, Population 550). Although not an island itself, the town faces a huge rock formation rising out of the Columbia that divides the current into rapids. The small community sprang up in 1888 when James Keane filed for land in anticipation of the arrival of the Great Northern Railroad. A ferry landing already existed and Keane expected his town to be a stopover for the line. The Great Northern bridged the gap between Spokane and Seattle in 1893, but Wenatchee was chosen as the main depot site instead. Rock Island still managed to get involved when its ferry was used to shuttle railway cars across the river until the Rock Island Bridge was built. The necessary stop allowed small stores and a trading post to develop.

Rock Island Dam has been producing electricity since 1931.

Rock Island Dam, two miles downstream from town, was the first hydroelectric facility on the Columbia. The Puget Sound Power and Light Company completed the project in 1931, calling attention to the tremendous energy potential of the river and leading the way for other dams.

The road bends south with the river, then east through miles of wheat fields that are supplied with water from the Columbia Basin Irrigation Project. The highway separates from the river at the burned-out ghost town of **Trinidad** and continues east. Legend has it that gold miners who had struck it rich stopped in the area of Trinidad in 1876 on their way to Oregon. While there for the night, they were threatened by Indians and in a panic buried their treasure and fled. They returned with their families in 1900, but failed to locate the nearly $100,000 worth of gold.

173~

As with most of the towns in the Columbia Basin, agriculture has always been the life-blood of **Quincy** (Elevation 1,301, Population 3,810), even though less than a foot of rain hits the ground here annually. In the early 1890s, investors poured money into a plan to construct pumps and wells for irrigation. Close on the heels of prospectors were dozens of optimistic farmers who broke the land, planted fruit trees, built homes and barns and waited for the water to flow. It

Mobile irrigation.

never arrived. The money well ran dry with the financial depression of 1893, leaving the young trees to wither in the sun. The collapsing, weathered remains of some of these once hopeful farms still dot the countryside.

Confidence returned in 1902 when the Great Northern Railroad rolled through and a post office was built. Mail service was one of the company's responsibilities: incoming mail was packed in a canvas bag and tossed from the speeding train; out-going mail was snared from a hook on a pole next to the tracks. If a railman's hands were not steady, the mail would have to wait for the next train. Peeved, the townsfolk would fine the Great Northern $5 each time they dropped the mail or refused to stop and pick it up. It is doubtful whether the fines were ever paid.

Efforts to bring water to the surface resumed the same year. The second try proved fruitful, and farmers flooded in after a water tank was erected. Shortly after the wells were dug the Great Northern opened its land for homesteads, causing a rush of squatters and a flurry of building. These original wells still nourish over 70 different crops grown in the Quincy area.

Ephrata (e-FRAY-tuh, Elevation 1,272, Population 5,550) is 14 miles east of Quincy and the largest town on Highway 28. The Egbert brothers of Oregon first settled the area in 1882 next to a fresh water spring. After planting an orchard and some hay fields, they sold their land to Frank Beazley, who started a horse ranch.

The Great Northern Railroad (since bought out by Burlington Northern) arrived in 1892 and obtained water rights from Beazley to operate their steam engines. A water tower was built next to the line, drawing water from the spring. An old boxcar was left to serve as both post office and depot, and the town was officially born. Only

Beazley and a few others were permanent residents, but there was a buzz of activity from the constant flow of farmers who used the town as a grain shipping point.

At one point the town was called Beazley Springs and later an imaginative railroad employee called the new station Number 11. The name that eventually stuck came from an inspired Great Northern surveyor who had recently visited the Holy Lands. Noting the similarities of the arid landscapes and the presence of the orchard, he called it Ephrata, which is Sanskrit for "fruitful." It is also the alternate name for Bethlehem.

At the ripe age of 61, Jesse Cyrus arrived from Springfield, Illinois in 1896 and purchased Beazley's land and house. After sending word for his family to follow, he started the first store in town and began platting in 1901. Anticipating growth, he bought large tracts of land from the railroad and within five years three schools, a real estate office, a doctor's office, a bank, a saloon, a hotel, a restaurant and several more stores were erected, in addition to the advent of a newspaper.

The last grand roundup - the stuff of history, myth and legend.

To make room for the mini-invasion of homesteaders and wheat farmers, the last great round-up of wild horses in Washington began in Ephrata in April of 1906 when about 300 cowboys roped nearly 5,000 animals in the area and drove them south to the mouth of Crab Creek. Most of the horses died en route due to a lack of food and water. The remainder were shipped by rail to horse ranges in Montana and the Badlands of South Dakota and some as far as the East Coast. Others were sold to glue and canned beef factories. At one time tens of thousands of the horses ran free over the Columbia Plateau. A story persists of one defiant, white-maned stallion that escaped the collection at the boxcars and led a few other horses back to a place where their untamed offspring still survive and roam the open spaces. The rearing stallion depicted above the entrance to the **Grant County Historical Museum** (First NW and C Street) is a tribute to this myth.

Despite the biblical name, the atmosphere of early Ephrata was far from angelic. Saloons never closed and gunplay was common, but without a jail or even an officer of the law, not much could be done to control the rowdy behavior of cowboys, railroad workers and rugged farmers. Not exactly an ideal setting to raise a family, but the town continued to attract settlers in increasing numbers throughout the first decade of 1900. The town's future was secured in 1909 when it became the county seat of the newly created Grant County. Rumor, suspicion and a whiff of foul play surrounded this legislative bill, as it was believed that elected officials were bribed and opponents of the measure were tricked into missing the final vote on the matter. Protest was voiced but nothing was ever proven.

The government office attracts lawyers, bureaucrats and other professionals, creating an interesting mix of urban and rural elements. Men in suits walk down the street chatting with farmers in overalls and John Deere hats, and hands, rough from working the earth, shake those accustomed to tapping computer keyboards. The standard of living is unusually high here, with the proximity of the Grand Coulee Dam to the north supplying residents with some of the cheapest electric power in the state. Retired folks comprise nearly a third of the population, while young families migrate in from larger cities to take jobs at the Public Utility District and Bureau of Reclamation, and to enjoy the slower pace.

Venerable trees tower over the oldest streets in town, providing shade and a sense of depth against a background of wheat. Impressive as they are, these are the few remaining elms, maples and cottonwoods that were planted soon after the town was incorporated in 1909. In 1911, the city council planted 1,100 trees up and down the streets, earning the town the nickname of "little oasis." Most of these had to face the ax to make room for the state highway; a reluctantly progressive step that nearly sparked riots at the time because many would have preferred the trees to pavement. Hundreds of other trees were uprooted or died slowly when wells were dug in the small canyon west of town, causing a stream to dry up.

Grant County: Ephrata is the county seat of Grant County, which was organized in 1909 and was formerly part of Douglas County. It was named after President Ulysses S. Grant. It is located in the east central part of the state and is bounded on the west by the Grand Coulee and the Columbia River. In the late nineteenth century, the county was traversed by railroads: the Great Northern; the Northern Pacific; and the Chicago, Milwaukee and St. Paul. The railroads brought settlers into the county, attracted by its rich soil and agricultural potential. The Columbia Basin Irrigation Project of the 1930s also made a significant impact on the county while the completion of the Grand

Coulee Dam opened lands for farming and furnished electric power for industry. Today the county is a major bean and pea producer and food processing center.

Courthouse: C Street NW, PO Box 37, Ephrata 98823, 509-754-2011 (Information), SCAN 551-1011, FAX 509-754-3639. Area: 2,680.2 square miles. State Ranking: 4th. 1993 Population: 60,300. Unincorporated: 30,456. Incorporated: 29,844. Density: 22.5 persons per square mile. **Cities and Towns**: Coulee City, Coulee Dam, Electric City, Ephrata, George, Grand Coulee, Hartline, Krupp, Mattawa, Moses Lake, Quincy, Royal City, Soap Lake, Warden, Wilson Creek. **Principal Economic Activities**: Food processing, agriculture. **Points of Interest**: Grand Coulee Dam, Dry Falls, Potholes Reservoir.

Climate: (Ephrata - elevation 1,272)

	Jan	Apr	Jul	Oct
Max Temp. F°	33.7	65.3	90.5	65.3
Min Temp.	21.1	41.4	62.4	42.9
Mean Temp.	27.5	53.2	76.5	55.8
Precipitation	1.05"	.56"	.20"	.77"

Average Annual Maximum Temperature: 63.1
Average Annual Minimum Temperature: 41.9
Annual Mean Temperature: 52.5
Average Annual Precipitation: 8.42"

Twenty or so miles up the road, **Stratford** is a good example of unfulfilled anticipation. One of many town sites that rose in the wake of the Great Northern's progress in the 1890s, a hotel, a school and a handful of homes were quickly erected for nearly 100 early residents. When irrigation projects floundered, most folks caught the first train out. By the 1930s, less than 20 people remained, and the population hovered around this mark for nearly 40 years. The string of grain elevators to the south summarize the area as little more than a stop-off for farmers.

Continue east past the tip of Brook Lake and on for seven miles to **Wilson Creek** (Elevation 1,276, Population 226) located on the eastern side of the creek that shares its name, and mostly hidden from the road. Crop dusters take off from a small airport just east of town to work the fields below.

About 18 miles past Wilson Creek sits **Odessa** (Elevation 1,540, Population 956). Cattlemen were the first to recognize the quality of the prairie land and began clearing the sagebrush for homesteads and grazing in the mid-1880s. Wells dug in this location continue to irrigate crops. Residue collected and pressurized during the last Ice Age created ideal soil for growing wheat, and fields quickly spread. Water was drawn from Crab Creek, around which the town was eventually situated. One rancher, George W. Finney, made his home here and watched his future spread before him as the Great Northern extended its tracks through his land in 1892.

As much as the arrival of the Great Northern, immigration proved the cornerstone of Odessa's growth. In order to attract settlers and ensure prosperity, the Great Northern began offering immigrants free passage to the country and the opportunity for homesteads if they would settle near the depot. Some were even given jobs laying westward track. Railroad representatives sent to Russia on recruitment trips found themselves with an easy task.

Farming all suitable land in Wilson Creek Canyon.

The program proved successful and the location was bursting with promise, so in 1898 Finney donated his land and platted the town. The vast majority of these early immigrants were Germans living in Russia along the Black Sea. The town took its name from a wheat-growing city in that region.

The immigrants paved the way for a steady migration of German-Russians that began in 1900 and lasted for a decade. Germans initially moved to Russia at the urging of Catherine the Great (herself a German) who promised them autonomy and exemptions from unfavorable Russian laws. When Catherine died the promises went with her, and the displaced Germans were faced with increasing taxes, government harassment and forced military service. America provided the perfect escape; an estimated half a million German-Russians entered the U.S. between 1880 and 1910. Since most were wheat farmers, they beelined for agricultural areas. Immigrants who came under the Great Northern's plan a few years earlier called for their families and friends, and soon entire extended clans got off the train at Odessa to start new lives. By 1910, Germans constituted nearly one-third of the total population of the county. Word spread of eastern Washington's growing German population (Ritzville, Endicott, and Warden were a part of this movement), and some of those who first landed in the Midwest later moved to the state.

In Odessa, over 80% of the current population are of Germanic descent, and until the 1950s, German was spoken more than English.

Three annual festivals celebrate this heritage in grand style, often attracting as many as 20,000 visitors in a weekend.

28
WASHINGTON

Following the ideals of "Kirche, Kinder and Kuche" (church, children and kitchen) the immigrants wasted no time in embracing their new home, rapidly constructing several churches and schools, as well as elaborate homes and barns. Part of Odessa's charm comes from the unusual combination of Victorian and Russian architecture. Many homes and downtown buildings built prior to 1910 have been immaculately maintained.

North and west of Odessa, rocky stretches of scablands interrupt and contrast with rolling fields of wheat. In 1991, the Bureau of Land Management established 8,500 acres as part of the **Lake Creek Recreation Wildlife Enhancement Project** for the preservation of endangered wildlife and vegetation. The lunar-like landscape was carved out by Ice Age flooding millions of years ago. Follow Highway 21 north of town for a sidetrip into some of the state's most unusual scenery.

The next 25 miles of Highway 28 showcase dramatic windshield scenes; from deep basalt canyons and desert rangeland to weaving scablands and golden acres of wheat. The only dot on the map during this stretch represents the whistle-stop of **Lamona**, but it is little more than a cartographic technicality. Named for the first store-owner John H. Lamona, the long abandoned depot sits frozen in time as if recalling more prosperous days. A few small homes hide behind trees and among the scattered sagebrush.

Harrington (Elevation 2,260, Population 494) breaks up a long stretch of asphalt. Named in 1882 for a wealthy banker in California who invested heavily in the area, the town's story echoes a recurring railroad theme. Encouraged by the financial backing of the distant prospector, settlers moved in expecting the Northern Pacific to stop by on its journey west. So confident were these few pioneers that they lobbied for a county seat just weeks after opening a post office. But they ran into a snag — the railroad never showed. Some families left for greener prairies, but the few who stuck it out were rewarded when the Great Northern laid tracks adjacent to the town in 1892. With transportation now available for their stable wheat crop, good times had arrived. The word spread like a virus and soon Harrington housed nearly 500 permanent residents eager to claim their piece of the railroad pie. Unlike other boom and bust towns in the general area, the town's population has remained relatively stable since the 1920s, though farms have modernized and grown. Otherwise, farmers continue to quietly plow their fields and send the wheat away to market as they have done for decades.

The final 13 miles of Highway 28 pass scrub brush and rolling hills until connecting with U.S. 2 in Davenport. ∞

State **Highway 31** from a junction with State Highway 20 in Tiger, north through Ione, Metaline and Metaline Falls, across the Pend Oreille River to the Canadian boundary. Route length: 27 miles.

Highway 31 begins its northward journey at Tiger, where Highway 20 turns south and the **Pend Oreille River** (Pon-der-ray) flows north. The river is the largest north-flowing river in the country. The name Pend Oreille, "ear-ring," was brought by French fur trad-ers who observed natives wearing shell ornaments in their ears. The river touches three states and two countries, begin-ning as the Clark Fork River (named

The "Pend Doreille" returning from an 1896 hunting trip loaded with deer.

by the Lewis and Clark Expedition) near Butte, Montana, traveling 300 miles to Lake Pend Oreille in Idaho, and entering Washington 35 miles west at Newport. After reaching Canada it heads west and reenters Washington as the Columbia River.

Ione (eye-OHN, Elevation 2,095, Population 490), four miles north of Tiger, was named for Ione Morrison, niece of the town's first post-master. Railroad passenger cars sit abandoned on the siding. A lum-ber mill on a small branch of the Pend Oreille River reveals the town's livelihood. Before timber, there was cement, or at least designs to produce cement after a large limestone vein was discovered. An English engineer with high hopes built a Portland cement plant in 1906, but the venture, one of the first attempts to make cement in Washing-ton, failed, and in 1934 the abandoned plant was destroyed by fire.

Box Canyon is seen from a turnout four and a half miles north of Ione. A railroad trestle spans the channel which stretches for 1,200 feet, its purple-gray rock walls 20 to 100 feet high. For years logs churned through the narrow canyon en route to mills in Metaline Falls.

Continue along the river to **Metaline** (MET-uh-leen, Elevation 2,000, Population 188) and **Metaline Falls** (Elevation 1,900, Popula-tion 235). Settlers here were obviously not blessed with creativity, as the towns stole their name from the 19-foot drop in the Pend Oreille called, you guessed it, Metaline Falls. The name Metaline was given by mid-eighteenth century miners and prospectors for the abundant valuable minerals which covered the area. At the foot of the falls is the Dewdney Trail, a common route for early fur traders.

Metaline, perched above the waterfalls, proclaims itself the oldest town in Pend Oreille County. There is a quaint, little waterfront park and not much else but the view.

Until recently, the Portland Cement Plant employed most of Metaline Falls. Its grey, large, silent form overshadows the entire town; the former hum of industry is almost audible. Dust from the plant permeated the air, which, unless residents took care to wash off their cars, would harden into cement at the first rainstorm.

Mill Pond flume, 12,280-foot-long. The ultimate waterpark.

The highway climbs steeply out of Metaline Falls to Sullivan Lake Road. Take the road one mile to **Mill Pond**. In 1920 a 12,280-foot-long flume was built from the pond to Metaline Falls, providing power to the cement plant. Construction equipment for the flume traveled down the Pend Oreille River by steam boat from Newport to Ione. Then it was rafted through treacherous Box Canyon to arrive at last in Metaline Falls.

Maintenance of the flume was a daunting and dangerous task. The flume had been built across a steep slope alive with springs and seepages. Ground slumps and slides were a frequent threat. Chronic leaks forced workers to spend hundreds of hours jamming oak-oil treated rope into cracks between boards, or shoveling sand through trap doors in an attempt to plug leaks. As the ground shifted workers would use tracks, blocks and tackles to hoist the sagging flume back into position. Martha McDougal recalls her father's stint as a flume tender:

My father would patrol the flume on snowshoes in the winter looking for leaks and potential slides. He would use a .405 caliber rifle, the elephant gun, to shoot off large icicles. He used to come home in the evening with a black and blue shoulder from the recoil. Once while plowing snow off the top of the tall flume the horse, plow and McDougal slid over the side. The horse landed on a stump and was killed. McDougal survived only because he happened to land on the horse.

When the cement plant covered the flume with boards to give its workers access it also created a popular public thoroughfare. In an age before automobiles were commonplace the boardwalk had advantage over the Sullivan Lake road of being flatter, more scenic and one mile shorter. For the first time picnickers, fishermen, photographers and Sunday strollers all found beautiful Sullivan Lake within a day's hike. In the 1930s the Civilian Conservation Corps camp was built at Sullivan Lake. The CCC crews, mostly young men, walked the flume into Metaline Falls on weekends. One of their companions was a tame elk called "Minni the Moocher." Minni hiked the flume with them into town and then waited and mooched food from town folks until her friends were ready to return to the lake.

Two miles before the Canadian border take East Side Access Road two miles to **"Z" Canyon**, Boundary Dam and Crawford State Park. The canyon was named for its zigzag contour and is striking for its unusual parameters. Only 18 feet wide but 400 feet deep, the river gushes with phenomenal speed.

Continue over **Boundary Dam** (Seattle City Light Company's largest dam) to the west bank of the Pend Oreille River and **Crawford State Park**, which focuses on Gardner Cave, the longest limestone cave in Washington. Guided tours explore the upper 494 feet of the 1,055-foot-long cave and reveal formations with names like "Fried Eggs," "Christmas Tree," and "Queen's Throne." The 90,000-year-old formations grow at a rate of one-half inch every year. The cave was shaped by erosion and the limestone-dissolving reaction of acid.

Ed Gardner, a bootlegger who kept stills in the area, discovered the cave in 1899. He later lost it in a poker game to William Crawford, who would donate the property to the state in 1921.

Highway 31 ends 12 miles from Metaline Falls, at the International Boundary.

"Z" Canyon's narrow chasm.

cs

Interstate **82** from a junction with Interstate 90 south to Yakima, east to Kennewick, then south to the Washington-Oregon border at Plymouth. (Overlaps U.S. Highways 97, 12 and 395.) Route length: 126 miles.

I-82 may suffer from an identity crisis; information for the road is covered on U.S. 97, 12 and 395. ☙

Interstate **90** from a junction with Interstate 5 in Seattle, east across Lake Washington to Mercer Island, then southeast through Issaquah and North Bend, over the Cascades via Snoqualmie Pass, continuing through Cle Elum, Ellensburg, Kittitas and Vantage, across the Columbia River, north to George, then east through Moses Lake to Ritzville, and northeast through Spokane to the Washington-Idaho border. (Overlaps U.S. Highways 97, 395 and 2.) Route length: 327 miles.

Lacey V. Murrow Memorial Bridge and Mercer Island.

Cutting the state in half, I-90 begins with Seattle's skyline in your rearview mirror. You'll cross Lake Washington on the **Lacey V. Murrow Memorial Bridge**, known locally as the Mercer Island Bridge. Lacey Murrow, brother of famous broadcast journalist, Edward R. Murrow, was the State Department of Highways Director who proposed linking Mercer Island and Seattle via a concrete bridge. Previously, Mercer Island citizens intent on reaching Seattle crossed a bridge to Enetai on the east side of Lake Washington, then drove around the south end of the lake. When Murrow's bridge opened in 1940, it was the world's largest floating bridge and first to float on anchored pontoons, but more importantly, it provided an opportunity for eastside suburban growth. A twin floating bridge was recently built beside the existing one.

The Duwamish Indians were afraid of **Mercer Island** (Elevation 15, Population 21,260). Although they regularly raided the island for berries, roots and nuts, they believed evil burial spirits lurked nearby, and at night, the island submerged into Lake Washington's murky waters, only to rise again each morning. Mercer Island's blue clay soil erodes easily when wet, causing occasional landslides and accounting for the Indian's sinking island theory. There are also three submerged forests surrounding the island — one off the west central shore, and one each near the south and north ends. Geologists believe that rain caused the clay layers to slide away from the underlying hardpan, taking the trees upright into the water.

Mercer Island is a popular and affluent residential neighborhood five miles long, an average of one mile wide, and is situated seven miles east of Seattle. It was named after Judge Thomas Mercer, an early Seattle pioneer who arrived from Illinois in December of 1852. Mercer brought the settlement's first horse, Old Tib, and a covered wagon; with these he provided Seattle's first express and milk delivery service.

The judge often employed a Duwamish Indian to row him to the island in the morning and return in the evening to take him back. He loved the quiet, rugged beauty of the heavily wooded island, spending hours picking berries and walking its shoreline. On one occasion, when the Indian returned, Mercer was nowhere to be found. Lost in his thoughts and enjoying the island's tranquillity, he had decided to spend the night. The Indian waited until dark, fled what he perceived to be a haunted island, and returned in the morning to find Mercer patiently waiting. Since Mercer's clothes were not wet, the Indian concluded that the judge had supernatural powers — after all, he had just spent the night on a submerged island!

For a scenic drive take West Mercer Way. The road circles the island, winding along Lake Washington's wooded shoreline.

Wedged between Lake Washington and the Cascade foothills, **Lake Sammamish** takes its name from an Indian tribe that lived lakeside. *Samma* means "the sound of the blue crane," and *mish,* "river." Another tribal name was *Xa-tcx-atcu,* or "small lake," a size comparison to Lake Washington. The lake is eight miles long, one to two miles wide, and shaped like a coiled snake.

Southeast of the lake, **Issaquah** (IS-uh-kwah, Elevation 55, Population 8,326) is a blend of suburbia and small town living. Population has sharply increased in the past several years with those seeking shelter from city life, and this growth has created an odd juxtaposition of wilderness and commercial sprawl. The wooded foothills of the Cascade Mountains provide a backdrop for the recent explosion of stripmalls and outlet stores.

During the first World War, the German Count von Alvenslaben sank over one million dollars into the Issaquah and Superior Coal Mining Company, placing bread on many tables, before abruptly abandoning the project. By that time coal was already old news in town, but past enterprises had been relatively small. Mining began as early as 1863, when Lyman Andrews walked to Seattle with a flour sack full of Issaquah coal. A small core of optimists grabbed their own sacks and followed Andrews back, but most turned to farming within the first year due to the difficulty of the work and lack of money in small-scale mining. They toiled in the mud along Issaquah Creek to

Issaquah's historic depot, built in 1888, looks over a small park and a public library.

clear trees and make room for hops needed in Seattle and Olympia breweries. Small dairy farms, originally intended to feed the local community, grew into large commercial ventures. Coal made a comeback in the mid-1870s, bringing the first mini-boom and a few permanent residents.

The Seattle, Lake Shore and Eastern Railroad was organized in 1885 by local investors and intended to run east over Snoqualmie Pass and continue to Spokane, with a connection running north to the Canadian border. The line was deemed necessary when the mighty Northern Pacific overlooked Seattle as a depot site. Tracks extended through Issaquah and 12 miles further to North Bend before money ran out and construction ceased. Though short of their original goal, the line brought business and prosperity to Issaquah, finally creating an efficient method for carrying out the substantial coal deposits that had been relatively untapped since the 1870s.

The independent line was eventually bought out by the Northern Pacific and abandoned in 1974. It has been converted into a small sightseeing train and trail system. The old depot (corner of First and Sunset Way), built in 1888, looks out over a small park and a public library. The old tracks are still embedded in the streets.

The worn remains of **Preston** are located five miles further east. Hidden from the highway, it has the feel of a ghost town on the verge

185~

of being swallowed by blackberry thickets. Minus scattered homes and a dilapidated sawmill, the community probably looks the same as it did when the families of August and Emil Lovegren and Olaf Edwin arrived in 1890. Immigrating from Sweden to escape religious persecution, they made their homes along the newly-constructed Seattle, Lake Shore and Eastern Railroad line.

Preston's sawmill attracted settlers for decades.

A sawmill was ready to run in 1896, attracting hundreds of new settlers for its work opportunities and proximity to the tracks. The first structures erected with local timber were a Baptist church and the Vasa Lodge, used for social gatherings and community meetings. The small sawmill ran continuously until after World War II when a lack of technological advancement forced its closure.

A few weather-beaten log cabins and A-frames carved into the steep cliffs are visible along the Raging River, but most are abandoned. The Victorian home built by August Lovegren in 1904 has been preserved, along with a community center built under the Works Progress Administration. A minor logging operation has risen from the remains of the old Preston mill, running alongside rusted cranes, twisted tracks and piles of rotted logs next to the collapsed structure that once served as an office.

Continue east for six miles through forests of western hemlock, birch, cedar and Douglas fir to **North Bend** (Elevation 440, Population 2,620). At the gateway to the Cascades, large swaths of cleared timber come into view on the hills surrounding the highway. Iowa-born William H. Taylor took a long journey through San Francisco, Victoria, B.C., and Seattle before arriving here in 1872. Mining opportunities led the adventurous 19-year-old back to California a few years later, but he returned in 1880 to start a farm and a trading post for those traveling over Snoqualmie Pass. It was around this small store  that North Bend eventually grew. Taylor would walk to Seattle for supplies and return with the goods strapped to his back, a four-day round trip. He platted the town in 1889, donating a stretch to the Seattle, Lake Shore and Eastern Railroad that was heading their way, encouraging the company to build a depot.

In the 1880s, thousands of workers invaded North Bend annually to participate in the hops harvest. An even larger invasion of aphids in 1890 destroyed the farming industry, but many stayed in town to work in logging camps and sawmills. The Snoqualmie Mill, built in 1917, still runs and is the second oldest all-electric mill in the nation. The hills surrounding town, now owned by the Weyerhaeuser Company, are all on their second or third cut, and so immune to federal old-growth logging regulations.

Located on the South Fork of the Snoqualmie River, North Bend was constructed with a Bavarian theme; its buildings and shops look like colorfully decorated gingerbread houses. Even the Chinese restaurant has a distinctive Germanic architectural flavor. Several years ago the popular television series Twin Peaks was filmed here, and partly as a result, tourism emerged as the economic backbone of this scenic town.

The 4,197-foot sheer walls of **Mt. Si** loom directly north of town, adding to the panoramic setting. The Indian name, *Kelbts*, means "camping place," but the peak was named for pioneer Joseph Merritt,

Mt. Si receives the most hikers per year in the state.

a loner known as "Uncle Si" who built a small cabin at the base of the cliff in 1862. An Indian legend details the creation of the mountain. Snoqualmie (or moon) was the king of the heavens and one night S'Beow (beaver) climbed into the sky and brought the trees and fire

187~

back to the earth. To retrieve the stolen goods, Snoqualmie descended a rope from the heavens that broke during his pursuit. Mt. Si was the result of his crash to the ground and his face was carved into the summit.

A hiking trail leading up Mt. Si is the most popular in the state, heavily used by weekend warriors from Seattle and those in training for a late summer expedition of Mt. Rainier. The mountain's proximity to Seattle, plus views of the Cascades, the Puget Sound Basin and the distant ridgeline of the Olympics account for the trail's attraction. Hang gliders are often seen taking flight from a flat ridge near the summit. (Follow North Bend Way a half mile from North Bend to Mt. Si Road. Turn left and continue two and a half miles to the trailhead. The hike is an eight-mile round trip.)

Top-of-the-world Cascade Lake.

Stretching all the way from the Sierra Nevada foothills in California to the Fraser River in British Columbia — approximately 700 miles — the **Cascade Mountain Range** (with 5 volcanic peaks varying in elevation from 8,364 to 14,411 feet) divides Washington into two distinct climate zones. When naturalist John Muir stood atop Mt. Rainier and viewed the majestic summits of Mt. St. Helens, Mt. Adams, and Mt. Hood protruding from a low-lying cloud bank, he described them with reverence as "islands in the sky."

The range is shaped somewhat like an hour glass, with the 100-mile-wide sections beginning at the Canadian and Oregon borders, and the narrower, 50-mile-wide middle portion, located in central Washington.

Because of their origin, the northern and southern Cascades are quite dissimilar. The rugged southern portion resulted from volcanic activity, while the northern portion, once a great ocean floor before being raised up, is more uniform. It's not uncommon for climbers to find an abundance of fossilized shells near the top of the range's northern peaks.

INTERSTATE 90

The Cascade, Rockdale, and Stampede tunnels were carved through the mountains to facilitate rail transportation, while the Chinook, Stevens, and Snoqualmie passes make this once difficult barrier to western migration easily accessible by highway. And almost anywhere travelers might find themselves in the state, the dramatic Cascade range constitutes an ever-present part of the scenery.

Previously known by the unofficial monikers the *Sierra Madras de San Antonio,* the *Snowy Range,* the *Snowy Mountains,* and the *Klannet Range,* the Cascades were given their current name by British botanist David Douglas, who was moved by the waterfalls of the same name along the Columbia River. Seven years later, a Boston school teacher by the name of Hall Kelley failed in his efforts to have the range renamed *President's Range,* with its individual peaks to be named after former presidents.

The volcanic peaks that dominate the Cascade Range are dormant, not extinct. Because both Mt. Rainier and Mt. Hood are near populated regions, geologists have speculated that an eruption — especially one that triggered a massive mud slide — might have disastrous consequences. Seattle and Tacoma could be totally destroyed if Rainier were to erupt, and Portland laid to waste if Mt. Hood blew its top again. Further catastrophes would likely occur if dams in the vicinity of an eruption were destroyed, releasing devastating walls of water.

Regardless of these apocalyptic predictions, the Cascade Range still remains a climber's and hiker's dream come true, a wonderfully diverse ecosystem, a study in geological formations, and one of the scenic gems of the Northwest region.

Snoqualmie (snoh-KWAHL-mee) **Pass** is the most frequently crossed pass in the state. Its moderate elevation (3,010 feet) is deceiving. Pacific Ocean-born storms get caught in the Cascades bringing heavy rain or snowfall and making driving treacherous. Only an hour from Seattle, the pass is a popular winter destination for alpine and nordic skiers.

Snoqualmie Pass ski area.

'Snoqualmie' was the name of an Indian tribe who lived in the area. The word derives from *sdoh-kwahlb-bhuh. Sdoh-kwahlb,* meaning moon, was the life source of the tribe. The Snoqualmies terrorized other tribes in the region, and a translation of the name given them by other Indians indicates fear, dislike and respect.

90 Three miles east of the pass you'll drive by five-mile-long **Keechelus Lake**. Nestled at the head of the Yakima River, Keechelus is an Indian name meaning "few or less fish." Skeleton tree stumps rise from its shallow waters. For several years during the late 1800s, the lake boasted a summer population of 1,500 dam and railroad construction workers.

Lake Keechelus, an Indian name meaning "few or less fish."

Kachess Lake, two miles away, but not visible from the freeway, contrasts from Keechelus in meaning, "many fish," but is similar in size, shape and direction. Both lakes were formed when glacial run-off collected at the base of a thick pile of volcanic rocks, a basalt and sandstone ridge that is part of the Naches formation. There are good exposures of the rock along the east side of Keechelus Lake and on both sides of the pass.

Easton, one mile past Kachess Lake, began as a lumber community. Although market accessibility dramatically increased with the arrival of the Northern Pacific (1888) and the Milwaukee, Chicago, St. Paul and Pacific (1911) Railroads, Easton gradually evolved into a railroad service town as the last station for Northern trains heading over Stampede Pass and Milwaukee trains en route to Snoqualmie Pass.

Easton was named for its position at the east end of the two-mile-long Stampede Tunnel. The tunnel, completed May 3, 1888, took two years of work, cost $1,000,000 and at least 13 lives. Its name derives from a crew of trail cutters driven so hard by their foreman that they abandoned their tools, rolled their blankets, and *stampeded* down the trail. The tunnel's completion made possible the first transcontinental route across the Cascades. Previously, Northern Pacific's lines followed the Columbia River to Portland, Oregon and then north through Kalama to Tacoma.

Iron Horse State Park, just past Easton, is 113-miles long and 100-feet wide. The park is also the trailhead for the **John Wayne Memorial Trail** which crosses the state from Easton to Tekoa near the Idaho border. This trail follows the Milwaukee Corridor, formerly the roadbed of the old Chicago, Milwaukee, St. Paul, and Pacific Railroad and is used by hikers, bikers, cross-country skiers and equestrians.

The search for fuel sources to power their locomotives over the mountains led Northern Pacific geologists to coal fields near present-day **Cle Elum** (klee-EL-uhm, Elevation 1,980, Population 1,785), at the confluence of the Cle Elum and Yakima rivers. Abundant coal was discovered in 1884 and two years later a railroad station was built. Tracks soon connected Cle Elum and the Puget Sound region. The name Cle Elum derives from the Indian word Tle-el-Lum, which means "swift water," a reference to the Cle Elum River.

From Cle Elum, the interstate leaves the pine-clad foothills and enters the open prairie and farmland of central Washington. Laid out on the flat floor of the Kittitas Valley, **Ellensburg's** (Elevation 1,597, Population 12,770) development began around 1870, when Andrew Splawn, an adventurous young cowboy, bought a small cabin from horse thief Wilson the Renegade and opened a trading post near the confluence of the Yakima River and Wilson Creek. He called the store Robber's Roost, after his outlaw predecessor, and traded with local Indians and travelers en route to Snoqualmie Pass. In 1872, the store was sold to John Shoudy. Shoudy platted a townsite and named it "Ellen's Burgh" after his wife, Mary Ellen. The "h" was eventually dropped by order of the Postal Department. The two-story brick **Shoudy Building** (Third and Main) stands where Robber's Roost once operated.

The Davidson Building, built after the '89 fire.

In 1886, the Northern Pacific Railroad came to town. With low-grade iron ore and coal close by, and rail transportation secure, Ellensburg was being talked of as the "Pittsburgh of the West." The population had risen to 600 and the town was soon incorporated. Furthermore, because of its central location, many considered it a natural site for the capital of the soon-to-be state.

Disaster struck on July 4, 1889 when a fire destroyed most of the business district and many homes. The state's capital could not exist in a burned-out community so the citizens began rebuilding. In a matter of days a new city of brick began to emerge. The **Davidson Building** (Pearl and Fourth) has a three-foot phoenix perched on top symbolizing the city rising from the ashes.

The candidates for the state's capital were Ellensburg, Yakima and Olympia. It is likely that Ellensburg would have defeated Olympia but the presence of another central Washington city split the vote and Olympia won handily. The optimistic local newspaper declared: "Capital or no capital, Ellensburg speeds along and will get there just the same. No grass on her streets, no flies on her back, no lard on her bangs. Whoop her up again, boys!"

In 1891, as a sort of consolation prize for losing the capital competition, the state legislature chose Ellensburg as the location for the Washington State Normal School, now **Central Washington University**. CWU is known for its education programs and specializes in training teachers. Its oldest building is **Barge Hall**, built in 1894 and named for Professor Benjamin Franklin Barge, the school's first principal. The building is a blend of Victorian and medieval architecture.

Ellensburg's downtown is a National Historic District best seen on foot. The majority of the structures were built after the fire of 1889. Gargoyles and sheaves of wheat adorn the **Land Title Building** (Fifth and Pearl), formerly the Farmer's Bank and erected in 1911. The **Cadwell Building** (114 East Third) was built by Edward Cadwell in 1889 and houses the **Kittitas County Museum**. Cadwell was an attorney for Northern Pacific who invested substantial capital into rebuilding Ellensburg.

The **Clymer Museum** (416 North Pearl) features the work of **John Ford Clymer**, an artist who revealed the Western frontier through "story-telling pictures." He also shared covers on the *Saturday Evening Post* with Norman Rockwell. Clymer's art adorns more than 80 *Post* covers. The old, black furnace at the entrance to the museum was once a gathering spot for men seeking warmth and companionship. One venerable local recalled, "My pop used to take me along when I was just a boy. I remember the men with mouths full of tobacco and the sound of the furnace sizzling as it was pummeled by spit."

An old stove in the Clymer Museum.

The Ellensburg Rodeo, billed as "the Greatest Show on Dirt," comes to town every Labor Day weekend. Wild cow riding, Brahma bull riding and barrel racing are a few of the events that occur at Washington State's largest rodeo. On a related note, Ellensburg is also the state's beef capital.

Kittitas County: Ellensburg is the county seat of Kittitas County, which was organized in 1883 from portions of Yakima County. The county is located east of the Cascade Mountains in the geographical center of the state. The county was first visited by Europeans in 1812 when members of the Pacific Fur Company passed through the region. Prior to the Civil War, Captain George McClellan supervised military road construction through the county. In 1905, the U.S. Reclamation Service's project in the county opened up 72,000 acres for agricultural development and was of major importance to the county's economic development. Today, Kittitas County is an important food processing, mixed agriculture and stock raising center. Mining and timber also add diversity to its economy. Central Washington University at Ellensburg is the area's higher education and research center.

Courthouse: 205 West Fifth, Ellensburg 98926, SCAN 460-7508 (Commissioners), FAX 509-962-7650. Area: 2,320.0 square miles. State Ranking: 7th. 1993 Population: 29,200. Unincorporated: 12,260. Incorporated: 16,940. Density: 12.6 persons per square mile. **Cities and Towns**: Cle Elum, Ellensburg, Kittitas, Roslyn, South Cle Elum. **Principal Economic Activities**: Food processing, agriculture, wood products, metal fabrication. **Points of Interest**: Ginkgo Petrified Forest, Yakima River Canyon, Olmstead State Park.

Climate: (Ellensburg - elevation 1,597)

	Jan	Apr	Jul	Oct
Max Temp. F°	35.2	61.8	83.9	63.0
Min Temp.	19.3	35.2	52.8	36.1
Mean Temp.	24.6	48.1	68.9	48.9
Precipitation	1.26"	.49"	.13"	.66"

Average Annual Maximum Temperature: 60
Average Annual Minimum Temperature: 35.9
Annual Mean Temperature: 47.7
Average Annual Precipitation: 8.86"

Four miles east of Ellensburg, **Olmstead Place State Park** preserves the legacy of the family farm. In 1875, Samuel and Sarah Olmstead crossed the Cascade Mountains on horseback with their young family and established one of the first homesteads in Kittitas Valley. The 200-acre farm still produces wheat, oats and hay, as well as dairy cattle and chickens. The original Olmstead log cabin stands near the southern end of the park and has been renovated along with a single-room school house where the Olmstead children and others learned to read and write. The house has been restored with many Olmstead belongings such as a 1870 Scottish spinning wheel. One corner of the school house has been decorated as a schoolroom, complete with benches, a desk and some books. To the west, behind the house are the chicken coops. A wagon shed, granary, milkhouse and dairy barn are contained inside a fenced field nearby. North of the house is a large red hay barn that was built in 1908.

Samuel and Sarah Olmstead's log cabin.

About one mile from the park, **Kittitas** (Elevation 1,500, Population 1,010) is from the Indian word *K-tatus*, meaning "gray gravel bank"; it refers to a gravel bank on a river shoal near Ellensburg.

The road passes prosperous-looking farms, neat houses and spacious barns, fields of hay and alfalfa, and herds of sleek cattle before leaving the valley and climbing the sage and ryegrass covered hills. The highway drops to the Columbia River and **Vantage**, 30 miles east of Ellensburg. Stunning views of steep, basaltic cliffs rising from the mighty Columbia lend credence to the naming of this fuel and camping stop.

Basaltic cliffs rising from the mighty Columbia at Vantage.

Perched high atop the somber bluff on the west side of the Columbia is the **Ginkgo Petrified Forest State Park**, considered to be one of the most unusual fossil forests in the world. Discovered by Ellensburg geologist George F. Beck in 1932, this particular petrified forest generates interest among scientists for several reasons First, there are over 200 species of fossilized trees in the area. Second, since the fossil beds are young by geological standards (the Miocene Age of the Tertiary Period), the area provides the last examples of the fossilized wood of the prehistoric gymnospermous (a tree with naked seeds, i.e. not encased) ginkgo tree. Descendants of the ginkgo tree can still be found in the Orient, where they can reach 100 feet in height. Third, petrified trees are seldom found in previously active volcanic areas because the logs would usually tend to float up through the lava and burn once coming in contact with oxygen. But the fact that waterlogged trees in the Ginkgo Petrified Forest were buried in the lake-bottom mud, allowed them to survive the inferno, at which time the petrifaction process began. (It's a common misunderstanding that petrifaction involves a straight molecule-to-molecule substitution of wood by silica. In truth, most of the wood fiber remains, acting as a blotter of sorts that absorbs the silica minerals.)

Although the fossil beds — containing an estimated 7,500 logs, as well as the fossilized remains of prehistoric mastodon, deer, antelope, three-toed horses, large cats, wild pigs, etc. — are at least 10 million years old, the fact that the logs show little sign of having been crushed before fossilization occurred, suggests that they petrified rather quickly.

After the interstate crosses the Vantage Bridge, search the eastern foothills for an unusual sculpture called "When Grandfather Cut Loose The Ponies." The life size monument displays 18 wild horses running from an overturned basket and commemorates the "Great Spirit's gift to our planet."

The highway rises north, northeast 12 miles to **George** (Elevation 1,300, Population 336), located on the western edge of the Columbia Plateau. George, Washington — the two belong together — is the only town in the nation bearing a president's full name. The town's streets are named after different types of cherry trees. The world's largest cherry pie is baked at the annual George Washington 4th of July Celebration.

George has most recently gained fame as a venue for summertime concerts. Located on the former grounds of the Champs de Brionne Winery, crowds gather on dirt terraces and watch world-famous acts perform in an amphitheater with the Columbia River and towering canyon walls as a backdrop. Since concerts are usually scheduled in the evening, sunsets accentuate the panorama.

From George the highway travels directly east, passing through large farms and the **Winchester Wasteway** area, 2,000 acres of streams, ponds and small lakes used for irrigation, and by hunters and fisherman. During the Christmas holidays, farmers take part in an informal competition, setting up giant light displays that help break the monotony of this long, straight stretch of road. Late night cross-state travelers work overtime as judges.

The city of **Moses Lake** (Elevation 1,039, Population 11,700) is 26 miles from George. Both the city and the lake on which it lies were named after **Chief Moses**, whose Sinikiuse and Wenatchee tribes camped on the shores of the lake for generations. The famous warrior/diplomat was one of the most influential Indian leaders in eastern Washington and northern Idaho in the mid-to-late 1800s. His commitment to fairness earned him respect among both Native Americans and whites: "When the sun comes up one day I do not talk one way and the next day another, I have only one straight way, my mind is to go along the road with good men, those who tell the truth and do not lie."

In 1878, Chief Moses traveled to Washington D.C. and counseled with President Rutherford B. Hayes, reluctantly relinquishing control of the Columbia Basin to the government, which opened the basin for homesteading.

Pioneer farmers who had settled on the lake formed a community called Neppel, after a pioneer's hometown in Germany. Farmers were challenged by the aridity of the region, a condition that would continue until the Columbia Basin Irrigation Project was realized in the 1950s. One alternative industry in the early days was shipping carp caught in the lake to Jewish settlements in Chicago and New York. On September 9, 1938, a population of 370 voted to incorporate Neppel and change its name to Moses Lake.

Economic growth improved when an army air force base was established in 1942. The military left briefly after the war but returned in 1948 to protect the Hanford Atomic Works, Grand Coulee Dam and the entire Pacific Northwest. During this time the town also prospered from the development of sugar beet and potato processing plants. Japanese-Americans, forced to relocate during World War II, provided labor for these plants.

In 1966, Boeing purchased the airstrip and has since used it to train its flight crews. The airport has the most advanced radar system in

Digging potatoes at 500 bushels per acre, circa 1920s.

the world, the ASR-9 system, allowing them to monitor both air traffic and weather on separate channels. Japan Airlines shares the airport, basing its flight training school there.

INTERSTATE
90

Moses Lake, the city, is accessible via State Highway 171. Artifacts from Chief Moses' tribes and other Indian groups in the Columbia River Basin are contained at **Adam East Museum** (Third and Ash).

Moses Lake, the lake, is made up of three arms, which are over 18 miles long and up to one mile wide with over 120 miles of shoreline. It is a shallow lake with a maximum depth of 30 feet. Its waters attract recreationists, and the sand dunes south of the lake are the most extensive dunes open to off-road vehicles in Washington.

The interstate collides with U.S. 395 at Ritzville 41 miles further. The two highways then travel together 60 miles northeast to **Spokane** (Elevation 1,982, Population 183,800), the second largest city in the state and largest in a region known as the Inland Empire.

In the early decades of the nineteenth century, this region was the domain of the Spokane and other Indian tribes. A few explorers had passed through, and fur traders from Great Britain and the United States were trickling in, foreshadowing the army of settlers to follow. But these men had no desire to stimulate settlement, for their source of income — fur-bearing animals — depended upon the preservation of the wilderness.

The Hotel Davenport, designed by Kirtland Cutter.

In 1810, Washington's first permanent white settlement, the **Spokane House**, was built along the banks of the Spokane River. The fur-trading center was also a popular meeting place for trading parties, Indians and company employees. One employee described its social appeal, "At Spokane House there were attractive buildings, a ball-room even; and no females in the land so fair to look upon as the nymphs of Spokane; no damsels could dance so gracefully as they; none were so attractive."

Although the post was dismantled in 1826, fur traders and missionaries continued to drift through into the 1830s. In 1873, **James Nettle Glover**, the "Father of Spokane," purchased a water-powered sawmill by the Spokane Falls from two squatters. The mill was improved and a store built. Platted by Glover as Spokane Falls in 1878, the town's population grew to 1,000 by 1881 with incorporation and the promise of a Northern Pacific branch line.

Originally the town was called Spokan Falls, without the 'e.' Lt. T.W. Symons explains: "whether to put the final e on this word has been a much discussed question and has divided the people of the Spokane Region into 2 parties. The majority, however, seem to desire the e, and so will finally be adopted, and in all probability, go down to futurity."

There was much talk of the improvements that would follow the establishment of rail connections and of profits to be made. The town's first bank owner, A.M. Cannon, observed, "The N.P. is coming this way, and there will be all sorts of checks to cash and I might as well be ready to take care of them."

In 1883, the Northern Pacific was completed through Montana, thus establishing transcontinental mail service. Pamphlets back East were publicizing "the luxuries of limitless wealth" that "the manufacturing center of the Great Northwest" offered. The N.P. was followed by several transcontinental and local lines including the Union Pacific, the Great Northern, the Milwaukee, the Canadian Pacific, and the Washington Central. Spokane was the major railroad center in the west.

Gold, silver, copper, lead and zinc found in Couer d'Alene mines and the area's only direct connections to the East made Spokane Falls the region's gold rush capital during the 1880s. Northern Pacific's promotion of the region was emphatic: "The wonderful rich mineral wealth of the Coeur d'Alene Mountains and the tributaries of the river of that name has been heralded to the world and all old prospectors and miners stand amazed at these new fields which are unequaled in richness and extent. There's more than enough for all who come."

The boom was different than an earlier one in Walla Walla; it was based on lode and not placer mining. Lode mining excavates hard rock mineral veins while placer mining usually takes place in streams or gentle waterways. Mansions of wealthy and lucky investors soon lined the hills above the Spokane River.

In a letter to his wife and child back in Minnesota in 1883, John F. Sprague wrote: "There's big excitment about the gold mines, they ar about 90 miles from here. Most everyboddy around here ar going in the spring. They clame that they ar the richest mines that ever was discovered in the United States... I have not got the mine fever yet, It will be a rough place [sic]."

By 1884, at least 1,000 new settlers had arrived; the dusty streets were crowded with stagecoaches and lumbering prairie schooners. Heavily laden freight wagons and strings of pack horses and burros set out almost daily for outlying settlements and mining camps. Miners, lumberjacks, construction workers, and Indians jostled each other on the wooden side-walks, in stores, and on the dance floors of the local amusement halls. Brawls were a daily occurrence, and guns were frequently drawn, occasionally with fatal results.

On one bitterly cold and wintery day in 1878, Clara Gray found her black silk dress frozen to the closet wall. After removing it with a hot iron, she put it on, and danced Spokane Fall's first waltz. Other cultural developments accom-panied the burgeoning town's growth. Several newspapers were form-ed, the *Spokane Re-view*, the *Spokesman*, the *News-Democrat*, the *Spokane News*, and the *Spokane Weekly Times*. Libraries were raised, and by 1890 17 religious denomina-

There must be a damsel in distress somewhere in the Spokane Courthouse.

tions had formed and nearly as many churches had been built. A favorite place for elaborate social functions and for theatrical attractions was Concordia Hall, a building owned by the Concordia Singing Society, a German organization. The Bachelor's Ball, the social event of the winter, was held here in 1886.

On a sultry, summer evening on August 4, 1889, pork chop grease started a fire in an eating house on Railroad Avenue. The city's down-town business area was virtually wiped out by the "Great Fire." A newly-installed water system proved useless, the hoses leaked and the only man who knew how to operate it was the vacationing water superintendent. The 32-block business district was destroyed, with an estimated loss of $6 million. No lives were lost, but the city was a mass of blackened ruins.

Reconstruction began at once. Within a year more than $4 million was invested in construction. Brick and granite replaced the tent-cities that had risen after the fire. The period was marked by great civic improvements, sewers were laid, street lighting improved, and bridges were built. The population exploded once more as 25,000 people called the sparkling new city home. The city charter in 1891 decreed: "The name of the municipal corporation now existing and known as the city of Spokane Falls, shall be and is hereby changed to the name of city of Spokane."

Variety theaters flourished like weeds after a spring rain. Soon the town was more wide open than ever; proprietors of shows paraded the streets with bands, followed by their box-rustling ladies in carriages. Local disapproval of this type of entertainment mounted, and, led by local ministers, an aggressive campaign was directed against the variety theaters. In 1897, Mayor Olmstead called for the enforcement of regulatory laws. "While I am not a puritan, I am convinced that vice and immorality have put on too brazen a front."

Bing Crosby and Father Clifford Carroll, 1957.

One of the best-known and most popular characters of this lusty period was Jimmy Durkin. Everyone knew and liked this genial saloon keeper, who boasted that he would cash any check offered to him. He had advertisements to that effect painted on roadside rocks, until a miner brought in a rock one day and asked: "See anything peculiar about that rock, Jimmy?" — "No. I can't say I do," answered Durkin. — "Well," said the miner, "I found that rock 4,000 feet below the surface and it's the only one in this part of the country without your name on it." When denounced by a crusading minister, Durkin promptly offered window space for an antisaloon display. The display only served to attract larger crowds, and the minister admitted that Jimmy was a "man of his word."

Spokane survived the Panic of 1893 as mines in Couer d'Alene continued to prosper and new ones opened in the Kootenai district of British Columbia. Acres of valuable pine stretched northeast and east of Spokane. Land-hungry immigrants, particularly from Germany, Poland, Russia, and the Scandinavian countries, came in a steady stream as the fertility of the Palouse soil was no longer a secret. A 1906 edition of the Farm Fortunes brochure wrote:

> There was a time, less than a generation ago, that emigration to Washington was accompanied to some of the earmarks of pioneering; that the settler was confronted by certain hardships; that the educational and social advantages

were not on a par with those on the east and middle west. The west has developed rapidly. It is no longer an Indian... for the man of moderate means the difference between living in the east and living in the west is the difference between getting along and getting rich.... Bring your old folks and your children to the Spokane country. Do not delay.

Spokane's population had grown to 104,402 by 1910. The city had become the largest and most important community in the north between Seattle and Minneapolis-St.Paul.

Turn-of-the-century prosperity, stately architecture committed to a 1904 "City Beautiful" program, and the area's natural beauty have combined to make Spokane a great walking and exploring city. Spacious hilltop homes overlook the city, river and pine-covered hills. The downtown features many brick and stone business blocks and tall, terra-cotta-faced, neoclassic office buildings. The river is the site of Riverfront Park, developed for the 1974 World's Exposition Fair.

Situated on a bluff south of downtown, **Browne's Addition** is an historical, residential district named for J.J. Browne,

St. John's Episcopal Cathedral.

an early homesteader who possessed and purchased a great deal of property. Many of the mansions in the area, and several downtown buildings, were designed by prolific architect Kirtland Cutter, who was educated on the East coast and from European travels. Cutter was told to spare no expense when designing the home of mining magnate **Patsy Clark** (West 2208 2nd Avenue); a command he apparently heeded. Windows from New York's Tiffany Company, grandfather clocks from London, and hand-sculpted column caps from Italy grace this mansion turned restaurant, now open for tours and meals.

The **Amasa B. Campbell House** (West 2316 1st Avenue), an English Tudor Revival structure built in 1898 by Cutter, is notable for its well-maintained, and somewhat cluttered, interior. An Oriental fountain bubbles outside. Next door the **Cheney Cowles Memorial Museum** collects, preserves and interprets the history of Eastern Washington, the Inland Northwest, and local Indian cultures.

The majority of houses on this and adjacent blocks are worth seeing; descriptions of architectural styles are highlighted on frontyard displays.

Cutter continued his work downtown with his design of the **Davenport Hotel** and the adjoining **Matador Restaurant** (West 808 Sprague). The California Mission-style restaurant contrasts sharply with the eclectic hotel, and shows the imagination of the architect. Inside the lobby of the Davenport, singing caged birds, a giant stuffed polar bear, rams' heads and knights' helmets once greeted famous visitors such as Theodore Roosevelt, John F. Kennedy and Mahatma Gandhi. The Davenport closed in 1984.

West of Monroe Street, in an area known as *Civic Center,* Riverside Avenue breaks from the city's grid-like pattern and follows an S-curved shape. A median strip planted with Linden trees divides the street. On the south side of the street, tranquil **Our Lady of Lourdes Cathedral** (built from 1902-1908) and the adjacent **Catholic Diocese Chancery** (1924) face the **Masonic Temple** (1905), colonnaded in gray cast stone and stretching for 222 feet along the curves of the street. Eighteen columns support a stone-railed promenade that extends the length of the building. Busts of Senmut, an Egyptian builder of temples, flank the entrances.

Life is a carousel.

The **Elks Club,** from 1919, and the **Chamber of Commerce**, begun in 1933 are harmonious with, but different from, the temple which separates the two buildings. The Elks Club was constructed of gray cut stone and is sheltered by a copper alloy roof.

The commerce building was built in a Florentine Renaissance-style and is topped by a tile roof and columns featuring masks of Native American chiefs.

The **Spokane Club** (1910), Spokane's oldest, neighbors the Chamber of Commerce. The club was organized in 1890 as a men-only retreat where members could enjoy a smoke, a good book, or each other's company. Escorted women had a separate entrance; several rooms were off-limits.

The **Spokesman-Review Building** (1891, West 927 Riverside Avenue), a five-story building of red brick and gray Montana granite, highlights the street east of Monroe. The *Spokane Review* and the *Spokesman* merged in 1893 to form the *Spokesman-Review*, Spokane's major newspaper. Although the *Spokesman-Review* currently has a fine reputation, during his presidential term, Harry Truman identified the paper, along with the *Chicago Tribune* as the "two worst newspapers in America."

A few blocks east, Spokane's retail and financial district begins, covering 15 blocks and connected by an organized system of skyways. Although Spokane's climate is generally agreeable, winters are cold and snow is common. The enclosed skyways make it possible to shop all day and never set foot outside.

Across the river, the **Spokane County Courthouse** (West 1116 Broadway) looks more like a European castle than a center of local government. In the 1890s the County Commissioners decided they needed a new government building. They offered a prize to the person who submitted the most original design. The winner was 29-year-old, pseudo-architect Willis Ritchie, whose background consisted of a correspondence course conducted by the United States Treasury Department.

The building resembles two famous 16th century French chateaux; Chateau de Chambord, built in 1519 and Chateau d'Azay Le Rideau built in 1516. In 1895 the cost of construction was $273,600; it is now worth more than $4,000,000.

Northeast of downtown, **Gonzaga University** (East 502 Boone) was founded in 1887 by Father Joseph Cataldo. After choosing the site for the school, Cataldo's superiors wrote:

> You have seen the place and know of its healthfulness and the beauty and even grandeur of the surrounding scenery. No where perhaps could be found a location more healthful and with more beautiful and attractive surroundings — the undulating gravelly prairie, the river, the falls, the wooded hills and mountains nearby, all contribute to the beauty of the location as well as to its healthfulness.

The school was named after Saint Aloysius Gonzaga, son of a noble Renaissance family who attended to the sick and dying in plague-stricken Rome. He died of exhaustion at the age of 23 on June 21, 1591, and was declared the patron saint of youth in 1726.

Sights on campus are the **Saint Aloysius Church**, a Roman-style church built in 1909 with impressive Corinthian columns; and the **Crosby Library**, featuring memorabilia of Gonzaga's most famous alumnus, **Bing Crosby**.

Born in Tacoma in 1901, Harry Lillis Crosby was raised in an Irish-Catholic family of seven children. As a child he was described as "tough, mischievous and addicted to pranks." Crosby attended Gonzaga in 1920 where he was a member of the varsity baseball team. He played drums in a local band known as the "Musicaladers."

In 1925, Crosby borrowed some gas money from a friend, filled the tank in his $8 Model-T and took off for California. Two years later, he was working in the biggest orchestra in the country. Within four years Crosby was both a movie and radio star, becoming one of Hollywood's biggest box-office attractions after the release of his first film, *The Big Broadcast*, in 1932. His celebrated "Road" pictures with co-stars Bob Hope and Dorothy Lamour included *Road to Singapore* (1940), *Road to Zanzibar* (1941), *Road to Morocco* (1942), and *Road to Rio* (1947). In 1944 Crosby earned an Oscar as best actor for his performance in *Going My Way*.

In his musical career, he recorded over 1,500 songs and exceeded $300 million in sales. His most famous recording, "White Christmas," has sold 30 million copies.

After playing a round of golf in Madrid, Spain, Bing Crosby collapsed to the green on October 14, 1977, dying of a heart attack.

The **Spokane River Centennial Trail** runs across Gonzaga's campus at the river's edge and is used by pedestrians and bikers. Its 39 miles of pathway connect Spokane to the Washington-Idaho border.

The roots for Spokane's extensive park system were planted in 1904 with the organization of the City Beautiful Committee. Park designs were commissioned from the Olmsted brothers, renowned landscape architects, who formulated the Olmsted Plan. In the "Need for Parks" the Olmsteds wrote:

> ... city life involves a continual strain of the nerves, through the need of avoiding dangers of the factory and street, owing to the multitudinous harsh noises and the vivid and eye-tiring sights and through having to give attention to so many things and to talk to so many people. Even to the well this is tiring to the nerves... it is to those whose nerves are tired and they are a large proportion of the dwellers in a city, that the parks are most immediately beneficial.

Manito Park and Botanical Gardens (17th and Grand), southeast of downtown, is one such park established by the Olmstead Plan. Within the park, Duncan Garden features an array of formal floral displays typical of 19th-century plantings. The four-acre Rose Garden contains more than 1,500 roses and a perennial garden blooms spring through fall. Exotic plantings, wooden bridges and walkways, and metal and stone lanterns are found in the Nishinomiya Japanese Garden.

Near the gardens, **Saint John's Episcopal Cathedral** (East 127 12th Avenue), a 20th-century gothic structure, is perhaps the most recognizable landmark in Spokane. Begun in sandstone from Tacoma and Boise and completed in Indiana limestone, the elaborately detailed building took over 50 years to complete. On either side of the main entrance arch are triangle spandrels, ornamented with the rose as a symbol of love and the pomegranate for unity. Medallions in the aisle windows illustrate the development of Christianity from apostolic times to the present.

Once fishing grounds for the Spokan-ee Indians and the original location of white settlement, Spokane's riverfront had lost importance by the mid-1900s. When Spokane was chosen as the site of the 1974 World's Fair, train tracks, trestles, freight sidings, warehouses and slum areas were torn out and replaced with **Riverfront Park**. The only structure spared destruction was the 155-foot, granite clock tower from the original Great Northern passenger depot, a symbol of the railroad's importance to the city. Today the park contains numerous family attractions including an IMAX theater, miniature golf, a gondola ride over the Spokane Falls, an opera house, a Ferris wheel and 100 acres of open fields.

The majority of the park's attractions lie on Havermale Island, a giant rock in the Spokane River just above Spokane Falls. In 1877, news that the Nez Perce Indians were on the warpath sent settlers into a panic. Those within a radius of 25 miles sought refuge on the island.

"Joy of Running Together" by artist David Giovedare.

The most popular attraction is a 1909 merry-go-round, which was installed one year after the world's fair. Designed by Charles I.D. Looff, the carousel spent its original years entertaining youngsters at nearby Natatorium Park, which closed in 1968. The ride collected dust until 1975, when a fund-raising campaign brought the carousel to the river.

Bloomsday, one of the largest road races in the nation, winds through Spokane on the first Sunday of every May. Contestants finish at Riverfront Park, where a collection of iron statues of every size and shape commemorate the "Joy of Running Together." The artist, David Giovedare, also created "When Grandfather Cut Loose the Ponies," a pack of galloping horses running across the foothills east of Vantage. Just west of the park, a short walk, the first hydroelectric plant west of the Mississippi was built along the thundering Spokane Falls. The falls are most powerful in the spring. A good vantage point is the **Monroe Street Bridge**; its concrete arches were the largest in the world when built. Concrete buffalo designs are affixed to the side of the bridge. Plans and drawings of the bridge are on exhibit in the Sorbonne, Paris.

Spokane County: Spokane is the county seat of Spokane County, which was the first county organized in 1858 from part of Walla Walla

Entering downtown by way of the award-winning Monroe Street Bridge.

County. Five years later it was voted out of existence by the Territorial Legislature and merged into Stevens County. In 1879 it was recreated and named after the Spokane Indians; the name means "child of the sun." It is located in the northeastern part of the state and is bounded by Idaho on the east. The county was first visited in 1810 by fur traders who established Spokane House as a trading center. Two years later the Pacific Fur Company built Fort Spokane. Missionaries arrived in the county in the 1830s. The first permanent settlements in the county were established in the 1870s and the county's prosperity was assured with the arrival of the Northern Pacific Railroad in 1890. Today, Spokane County has a prosperous and varied economy based on manufacturing and agriculture. Spokane is the second largest city in the state and is a regional transportation, financial and cultural center.

Courthouse: West 1116 Broadway, Spokane 99260, SCAN 272-2265, FAX 509-456-2274. Area: 1,758.3 square miles. State Ranking: 19th. 1993 Population: 383,600. Unincorporated: 180,051. Incorporated:

203,549. Density: 218.2 persons per square mile. **Cities and Towns**: Airway Heights, Cheney, Deer Park, Fairfield, Latah, Medical Lake, Millwood, Rockford, Spangle, Spokane, Waverly. **Principal Economic Activities**: Food processing, apparel & textile manufacturing, publishing, metal fabrication, agriculture, electronics machinery manufacturing, wood products. **Points of Interest**: Long Lake Dam, Mt. Spokane, Spokane Plains Battlefield, Spokane House.

Climate: (Spokane - elevation 1,982)

	Jan	Apr	Jul	Oct
Max Temp. F°	35.5	61.4	88.4	61.8
Min Temp.	24.2	38.4	56.7	39.6
Mean Temp.	29.9	49.9	72.6	50.7
Precipitation	2.03"	1.31"	.40"	1.17"

Average Annual Maximum Temperature: 60.9
Average Annual Minimum Temperature: 39.7
Annual Mean Temperature: 50.3
Average Annual Precipitation: 17.41"

Interstate 90 leaves Spokane and travels 21 miles to the Washington-Idaho border. ○<

State Highway 92 from a junction with State Highway 9 northeast to Granite Falls. Route length: eight miles.
　　Highway 92 cuts through a narrow valley between the South Fork of the Stillaguamish River and the Pilchuck River on its way to **Granite Falls** (Elevation 396, Population 1,395). Settled in 1885, the town was named for the falls one mile north where the Stillaguamish plunges over a smooth granite ledge onto huge boulders below. Neighboring mines once produced modest amounts of copper, silver and gold that were shipped by rail west to Everett, carrying with it high hopes for growth. When the ore deposits failed to make the grade, logging became the mainstay. Most of the prime timber was cut long ago, but the surrounding second-growth is approaching heights suitable for harvest. To view the falls, take the scenic Mountain Loop Highway from the eastern edge of town. ○<

State Highway 96 from a junction with Interstate 5 east to a junction with State Highway 9. Route length: five miles.
　　A short connector from south of Everett to south of Snohomish. ○<

US 97 **Highway 97** from State Highway 14 at the Columbia River and Maryhill, north through Goldendale, Toppenish, Wapato, Yakima, Ellensburg and Liberty to a junction with U.S. Highway 2, then east across the Columbia River, northeasterly recrossing the Columbia River at Chelan Falls, and continuing through Pateros, Brewster, Okanogan, Omak, Tonasket and Oroville to the Canadian boundary. (Overlaps Interstates 82 and 90, and U.S. 2.) Route length: 317 miles.

Driving north on U.S. 97 you begin to gain a perspective of the dramatic cut the Columbia River makes through the wheat-covered plateaus of Washington and Oregon. On clear days, a pull-out two miles south of Goldendale provides views of the gorge's high basalt cliffs and four mountains: Rainier, Adams, Hood, and St. Helens. To the east, the Horse Heaven Hills plateau forms a gently rolling plain that slopes southward to the river.

Goldendale (Elevation 1,600, Population 3,375) is a town whose charm is not revealed from the highway. Beyond the roadside McDonald's and the corner filling stations competing for business, lies a quiet, self-sufficient community with comfortable Victorian-era homes and an authentic downtown. Diversity has played a key role in Goldendale's success; raising stock, growing wheat and alfalfa and processing timber have all sustained the economy. The recently-closed lumber mill has been replaced by an aluminum mill.

When John J. Golden arrived in 1863 with his family and a long string of cattle, he found himself surrounded by acres of waist-high grass reaching to the horizon in every direction; a good sign his stock and family would not go hungry. Following the waves of cattlemen to the region were farmers who figured that their counterparts were onto something good. They were right. Underneath all that grass was a blanket of rich soil ready to be plowed and planted. After a brutal

The Presby Mansion and the Klickitat County Museum combined into one.

winter in 1860-61 wiped out most of the cattle population, sheep were introduced, and by 1888, 86,000 head were counted. All parties benefited in 1903 when the Columbia River and Northern Railroad built a line through Klickitat to Lyle's waterfront. From there, goods were transferred to steamboats and shipped down the Columbia River to profitable, West Coast markets.

Much of the region's history is preserved at the **Presby Mansion** (127 Broadway), now the Klickitat County Historical Museum. W. B. Presby was a lawyer and state senator who helped frame Washington state's constitution. Inside is an authentic collection of pioneer clothing and artifacts of the area's early immigrants. Also a pretty amazing collection of coffee grinders.

Another site worth a peek is the **Old Red House** (Sentinel and Columbus). Built in 1890 by Charles Newell, this is an architecturally interesting building with fire engine-red walls, stained-glass windows, "gingerbread ornaments" and multiple chimneys. Newell gained fame as Washington's "horse king," rounding up hordes of wild horses from the Yakima Reservation and shipping them back east for a substantial profit.

Continue north on Columbus Avenue one mile to **Goldendale Observatory State Park**, home of the country's largest public telescope. The telescope was the brainchild of four Vancouver, Washington astronomers who, in the late 1960s, constructed a 24-1/2" reflecting Cassegrain telescope for Clark College in Vancouver. In 1973, attracted to Goldendale's clear night skies and minimal light pollution, they found a home for the telescope on a hilltop above town. A Celetron telescope and six portable viewers have since been added to the park. Long recognized as an optimal viewing spot, a team of star-gazers from California's Lick Observatory were sent here in 1918 to witness a total eclipse of the sun.

The Klickitat or "robber" prairie.

Klickitat County: Goldendale is the county seat of Klickitat County, which was founded in 1859 from part of Skamania County. It was named after the Klickitat Indian Tribe and the word means "robber" or "thief." The county is located in the extreme south center of the state and is bounded on the south by the Columbia River. The county was first settled in 1852 by Erastus Joslyn. However, not until 1867 was an effective county government organized. Transportation played an important part in the county's history. A U.S. Army wagon road crossed the county in 1855, and later the Columbia Railway and Navigation Company's railroad and competing Columbia River steamboats provided a colorful chapter in its history. Today, Klickitat County bases its economy on food processing, agriculture and wood products.

Courthouse: 205 South Columbus, Goldendale 98620, FAX 509-773-4244 (Auditor), FAX 509-773-5713 (Public Works). Area: 1,907.8 square miles. State Ranking: 15th. 1993 Population: 17,500. Unincorporated: 11,565. Incorporated: 5,935. Density: 9.2 persons per square mile. **Cities and Towns**: Bingen, Goldendale, White Salmon. **Principal Economic Activities**: Wood products, metal industries, agriculture. **Points of Interest**: Maryhill Museum, Stonehenge, Goldendale Observatory.

Climate: (Goldendale - elevation 1,635)

	Jan	Apr	Jul	Oct
Max Temp. F°	36.5	61.5	84.3	63.4
Min Temp.	22.3	34.4	49.5	36.0
Mean Temp.	29.4	48.0	66.9	49.7
Precipitation	2.93"	.85"	.15"	1.64"

Average Annual Maximum Temperature: 61.0
Average Annual Minimum Temperature: 35.9
Annual Mean Temperature: 48.4
Average Annual Precipitation: 17.41"

From Goldendale you can continue north to Yakima, or for those who appreciate their scenery mixed with desolation, take the Goldendale-Bickleton Road 40 miles northeast to **Bickleton**. This sidetrip is also a must for ornithologists; Bickleton declared itself the "Bluebird Capitol of the World" in the 1960s. Thousands of Blue Mountain and Red-breasted Western Bluebirds begin arriving every February and stay until October. A migrating bird, they gather in separate groups of males and females and sometimes travel as far as Mexico before returning in the spring. The community maintains over 2,000 blue and white birdhouses which are perched on fenceposts throughout the town.

Charles N. Bickle and Samuel Flower settled Bickleton in 1878, hoping to attract newcomers by opening a general store. Flower left in 1884 to help establish Mabton to the northeast, but Bickle stayed behind, maintaining the store and opening a successful horse trading operation. Bickle was also responsible for delivering the mail to and from Goldendale, a two-day horseback trip each way.

Today's Bickleton is a small farming community set deep in the Horse Heaven Hills, a reference to the abundant bands of wild horses that once roamed this wide-open country. Rolling hills covered in sage and bunchgrass reach to the horizon.

The Mabton-Goldendale Road continues through long, barren stretches for 26 miles before dropping into the fertile Yakima Valley at Mabton on State Highway 22.

Back in Goldendale, U.S. 97 heads north, climbing the foothills of the Simcoe Mountains. A thick canopy of ponderosa pine (yellow pine), Douglas fir and Oregon oak provides a sudden but welcome relief from the hot, treeless fields of the Columbia Hills and Klickitat Valley. Along the 16-mile stretch of highway between Goldendale and **Satus Pass** (SAY-tus, Elevation 3,149) are several lodges and mini-resorts that probably attract patrons for their ability to guarantee peace and quiet. The word *Satus* derives from a band of the Yakima Indians known as the Setaslema, or "people of the rye grass prairie."

After summiting, the highway enters the **Yakima Indian Reservation**. Covering 1.4 million acres, the reservation is the largest in the state. Meeting at Walla Walla for a two-week council in 1855, chiefs and representatives from 14 area tribes (collectively termed the Yakima tribes) sat face to face with delegates from the U.S. government. The Indians, unable to relate to the concept of land ownership, found their backs against the wall as cultures collided. One leader, Ow-hi, verbalized the conflict: "...What shall I do? Shall I give the land which is a part of my body and leave myself poor and destitute? Shall I say I will give you my lands? I cannot say so." Left with little choice, the Indians signed the agreement and the Yakima Reservation was created, but it would be four more years of conflict and bloodshed before the treaty was ratified.

In 1935, the 14 tribes achieved self-governance by forming the Yakima Indian Nation, establishing a Tribal Council empowered to make business and judicial decisions. Their reservation includes nearly half a million acres of timberland, giving the Yakima's the largest commercial timber venture of any reservation in the country. They also harvest cash crops worth hundreds of millions of dollars, leaving little doubt as to their ability to sustain themselves.

A trilbute to Lou Shattuck, a Bikleton native from 1892 - 1978.

211~

Mural entitled "When Hops Were Picked by Hand."

US 97

The road continues north, leaving the protective covering of lodgepole pine until soon the only vegetation found is just off the road in the shallow canal through which Satus Creek runs. The remaining terrain is rolling desert, a mixture of rock, sage and dirt. After a long hot stretch, one that will make those low on gas sweat, the road drops out of the desert, and passes through the **Toppenish Wildlife Refuge**, 1,763 acres of brushy creek bottoms, wet meadows, sagebrush uplands and croplands located along Toppenish Creek.

Rows of corn fields lead into **Toppenish** (TAH-puhn-ish, Elevation 763, Population 7,550), where dozens of murals tell the story of life in the 1800s. Similar to other theme towns in the state, a sagging economy prompted Toppenish to embrace tourism. Unlike most theme towns, Toppenish has made the transition without appearing chintzy.

The best way to learn the history of the area — besides reading *Washington for the Curious* — is to take a tour of Toppenish's murals. The first mural, "Clearing the Land," was painted in 1989, and shows a homesteader furrowing the earth with his plow. Since then artists have added dozens of murals and continue to do so. Each June, one day is selected as "mural-in-a-day" day; thousands come to see the joint effort of some of the best artists in the Northwest.

Before murals there were sugar beets. Between 1935 and 1980 the **Utah-Idaho Sugar Beet Company Plant** ran with might and main, processing great quantities of the vegetable for its sugar content. Beets were fed by conveyors through washers and shredders and then dropped into a hot water bath to extract the juice. Intense heat and vacuum pressure produced a syrup, which was then clarified with lime and sulfur gas. After reaching the proper consistency, spinners would separate the molasses from the white sugar. The sugar was then crystallized, sacked and thrown onto another conveyor belt that led to a railroad siding. The factory ran 24 hours daily, and would operate for years at a time without a shutdown.

Toppenish is a contraction of the Yakima Indian word *Xuupinish*, meaning "sloping hill." The city lies on the edge of the Yakima Reservation, and serves as its headquarters. The **Yakima Indian Cultural Center**, just south of town on U.S. 97, is one of the most impressive of its kind in the country. Inside the towering, shake-roofed winter lodge, the history of the Yakimas is explained through dioramas, lectures and an extensive library. Fourteen giant teepees surround the building, each representing a tribe of the Yakima Nation confederation. The teepees, decorated with Native American symbols, accommodate overnight stays; reservations are made months in advance.

After a hard day picking hops these guys are probably thinking of an ice cold beer.

If there is still enough light left in your day, visit the **American Hop Museum**, (22 South B Street). Filled with anecdotes, photos and various memorabilia, the museum tells you everything you ever wanted to know about the hop industry (more interesting than it sounds). One story describes how pickers attempted to make their sacks of hops heavier, since they were only paid one or two pennies per pound. Dirt clods, rocks, or even watermelons were stuffed in the middle of the sack where the objects were least likely to be discovered by the farmer. One family would hide their overweight daughter in the bottom of the picking box, which took up about a third of the space. She would then be covered with picked hops. After a few days, envious pickers revealed their competitor's plot to the farmer who, without saying anything, began stabbing and stirring each box of hops with a pitchfork. Watching through a crack in the sideboard, the daughter weighed her options and just before the farmer laid his pitchfork into the box, decided she was no longer interested in the hop business and expeditiously abandoned her hiding place. The family was never heard from again.

The role of hops as a herbal medication dates back to Babylonian times when a hop beverage was considered a cure for leprosy. The monks of Picardy in Weser, Germany and the Abbey of Corbay used hops for brewing as early as 822. Beer was consumed mightily in the old world and considered a staple in the sailor's diet during long voyages as a source of vitamins, energy and hydration.

Originally planted for profit in New York state over 300 years ago, the crop moved westward with settlers in the 1850s. Since about 1860, hops have been one of Washington's top ten cash crops; the Yakima Valley, where dryer climates produce substantially higher yields and less chance of mildew damage, currently supplies 25% of the world's demand. Washington is second only to Germany in production, exporting 60% of the state's annual crop to over 70 countries.

Continue north past miles of fruit stands. The area is fertile but dry; the road crosses several man-made canals, which provide irrigation for the orchards, vineyards and hop fields.

Wapato (WAH-puh-toh, Elevation 875, Population 3,760) lies on the eastern edge of the Yakima Indian Reservation, seven miles past Toppenish. Fruit and vegetable storage facilities are the town's largest buildings, and attract a line-up of trains and trucks to transport hops, grapes, apples and cherries to market. Reflecting its agricultural dependence, *Wapato* comes from the Yakima word for "potato."

From its early beginnings as a trading post for Indians and settlers, Wapato has always been a cultural collage. After the town was platted in 1902, tracts of reservation land were leased to white farmers who often hired Japanese and Filipino laborers. When Japanese-Americans were confined to internment camps during World War II, Mexican migrant workers replaced them in the fields. Sun-bleached adobe homes and Mexican restaurants reveal the influence of a large Hispanic population that has moved away from the migrant life and established roots here.

From Wapato, U.S. 97 hooks up with I-82, passes through Yakima (U.S. 12), and crosses Manastash Ridge to join I-90 just south of Ellensburg. Coursing west of that community, it leaves the interstates, resuming its northerly direction across the Kittitas Valley and up into the foothills of the Cascade Range along Swauk Creek. Once a fairly important mining district, the area around Liberty is now better known for its mineral-hunting opportunities. Collection sites at First Creek, Crystal Mountain, Lion Rock and Red Top are all enough to make any rock-hound sit up and bay! The Ellensburg Blue Agate present in these hills is found nowhere else on earth. This rare gemstone ranges in color from a light, sky-blue through a corn-flower blue to an almost  purple-royal blue.

The tiny settlement of **Liberty**, now a National Historic District, sits quietly rusting away two miles off of U.S. 97. Tiny sparkling specks of gold in Swauk Creek led miners here as early as 1873 looking for riches in the bottom of a pan. Moderate success washed in and out for nearly 40 years until a larger-scale operation brought in steam power to hit those hard-to-reach spots in the 1920s. Briefly hovering somewhere between boom and bust, efforts were eventually abandoned along with cranes and other pieces of equipment. A much valued form of wire gold can still be found along Swauk and nearby Williams creeks, bringing weekend-49ers and collectors to try their luck in the manner of old.

Pushing north from the Liberty junction you start to climb **Blewett Pass** (Elevation 4,102). The much improved new section of road circumvents the old snake track that used to keep teamsters awake at night. The old road remains for the more adventurous.

Dropping into Blewett, watch for the remains of one of the largest stamp mills in the state on the west side of the highway. The remnants of an old mining arrastra can be seen at Peshastin Creek. An arrastra is a drag-stone mill contraption that crushes ore for mercury recovery, a method practiced by miners of that era. Though once holding much promise (the stuff miners eat and breathe), the Blewett area never matched the big California or Canadian strikes made in the West.

U.S. 97 junctions with U.S. 2 halfway between Leavenworth and Cashmere, sinking east to Wenatchee where it once again heads north, branching into two highways. U.S. Highway 97A (Alternate) runs along the west side of the Columbia River and U.S. 97 remains with U.S. 2 on the east side as far north as Orondo. After Orondo, U.S. 97 again regains its own designation and dignity, except for a short sojourn with Highway 20 out of Okanogan, clear to the Canadian border.

Skirting along the river through fruit orchards under the western rim of the Waterville Plateau, the highway crosses west at Chelan station and rejoins its errant twin U.S. 97A just below **Wells Dam**. The dam, owned by Douglas County PUD, is unique in its design, combining the

Wells Power Dam on the Columbia.

215~

powerhouse, spillway, switchyard and fish facilities into a single structure, thereby saving millions of dollars over conventional design. The guidance efficiency for migrating juvenile steelhead and salmon exceeds the level sought by fish agencies and is the highest on the Columbia.

Moving on towards Pateros, keep an eye out for a sign that points out the **China Ditch**. This ditch, still visible below the highway, was built by Chinese miners sometime between 1860 and 1880. Water flowed down this chute from its diversion point three miles up the Methow River to sluice sandbars two or three miles downstream on the Columbia. After the Chinese moved on, the ditch was used by settlers to irrigate orchards until a 1948 flood destroyed two miles of canal and flume. History proved that the China Ditch produced far greater value in apples than it ever did in gold.

Above Wells Dam, **Pateros** (puh-TIAR-uhs, Elevation 812, Population 580) sits on a bench surrounded by orchards and is the jumping off place for State Highway 153 into the Methow Valley. The community, though small, is a major fruit storing and shipping area. Situated at the mouth of the Methow River, it was once considered the home of some of the most dangerous rapids on the Columbia River. Artifacts discovered here point to the existence of an important native settlement in the past.

As you press on towards **Brewster** (Elevation 812, Population 1,645), the terrain changes from the steeper cut of the Columbia to the broader expanse of the Okanogan Valley, with vast orchards sweeping gracefully down to the river banks. On a thumb of land jutting into Lake Pateros, Brewster (originally Bruster) languishes quietly in the heart of orchard country. Once an important steamboat landing, the town was dragged here from its original location and name (Virginia City) a mile away. It took a 32-horse hitch to drag the hotel over, and at least a like number of drinks to site it properly. There is a handsomely-aged Oddfellows Hall at the end of Main Street, next to a small park with a Tomahawk missile whose inscribed base states: "Honoring the men and women, our role call is many blends of color, race, creed but our belief in duty, honor, country, is a common denominator." The old Rio Theater on Main Street still presents a picture show Friday through Sunday.

Leave Brewster and drive across the estuary formed by the joining of the Okanogan River and Lake Pateros. Turning east on State Highway 17, the road rises about a mile to **Fort Okanogan State Park and Interpretive Center** operated by the Colville Confederated Tribes. In September of 1811, a party from the new Pacific Fur Company, an offshoot of John Jacob Astor's American Fur Company, landed and built a driftwood fort at the confluence of the "Oackinacken" and

Columbia rivers. Their purpose was to compete in the lucrative fur trade with Canada's Hudson's Bay and North West fur companies. Soon the party departed, leaving one, Alexander Ross, without so much as a hand mirror for another man's company, to winter and establish trade. At least the trading was good; for merchandise worth $160 he received $10,000 worth of pelts, but he would have gladly swapped the isolation. He wrote "I pined, I languished, my head turned gray, and my only consolation was my bible." Facing stiff competition and the War of 1812, Astor's company sold out to the North West Company in 1813, which was forced to merge with its fierce rival, the Hudson's Bay Company, eight years later. Hudson's Bay then operated Fort Okanogan, moving it once, until pressed to withdraw from all its holdings on the Columbia in 1860. The two sites, now under water or fill, were acquired by Washington state in 1951 and excavated in '52 and '57. The Interpretive Center was erected in 1960 and is well worth the short drive to gain the interesting early history of this area. A bonus is the magnificent view from the center's highland location.

Back on the highway you can cross the Okanogan River at Malott and join old U.S. 97. **Malott** was once a trailhead on the Chiliwist Trail, one of the main routes used by natives and early explorers into the upper Methow Valley. You can continue north here or cross back to the main highway and drive into the town of **Okanogan** (Elevation 829, Population 2,390). Here U.S. 97 hooks up with Highway 20; the city ranges along the west side of the river. Eye-catching sites include the courthouse on a knoll west of the commercial center; First Methodist Church on Queen Street, especially if you have an interest in stonemasonry; and the historical museum at the north end of town. One early description of the area west of town up on Pogue Flat reads: "In April and early May the valley is a fairyland; apple blossoms, with their beautiful tints and sweet aroma, contrast with drab hillsides and the pungent odor of sagebrush." At one time the town was reached by an unusual and much-ridiculed high bridge across the river, steeply inclined to allow passage of even the tallest steamer stacks of the day.

Okanogan County: Okanogan is the county seat of Okanogan County, which was created in 1888 from Stevens County, and is an Indian word for "rendezvous." It is situated in the north central part of the state west of the Cascades and bounded on the north by Canada. In 1859 the county experienced a gold rush when placer gold was discovered on the Similkameen River. Steamboats reached the town of Okanogan two months of the year in the 1880s, but it was not until 1915 that the county had regular transportation service when the Great Northern Railroad ran a branch line from Wenatchee to Okanogan. Today, mining is an important part of the county's economy along with timber products and agriculture.

Courthouse: 149 Third North, Okanogan 98840, SCAN 336-1228, FAX 509-422-3523. Area: 5,300.6 square miles. State Ranking: 1st. 1993 Population: 35,400. Unincorporated: 21,052. Incorporated: 14,348. Density: 6.7 persons per square mile. **Cities and Towns**: Brewster, Conconully, Coulee Dam, Elmer City, Nespelem, Okanogan, Omak, Oroville, Pateros, Riverside, Tonasket, Twisp, Winthrop. **Principal Economic Activities**: Wood products, agriculture. **Points of Interest**: Fort Okanogan, Grand Coulee Dam, St. Mary's Mission, Colville Indian Reservation.

Okanogan County Courthouse.

Climate: (Okanogan - elevation 835)

	Jan	Apr	Jul	Oct
Max Temp. F°	31.0	67.8	92.1	65.2
Min Temp.	17.4	38.4	57.9	38.6
Mean Temp.	24.2	53.1	75.0	51.8
Precipitation	1.23"	.88"	.28"	.89"

Average Annual Maximum Temperature: 63.2
Average Annual Minimum Temperature: 38.2
Annual Mean Temperature: 50.7
Average Annual Precipitation: 11.65"

Omak (OH-mak, Elevation 750, Population 4,150) Cheek by jowl with Okanogan and nearly twice its population, it has nearly swallowed its closest neighbor. A substantial part of the town rests on the Colville Indian Reservation. Possessing an economy built on timber products, tree fruit and livestock production, it is the shopping and business hub of the north central Washington area.

Most anywhere in the West when you say "Omak," you also add "Stampede" and then "Suicide Race." This famous event closes out each day of the rodeo (always the second week in August) and has been a tradition for over a half a century. A rite of passage for the local tribal members, the race hurtles down a steep bluff, crosses the river and finishes inside the rodeo arena in front of the attending crowd. It's hell on men and horses, and on animal activists, but there are tales of men who have escaped the law and risked recapture just to ride in this race.

Once head of navigation and a bustling supply center for the upper valleys, the little town of **Riverside** now sleeps quietly in a corner of the Okanogan like a cat in the sun. When the railroads killed steamboat traffic the economy drowned, perhaps not for the worst. One account reads: "it has an air of rustic serenity, emphasized by yellow roses and hollyhocks and vine-covered houses." Beats "bustling" any day of the week!

Riverside Park.

Around Short Mountain the highway turns up Wagon Road Coulee, crosses the river and straightlines into **Tonasket** (Tuhn-as-kuht, Elevation 900, Population 985). Here U.S. 97 and Highway 20 part company, as 20 climbs east to the Okanogan Highlands, leaving 97 to work its way alone to the Canadian border. Named for an Okanogan chief who relocated his band to Curlew on the Colville Reservation, Tonasket stretches along a narrow shelf next to the river beneath the rising hills. The chief ceded his land for the promise of a boarding school for natives, a doctor, a gristmill, a sawmill and a $100-a-year stipend. The school burned down after a couple of years, and the chief eventually sold his rights to the town. North of Tonasket the road remains straight but the river begins to twist and writhe out through the Okanogan trench.

Tonasket apple crates. In New York City, this might be art.

219~

At **Ellisford**, Father Etienne de Rouge ensured job security by rebuilding the church that seemed to burn down every few years. The surviving bell is still housed in town. Another denomination, the Dunkards, moved first to Pennsylvania then here during World War I to escape religious persecution. They celebrated love feasts and refrained from oaths, lawsuits and military service, practices that were ridiculed and condemned. (Of course they were persecuted, how could they not be for such deviant behavior?)

The last stretch (or the first depending on your direction) of U.S. 97 passes through **Oroville** (Or-vil, Elevation 918, Population 1,515). The community sits above where the Similkameen and Okanogan rivers conjoin. Lake Osoyoos laps placidly against the northern edge of town. A roaring start as a mining district (one store, 20 saloons), eventually gave way to the present-day base of fruit processing. Agriculture and cross-border traffic aid the economy. The original "Oro" (gold) discoveries were enhanced by a number of diverse mineral strikes. Pure epsom salts (magnesium sulfate), silver, lead, and arsenic as well as limestone and terra-cotta clay have been taken out in commercial quantities. A Kalispel Indian word for narrows, *soyoos* and an Irishman's "O" combined to form the name given to the lake that borders the town and crosses the border (most of the water is in Canada). A broad flat that once held Indian encampments and a place to race their horses is now the location of **Veterans' Memorial State Park**, a popular stopover for inter-country travelers, and just a stone's throw to the U.S.-Canadian border and the end of U.S. Highway 97. ⌘

US **Highway 97A** from a junction with U.S. Highways 2 and 97 in Wenatchee, north along the Columbia River through Entiat, Winesap and Chelan to a junction with U.S. 97. Route length: 40 miles.

This highway is an alternate to U.S. 97 and runs along the west side of the Columbia River, passing through fruit orchards and the shadows of steep hillsides. Three miles north of Wenatchee, the **Ohme Gardens** are perched high on a rocky bluff overlooking the Wenatchee Valley, the Columbia River and the Cascades. The nine-acre alpine garden is surrounded by tall evergreen trees that sharply contrast the adjacent, barren hills. Flower-lined paths wind between small ponds, rugged rock formations and low-growing alpine plants.

Four miles further, an equally impressive collection of meticulous gardens and lawns helps reduce the grey starkness of **Rocky Reach Dam**, a 2,860-foot-long structure comprising over one million cubic feet of concrete. A fish ladder makes a long, graceful curve from the base of the dam and rises to its upper level.

The Chelan County Public Utility District began construction on the dam October 2, 1956 and dedicated it July 20, 1969 with seven generating units. There are now 11 units with a generating capacity of 1,287,000 kilowatts. The dam features several exhibits of geological and archaeological significance, a Nez Perce Indian portrait collection, the "Look a Salmon in the Eye" fish viewing room, and two interpretive museums; Gallery of Electricity and Gallery of the Columbia.

Continue one mile to **Lincoln Rock** and notice its eerie resemblance to Abraham Lincoln. **Lincoln Rock State Park** is located across the river and accessible by bridge.

The waters flowing beside **Entiat** (EN-tee-at, Elevation 800, Population 465), "rapid water," are calm now, but before dams blocked the river the town was accurately named. For years, treacherous rocks and strong currents combined to

Lincoln look-alike.

cause numerous shipwrecks. Follow the Entiat River Road from town into the rugged and bountiful Entiat Valley, long known as the "Gateway to Sportsmen's Paradise."

A historical marker four miles north of Entiat designates **Earthquake Point**, the site of a violent 1872 earthquake. The quake caused a massive landslide, stopping the flow of the Columbia River for several hours until a 15-foot wall of water broke through.

A few miles past **Winesap**, named for the predominant type of apple in the area, the road departs from the river and heads north. It is possible to reach Lake Chelan via State Highway 971, or continue eight miles along U.S. 97A through the Knapp Coulee, the more direct route to **Chelan** (she-LAN, Elevation 1,100, Population 3,150), two miles west of the Columbia River at the southeast tip of Lake Chelan.

Town of Chelan and lake circa 1905.

Alexander Ross and David Thompson first explored the area in 1811 looking to expand their fur trading territory. They found not only friendly natives in the Tsill-ane tribe, but a spectacular and isolated location. Repeated attempts over the next 50 years to connect the lake with a road failed due to the severity of the terrain. Even the military outpost of Camp Chelan lasted less than a year when transporting men and supplies became a battle in itself.

But while the steep, wooded hills offered challenges, they also presented opportunities. Ample resources existed for logging and mining — if only one could reach them. Attempts to access the bounty of thick forest required a creative approach, bringing about long slides and chutes that sent logs racing down hillsides and splashing into the lake below where they were loaded onto waiting boats. Minor logging companies began operations after reservation lands were opened in 1886, but transportation remained a problem. Reliable railroad service did not exist until 1914. Much of the surrounding area now falls within National Wilderness boundaries, and thus off-limits to logging.

The first major industry arrived with J. Harry Holden in 1896, who staked and dug the Holden Mine. Nearly all of the copper, 50% of the gold and 40% of all silver in the state came from these mines during the 1930s and 40s, bringing statewide exposure to the area for something more than the scenery. The mine employed over 400 local residents and generated a mill capacity of nearly 2,000 tons a day, shouldering much of the town's economy during the peak of the company's production. When the mine closed in 1960, the buildings were donated to the Lutheran Church and converted into the Holden Village Retreat Center.

Chelan's economy is now primarily grounded in apple-harvesting and tourism. In 1887, two years prior to the town's platting, Richard Hinton Lord planted the first apple orchard, introducing an industry which has grown steadily for over a century. Orchards covering nearly 10,000 acres of shoreline produce world-famous apples, and some farmers swear the secret lies in the purity of the ice-cold lake water used to irrigate the trees. Smaller groves of cherries, pears, apricots and peaches are nestled among the apple orchards.

A glance is all that's required to see why tourism is big business here. Wedged among the Cascade Mountains, the deep green of thick forested slopes is highlighted against the backdrop of glacial peaks and snow-capped mountains. In spots, waves splash against rocky, arid cliffs that rise hundreds of feet from the water. Another glance reveals the abundant shops, restaurants, hotels and resorts that welcome hordes of vacationers, and their wallets, each year.

Still, it is the presence of **Lake Chelan** that accounts for the annual influx of tourists. As far back as 1888, boat trips around the lake began with the launching of the wood-powered steamer the *Belle of Chelan*. Twelve years later the original *Lady of the Lake* began her runs. By 1946, the boat was making daily mail, passenger and freight service. A 100-foot cruise ship dubbed *Lady of the Lake II* started tours in 1990, creating a wake that during hot, dry summer months, speed-boats and jet skis must negotiate. Countless kayaks, paddle-boats and canoes also compete for a space on the water.

The lake is not only beautiful, but geologically interesting. During the last ice age a gigantic glacier receded northward, straightening

Lady of the Lake on Lake Chelan from 1900 to 1915. A round trip took 8 to 10 cords of wood.

223~

the curved valley and carving a deep depression now filled by the lake. Located in one of the deepest gorges in North America, Lake Chelan is fed by 27 glaciers and 59 streams. Chelan is a native word for "deep water," and at 1,486 feet, it is the third deepest lake in the United States behind Crater Lake (1,962 feet) in Oregon and California's Lake Tahoe (1,645 feet). Shaped like a long, thin ribbon and fjord-like in appearance, the lake stretches for 55 miles and is no more than one mile wide.

Roads edge only the northern and southern extremities of the lake, leaving the majority of the shorefront accessible only by boat, so isolation is still the rule for parts of Lake Chelan. An example of this solitude is found at the remote wilderness community of **Stehekin** (Stuh-hee'-kin), located at the northwestern end of the lake. The word means "the way through," a reference to Indians who camped here while traveling the east-west route through the Cascade Mountains. The only way through now is by boat or floatplane.

Hotel Field in 1906 at the head of Lake Chelan.

Originally discovered by gold miners, the tiny outpost is a throwback to simpler times. The secluded spot was not actually settled until John Horton, a Civil War veteran, arrived in the mid-1880s. Prior to the 1950s, there was rarely any exchange of money, and the barter system was standard practice to Stehekin inhabitants. The 100 or so current year-round residents remain self-sufficient; they grow their own food, make their own clothing, maintain their own equipment, use wood as their primary source of heat and continue to barter on a small scale. When the store closes at the onset of winter, a sign in the window reads, "Open Next Spring." Fortunately, residents are able to send a grocery list and a blank check to the store in Chelan for their order to be filled. Their groceries are then picked up and delivered by boat. Phones are scarce in Stehekin, lest the ringing disturb the pristine wilderness and primitive character.

Back at the "civilized" end of the lake U.S. 97A heads northeast of Chelan to rejoin U.S. 97, already in progress. ⁓

S tate **Highway 99** from Fife north via Federal Way, SeaTac, Seattle and Lynnwood to a junction with Interstate 5 in Everett. Route length: 55 miles.

One claim that can be made about Highway 99 is that it has character, loads of it. The endless string of stoplights and relentless traffic jams allows the frustrated driver to soak in an eclectic mix of used car lots, fast food joints, pawn shops, funeral parlors, strip clubs, taverns and hole-in-the-wall diners.

A typical stretch of Highway 99.

Before urbanization took over the road like cheatgrass invades a farmer's fields, Highway 99 was the main and fastest route up the state's population spine. I-5 has since taken over the thoroughfare role.

The region's history is mostly discussed along I-5 from Tacoma to Everett. ⁓

S tate **Highway 100** from a junction with U.S. Highway 101 in Ilwaco south to Fort Canby State Park then north back to Ilwaco. Route length: six miles.

Beginning at the western edge of Ilwaco, this hairpin loop covers the extreme southwestern tip of the state, highlighted by dramatic, lofty views of the mouth of the Columbia River and Pacific Ocean waves crashing against rocky cliffs. The cape is defined by a wildness that is no less apparent now than it must have been two centuries ago when British and American vessels roamed the West Coast, eyes trained for requisition. From a navigational standpoint, the weather is consistently unfavorable, if not unbearable; the wind howls with a vengeance, a moist blanket of creeping, soupy fog rolls in almost daily and the currents are among the most feared on the Pacific coast. But in spite of all the climatic rage, or perhaps because of it, this finger of land between river and ocean retains a rare rugged beauty.

Take Highway 100 (Fort Canby Road) from Ilwaco along the shore of **Baker Bay**, a protected cove that elicits a sigh of relief from captains entering the mouth of the Columbia River. The timing and discovery of the bay is an interesting twist in American history, and one that could have changed the boundaries of the United States. There is significant evidence that suggests British Captain James Baker discovered the mouth of the Columbia prior to Captain Robert Gray, (it does, after all, bear his name), but no documented proof is available. His ship, *Jenny*, was rumored to be in the slave running business, a venture formally condemned by the British government, and so Baker was ordered to refrain from keeping a captain's log or discussing his travels. As a result, Gray's find was deemed the official discovery and the land fell under American control.

In 1848, Congress created the Life Saving Rescue Team (a forerunner of the modern-day U.S. Coast Guard) to patrol U.S. shores in search of shipwrecks, and in 1874 a unit was commissioned to Baker Bay. The national Motor Lifeboat School operates from this station because the consistently turbulent weather offers the ultimate training for life saving exercises. The station can be seen from the highway, but it is not open to the public.

Follow the signs along Fort Canby Road to the **Lewis and Clark Interpretive Center**, which details each stage of the explorers' epic wilderness trek, along with exhibits explaining the numerous shipwrecks and military activity in the area.

William Clark.

The walls of the interpretive center are covered with photographs, murals, maps and quotes from members of the Lewis and Clark party (formally termed the Corps of Volunteers for Northwest Discovery), outlining the difficulty and significance of their heroic efforts to stretch the boundaries of the U.S.

In January of 1803, President Thomas Jefferson sent a secret memo to Congress requesting $2,500 to finance a mission to the Pacific Ocean in order to claim territory and assess natural resources; although he "officially" told wary foreign powers the expedition was strictly for scientific research and "literary purposes."

The **Lewis and Clark Expedition** was one of the most dramatic and significant episodes in U.S. history (and no small event in the history of Washington state, either). Beyond a doubt, it stands as our nation's epic in documented exploration of the American West. In two years (1804-06), the 33 individuals who made up the expedition party fired the imagination of the American people and made them aware of the full sweep of the continent on which they lived.

In 1803, President Thomas Jefferson had sent James Monroe and Robert R. Livingston to France to finalize a deal that enabled the U.S. to purchase New Orleans and western Florida for $2 million. Much to the envoys' surprise, the normally aggressive Napoleonic French seemed to view the vast Louisiana territory (recently acquired in a secret deal with Spain) as more of a burden than a benefit, and offered to sell the enormous 838,000-square-mile region for $15 million. The resulting Louisiana Purchase — extending from the Mississippi River to the Rocky Mountains, and from the Gulf of Mexico to British North America — doubled the area of the United States!

Although Jefferson had previously proposed exploring the West, the consummation of the Louisiana Purchase provided the impetus to move forward with large-scale settlement. A primary objective was to find a practical transportation (and hence, trade) link between the Louisiana Territory and the "Oregon Country," claimed by the U.S. following Captain Robert Gray's discovery of the mouth of the Columbia in 1792.

The expedition was more than just geographic exploration. President Jefferson was also interested in information on the resources and native inhabitants of the new territory. The party was instructed to scientifically observe and, if possible, collect plant, animal, and mineral specimens; record weather data; study native cultures; conduct diplomatic councils with the tribes;

Meriwether Lewis.

map geographic features "of a permanent kind" along their route; and record all important observations and events in a daily journal.

By choosing Meriwether Lewis and William Clark as co-commanders of the expedition, Jefferson gave the challenging and risky undertaking its best chance of success. Lewis, born and raised in Charlottesville, Virginia, had been a boyhood neighbor of Jefferson's. In 1794, at the age of 20, Lewis joined the militia, where he served under Lieutenant William Clark, four years his senior. Seven years later, Lewis, by then an Army captain, received a letter from President-elect Jefferson offering him a position as secretary-aide. Two years after that, once Congress had appropriated funds for the expedition, Lewis was commissioned one of its leaders.

Both Lewis and Clark were experienced woodsmen/frontiersmen and seasoned officers who were cool in crises and quick to make decisions. In temperament, however, they were opposites. Lewis was introverted, melancholic and moody; Clark was extroverted, even-tempered and gregarious. The better-educated and more refined Lewis, who, like Jefferson, possessed a philosophical, romantic, and speculative mind, was at home with abstract ideas. Clark, on the other hand, was more of a practical man of action. Each supplied vital qualities that balanced their partnership.

The epic journey began in Washington, D.C. on July 5, 1803, and eventually reached the Missouri River, where in two pirogues and six dugout canoes the party forged westward through country "on which the foot of civilized man had never trodden [sic]." Whether on foot, horseback, or by boat, the journey would take the explorers over massive mountain ranges, across seemingly endless plains, through dense forests, and against powerful currents of raging water. Hunger, fatigue, privation, and sickness were often the order of the day.

While wintering at Fort Mandan, North Dakota, Lewis and Clark recruited French-Canadian fur trader Toussaint Charbonneau and his Shoshoni wife, Sacajawea (together with their newborn son, Jean Baptiste), as interpreters. Sacajawea's contribution to the ultimate success of the mission was significant. In his journal, Lewis noted the importance of her presence when the party found itself in potentially hostile territory: "This Indian woman . . . confirmed those people of our friendly intentions, as no woman ever accompanies a war party of Indians in this quarter."

By mid-October, 1805, the party finally reached one of "the great objectives of our journey," the Columbia River, near what is now the Tri-Cities area. A month later they reached the "great Pacific Ocean which we been so long anxious to see [sic]." The north shore of the Columbia estuary proved sparse of game and too exposed to winter storms, so they crossed to the south side of the river into what would later be Oregon. There they constructed Fort Clatsop near Astoria. On March 23, 1806, after the disappointment of failing to make contact with coastal trading vessels, the party began the long trip home.

In the two years, four months, and nine days of the expedition, the Lewis and Clark party traveled more than 8,000 miles.

After completing the expedition, Clark was promoted to Brigadier General and appointed to the Superintendency of Indian Affairs. He lived a long and productive life, dying at age 68. Lewis, on the other hand, who served briefly as governor of the Louisiana Territory, died tragically (possibly suicide) three years after finishing the expedition. Thomas Jefferson is credited with the Latin inscription on Lewis's tombstone: *Immaturus obi: sed tu felicior annos Vive meos, Bona Republica! Vive tuos.* (I died young: but thou, O Good Republic, live out my years for me with better fortune.)

A short walk from the Lewis and Clark Interpretive Center is **Cape Disappointment Lighthouse,** completed in 1856 after three years of mishap and misfortune. Before its creation, men were sent ashore to set the tops of trees on fire to help guide ships onto the harbor, often with the assistance of local Indians. The first vessel carrying construction materials for the lighthouse arrived on September 18, 1853 and was forced to wait eight days for a pilot to arrive to lead the ship in. Immediately after the captain was taken aboard the current turned ugly, forcing the ship into the breakers. The *Oriole* sank along

Waikiki Beach and Lighthouse at Cape Disappointment.

with its entire cargo. Then, after a year of waiting for new supplies, it was discovered that the lighting system ordered from France was not compatible with the structure and needed rebuilding. Halfway through the second attempt the tower was determined too small and the present materials inferior. Back to the drawing board. The construction of two other state lighthouses was eventually halted so the money could be re-appropriated to raze and raise for a third and final time. Talk about your tax dollars at work. Cape Disappointment Lighthouse was originally scheduled to be the first on the West Coast but these lengthy delays allowed a lighthouse in California to win this distinction. It is, however, the oldest in Washington state.

The views from **Cape Disappointment** are hardly indicative of the name; from here one can peek down the river corridor, out across the Pacific and over to the low mountains of the Oregon coast. Some of the best vantage points come along the stretch of highway running along the bluff on the east side of the cape.

Notorious sandbars and veiled currents make the transfer from ocean to river precarious even in fair weather, but captains with a schedule to keep and money to pocket often risked their lives to save time, and ended up losing both. Long considered the "Graveyard of the Pacific," the remains of over 2,000 vessels litter the sandy bottom to serve as unseen reminders of the mouth's deadly entrance and the need to navigate on its terms.

Rusted portions of one such vessel, the British *Peter Iredale*, can still be seen permanently wedged into the surf. Another sunken British ship, the *Isabella*, went down in 1829 and was discovered in 1985 when a fisherman snagged his nets on the hull. After close underwater inspection, it was found that the wooden vessel was nearly completely intact, along with the over 10 tons of cargo and trade items she carried. The archaeological treasure is now on the National Register of Historic Places.

Mariners would regularly wait as long as six weeks for a safe chance to enter the river mouth, often to find they had not waited long enough. Commander Charles Wilkes aptly described the Columbia sandbar when he wrote: "Mere description can give little idea of the terrors of the bar . . . one of the most fearful sights that can possibly meet the eye." And he should know. His ship *Peacock* (under the command of Lieutenant William L. Hudson) ran aground and sank in 1841 while attempting to round the cape, earning him the probably unwanted distinction of having the scene named for his lost vessel. Peacock Spit is still known as the most deadly section of the Columbia River sandbar. With 50-mile-an-hour winds and 20-foot swells not uncommon, even the Coast Guard refuses to risk navigation in these waters except in cases of extreme emergency. Such treacherous conditions caused many explorers to doubt whether the area surrounding the Columbia would ever be settled. The British abstained from haggling for the coastline when they decided they did not want to bother setting up a port at such a deadly location, effectively conceding it to the United States by looking north and choosing Port Vancouver instead.

The name Cape Disappointment stems from the experiences of Englishman John Meares, who followed the trail documented by the Spaniard Bruco Heceta in 1775. Failing to discover the mouth of the Columbia in 1788, Meares hastily dismissed it: "Disappointment continued to accompany us . . . we are now with safety able to assert that no such river exists as laid down in the Spanish chart." Four years later, 34-year-old Captain Robert Gray located the elusive river (presumably on a fair-weather day) and named it for his vessel, the *Columbia Rediviva.*

The end of the cape marks the spot where members of the Lewis and Clark Expedition first touched the waves of the Pacific Ocean in November of 1805. Shortly after reaching the long-awaited destination President Jefferson had set for them, the mood soured as the realities of the harsh climate set in. Sounding less than enthusiastic in a journal entry dated November 22, 1805, Captain Clark documented the weather that continually pounded them:

> A moderate rain all the last night with wind . . . a little before Daylight the wind which was from the S.S.E. blew with Such Violence that we wer almost overwhelmed with water blown from the river, this Storm did not sease at day but blew with nearly equal violence throughout the whole day, accompanied with rain. O! how horriable is the day . . . [sic].

The strategic location as the mouth of the Columbia River made Cape Disappointment a natural choice for inclusion in the first wave of the Coast Artillery Defense. As part of this effort to secure U.S. shores, **Fort Canby** was built in 1852 on the rocky bluff to serve as a protective and watchful eye. Originally established as a military reserve, the fort later received a supply of cannons at the outbreak of the Civil War to prevent Confederate gunboats access to the Columbia; a fear that was never realized. Gun batteries and long-range artillery were later added to the grounds, but the fort was deactivated shortly after the end of World War II without ever experiencing battle.

In 1957, the 584 acres covering the southernmost point of the peninsula underwent a peaceful conversion and became **Fort Canby State Park**, and the now defused gun batteries are open to exploration. Nearly 200 campsites are available, along with hiking trails through old-growth forest of 300- to 500-year-old Sitka spruce and hemlock trees. Beaches are open for swimming, boating and fishing.

On the return trip, follow Robert Gray Drive north to **North Head Lighthouse**. Facing the ocean and on the opposite side of the cape from Cape Disappointment Lighthouse, this accompanying beacon was built in 1898 after captains had difficulty determining which headland signaled the entrance to the river. The close proximity of these two lighthouses further stresses the navigational nightmare presented here, especially when poor weather limits visibility. The brightly-painted red and white tower is a short walk from the highway. Standing in front of this lighthouse affords a panoramic view of the Pacific Ocean horizon and the Olympic Mountains to the north. Layer after layer of waves break violently against sandbars, recently-constructed jetties, and eventually the jagged rocks directly below. From this perspective you can actually see the zigzag currents at work, where even the breakers seem to be in a state of confusion.

To complete the loop, follow Robert Gray Drive back to Ilwaco and a connection with U.S. 101. ℭఔ

North Head Lighthouse illuminates a navigational nightmare.

US **Highway 101** from the Columbia River and Chinook west through Ilwaco and Seaview then north through South Bend, Raymond, Cosmopolis, Aberdeen, Hoquiam and Humptulips. West to Queets, north through Forks and then east through Sappho, Port Angeles, Sequim and Blyn to Gardiner. South from Gardiner through Quilcene, Brinnon, Lilliwaup, Hoodsport, Shelton and into Olympia and a junction with Interstate 5. Route length: 363 miles.

The Columbia River bends and breaks 1,243 miles before pouring 150 billion gallons of water a day into the Pacific Ocean. Transfers of this magnitude are rarely placid, and this violent collision is no exception. Nearly four miles wide at the mouth and dragging a state's worth of momentum, one of the country's largest rivers rams head-long into the ocean tide, causing swirling currents and continually shifting sandbars. Crossing the four-and-half-mile Astoria-Megler bridge that connects the western edges of Oregon and Washington affords a lofty view of the turbulent water, while the wind whips at such a clip it causes a car to shake flimsily.

U.S. 101 begins its tour of the coast here on the river heading north past crooked pilings and the rotted remains of a ferry dock rising from the waves. These timbers mark where the town of **McGowan** once stood and where in 1853 Patrick McGowan started the state's first salmon-packing company. The company proved more successful than the settlement and moved its headquarters to Ilwaco at the turn of the century, effectively turning McGowan into a ghost town. All that remains to-day are two ragged buildings and the stately McGowan home.

A mile down the road a tunnel runs through rock, above which sits **Fort Columbia**, constructed in 1898 at the beginning of the Spanish-American War and active during World War II.

Fort Columbia State Park Lighthouse.

The closest the fort ever came to experiencing an actual battle came when a Japanese submarine fired upon Fort Stevens just five miles across the river in Oregon. The land is now **Fort Columbia State Park and Interpretive Center**, complete with historic walk and exhibits on early Northwest exploration and history of the Chinook Indian tribe.

233~

Next door you'll find **Chinook**, a classic fishing village ideally located at the aqua turnpike between river and ocean. Chinook was given the county seat in 1851, reflecting local expectations of becoming a fishing and transportation hub for the newly exploited West Coast. At that time salmon runs were thick and steady, and fish weighing 75 pounds or more common. The only real concern was how to haul them in with the greatest speed. Efficiency was maximized with the advent of fixed rigs, a type of fish trap that funneled them along a channel of pilings into a pot which they could enter but not exit. Due to its staggering catch capacity, this quickly became the preferred fishing method of the area, bringing equally staggering economic prosperity and a claim to the highest income per capita of any town in the U.S. Several ornate old homes hearken back to that prosperous era.

In an attempt to equalize give and take, the first state-run salmon hatchery began on the Chinook River in 1895, but the effort hardly counteracted the increasing number of traps. A prophetic article from the *South Bend Journal* of 1910 discussed the effect of the hatchery on the future of salmon fishing:

> It is thus noticeable that the hatcheries are more than maintaining their average annual output (31 million fry per year), which is in itself a hopeful sign of a reasonably wholesome condition, showing that the salmon supply can be maintained provided the advancing wave of civilization does not engulf the industry with its destructive tendencies.

The hatchery now operates as a non-profit organization. A fish conservation act outlawed fixed rigs in 1934, permanently halting momentum and leaving only the symmetrical pilings as a reminder of glory days. Salmon processing and packing is still the primary industry, approached with a mixture of necessity and nostalgia.

Continue along the shoreline to **Ilwaco** (il-WAH-koh, Elevation 16, Population 890). Originally settled in the 1840s, it was not until the 1870s that the fishing town in-waiting accumulated a significant population. Known in early times for its rustic, if not primitive, accommodations and services, rowdy fist-fight atmosphere and a male-female ratio heavily on the side of the men, prosperity eventually arrived with the dual saviors of the railroad and the fishing industry.

Early funding for the town (named in 1876 for Elowahka Jim, the last Chinook Chief in the area) came from an unlikely source. Part myth and part miser, Scottish-born James Johnson took a donation claim in 1845 on the acreage that now includes most of Ilwaco. It was known that Johnson possessed a fortune of some $20,000 in gold slugs which he had buried somewhere on his land, but the origin of this treasure was open to debate. One story maintained that Johnson was

once the captain of a ship carrying a cargo of gold when he inten-
tionally wrecked the vessel and escaped with the goods. Another
version traces the path of the gold as it slipped through several hands
on its way to Johnson. Allegedly, a vessel of 49ers arrived victorious at
Ilwaco, and when coming ashore with their prize their small boat
capsized, killing all but one of the men. Indians who witnessed the
event then finished off the survivor and took the gold. When Johnson
caught wind of this he began selling illegal whiskey to natives at prices
as high as an ounce of gold for one pint of his home-grown moonshine. He kept them in a state of perpetual inebriation until he had
collected the entire booty.

Whatever the source, some of this wealth trickled down to the
fledgling town. On several occasions Johnson lent portions of this
money to Bill McCarty, a civic-minded Irishman who settled his claim
a year prior to Johnson. McCarty, the son-in-law of Chief Carcowan of
the Chehalis tribe, used these funds and his Indian connections to
start up fishing and logging companies which eventually brought
income and new settlers to the area. When Johnson drowned in the
Columbia River in 1855, a search began for the hidden treasure that
would continue for over a century. Since he never confessed its location to anyone — including his wife and sons — fortune seekers
fueled the myth by digging countless holes and concocting theories
long after the land had been divided. One man was granted permission to try his luck with the aid of a bulldozer.

An influx of entrepreneurial spirit thrust Ilwaco into the role of the
area's transportation center in the 1870s. One such forward-thinking
individual was **Lewis Alfred Loomis**, a businessman who traveled
westward from New England in 1872. After starting a steamship company in 1875, he secured a mail contract and used stagecoaches to
bring the region's parcels in from Olympia. Finding this method too
slow, he began raising money for a railroad line in 1882. At a time
when nearly every town on the Washington coast was scrambling for
the sacred locomotive, Loomis forged his own by sheer will and a
refusal to wait for larger existing lines to arrive. The success of the
line increased in proportion to its length; trees cut to make way for
tracks were used to build crossties on the spot, while a locomotive
and flatcars followed close behind with the rest of the materials. In
addition to mail, the railroad was commissioned to move salmon,
oysters, clams, cranberries, timber and even passengers and livestock.
Fully completed in 1889 and named the Ilwaco Railroad and Steam
Navigation Company, it earned the distinction of being America's
westernmost line. Summer brought the heaviest business when it
shuttled hordes of inlanders to the coast for summer vacations; some
even brought their dairy cows along for the holiday.

Surprisingly, the railroad encountered little opposition from larger
rail companies as they forged ahead with their plans. Complaints

usually were made by homesteaders displeased with watching and hearing a train rolling through their front yard. One such dissenter staged a primarily symbolic protest by building a fence across the track in the middle of the night. In the morning, the dispute was settled with brute force and the train's own version of Manifest Destiny when the wooden fence failed to stone-wall the locomotive.

The proud but unorthodox Ilwaco Railroad and Steam Navigation Company.

As might be expected of such an unorthodox operation, service on the railroad was casual and quirky; trainmen wore no uniforms; a schedule was determined by tide tables (in some areas the track was laid on pilings directly over the water); and trains regularly picked up folks at virtually any location, especially women with young children who often rode free. It also featured luxuries rarely found on modern lines, including geese and turkey hunting from passenger car windows (the train would halt so those with good aim could collect their dinner) and a stop at "Loomis Station" located suspiciously close to L.A. Loomis' front door. Irritated passengers often waited for Loomis to finish a meal or get dressed before he would board the train and allow it to continue. Dubbed the "Clamshell Railroad" and the "Irregular, Rambling and Never-get-there Railroad," Loomis sold his empire to the Oregon Railroad and Navigation Company in 1900 for $142,000 and retired. The advent of the automobile drove the line to obscurity in 1930.

Paralleling the rise of rail transit was the emergence of wholesale salmon fishing, the nerve-center and life-blood of early Ilwaco. The continuous rows of split pilings that extend from the shore are the skeletal remains of a once rabid machine known as the fishing industry. Up until the late 1920s, the Columbia River swelled with salmon rushing in and out of the ocean in numbers that can only be imagined now, while men stood poised to haul in the enormous bounty. A single boat could often bring in 100 large salmon a day. At times the generosity of the sea was so overwhelming that entire catches had to be dumped overboard because plants could not process them fast enough. The work was truly wretched, exhausting and downright dangerous (19 men drowned in just two days in May of 1880), but it was the way of life for the residents of Ilwaco, and on several occasions violence erupted to maintain it.

US 101

Like the Native Americans before them, the first white fishermen used gill nets and drag seines to do their work. Profit-minded settlers then made improvements on these methods and brought in quantities of fish that shocked and impressed the Indians. One such method, horse seining, employed work horses to haul great stretches of camouflaged netting onto shore, where the catch was immediately loaded onto wagons and skiffs and delivered to canneries. As men, horses and fish struggled on the beaches, expansive gill nets crisscrossed sandbars like a gauntlet for the salmon's run to the sea.

In 1879 a technique was borrowed from the Great Lakes area when fish traps were introduced to the area. Within a decade, over 120 traps stood like pegs on the sandbars, stretching all the way back to the town of Chinook. This new method made a tight working condition even tighter, and the new powerhouse traps, coupled with existing nets, brought about record season catches. It also brought trouble.

Drag seine fishermen piling up a day's catch.

With the introduction of mechanized pile drivers, the timbers leading from shore became permanent fixtures in the sandbars and mudflats. Huge pots sat at the end of pilings to collect the constant salmon flow, and countless traps were dumped and refilled.The problem was not only that the riggings prevented the free movement of the gill-netters, but that they were often located at tried-and-true spots along the river. Their presence placed prime fishing

holes out of the reach of their nets, jeopardizing their production capacity and, in essence, the gill-netters way of life.

Armed with the distinction of being the first men on the river, the gill-netters declared war on the invading competition by sabotaging traps and terrorizing night watchmen instructed to guard fishing areas. This intimidation was often successful enough to cause some to seek out new employment and distant residences. The rough-and-tumble reality of Ilwaco took on new meaning in 1884, beginning 25 years of guerrilla attacks and increasingly bad-blood between rival fishermen. When the cost of damages continued to mount, armed ships began patrolling the harbor and several men were killed attempting to damage traps.

As if tensions were not high enough, a strike by gill-netters and trappers brought the Washington National Guard to the area. The troops stopped and inspected all boats entering and exiting the river mouth, incensing the fishermen and causing a new wave of defiant attacks against fish traps. One particularly rebellious contingent even proposed a midnight raid on the soldiers themselves, whom they considered to be traitorous cowards out of their element. Not to be outdone by their sea-going counterparts, strikes by cannery workers brought federal troops to Ilwaco to maintain the peace. Their stay served to defuse the violence, although tempers remained red-hot. The federal ban on traps in 1934 and the gradual disappearance of drag seines caused many fishermen to move elsewhere, returning Ilwaco to a quiet sea town. Fishing activity is mostly confined to the deep-sea and sport variety now, and efforts to attract tourists to the beaches are increasing.

Ilwaco in a time of peace.

From Ilwaco, continue north past the summer resort town of **Seaview** and east into water-logged farmland. The contrast between the east and west sides of the road offers a thumbnail sketch of the region. Steep hills on the eastern side appear untouched, blanketed by fallen trees and a mossy, tangled underworld. On the west side, lush lowlands, an occasional stately farmhouse or Scandinavian style barn and a modest bovine population dot the landscape. Some of the scattered farms on this thin patch of land between the Columbia River

~238

and the bay have been active in dairy farming and grain production for over two centuries. There is evidence of human exploitation, but surprisingly few people or homes, leaving the landscape both pristine and ravaged. The land opens to reveal hearty forests in the near distance that border large clear-cut sections laid in a checkerboard pattern. By the early 1920s it was estimated that 25 billion board feet of quality timber was available in the Willapa Bay area, and mills were capable of producing about one million board feet per day. The creation of the Willapa National Wildlife Refuge protects portions of this land now, while the rest is on its second or third cut.

A collection of small rivers and streams run off the hills and spread out like fingers to feed the flatlands that run east towards **Willapa Bay**. Fresh and salt water mingle at the mouths of these streams, bringing them under the influence of tides that fluctuate as much as 10 feet. At low tide the bay looks like a mudflat; high tide causes the rivers to spill over, creating a pattern of sloughs. During this time, branches from small, semi-submerged trees and long thin reeds extend from the water, and cattle grazing in fields are surrounded by overflowing moats of irrigation ditches as if marooned.

A feeling of isolation is associated with this region, and **Long Island** is a reflection of that sentiment. Although located just a short distance from shore, portions of the seven-mile-long island are far removed from human civilization. Considered part of the **Willapa National Wildlife Refuge**, the island is a good example of land management, harboring red cedars up to an astonishing 1,000 years old, timber farms without a tree over 30 and a varied population of aquatic and migratory birds. Black bear, elk, deer, river otter and other wildlife coexist in a section of old-growth forest that has flourished without interruption for over 4,000 years. Steady rainfall and its location

The fertile mudflats of Willapa Bay separate lush vegetation and productive clam beds.

within a sheltered bay have helped spare this ancient cedar grove from the natural perils of fire and windstorms, making the southern part of the island one of the few coastal forests left in the state.

Chinook Indians hunted, fished and gathered shellfish on Long Island centuries before explorers arrived, but only one bona fide settlement was ever established. **Diamond City** was built on the northern tip of the island in 1867 for the sole purpose of harvesting oysters. And harvest they did. So thorough were these tideflat farmers that within 10 years the beds were systematically depleted. Named for the sparkle created when the sun struck the oyster shells at low tide, when the glitter eventually disappeared, the folks packed up and left and the town ceased to exist. Even less enduring were loggers who lived on houseboats and worked the area around 1900, but they too are long gone. The only way to reach the uninhabited island is by private boat.

The oyster also inspired the first permanent settlement along the shores of Willapa Bay. After stories of their abundance spread all the way to San Francisco, the schooner *Robert Bruce* arrived in 1851 in search of fortune, and while not the first to arrive, it was the first boat to stay. Not that they had much choice, considering the bizarre circumstances surrounding their landing site. An ongoing quarrel between the captain and the cook determined the location of what was to be known as **Bruceport**. This temperamental chef, angered at mounting insults and affronts, drugged the captain and crew via the stew, then set the ship ablaze and escaped in the only available row boat, never to be heard of again. Thanks to an ebb tide and a timely rescue by resident Indians, the unconscious men were saved, but their entire ship and cargo burned and sank.

Beached as they were, the "Bruce boys" proceeded with plans and set up shop where they stood, eventually constructing two hotels, a saloon (of course) and a schoolhouse. Indians employed by the outfit loaded oysters onto schooners bound for San Francisco, and for a spell Bruceport became a major contributor to the oyster boom that continued until 1880. By 1890 the town was just a memory, and all that remains is a roadside marker located miles from the original site.

As the bay narrows and meets the sheltered entrance of the Willapa River, two signs welcome you to **South Bend** (Elevation 11, Population 1,570). The first announces the town as "An ideal place to raise a family and a fine place to retire," while the second hails South Bend as "The Oyster Capital of the World." Two big claims for one small town, but they are not unsubstantiated. In reference to the first, a modest proportion of the population are indeed those happily unemployed, while many natives take pride in the fact that they have lived their entire lives in this scenic village. As far as the oyster proclamation is concerned, the significance of the mollusk can be seen everywhere; from clouds of seagulls descending on mountains of discarded shells to crushed-shell driveways and various landscaping uses that are the coastal alternative to beauty bark. Processing plants line the shore, where cranes hoist racks of oysters from boats and dump them on conveyor belts. Low tides reveal rows of stakes and pilings that mark the boundaries of oyster beds. A healthy industry boost occurred in 1986 when neutered oysters were developed, thus avoiding the loss of texture and flavor that comes with spawning and also allowing lucrative year-round harvests.

Founded in 1869 and later coined the "Baltimore of the West," the town's first 20 years were filled with equal parts anticipation, prosperity and disappointment. Sawmills rose almost immediately to take advantage of the quality spruce and cedar surrounding Willapa Bay, and a steady stream of schooners followed the narrow, S-shaped channel into the river to haul the goods away. The timber is on its second and third cut and not considered part of a national forest, so some of the problems that affect other logging communities on the coast do not apply here.

Echoing a recurring theme here in southwestern Washington, representatives from the Northern Pacific Railroad purchased land in South Bend with plans of connecting the Yakima Valley to the coast, inciting a riot of enthusiasm and town expansion. But as was often the case with railroad speculation, plans quickly changed. The national economic "Panic of 1893" brought the line to a halt in Centralia and froze hasty construction projects in their foundations.

Glimpses of prosperity, often known to attract a crowd, caused the population to swell from 150 to over 3,000 in the years just prior to the financial crash. With these new citizens came political aspirations, culminating in an 1892 ballot that proposed moving the county seat from Oysterville — located directly across Willapa Bay — to South Bend. When election results gave South Bend a suspiciously lopsided victory, fried Oysterville residents cried foul and refused to forfeit the official county seals and records. They complained, quite justifiably, that transient railroad workers had voted illegally to fix the outcome, thus making the election invalid. Ignoring their protests and a pending lawsuit, roughly 80 men from South Bend crossed the bay in two steamers on Sunday, February 5, 1893 while most of Oysterville's residents were in church. After eluding an armed guard by agreeing to buy a round of drinks in his tavern, the party proceeded to the courthouse. Brazened by a lack of resistance, the "invaders" looted the building like weekend Vikings until Auditor Phil D. Barney, brandishing a wooden chair leg, broke up the raiding party. The South Benders then collected the coveted paperwork (along with some furniture) and returned with the bureaucratic treasure. Some time later the election fraud was verified, but in the interest of practicality, little attention was paid this fact and the county seat remained in South Bend.

The **Pacific County Courthouse** (300 Memorial Avenue) was erected between April of 1910 and June of 1911 to accommodate the town's new civic responsibility. An impressive structure now on the National Historic Register, this two-story building is highlighted by a glass dome and immaculate landscaping, complete with pond and waterfall. Inside, murals depicting local scenes were painted by Bert Boxtodder, a jail inmate, in January of 1942. Locals have dubbed it "The Gilded Palace of Extravagance."

Sketch of the Pacific County Courthouse, the "Gilded Palace of Extravagance."

Pacific County: South Bend is the county seat of Pacific County, which was organized in 1851 by the Oregon Territorial Legislature from Lewis County. It is named for the Pacific Ocean and is located on the far southwest corner of the state facing the Pacific Ocean. The county around Willapa Bay was explored by Lewis and Clark in 1806 and during the state's territorial days was a key point in the Washington Territory's water and stagecoach transportation system. Today, Pacific County's economy is based on wood products, agriculture and fishing.

County Seat: 300 Memorial Avenue, South Bend 98586, FAX 206-875-9377. Area: 908.2 square miles. State Ranking: 30th. 1993 Population: 19,800. Unincorporated: 13,180. Incorporated: 6,620. Density: 21.8 persons per square mile. **Cities and Towns**: Ilwaco, Long Beach, Raymond, South Bend. **Principal Economic Activities**: Wood products, seafood processing, agriculture. **Points of Interest**: Willapa Bay, Fort Canby, Willie Keil's Grave, Willapa National Wildlife Refuge.

Climate: (Long Beach - elevation 10)

	Jan	Apr	Jul	Oct
Max Temp. F°	48.5	56.0	66.5	61.8
Min Temp.	35.5	40.3	50.3	43.9
Mean Temp.	41.8	48.0	58.4	52.8
Precipitation	12.62"	6.1"	1.09"	7.91"

Average Annual Maximum Temperature: 58.2
Average Annual Minimum Temperature: 42.4
Annual Mean Temperature: 50.2
Average Annual Precipitation: 80.79"

Long before the asphalt was laid for U.S. 101, an electric trolley nicknamed "Galloping Gertie" connected the four-mile-stretch between South Bend and its neighbor **Raymond** (Elevation 14, Population 2,870). In rainy weather water filled the depression where the tracks were laid, causing the little street car to lurch and bounce along, leaving a rooster tail of cascading mud behind. The line was laid in 1912 and ran on a street that today is graced by a giant logger carved from wood. This piece of work welcomes visitors to Raymond and offers a clue to the town's background, as do the heaping mounds of sawdust that are taller than most of the surrounding buildings.

When the ship *Willamette* wrecked in the shallow waters of the Willapa River in 1861, Captain John Vail decided it was fate and called the place home, planting the seeds that would grow into Raymond. Great crowds followed, filling the valley with smoke, noise and bustle. Logs were rafted downriver where pilings guided them to mills built on stilts on the water's edge. To maximize efficiency, the timber was then cut and loaded directly onto ships docked at connecting piers. When the Northern Pacific Railroad extended track though the area in 1895, logging efforts sharply increased with the opportunity for overland delivery. Typical of the haphazard rambling of the railroad, the settlement was poorly organized to meet the line heading to meet them, while next door, South Bend had called out the band and welcoming party years earlier only to watch the fickle engines pass them by.

With all the activity, no one had bothered to officially plat the town. This void was filled in 1904 by Leslie V. Raymond, the town's first postmaster. Taking a cue from the mills, the rest of the town was constructed on pilings above the changing tideflats. Stella Raymond, recalling the early wide-open town, wrote:

> First street. . .truly a fearful and wonderful street, with its board sidewalks and stilts with the growing number of stores, rooming houses, saloons and dance halls looking across a muddy and passable void — sometimes an unsteady patron of a saloon might topple into the void . . . there for removal by the city's unpaid street cleaner — the tides.

These "sea-legs" continued to support the residents until an ambitious and clever project was initiated which brought both financial and physical stability.

Following announcements that free waterfront sites were available, nearly 20 saw and pulp mills descended on Raymond shortly after it was platted. The land was free, but there was a catch — the sites were located on mudflats. Recognizing the land's potential (and since they were already there), mill owners pooled their money and filled the underside of the elevated town with sediment dredged from the harbor, enlarging the waterway and allowing the business area room to expand. This deeper, more accessible channel brought shipyards with it, adding to the town's first major boom. Pursuing the call of ready employment, wandering workers and journeymen poured into Raymond to earn a living, causing a severe housing shortage. Ragged tents and hurried shacks sprang up on the outskirts of town, where weathered displaced men drank, fought and plotted their next move.

During the Great Depression years, Raymond was forced to issue its own script. They called this currency oyster money, even though they had no industry of the kind there, and gave new meaning to the phrase "shelling out a few bucks." (Similarly, South Bend used wooden coins portraying fir trees and Ilwaco issued salmon money.) Further ingenuity helped the staggering economy in 1937 with the creation of the first stud mill, which cut timber into standard eight-foot 2x4s used for building houses. This idea quickly caught on, and soon similar mills sprang up across the peninsula. Eight-foot studs have since become lumberyard essentials.

Leaving Raymond, the next 18 miles lead north through hills that have made the area famous for logging. The two-lane highway passes assorted remnants of the timber industry: clear-cuts, tree farms, isolated patches of thick, mature trees and logging road intersections before meeting the Chehalis River in Cosmopolis.

Cosmopolis (Elevation 11, Population 1,375), Greek for "City of the World," established itself early on as the boot camp to the timber industry's army. Pioneers arrived in the early 1850s and platted the town in 1861. After failed attempts at tanning and a wheat mill, homesteaders looked to the forests for their livelihood and built the harbor's first water-powered sawmill in 1879. By the time the railroad arrived 13 years later, one company controlled the entire town, turning it into the production king of the region. This single business, the Grays Harbor Commercial Company, was interested only in harvesting logs for profit, not building a prosperous or well-rounded town. Competition was strongly discouraged, no land-grants were issued and wages were kept as low as possible. If a worker voiced a complaint or even spoke of organized labor, he was simply told to move on. But complaints were rare because it was well known that Cosmopolis offered one  thing: work, and plenty of it.

Loggers labeled the outfit the "Western Penitentiary" because of the poor working and living conditions and the armed guards hired to keep workers in line. Men were generally treated as necessary fuel for the constantly running machine; and the machine did not stop. Two shifts a day kept sawdust flying around the clock, and men were constantly pushed to increase production. Accidents were frequent and worker turnover was continuous; the prevailing attitude was to endure the work, pocket the money and get out — ideally with all fingers still attached. The only significant change came when the work day was trimmed down from ten hours to eight. Countless vagabonds, hard-luck hobos and green-horned loggers combined to form the cheapest labor force and most productive sawmill on Grays Harbor. There may not have been an annual

Cosmopolis February 25, 1855 Treaty Council.

company picnic on the river, but there were results and always an available job for those willing to accept the lower pay.

Cosmopolis was also the site of the first Treaty Council on February 25, 1855 between Isaac Stevens, Governor of the Washington Territory, and Indian representatives from the Quinault, Quileute, Chehalis, Queets, Satsop, Cowlitz and Chinook people. Despite a week of interpreted discussion, the meeting failed to produce a signed treaty or solve territorial disputes. The event marked a shift in attitude between natives and the encroaching whites. Settlers were seen as an aggressive enemy not to be trusted, and the Indians were considered a hindrance to progress. Only the most isolated of tribes were considered safe from the threat of reservation living. A mural depicting the scene is painted on the side of a water tower visible from the highway.

At the turn of the century Washington harvested over one-sixth of all timber cut in the United States. Railroads carried valuable Douglas fir, cedar, spruce and hemlock to the midwest, while ships set sail for markets around the world. Riding each boom and bust of this giant industry were the towns of **Aberdeen** (Elevation 12, Population 16,665) and Hoquiam, at one time two of the world's largest timber ports. Originally located four miles apart, their borders have since merged.

Similarly, their histories are meshed in the thick forest surrounding Grays Harbor. Both grew steadily around the mills that began operation in the mid-1880s, relying on the connecting Chehalis, Wishkah and Hoquiam rivers to transport logs felled deep in the hills to awaiting sawmills. And, of course, both lobbied furiously to sell land to the railroads. In the end, Aberdeen's ability to acquire a rail link just four years prior to Hoquiam made the difference, and subsequently Aberdeen, perhaps more than any other town in Washington, symbolizes the logging industry.

Sam Benn traveled from San Francisco to the Northwest in 1859 and reached a wooded wonderland beyond his comprehension. Through trades and purchases he acquired 740 acres of virgin forest land that included two powerful rivers and access to Grays Harbor for shipping. Aware of the wealth of natural resources, Benn encouraged settlement by offering free plots of land to perspective industrialists and businesses. The first to accept this generous offer was a large fish canning operation which opened its doors on the shores of the harbor in 1873. When the town

A look down Aberdeen's Heron Street. Notice the similarity of the automobiles.

was platted in 1884, a donated site was offered to anyone interested in setting up a sawmill. One taker arrived that same year and finished timber rolled from the mill before the structure's roof was completed.

Only the Northern Pacific's decision to stop first in Cosmopolis managed to slow growth during the town's early existence, but even this proved a minor, temporary setback. In an attempt to control their own destiny, several Aberdeen businessmen and mill owners purchased used railroad tracks and ties and donated them to the town to secure their own line. Benn then donated space for a mill yard and train depot, along with free land to those who supplied the labor. A short time later, this stretch of community track was given to the Northern Pacific which soon sent the first train. Aberdeen had struck pay dirt. This connection allowed timber to be sent to the international ports of Seattle and Tacoma, and to far-off cities like Chicago and San Francisco, ushering in a decade of growth and economic stability.

Not even devastating back-to-back fires in 1902 and 1903 halted Aberdeen's progress for long.

In 1900, six sawmills, two shingle mills and two shipyards lined Aberdeen's shores; the number jumped to 34 mills 10 years later. The town held around 17,000 people in 1910, large enough to have distinct neighborhoods and attractions. One section, dubbed "The Line," was a muddy street packed with saloons, brothels and an assortment of entertaining trouble. When overworked men came out of the backwoods or rubber-legged seamen hit land for the first time in weeks, they often went for a jaunt down "The Line" to ease, if not explode, their tension. A month's pay could easily be spent in a weekend worth of revelry. Whether it was whiskey, wanton women or a little five-card draw, plenty of ways to blow off steam were available at all hours, and drunkenness, fist fights and gunplay were as common as fir trees.

Districts of a seedier nature existed in most logging towns, but what separated Aberdeen from, say Cosmopolis, were the tailors, shop-keepers, teachers, farmers, fishermen and families that made up the rest of the permanent population. Salmon and clam canneries and a World War I-inspired shipbuilding industry rounded out the local economy.

The year 1926 saw a record timber crop of over one-and-a-half billion board feet slide beneath the saws of Aberdeen's mills and onto ships and steamers bound for ports across the globe. The year also signaled the beginning of the end. Although enormous harvests would continue until 1929, much of the clear-cutting proved unnecessary. Many ships built for the war effort were burned in the mid-1920s after lying dormant. The period of gluttony ended in 1930 when business dropped like a topped spruce and several mills closed operations for good, sending the unemployed in search of greener forests. Though logging would never be the same (not to mention the forests), new industries such as plywood plants, pulp and paper mills and chemical corporations rose from the sawdust to maintain a faint economic heartbeat in Aberdeen.

Due west on U.S. 101 is **Hoquiam** (HOH-kweeuhm, Elevation 14, Population 8,970), the older brother of Aberdeen that shared the same appetite, but never grew as tall. The name originates from *ho-qui-umpts*, meaning "hungry for wood," an Indian phrase that would adopt a whole new meaning once white settlers arrived. The Native Americans used the term to describe the ample driftwood that collected at the mouth of the Hoquiam River, but this naturally accumulated timber paled in comparison to the amount of wood that rushed from logjams leading to mills along the shoreline in Hoquiam.

First settled in 1859 by James Karr and four Scottish brothers by the name of Campbell, these men began grazing cattle on the tideflats, running a modest amount of beef and dairy products to Olympia and British Columbia. But the surroundings told them the future was in timber. What they did not know was that it would require the power of blackberry pie to jump start the logging industry.

When Ed Campbell became postmaster in 1867, his home on the Hoquiam River evolved into a bed and breakfast for trappers, travelers, mail-runners, fishermen and other visitors. Mrs. Campbell quickly earned a reputation for her deluxe feather-bed accommodations and fare that would prompt some to spend an extra night for seconds and thirds. In 1880, George Emerson found himself at the Campbell home during a speculative trip representing timber mogul Captain Asa M. Simpson of San Francisco. After a memorable supper Emerson tasted Mrs. Campbell's blackberry pie and that was it — the site for the new mill was thus chosen. Not only was there a deep-water port and some of the most impressive forest he had ever seen, but irresistible pie to boot. He purchased 300 acres of land in the name of Simpson, creating the Northwestern Lumber Company, the first in Hoquiam and the second on the harbor behind the Cosmopolis mill.

The first lumber was cut in September of 1882, attracting new settlers and businesses almost instantly. At that time, landowners in Hoquiam were required to build on their parcels, a forward-thinking move that resulted in many mill workers donating portions of their claims to logging enterprises, ensuring their own job security and helping the town at the same time.

Logging encountered such a meteoric rise that some were simply drawn into fortune. Two such men, Robert and Joseph Lytle, were running a grocery store when they were forced to accept a fledgling logging operation as payment for goods. Originally peeved by the acquisition, they eventually decided to keep the mill running by purchasing a small cache of cedar logs. Capitalizing on low prices and an optimistic economy, in a few short years the Lytles went from modest store owners to timber tycoons. In 1907 they organized the Hoquiam Lumber and Shingle Company, and later the Woodlawn Mill and Boom Company.

Another pair of brothers also found their fortune in the sawmill trade. Alex and Robert Polson, descendants of Nova Scotia, arrived in Hoquiam in 1882 and 1887 respectively, forming the Polson Brothers Logging Company in 1891. Starting out with jacks and a team of oxen, the brothers gradually modernized their facilities and eventually became the largest logging company in the world. The Polsons brought the first log-driving splash dam and the first logging railroad to the area, two introductions which accelerated the rate timber could be removed from the forest, while allowing longer trips into the back-woods. At one time, the Polson brothers controlled two sawmills, a shingle mill, a logging railroad and a dozen logging camps, adding significantly to the overall production of the area. A community leader,

Alex Polson was Hoquiam's first tax assessor and served a term as a state senator, where he helped set aside a large tract of school-owned timberland to provide the institution with a necessary future income.

In 1924 Robert Polson gave his nephew Arnold a mansion built entirely of Polson timber as a wedding gift that serves as a testament to that prosperous era. The **Polson Park and Museum** (1611 Riverside Avenue) offers a look back when logging camps buzzed in the woods and Hoquiam and Aberdeen were just getting on their feet. Information on Indians of the area, folk tales and the discovery and navigation of Grays Harbor are on display, including a re-creation of a logging railroad complete with model train set.

As in Aberdeen, take a personal historic driving tour by locating the large murals that decorate various buildings downtown, ranging from logging scenes to images of Hoquiam at the turn of the century. Over the years, many old buildings downtown have met the wrecking ball to make way for modern structures, taking history and character with them. This urban renewal — or "bourbon removal" — as one former restaurant owner phrased it, affected an area largely occupied by taverns and restaurants that had long been considered local landmarks. Older residents speak of the renovations with a mixture of nostalgia and bitterness.

Surrounding Grays Harbor for most of its early history were logging camps that kept the timber industry alive and kicking. In stump-covered clearings amidst the objects of their toil, men lived in a world with different rules and protocol, where arms and backs did work now reserved for machines, and where a livelihood became a way a life. The turn-of-the-century logger was a unique breed of animal: pioneer at heart, adventurous in spirit and highly tolerant of pain, discomfort and fear. Their towns consisted of little more than bunkhouses, a mess hall and timber skyscrapers as far as the eye could see.

Working from "can to can't" — that is, from can see to can't see — the camps were strictly regimented for efficiency. The day would begin well before sunrise with a foreman's call of "daylight in the swamp!" and a hearty breakfast, and end with a weary twilight walk back to camp for a quick clean up and a well-deserved dinner. Evenings were spent exchanging gold coins in heated poker games, with the occasional fiddle or harmonica adding to the ambiance before lights out at 9:30. This schedule ran from Monday to Saturday; the Sabbath was devoted to wash-board scrubbing of clothes in an effort to rid the bunkhouses of the unholy odor of damp wool mixed with sour sweat. Aching muscles, perpetual blisters and king-size slivers were exchanged for a "monthly insult" (paycheck) that hardly turned loggers into wealthy men, and the labor was performed with a sense of pride and camaraderie.

Nestled among the ancient wooden giants of the coast for six months at a time turned simple pleasures into objects of obsession; and these were not to be tampered with. Two such staples were the loggers' beloved chow and chew. A good cook was about as valuable as a whole team of oxen, because near-riots would ensue if the food failed to satisfy a famished group of ax-swingers with cedar-sized appetites. Full plates were thrown on the floor or even out of windows if the fare was deemed unpalatable, a warning not taken lightly by cooks or foremen. Serving cold potatoes or leathery meat was a sure recipe for disaster, and entire crews were known to walk out of camp in a flurry of cussing and tossed utensils to protest subpar grub. A pair of cold flapjacks nailed to a cook's bunkroom door served as a backwoods pink-slip; a not so subtle signal that it was time to hit the road — and fast.

Seasoned veterans had first crack at loading their plates, while the new men, or "flunkies" often helped to serve the chow and refill emptied platters. The cookhouse was the most important building in camp, and the reputation of a cook could determine which outfit a logger would work for.

Nearly as essential as food was Copenhagen snuff, or "snoose" as it was called in the woods. Cans of snoose were as much a part of the logger's equipment as an ax or wedge for all the importance they attached to it. Pinches of snuff were placed between cheeks and gums across the peninsula, and a shortage of chew could bring a sit-down strike until the supply was replenished.

Perhaps only a logger's zeal for work (read: life) could explain his fiery reliance on snoose. Living in the woods exposed them to constant danger, but they thrived on this tension. With tons of timber constantly falling around them, and cables and chains snapping and breaking through the underbrush, crushing anything in its path, a lack of attentiveness could mean certain death or disfigurement. The loggers countered the daily risks with skill, speed and precision, relying on what could rightly be considered a sense of duty and pride. What else could possess a man to drag a heavy saw 200 feet straight up a tree to lop off the top in preparation for his comrades below to drop the massive structure exactly where they planned? Certainly not the money. Perhaps it was the snoose.

From Hoquiam, U.S. 101 winds north through steep hills displaying the various stages of logging, from 30 to 50-year-old trees awaiting future harvest, to acres of young saplings, to giant clearings of stumps and blackened soil. The checkerboard pattern seen today is a reminder of the original method used to distribute land in the late 1800s. To encourage rail connections and expansion to the West, the government would compensate railroad companies with land for laying track. The railroads would often sell sections of this land to timber companies

Loggers in 1915 showing confidence in the stability of the timber.

anxious to tap into the virgin timber supply. These plots usually came in smaller squares rather than large, continuous plots, so the cleared areas were often separated.

About 20 miles north of Hoquiam the highway crosses the **Humptulips River** (huhm-TOO-lips) which once served as the primary thoroughfare for a particularly impressive plot of Douglas fir known simply as "21-9" (Township 21 North, Range 9 West). Packed into an area of just over 23,000 acres, the forest was so thick and tall that it was virtually impossible to cut down a towering fir without damaging it and others as it fell. The density was such that a man would often have to turn sideways just to squeeze through. After logging companies moved in to exploit this natural wonder, the Humptulips Boom and Driving Company was created in 1909 to shuttle the timber to the mouth of the river on Grays Harbor. The company built 27 splash dams on the Humptulips (Quinault for "hard to pole") and its tributaries, and production hit its peak in the late 1920s with over two billion board feet, the most ever moved from any port in the world.

A splash dam functions as a kind of holding tank for raw timber. Logs that collect in the standing water are packed so tightly that it is possible to walk across them from one side of the river to the other. When the water is released, enough pressure has built up to propel the logs downstream to another collection area, and so on until reaching the harbor mills.

Despite their transportation possibilities, splash dams were destructive forces. Farmers cursed the dams with considerable venom for ruining prime cultivation areas located close to river banks. Overflowing logs often caused rivers to flood, washing out or crushing large area of crops when logs were thrown over the banks. Considerably worse off, however, were the salmon. The concept of a fish ladder was foreign at this time, and some dams were so dense that many salmon runs were eliminated.

A marked contrast in the landscape begins about 10 miles north as the road rolls into the **Olympic National Forest**. Devoid of anything remotely resembling a clear-cut, it appears that every square-inch is occupied by a different shade of green. Created in 1897, the nearly 700,000 acres of virgin forest almost completely envelops the Olympic National Park.

Eight miles into the forest U.S. 101 skirts the western edge of **Lake Quinault**, a four-mile-long salmon-spawning ground owned by the Quinault Indians. From this point, South Shore Road connects with the 30-mile loop around the lake and into the Quinault Valley. This stretch of road offers a windshield to the world of the rain forest. Approximately 140 inches of annual rainfall (some areas register as much as 200 in a year), mild temperatures and an unusually long growing season all combine to make this section of forest one of the most fertile in the world. Plant and animal life

The cool, green Olympic National Park rainforest.

is so abundant that many species have not yet been classified. This integrated system controls its own micro-climate, causing cool summers and warm winters. Mosses and ferns grow rampant beneath the tallest Sitka spruce, western hemlock and Douglas fir on earth. Bald eagles, blue herons, swans, coyotes, black bears, cougars, deer and elk are just a fraction of the wildlife species that exist here.

From Lake Quinault the road bends west to reach the Pacific and the mouth of the **Queets River** (KWEETS), known throughout the state for excellent steelhead fishing. A shaded road leads into the rain forest valley, offering a quick peek at moss-covered trees, the occasional bounding deer and elk and what seems like centuries  worth of silence.

Once past tiny **Queets** — "people made of earth" — the highway again finds the coastline and heads due north for 15 miles. The elevated views makes it a challenge to stay focused on the road, so rather than swerve wildly, take advantage of the available viewpoints

This isn't a holiday at Ruby Beach; look closely and you'll see their large fishing nets.

to park and gaze out across the Pacific. From a parking lot at **Ruby Beach** you can access the waterfront for an up-close look at the ocean. Here, whitecaps smash into the rocky cliffs, and hefty logs are tossed onto the beach. Tidepools form in hidden nooks and crannies while swarms of seagulls fight the constant wind to collect clams at low tide. Sitka spruce grow clear to the edge of the cliff, their tangled roots peeking over the brink; a few extend horizontally from the rock and over the water below.

Offshore, sea stacks in a variety of shapes and sizes protrude from the ocean, some several miles from land. One of the largest, **Destruction Island**, lies directly in a gray whale migratory path. The massive creatures can be viewed on their journey southward to their wintering grounds from late December to early February, then back northward from March through May. Captain Bodega y Quadra attached the grim title to the 40-acre rock in 1775 after losing seven men aboard the Spanish *Sondra* to Indian attacks. They originally went ashore to collect wood and fresh water, but when they tried to escape with a collection of stolen dried fish, they paid the ultimate price for the salmon. In memory of the massacre, Quadra named the island "Isla de Dolores," the Island of Sorrow. Twelve years later six men from the British ship *Imperial Eagle* were killed while exploring a nearby river that Captain Barkley then named Destruction River. The apt name was also applied to the island.

The **Hoh Indian Reservation** begins where the road curves inland at the mouth of the Hoh River. Just one square mile, the reservation is the smallest and least populated in the state. Dependent upon salmon for their survival, this quiet tribe has introduced several programs to conserve salmon runs and enhance future spawning.

Eight miles further take Upper Hoh Road, a 20-mile spur off U.S. 101 that leads into the **Hoh Rain Forest**, the only coniferous rain forest in the world. The first few miles provide evidence of the heavy hand of logging, complete with the charred remains of slash burning, but the point at which the forest falls under the protective blanket of the Olympic National Park is starkly obvious. Mushrooms, ferns and moss create an emerald carpet for massive trunks, whether vertical or horizontal. Fallen trees sprout new life as saplings, countless shrubs and vines take root in the decaying bark. Ground roots often graph together to share water and mineral resources, resulting in one super tree. The **Hoh Rain Forest Visitors' Center** is at the end of the paved road, and offers an interpretive trail that explains the complex and vibrant ecosystem thriving underfoot and overhead. Several different hiking trails also commence here, some leading up to ridges, and others that wind into the valley and along the rivers and creeks sparkling with steelhead and trout.

Logging on the South Fork of the Hoh River in 1942.

Back on U.S. 101, five miles past **Bogachiel State Park**, the only developed park on the peninsula, you find the town of **Forks** (Elevation 300, Population 3,335). Once a bustling, raucous town of gruff loggers and salty dogs, two 24-hour restaurants and round-the-clock rambunctiousness, the streets of Forks have quieted as the logging industry has declined. Tales of its dangerously jubilant heyday are in abundance, revealing the character of the people who live here.

Fourth of July in downtown Forks of old.

One local tavern owner recalls a time when every barstool was occupied and crowds of drunken woodsmen had to be herded to the door at closing hour. Her motto — "If there ain't a fight, it ain't a good night" — colorfully relates the manner in which loggers blow off steam.

One hot Fourth of July afternoon in the mid-1970s, a motorcycle gang of 40 or so riders roared into town with intentions of aggressive part-time conquest and probably expecting little resistance. Wrong town, boys. After several hours of loud insults and threats, sidewalk wheelies and broken glass amusement, the folks of Forks had seen enough. As pick-ups blocked the street, the local fire-fighters arrived and unleashed their hoses on a good portion of the unwanted visitors as they stumbled from a bar. The rest met a similar fate when they came to check on the commotion. Mayhem ensued and fist-fights erupted, but order was soon achieved when a logging truck arrived promising to roll over any two-wheeled chrome vehicle that was not immediately removed from town. Soaked, shocked and quickly sobered, the bikers decided to take their leather elsewhere.

Although most interest now revolves around trees, it was a farmer, Luthor Ford, who first settled this area with his family in 1878. After the long journey from San Francisco, he built a log cabin and started a dairy herd on the fertile prairie land, eventually attracting others. To get the cattle to his land he had to transport them by schooner, and then drive 12 miles along the beach before heading inland.

A good living could be made in logging at the turn of the century, but only the resilience of its citizens kept Forks from becoming a ghost town after experiencing three major disasters. First, in January of 1921, the "Big Blow" toppled over five million board feet of timber, creating a twisted mess of branches and roots that took years to clear. Then, in January of 1925, fire destroyed most of the buildings in town. Later, in 1951, three-and-a-half months of drought set the stage for another fire that torched the surrounding forests, most of the homes, four sawmills and all the logging equipment. Were it not for a last minute change in wind direction, the inferno would have engulfed the rest of the town as well.

Located on a prairie between the Calawah and Bogachiel Rivers, farming and sport fishing are attempting to pick up the economic slack left by more than a decade of logging cutbacks and regulation. Simply mention the endangered spotted owl or marbled murrelet and a heated discussion is bound to erupt. The **Forks Timber Museum** (along U.S. 101 at the south end of town) was built by the high school carpentry class and details the events and personalities that shaped the timber trade, which peaked in the 1920s and 30s when they produced up to one million board feet per day. Once the self-proclaimed logging capital of the world, the moniker now serves as a proud reference to the past.

The Solduck River trickles out of the Olympic Mountains and picks up considerable size and speed before combining with the Bogachiel River to form the Quiluete River which releases into the ocean at La Push. Fourteen miles past the one-horse town of **Sappho** (SA-foh), a spur off U.S. 101 leads south to the refreshing waters of **Solduck Hot Springs**. The name means "magic waters" and was adapted from an Indian legend. Long ago, two dragons, Solduck and Elwha, engaged in a ferocious and lengthy battle. After fighting to a draw and near exhaustion, both retreated to their caverns, permanently sealed the entrances and wept hot tears of shame at their inability to conquer the other. These tears are said to form the Solduck and Olympic Hot Springs. From the resort, a two-mile round trip hike leads to the Solduck Falls, and a dramatic view that is attained by crossing a bridge that spans the canyon below.

After the spur road, continue east on U.S. 101 and within minutes the picturesque **Lake Crescent** comes into view. The lake's calm setting is interrupted in summer by hordes of backpackers, campers, fishermen and Sunday drivers. The *Storm King*, a 150-passenger paddle-wheel boat conducts tours of the lake three times a day in summer. The narrow, winding road runs along the lake's 10-mile-long southern edge. A steep slope covered with deciduous and evergreen trees rises from the north shore. The cobalt blue lake is the only known home of Beardslee trout, a large species known for its fighting ability. Geologists claim the 600-feet deep lake was formed by a retreating glacier in the last ice age, but local Indians have their own version of how it came into existence.

According to legend, the Storm King gazed down from his perch atop the rock-carved cliffs to see two neighboring tribes consumed in battle. Angered at their foolishness, he threw a giant boulder down to separate them, damming the stream that ran through the valley and thus creating the lake. Mindful of the fury attached to its conception, the natives refused to visit the area, especially at night, fearing that evil spirits inhabited the shores.

This fear did not deter white settlers, notably Dr. Louis Dechmann, who viewed the surrounding area as an ideal location for achieving mental and physical health. In 1913 the German-born proponent of positive thinking opened a lakeside health spa he called *Qui Si Sana,* a rough Latin translation for "Here Find Health." For five years he catered to primarily wealthy city folk who flocked to the rustic setting to practice deep-breathing exercises, organized recreation and meditation in an effort to eliminate the stress and tension of urban living. Capitalizing on the late 19th century Romantic movement of finding spiritual fulfillment through Nature, many could be heard echoing the mantra of the doctor's feel-good resort: "Every day in every way I'm getting better and better." After closing the spa in 1918, Dr. Dechmann moved on to operate a sanitarium in another location. The facilities were later converted into a youth camp called Camp David Jr. that is still in operation.

During this same era an entirely different kind of exercise was begun in the Lake Crescent area, inspired not by meditation but by World War I. The use of aircraft in the conflict had risen steadily since 1914, and by the time the U.S. joined in the fray, full-scale airplane construction was underway. Spruce was an essential ingredient in this process due to its strength and light weight. This effort was threatened by a logger's strike in the summer of 1917, and in a panic the **U.S. Army's Spruce Division** was created. Soldiers flooded the woods of the Northwest to work with civilians in logging camps, sawmills and railroad construction. By 1918, 30,000 soldiers stationed in 234 camps across the Olympic Peninsula worked like men possessed to drop trees and stretch 130 miles of track from Forks to the banks of Lake Crescent and on to Port Angeles. On one line alone, some 8,000 men struggled seven days a week, 24 hours a day for over a year to complete the effort; all for a salary of $20 per month.

Although no soldier in the Spruce Division received a medal for bravery, several efficiency records were established: first, it became the most expensive railroad ever built in the U.S., running up a tab of over $30,000 per mile; second, it was built 75% faster than any previous rail line; third, and perhaps most impressive, it was completed ahead of schedule. Despite this Herculean effort, the Spruce Railroad did not haul a single log for the war effort. Adding to the irony, the last piece of rail was laid near Lake Pleasant on November 30, 1918 — the day the Armistice was signed. The line was eventually used by logging companies to reach untouched portions of the forest.

Steep coniferous hillsides line the highway for the next 22 miles as it rises and falls past Lake Aldwell and on to **Port Angeles** (Elevation 36, Population 18,270), the largest town on the peninsula and front door to the Pacific. Originally drawn to the protection of **Ediz Hook**, a three-mile sand spit offering relief from strong currents and breakers, Spanish explorer Francisco de Eliza lavished lengthy praise on the harbor, calling it "Port of our Lady of the Angels." A year later the ever-present Captain George Vancouver altered the name to its present, more convenient form.

Much of the town's early history can be summed up in an ongoing battle with neighboring Port Townsend for the distinction of

Folks say there's great surfing around here but they're cautious to reveal exactly where.

being the official port of entry on the peninsula. Victor Smith, an ambitious U.S. Customs Collector, waged much of this war personally, purchasing large tracts of land in 1861 and determined to make his fortune. Through gritty perseverance and a great deal of travel, he managed to persuade President Abraham Lincoln to reserve land for a town, a lighthouse and a military base, thus claiming the treasured national port status. But just as things were looking up for this fledgling town, disaster struck. First, all of the buildings, including the customs station, were swept away by a flash flood in 1863. Then the fiery Smith was lost in a shipwreck in 1865, drowning out the loudest voice in Port Angeles. Without his direction and persistence, the customs house was moved to Port Townsend rather than rebuilt in

Port Angeles and the town turned quiet once again. As a consolation, the military arrived in 1895 and the U.S. Pacific fleet spent its summers anchored here until 1930.

For the next 15 years, aside from a small amount of farming and cattle grazing, Port Angeles was a quiet seaside town surrounded by unoccupied land. In the late 1880s, the Northern Pacific Railroad was rumored to be looking for a new port location, causing a wave of opportunists to head north. Technically the land belonged to the federal government, but with Washington, D.C. so far away, many settlers conveniently forgot about the details of ownership and staked claims anyway. Anticipating a fight that could never really be won (and perhaps gaining a new appreciation of what the Indians had been experiencing), Congress waived their dated claim over the land and the squatters-turned-settlers were there to stay. Although a rail line did not arrive until World War I, ornate Victorian homes were constructed along the bluff overlooking the water, giving the growing town an optimistic aura.

The second coming of Smith occurred around the same time and a bit further east. This time, however, it was George V. Smith, a lawyer from Seattle who affected the area in a rather radical fashion. In 1887, Smith founded the Puget Sound Cooperative Colony, a utopian-inspired community with lofty goals and aspirations. Their motto: "Let the many combine in cooperation as the few have done in corporation" was warmly embraced, and in many ways the experiment proved successful. The first sawmill, pulp mill and sewage treatment plant in the area all originated in the co-op colony, along with their own school and publication. But while the ideas and philosophy took root, the crops did not, and poor harvests led to the disintegration of the community. The majority of the people relocated next door in promising Port Angeles as a welcome addition to the current population. This influx gave town planning a wider scope, and in 1914 much of the downtown area was raised and filled to prevent washout from the tides and to encourage expansion. A courthouse erected in 1915 now serves as the **Clallam County Museum** (Lincoln and 4th), which highlights the early days of maritime exploration and the rise of the timber trade. On the waterfront, a 90-minute ferry ride leads to Victoria, British Columbia and Vancouver Island.

Clallam County: Port Angeles is the county seat of Clallam County, which was organized in 1854 and was formerly part of Jefferson County. It was named after an Indian tribe and means "strong people." It is located in the far northwestern corner of the state on the Olympic Peninsula. Its county seat, Port Angeles, was named in 1791 by Captain Francisco Eliza. In May of 1798 the Spanish attempted to establish a fort at Neah Bay; it existed for only five months. In 1887 the Tatoosh Island lighthouse was built to aid navigation in the Strait of Juan de Fuca. Olympic National Park was created in 1938. Today the county has a varied economy base on wood products, food processing, mining and tourism.

Court House: 223 East Fourth, Port Angeles 98362, 206-417-2000, SCAN 575-1011 (Information), FAX 206-452-0470. Area: 1,752.5 square miles. State Ranking: 20th. 1993 Population: 61,400. Unincorporated: 35,725. Incorporated: 25,675. Density: 35 persons per square mile. **Cities and Towns**: Forks, Port Angeles, Sequim. **Principal Economic Activities**: Wood products, agriculture, tourism. **Points of Interest**: Olympic National Park, Cape Flattery, Hurricane Ridge, Crescent Lake.

Climate: (Port Angeles - elevation 36)

	Jan	Apr	Jul	Oct
Max Temp. F°	43.7	54.4	66.6	56.6
Min Temp.	33.5	40.1	51.0	43.6
Mean Temp.	38.6	47.2	58.8	50.1
Precipitation	2.87"	1.08"	.48"	2.48"

Average Annual Maximum Temperature: 55.3
Average Annual Minimum Temperature: 42.1
Annual Mean Temperature: 48.7
Average Annual Precipitation: 24.61"

At the southern end of Port Angeles, Mt. Angeles Road rises 5,200 feet in seven miles to **Hurricane Ridge**, a hypnotic viewpoint that stares at the Olympic glaciers and the Pacific Ocean. Named by pioneers who experienced the gale-force winds that often blow snowdrifts around, the road roughly follows the route taken by Lieutenant Joseph P. O'Neil and his crew in 1890 when surveying the interior of the Olympic Mountains.

The view from the top reveals the diverse combination of high peaks, dense forests, and chaotic topography that defines the rugged **Olympic Mountain Range.** Despite being compressed into a relatively small area (50 miles by 35 miles), the range is visible from most of western Washington. It divides the Olympic Peninsula and is surrounded by the Strait of Juan de Fuca and the Pacific Ocean. Several knife-like peaks exceed 7,000 feet, including Mt. Olympus, the highest, at 7,965 feet. These mountains have an exceptionally heavy rainfall, producing spruce, hemlock, cedar, and firs with soaring heights up to 300 feet. The U.S. Coast Survey could not contain their awe at the region's immense forests, reporting in 1858 that they were an "immeasurable sea of gigantic timber coming down to the very shores." Betty MacDonald, author of *The Egg and I*, a novel set on the peninsula, wrote that they were "the most rugged, most westerly, greatest, deepest, largest, wildest, gamiest, richest, most fertile, loneliest, and most desolate" woods in the country.

The Spanish explorer Juan Perez first sighted the mountains in 1774, but English explorer Captain John Meares named its highest peak in 1778. When Meares sailed into the Strait of Juan de Fuca and saw  the snow-capped mountains dramatically rising out of the sea, he was so impressed by Mt. Olympus that he named it after the mythical home of the Greek gods. "If that not be the home where dwell the gods," he wrote, "it is certainly beautiful enough to be." Fourteen years later it was made official when Captain George Vancouver entered the name on his maps and referred to the entire range as the Olympic Mountains.

The Olympic Mountains: "If that not be the home where dwell the gods, it is certainly beautiful enough to be.

Pioneers began settling around the area in the mid-1850s, but the mountainous interior continued to be a mystery. The inaccessibility of the inner Olympics inspired various myths; some envisioned a harsh land of war-like Indians or even cannibals, while others dreamed of miles of Paradise, or a sort of utopian valley. Elisha P. Ferry, the first governor of Washington, told the *Seattle Press* in 1889, "Washington has her great unknown land, like the interior of Africa." The newspaper responded by writing: "Here is an opportunity for someone to acquire fame by unveiling the mystery which wraps the land encircled by the snow-capped mountain range."

James Hellbal Christie, a Scotsman who had explored northwest Canada for three years, responded to the challenge, but led the *Press*-sponsored expedition to a disappointing conclusion. Although the explorers were experienced mountaineers geared with mules and sleds, the party of six nearly starved to death and netted only 20 miles in three months due to frigid temperatures and falling rock. In 1890, Lieutenant Joseph P. O'Neil of the U.S. Army led an expedition which also proved unsuccessful. This time the party brought enough provisions, yet nothing went as planned. Men were lost. The botanist deserted the party. The mineralogist and naturalist who attempted to place a copper box on the top of Olympus for scientific research never reached the summit. Even the copper box was lost, so it is unknown whether the men were ever close to their destination. Neither O'Neil's careful preparations nor the scientific expertise of the party could tame the rugged Olympics.

Estimated as one of the world's youngest mountain ranges at just over two million years old, thick glaciers buried all of the Olympics about 10,000 years ago during an ice age, and now only the peaks of the highest mountains remain uncovered. Deep valleys have been sharply sculpted by up to 70 glaciers. More than 36 square miles of ice and snowfields drape the summits, exhibiting some of the largest and best-formed glaciers in the United States. The Blue Glacier on Mt. Olympus is particularly remarkable with its intensely clear blue coloring and deep grooves in the striated surface.

At the heart of the Olympic Peninsula and engulfing the Olympic Mountain Range is the **Olympic National Park**, a rare combination of glacial peaks, ocean coastline and the largest virgin temperate forest in the Western Hemisphere, a distinction which led to its designation as an International Biosphere Reserve in 1976. The only other temperate rain forests (as opposed to tropical) are found in New Zealand and southern Chile. As with much of the peninsula, the area was seen as food for the hungry timber mills before being rescued by federal protection. The nearly impenetrable interior wilderness also served to save itself since turn-of-the-century miners and loggers could not negotiate the rugged terrain to exploit the resources.

Joseph O'Neil was so impressed with the terrain and complete absence of human interruption that he vowed to prevent its destruction by making numerous personal appeals to Congress requesting the area be declared a national park. His wish was partially granted in 1897 when President Grover Cleveland created the Olympic Forest Reserve, the first in a series of protective legislative moves. Next, in 1909, President Teddy Roosevelt formed the Mt. Olympus National Monument, primarily to save the Roosevelt elk, a rare species found only in the Northwest. These rain forest dwellers were a few bullets shy of extinction after years of being hunted because their teeth made attractive watch ornaments.

National monuments receive less protection than national parks, and as a result the area was trimmed down three separate times until only half of the originally declared area remained pristine. Finally in 1937, President Franklin Roosevelt toured the Olympic Peninsula himself to inspect the object of such heated debate between environmentalists and industrialists. After a two-day car tour of the peninsula, the stewing Roosevelt allegedly cried: "I hope the lumberman responsible for this is roasting in hell." So moved at its wonder and wildness, FDR set aside 898,000 acres as the Olympic National Park one year later; a 60-mile strip along the coast was incorporated in 1953. Park status prohibits any type of unnatural development, including logging, mining and road construction. In 1981 the park again received international recognition when it was designated a World Heritage Site.

A meteorological oddity exists around the town of **Sequim** (SKWIM, Elevation 185, Population 4,070) in the Dungeness Valley, 15 miles east of Port Angeles. Storm clouds that blow in from the ocean are blocked by the Olympic Mountains, creating a rain shadow over the area. This barrier leaves Sequim with an average of only 16 inches of precipitation a year compared to over 100 inches just 25 miles away, plus considerably more sunshine and higher temperatures. This 50-mile radius includes both the wettest and driest areas in western Washington.

Encouraged by the favorable weather, the first homesteaders arrived in 1854 with intentions of farming the then cactus-strewn Sequim Prairie. They soon realized that it is possible to have too much of a good thing, for ample sun with no water is not a good cultivation combination. This problem was addressed in 1880 when D.R. "Crazy" Callen spearhead-

ed an irrigation project using water from the Dungeness River. The community joined together to form the Sequim Prairie Ditch Company in 1895 and began digging irrigation ditches by hand that spread across the valley floor. A year later the water began flowing, and in a decade

Birds-eye view of Sequim.

the project converted over 5,000 acres of prairie land to cash crops and grazeland, bringing new life and new residents to the area. This prosperous collective venture is still celebrated at the Irrigation Festival held each May. With the arrival of the railroad in 1915, Sequim became a booming agricultural trade center.

As population has grown, so has the debate over how much water should be available for irrigation. The local S'Klallam Indian tribe has lobbied for years to limit the number of pipes draining the Dungeness River. As a result, some agricultural restrictions have been imposed. The tribe's interests lie in keeping the water in the river to save the salmon runs they depend upon. Farmers are concerned their lush fields will revert back to a desert landscape if further cutbacks are made.

Sequim, a native word for "quiet waters," experienced a spell of international fame in 1977 when mastodon bones were discovered just outside of town. Archaeologists from around the world flocked to a small farm to study the remains of these 11,000 year-old elephant-like creatures originally unearthed by the land owner as he was digging a small duck pond. The Manis Site, one of six in the area, offered the first concrete evidence in North America that early man hunted the woolly beasts for food when an arrowhead was found in the rib cage of one skeleton. Portions of this dig are on display at the **Museum and Arts Center** (175 West Cedar Street).

Dairy products constitute Sequim's largest agricultural venture, along with strawberries, raspberries and grape vineyards for local wineries. The town appears to be in a transitional phase; old farms peek out from behind the growing suburban facade, complete with strip mall and outlet stores on either side of the main street. Though modernization exacts a price on the once rustic feel, a small-town charm has endured on the prairie. Following the downsloping highway out of town, the prairie looks as it did a century ago, with the exception of giant wagon-wheel sprinklers in the fields, awash in a fabric of color against the backdrop of the ocean and the Olympic Mountains. Long considered a mecca for retirees from across the state seeking a relaxed pace and consistently favorable weather, the population of Sequim has risen steadily since the 1960s when large tracts of farm land were sold to make way for housing developments.

The Strait of Juan de Fuca and the Pacific Ocean are always close by.

From its intersection with U.S. 101, follow Sequim-Dungeness Way north for three miles to the 210-acre **Jamestown S'Klallam Indian Reservation**. As early as 1850 a steady stream of white settlers crowded this small tribal community off their land until they were forced to purchase a fragment of the original to avoid eviction. The Point-No-Point Treaty of 1855 assigned the S'Klallams to the Skokomish reservation at the southern end of Hood Canal in exchange for unlimited fishing and hunting rights. Despite the declaration, most members remained in the area and adopted a nomadic lifestyle to dodge the growing numbers of settlers. Threatened with inevitable removal, Chief Lord James Balch (not a hereditary chief) led the tribe in purchasing a plot of land in 1874 that they could call their own. Several families accumulated $500 and bought 210 acres of mostly clear-cut forest land and named it after their chief. Although they relocated again, it was not until 1981 that the federal government officially recognized the Jamestown S'Klallams as a separate entity, a right immediately exercised by drafting and adopting their own constitution. The tribe is also one of the first in the nation to be involved in the Self-Governance Demonstration Project, a law that grants them direct control over programs once managed by the Bureau of Indian Affairs.

Over the past decade the S'Klallams have purchased 175 acres of land surrounding **Blyn** on the southern end of Sequim Bay, constructing a Tribal Community Center and Tribal Administration Building there. Since ownership of the original Jamestown settlement was distributed to all tribal members, many later sold their lots and moved on, reducing the present population to around 250. After such attempts to remain independent, it is appropriate that S'Klallam means "strong people."

Two miles north of Jamestown on Sequim-Dungeness Way is **Dungeness**, a dilapidated town which lived a short life as a port for trading vessels. The biggest attraction now is the **Dungeness Spit**, the longest natural sand spit in the world. The slim, curved six-mile sliver of sand appears fragile and destined to wash away, yet effectively protects the shore from the aggressive surf of the Strait of Juan de Fuca. Captain George Vancouver moored here in 1792 to escape unforgiving currents before rounding the coast into Puget Sound. While anchored, they were amazed at the clouds of multi-colored birds hovering and diving around them, and demonstrated this fascination by using them for target practice from the ship. Such activity no longer occurs since the area was declared the **Dungeness National Wildlife Refuge** in 1915, supporting over 200 species of birds that feed on abundant shellfish, particularly the Dungeness crab and clams that inhabit the tidepools. A half-mile trail through the woods leads to the spit and a first-hand inspection of a thriving coastal ecosystem.

From Dungeness, follow Sequim-Dungeness Way five miles south to the connection with U.S. 101. Back on the highway, continue southeast across the Sequim Prairie and along the western edge of Sequim Bay. At the southern end of the bay the road cuts east across the wooded Miller Peninsula, then bends south for six scenic miles with a clear view of **Discovery Bay**. In 1792, Captain George Vancouver landed on these shores to select a needed spar for his vessel *Discovery*, after which the bay is named. He was not disappointed. The coast was covered with thick forest well suited for ship building and has since been heavily logged. **Gardiner** marks the spot where Vancouver first went ashore for exploration. Most of the tall trees still standing are rooted close to the road, but expansive cleared sections can be seen through the timber. The road winds along the top of the hill, offering a good vantage of the water. The steep cliffs and rock formations on the opposite side of the bay mirror what cannot be seen to the west.

At the intersection with State Highway 20, U.S. 101 moves south into the solitude of the forest, where the lack of human presence draws further attention to the contrast between patches of evergreens and larger sections of clear-cut. Logging companies have erected billboards on the side of the road that announce "Renewable Resources for Tomorrow" and give dates on when a forest was first cut, when planted and when next harvest will be. Countless small streams and lakes can also be seen from the road. The largest waterway, the **Quilcene River**, was packed with splash-dams a century ago to move timber to the harbor. Logging trucks are a common site along this stretch of highway, most of them heading north to the mills of Port Angeles and Port Townsend.

Quilcene (KWIL-seen) is nestled in a valley surrounded by forested ridges to the west and lower hills to the east. White granular mounds of shells are evidence of the oyster industry. Their year-round harvest is staggered so each oyster follows a four-year growing cycle, creating a high quality product and an international reputation as a restaurant supplier. The **Olympic National Forest Ranger and Information Center** is located just off the highway, easily the largest structure in this quiet waterfront town.

About two miles further, the **Quilcene National Fish Hatchery** is open to the public and worth a stop to see the fish ponds and to read the informative displays and exhibits. Decades worth of over-fishing, pollution, dams and poor logging practices nearly eliminated salmon and steelhead runs all over the peninsula. To combat the destruction, the hatchery releases approximately three million fish each year into the surrounding rivers and Hood Canal. The majority of these fish swim through the Strait of Juan de Fuca and into the ocean where they scatter and travel for two to four years. To return to their birthplace to spawn, salmon must run the gambit of dams and fishing nets. Less than five percent are estimated to successfully reach their destination and reproduce. Coho, Chinook, chum, steelhead and sockeye salmon all originate in the Quilcene hatchery.

A gravel road leading up to **Mt. Walker** branches from U.S. 101 three miles south of the hatchery. Though the drive is rugged, the 2,750-foot summit easily compensates for a few potholes and bumps by presenting views of the Olympic Mountains, Hood Canal, Puget Sound, Mt. Bangor, Glacier Peak, and, on clear days, Mt. Rainier and Seattle.

The next few miles cut into the eastern edge of the Olympic National Forest before again finding the water. Forgotten logging roads are quickly swallowed by vegetation if not regularly traveled, and even

A quiet cove on the Hood Canal.

the two-lane U.S. 101 is narrowed by wild blackberry and huckleberry bushes reaching for passing cars. Emerge from this Northwest jungle landscape and gaze directly out at **Hood Canal**, just a part of the maze of waterways that separate the peninsula from the mainland. First discovered by Captain George Vancouver in 1792, the canal is actually a long, narrow bay that stretches for 80 miles, dividing the Kitsap and Olympic peninsulas before hooking back northeast. Public beaches all along the canal offer clam digging and oyster picking at low tide; simply follow the ever-present seagulls to a choice location. The towns along Hood Canal swell with tourists and vacationers during the summer, but even in busy times the slow pace is preserved and the scenery remains the focal point. The contrast between modest, weathered beach houses and large modern summer homes reflect recent efforts by urban dwellers to escape the bustle of the city, if only for the weekend. The highway crosses dozens of rivers and streams with Indian names like Dosewallips, Hamma Hamma, Duckabush and Lilliwaup that drain into the canal. Not only are they wild and beautiful to explore, but they are fun to pronounce aloud while driving.

Brinnon is characteristic of life on the edge of the peninsula. A few waterfront houses, a Senior Center and an old restaurant combine with some impressive newer homes with long docks and yachts to round out the town. Perhaps the most aptly titled structure is the Geoduck Tavern, named for the famous four-pound clam that thrives in these waters and carries the local economy on its back (or shell). Tons of these beefy bivalves are shipped to Japan each year where they are considered a delicacy. The beach that stretches from Brinnon one mile south to Dosewallips State Park is a hot spot for geoducks; all clam digging requires is a shovel and a tolerance to mud. A cleaner route is to purchase clams and oysters in a town store or at a number of shellfish stands just off the highway.

Near the road a tangle of underbrush, fallen trees and expanding thickets grow out of control, feeding off constant moisture and summer sunshine. Where river mouths meet the canal, fresh and saltwater collide to create sloughs and marshlands. With the exception of brief spots of thick vegetation at Duckabush and Eldon, the road provides consistent views of the water as it winds along as if starring in a sports car commercial. Mini-resorts in Lilliwaup and Hoodsport offer scuba diving, fishing excursions, hiking and camping.

The **Skokomish Indian Reservation** occupies the southernmost tip of Hood Canal and includes 5,000 acres of swampy wilderness and forest. The reservation was created in 1855 under the Point-No-Point Treaty. The Skokomish River and smaller tributaries contribute to much of the marshland area that makes farming difficult, if not impossible, but provides for the fine salmon and trout fishing that is the tribe's mainstay. Most of the fish that make their run to the canal originate in a trio of hatcheries west of the reservation. Clams dot the mudflats at low tide and provide food as well as folklore for the tribe: When the world was young and animals possessed human-like qualities, Crow was known throughout the land for his skill as a basket weaver. When Dukwibahl (or Transformer) arrived to change the order of the world, he was so impressed with Crow's craftsmanship that he used the designs off the baskets to decorate clam shells, thus forever leaving Crow's mark on the world.

Examples of intricate cedar woven baskets can be seen at the **Tribal Center Museum**, along with photographs, authentic hand-carved canoes and logging and fishing tools. Basket weaving is considered one of the primary artistic expressions for Twana (a larger group that the Skokomish are a part of) women, and the designs carry religious and historical significance, as well as depictions of everyday life. A school attached to the tribal center teaches children the ancient Twana language in an effort to keep their traditions alive.

U.S. 101 crosses the Skokomish River and plunges again into logging territory. The next 15 miles roll by a collection of tree farms awaiting their next projected harvest in 20 to 50 years, depending upon their present size. Acres of saplings often sit between fields of blackened stumps and sections of lightly touched timber, softening the contrast.

After passing Shelton and the sleepy village of **Kamilche** (actually just a collection of houses), take Kamilche Point Road northeast to glimpse a tiny community scattered across a small peninsula separating Little Skookum Inlet from Oyster Bay. The two-lane road swerves and bends to Kamilche Point and isolated views of the water. Numerous sail boats and small fishing vessels weave between wooded islands on their way to southern Puget Sound. Though only a short drive, the landscape varies considerably. The first mile is marked by sloughs and marshlands created by Skookum Creek draining into the inlet. Grass and reeds rise from the shallow, stagnant water that collects in run-off areas adjacent to the creek. Amidst the sloughs cattle graze on modest size farms. A bit further, the road moves within about 30 yards of the shoreline, although the many tall trees between

The bridge at Eld Inlet.

 the asphalt and water obscure the view. Only rough logging roads connect the middle portion of the peninsula where most of the land has been logged and replaced with tree farms. Almost all of the homes here are loosely clustered around the point and within sight of the water. Many are fronted by stumps emblazoned with the homeowner's name.

Back on Highway 101, continue south past views of Totten and Eld inlets and the wooded areas separating the two slim waterways. To the west the Kamilche Valley separates low partially-wooded hills with lush green fields and crisscrossing streams. A tavern, bakery and hand-painted signs advertising fresh oysters and scuba rentals are next to a short bridge crossing the southern tip of Eld Inlet. The final four miles of U.S. 101 gradually leave the small towns and country setting behind as it meets I-5 at the state capital in Olympia. ⁌

Seastacks are a common sight on U.S. 101, one of the state's most scenic highways.

S tate **Highway 102** from a junction with U.S. 101 west to Sanderson Airfield. Route length: two miles.

The large commercial airplanes gathered on the tarmac at **Sanderson Airfield** are waiting to be dismantled, having completed their tour of duty. The airport also serves private small plane owners.

It is possible to continue from Highway 102 on the Dayton-Airport Road, rambling along heavily-forested back roads to a junction with U.S. Highway 12 near Satsop, about a 30 mile trip. Along the way you will find the Shelton Timber Company Logging Railroad and **Schafer State Park** (East Satsop Road), once a picnic site for a logging company run by the three Schafer brothers. The Schafers, in charge of one of the most successful logging operations on the Olympic Peninsula, obviously knew as much about scenic retreats as they did business. Sheltered by thick groves of old-growth forest, the park maintains a rural setting along the banks of the East Fork of the Satsop River. ❃

S tate **Highway 103** from a junction with U.S. Highway 101 north to the tip of North Beach Peninsula. Route length: 20 miles.

Billed as the "World's Longest Beach" at over 28 miles, the reasonably-named **Long Beach Peninsula** is a favorite sandy strip for tourists, sun-worshippers, kite-flying enthusiasts and beachcombers. Motels, bed-and-breakfasts and restaurants dot the peninsula; charter boats and fishing vessels line the shore. Small resorts fill their reservation books during the summer months, then close and shelve them during the wet, blustery winters, when locals go into hibernation. Until the 1960s, the speed limit was unenforced here, making the hard-packed sand a popular drag strip for would-be auto racers in flashy hot rods. The speedway days have pass-

Waiting for the train at Long Beach in the 1920s.

ed, but driving on the sand is still fair game by virtue of a 1901 law that declared the beach an official part of the state highway. Less than two miles wide and often shrouded in a fog bank thick as a smoke cloud, the slim sandbar runs parallel to the mainland, separating the Pacific Ocean from Willapa Bay.

271~

The city of **Long Beach** (Elevation 10, Population 1,290) is the first population center encountered on Highway 103, and the location of Lewis and Clark's westernmost exploration. Conducting a bit of trailblazing of his own, Henry H. Tinker journeyed all the way from the coast of Maine to start the town of Long Beach. Arriving with his wife and children in 1880, he constructed several small houses and cleared and filled enough of the woodland area to allow others the space to settle. Anticipating tourists, the gregarious founder built a hotel and actively promoted the idyllic beachfront property to all visitors. This tourism legacy has endured and is now the economic giant for most of the peninsula. Five murals painted on various buildings provide a pictorial history of early life on the coast.

A drive around Long Beach in October reveals workers in waders standing in knee-deep water scooping cranberries from flooded bogs. Forty percent of the state's total production of the tart, red berry — the "ruby of the bog" — comes from the peninsula, making it second only to tourism in local commerce. Contributing to the industry's success is the Washington State University Research and Extension Unit on Pioneer Road in Long Beach. Established in 1923, scientists at the unit work to develop improved methods of cultivation and to create crops more resilient to frost and disease. Their original efforts, under the direction of D.J. Crowley, directly led to the gigantic boom in the industry which resulted in a merger between co-op farms on the peninsula and the Cranberry Canners Company of Massachusetts in 1941. That union later changed its name and is now the popular Ocean Spray brand.

Continue past numerous small lakes, resort communities, RV parks and hermit hideouts to **Ocean Park**. It is now primarily a resort town, but its origins lie in a fundamentalist Christian revival movement. Isaac A. Clark became frustrated with the emphasis placed on economic rather than religious interests in Oysterville, a town he co-founded. Rather than attempt to reverse the trend firmly ingrained in that settlement, he decided to start a new community of like-minded individuals. In 1883, Clark proposed to Methodist church leaders that they establish a Christian resort where they could hold revivals and bible studies all year long. Praised for its vision, the plan was set into motion.

The Reverend William R. Osborn caught wind of the idea back East and signed on, purchasing 140 acres for the camp several years later. Reverend Osborn had previously started a similar movement in Ocean Grove, New Jersey and, encouraged by its success, was looking to spread the word. Clark then donated 20 acres and Ocean Park was born. The Methodist Camp Meeting Association was formed to oversee the movement. Saloons were prohibited in the new community, and all members of the Methodist colony were required to sign a document vowing abstinence from alcohol, gambling and other vices.

The revival center offered bible studies, sermons, singing, picnicking, camping and an unspoken promise of better living. An article in the *Chinook Observer* emphasized the resort's focus on the family:

> The businessman can leave his family here for an outing with an assurance that its members are associating with the best class of people, and that they are not coming in contact with an element that is too often in evidence at a great many of our summer resorts. The sport and tough are not made welcome at this place.

The resort's first several years were spent in relative isolation and tranquillity, but within a decade Ocean Park's secular population increased and a canning industry set up shop around the religious colony. The ideals of the camp remained, but they could not control the commercial element growing around them.

Visitors were welcome to the camp, but in the end the growing number of tourists created an atmosphere the colonists originally sought to avoid. Ocean Park's popularity as a vacation spot led to the wholesale construction of hotels, resorts, restaurants and campgrounds. A few saloons even opened their doors for service (though confined to a specified section of town). Ocean Park is now the largest unincorporated town on the peninsula and a favorite among retirees.

On the shoreline of Willapa Bay east of Ocean Park is **Nahcotta**. This settlement followed in the wake of an oyster boom that began in the 1850s when Chinook Chief Nahcati led early settlers to plentiful oyster beds on the bay. Soon after, companies arrived and hired imported

The steamer T.J. Potter taking on passengers.

workers and Chinook Indians who harvested the mollusks at an alarming rate. A steady stream of schooners transported the shellfish to San Francisco and ports worldwide. The town grew smoothly and steadily for decades, culminating in the arrival of the railroad in 1889. But in addition to the normal fanfare that came with a rail connection, the advent also brought conflict.

Nahcotta was the end of the line for the recently completed Ilwaco Railroad and Steam Navigation Company, referred to as the "Clamshell Railroad" by locals. Here the final tracks turned east and were laid on pilings reaching over the waves of Willapa Bay, splitting the town and dividing loyalties. Nahcotta lay south of the tracks and had the support of Lewis A. Loomis, the owner of the railroad. To the north a new township was started by B. A. Seaborg, a canning mogul from Ilwaco. Seaborg issued a direct challenge to Loomis by trying to gain control over the peninsula's oyster trade. In time, Loomis prevailed and Seaborg was absorbed into Nahcotta.

After the railroad terminal was secured, Nahcotta became a stop for a new ferry route, making it the transportation hub of the peninsula. Steamers arrived daily from South Bend and Raymond across Willapa Bay carrying mail, passengers and trade items. Looking to branch out economically, reliance on timber products grew around the turn of the century, taking some of the pressure off of the sinking oyster industry. Then disaster struck in the winter of 1915. A chimney fire started a hotel burning, which in turn engulfed an adjacent building. A strong wind then carried the flames the length of the business district. When the smoke cleared, Nahcotta's economic base had been reduced to ashes. The old town never regained its youthful vigor.

Settlement on Long Beach peninsula began at the sheltered northern end around rife oyster beds. The town that sprang up around these beds and inspired migration was called, appropriately enough, **Oysterville**. To reach the salty, wind-blown town, follow Highway 103 north along the bay for three miles. One of the oldest settlements in the state, Oysterville was founded in 1854 when Chinook Chief Nahcati shared the location of a protected oyster bed with Issac A. Clark and Robert H. Espy. Wasting no time, the two men platted the town shortly after the visit and were joined by over 500 others in a few months time. A year later the town had a thriving oyster industry and the county seat; continued prosperity seemed inevitable.

But the tide soon turned. When a transcontinental rail link was connected to San Francisco in the late 1870s, then the largest consumer of Willapa Bay oyster, competition from eastern oysters caused business to suffer. In addition, a combination of over-harvesting, parasites and near-freezing winter weather brought the oyster beds dangerously close to depletion. By the time the railroad ventured close enough to be of real value, the industry was nearly washed up. The final blow came when South Bend rigged an election and kidnapped the county seat in 1893.

Substituting native oysters with transplanted Japanese oysters at the turn of the century helped keep the shellfish industry alive, but at that point it was only a shadow of its mid-1800s self. The upside of the early fizzle is that the well-preserved town was never compromised by needs for renovation or expansion. The community is on the National Register of Historic Places, and boasts many homes and churches that date back to the 1870s and earlier. Some vintage structures were substituted when portions of a street were lost to eroding tides, but the authentic feel remains.

From Oysterville, Highway 103 continues north four miles to its conclusion at **Leadbetter Point State Park**. The park touches the shores of both the Pacific Ocean and Willapa Bay, and between is an unusual blend of ecosystems. Forests of spruce, cedar and hemlock border salt-water marshes and sand dunes, all rich in wildlife. Deer are plentiful and black bears are known to feed on blackberries and huckleberries. The Indians called the tip of the peninsula *Tsako-te-hahsh-eetl*, "land of the red-top grass and home of the woodpecker." Hiking trails weave throughout the park and some lead to the sand dunes of the Willapa National Wildlife Refuge on the northern cap of the peninsula. The refuge is an annual stopover for a wide range of migrating birds, and is closed from April to August to protect nesting snowy plovers. ᏸ

S tate **Highway 104** from a junction with State Highway 522 northwest through Edmonds and across Puget Sound via ferry to Kingston, continue through Port Gamble and over Hood Canal to a junction with U.S. Highway 101. Route length: 33 miles.

Bumper stickers that crow "It's an Edmonds' kind of day" may be boastful, but it's difficult to deny **Edmonds'** (Elevation 40, Population 30,970) charm, a result of its historic preservation and waterfront locale. Rising from a ferry landing that sends and receives tourists to and from Kingston, Edmonds is a mix of loyal natives who have vowed to spend the rest of their years here; wide-eyed tourists who promise to relocate; and entrepreneurs who make a living from the attention the city receives.

A storm brought logger George Brackett and his trusty canoe to the lengthy beachfront facing Puget Sound. While the timbered slopes offered Brackett shelter, they also promised opportunity. Brackett purchased the Elwell homestead claim, located midway between Seattle and Everett, and their rail and steamboat connections and built a sawmill and wharf. He later served as postmaster and mayor and

Plying the waters between the mainland and Bainbridge Island.

275~

selected the town's name for the widely-respected U.S. Senator from Vermont, George F. Edmunds. (The name was slightly altered by postal authorities in the 1880s.) Legend persists that in order to incorporate Edmonds, the names of two oxen, Bill and Bolivar, were added to the petition.

Of historical interest is **Old Mill Town** (5th Avenue and Dayton Street), joyfully cluttered with stores chock-full of antiques and various knickknacks. The venerable facilities occupy a former sawmill site. **Brackett's Landing**, adjacent to the ferry terminal, is a beachfront tribute to the town's founder. The **Edmonds Historical Museum** (118 5th Avenue) is also worth a visit.

The waterfront is further bolstered by an extensive marina and the largest chartered fleet in the Puget Sound. Divers travel to Edmonds from around the country to explore **Edmonds Undersea Park**, 32 acres of murky terrain surrounding a dry dock sunk to attract marine life.

From Edmonds a thirty-minute ferry ride is necessary (but hardly unpleasant) to reach **Kingston**. (In the summer be prepared to spend more time in line waiting to board than on the ferry itself.) Rising from the north banks of Appletree Cove, Kingston residents overlook a sailboat-filled harbor from homes with million-dollar views. Before its role as a ferry terminus, Kingston dabbled in some milling operations that were eventually swallowed up by those in Port Gamble.

Two miles from Kingston turn north on Hansville Road to **Point No Point**. The lighthouse and foghorn flash and blare their warning to help ships work their way through the Admiralty Inlet. Tours of the lighthouse are given in the summer. In January 1855, during Governor Stevens' treaty-signing tour of the territory, the Point no Point Treaty was signed between Stevens and members of the Chimakum, Skokomish and Clallam tribes. As for the name, nervous navigators occasionally lost sight of the promontory; sometimes there was a point, sometimes there wasn't.

Up the road five miles, the fragrance of wood chips and cut lumber leads to **Port Gamble**. Hailing from East Macias, Maine, Andrew J. Pope and Captain William C. Talbot found themselves in San Francisco at a time when lumber was in hot demand. The discovery of gold in California led to a massive influx of men and subsequently the need to build hotels, wharves, homes and saloons (not necessarily in that order), all of which required timber resources that California did not have. And so in 1853, with sights set on the timbered mecca of the northwest, Pope and Talbot boarded the *Julius Pringle* and sailed up the coast. Attracted to Port Gamble's deepwater port and a seemingly endless timber supply, the opportunists started the Puget Mill Company, and by their first year of full production, four million board feet of lumber were processed. The Pope and Talbot Mill, the oldest operating sawmill in

North America, produces more than 90 million board feet of dimension lumber annually.

The majority of the homes and buildings in Port Gamble are company-owned and were restored in the 1960s. Neatly painted in white and grey, the wood-framed structures are topped by steep, gabled roofs and fronted by historical reader boards. Tree seeds imported from New England have matured into sugar maples and Maine elms that shade the town's quiet streets. The goal was to re-create a New England coast lumber town. It seems to have worked.

Port Gamble's cemetery occupies a spacious bluff overlooking the Puget Sound, a short walk east from the town center. The

1901 shot of Port Gamble and the Pope and Talbot mill.

remains of **Gustav Englebrecht**, the first United States Navy man to die in action in the Pacific, are located here. Englebrecht was a member of the *Massachusetts* crew sent to investigate a disturbance on the shores of Port Gamble. Canoe-loads of Tlingit Indians from southeast Alaska landed here in February 1856 to round up fellow tribe members who worked at the mill. Previously they had attacked a village at Steilacoom. When the *Massachusetts* went to intervene, Englebrect was shot and killed. Twenty-seven Tlingits lost their lives, including the chief, whose death was avenged by the killing of Isaac Ebey at Whidbey Island one year later.

Return to Highway 104 and cross Hood Canal over the one and a half mile **Hood Canal Floating Bridge** to the Olympic Peninsula. When opened on August 12, 1961, the 6,471-foot long bridge was the second concrete pontoon floating bridge in the state and the first in the world on tidal waters. Part of the bridge sank during a major storm in 1979, but was rebuilt and reinforced in 1982.

Highway 104 meets up with U.S. 101 21 miles from Sequim. ∝

S tate **Highway 105** from a junction with U.S. Highway 101 in Raymond west through Tokeland, north through Grayland to Westport, then east via Grays Harbor to rejoin U.S. 101 in Aberdeen. Route length: 52 miles.

Beginning across the Willapa River from Raymond, the highway stretches west through sloughs and marshland lining the mouth of Willapa Bay. At low tide it appears as if no vessel larger than a rowboat could pass, but for over a century oyster schooners regularly slid through deep trenches in the mud flats and into the river to load up on bivalves. Though never as commercially important as the deepwater port at Grays Harbor, the bay played a supporting role in transporting record shipments of timber from the coast in the early 1900s. Remnants of docks and old oyster beds rising from the mud come and go with the tides.

A gauntlet of crabbers lie in wait.

A spur just off of Highway 105 leads two miles southeast to **Tokeland**, a small community resting on a toe of land jutting into the bay. From roughly 1890 to 1910 the town was a hopping resort and tourist trap advertising fun for all ages. Steamers tied up here daily in summer months to deliver full loads of vacationers to the sandy beaches for sun and frolic. It was the rage for a spell, but as Pacific coast resorts grew increasingly popular, the crowds at Tokeland thinned out.

The resorts at **North Cove**, one mile west of the **Shoalwater Indian Reservation** back on Highway 105, met a similar fate, but for a different reason — the tide up and carried the town away. Erosion of the coastline where the Pacific Ocean meets Willapa Bay was already severe, and man-made jetties constructed in the 1930s near the mouth further exaggerated and expedited these tidal forces. The jetties protected certain areas, but left other shores, like North Cove, open for prolonged attacks by the powerful current. Some houses were saved and relocated, but many other structures slipped below the waves like abandoned ships.

Bending north, the road runs past sand dunes, ocean views, **Grayland Beach State Park** and on to **Grayland**, the heart of nearly 1,000 acres of cleared marshland known as the *Cranberry Coast*. Grown on low-running vines, the berries range from bright pink in the spring to a deep red in the fall. The fruit was a staple in the diet of coastal Indians, and also used to heal wounds and dye clothing. Most berries are now destined for supermarket produce sections, juice bottles and Thanksgiving dinners.

Scattered homesteaders arriving in the 1880s found a swamp-land thick with the wild berries, and early efforts at cultivation were thwarted by the trees, brambles and undergrowth that shared the bogs. Months were spent toiling in knee-deep water only to have one frost wipe out an entire crop. The farming process is arduous but rewarding; cranberries require at least four years to mature, but once they reach full potential they can produce perennially for decades. Even small farms are capable of disproportionately large harvests. But the risks, frustrations and time requirements did not make the berries a good choice for a quick cash turnover, so many young crops were abandoned prior to 1910.

Realizing the potential of the crop and having the time and resources to invest, Sam Benn, the founder of Aberdeen, introduced the first successful wholesale cranberry cultivation to the coast in 1912. (Attempts had been made on the Long Beach Peninsula as early as 1872, but they did not last long.) After two years of preparing the land and planting starts imported from Massachusetts, he sold plots to several pioneer families. Exercising patience and plenty of back muscles, the efforts eventually produced hearty yields and an indus-try was born. Grayland is now one of the most productive areas in the country for cranberries.

At the highway junction near the entrance to **Twin Harbors State Park**, continue north four miles to the fishing hub of **Westport** (Eleva-tion 12, Population 1,970). Once the self-proclaimed sport fishing capi-tal of the world, dwindling numbers of salmon have recently tested the claim. Regardless of catch phrases, a walk around the marina illustrates that fishing is still the local king of business; commercial and charter boats bob next to creaking docks; large cranes lift crab pots onto the pier and workers mend nets and swab decks. Whale-watching boats and pleasure cruisers round out the wave parade.

Prior to becoming a fishing center, Westport served as a popular summer resort. Platted as "Westport Beach" in 1891 by Frank Peterson, steamers brought vacationing families to the peninsula, where hotels and campgrounds were consistently booked during fair-weather months. Travelers entering Grays Harbor generally made a stop in the port as well, adding to the bustle.

Westport is also considered one of the state's best surfing beaches. But be warned, even when the sun is shining the water is cold enough to take your breath away, consistently hovering around the 60-degree mark.

For beach access and a good view of breakers crashing against the rock jetties, follow West Ocean Avenue from town to **Westport Light State Park**. Before reaching the shore you pass the Westport Light, the tallest beacon on the West Coast at 107 feet high. Built in 1895, the tower continues to operate on most of its original components.

In clear weather, the light can be seen from as far away as 25 nautical miles.

Return to the main branch of Highway 105 and drive east over a bridge spanning South Bay and past the neighborhood of Bay City. At the hard right turn in the road sits the once-hopeful town of **Ocosta**. A case of terminal fever hit this shoreline in the early 1890s when the Northern Pacific Railroad bought land and laid track. With an announcement that Ocosta had been chosen over Aberdeen and Hoquiam as the Grays Harbor headquarters, prospectors fell over one another trying to snatch the surrounding land. Enough plots were sold to create a small city, and settlers swarmed the bay with construction materials to cash in on what seemed a sure bet. Then, at the height of expectations, the plan derailed. Horrendous weather damaged portions of the track and halted construction on the terminal. Before the Northern Pacific could rebuild, the financial crash of 1893 put an end to funding and Ocosta was chalked up as a loss. Meanwhile, Aberdeen had laid their own track to entice the Northern Pacific, and consequently, the terminal landed there.

Further east, the highway rolls through the forest and along the southern shore of **Grays Harbor** to its conclusion in Aberdeen. A myth surrounding the creation of the harbor involves legendary logger Paul Bunyan and his country-wide search for a bathing spot. He found the Mississippi River sufficiently long and wide enough, but lacking in depth. He continued westward across the country with no luck until he eventually hit the shores of the Pacific Ocean. As he stood surveying the water before him, a catastrophic whirlpool began around his ankles, and for the first time in his life he was thrown off of his feet and dumped into a sitting position. The tumble formed a deep, rounded impression in the earth. When water from the ocean rushed in to fill the crater, he had finally found a bathtub large enough to contain him.

As the only deepwater port on the Washington coast, Grays Harbor served as a turnpike for some of the largest shipments of timber the world has ever seen during the logging heydays after 1900. A protected, nearly enclosed entrance made passage safe and relatively unpredictable. Deep, dredged channels allow large vessels to land even during low tides that expose mud flats and sandbars. The Chehalis, Wishkah and Hoquiam rivers drain into the harbor, along with numerous smaller waterways that trickle from every direction. The bay is the namesake of Captain Robert Gray, who anchored in the harbor on May 7, 1792. (Gray originally called it Bullfinch Harbor, but Joseph Whidbey of the Vancouver Expedition later changed it to the present name as a gesture of respect.)

Though he considered himself a fur trader, **Captain Robert Gray** became one of the most important American explorers by laying claim to vital points along the Pacific Northwest coast. Born in Rhode Island in 1755, Gray began his life at sea early, serving in the Continental Navy during the Revolutionary War. In 1787 he embarked on his first voyage to the West Coast on a trading mission, and on his return in 1790 he became the first American to circumnavigate the earth. Though the trip was not a commercial success (he arrived in Boston Harbor with a load of rotten tea), the feat made him famous.

After a rest of just seven weeks, he again set out for the Northwest with sufficient items to barter and a solid understanding of the fur trade. It was on this journey that he would make his most significant find: the mighty Columbia River. The discovery cemented the United States' hold on the region; a claim later secured by the creation of the 49th parallel as the international boundary line. Without this discovery, Washington state would not exist (and we, the authors of this book,

Cold waters only a purist could love.

would be out of a job). After securing a trade route with China on the return trip, he arrived in Boston in 1793 with a wealth of pelts and spent the remainder of his days sailing the Atlantic seaboard. Like a true mariner, he died at sea in 1806. ༀ

State **Highway 106** from a junction with U.S. Highway 101 northeast through Union to a junction with State Highway 3. Route length: 20 miles.

Branching off from U.S. 101 at the Skokomish Indian Reservation, the highway rounds the Great Bend (or south hook) of Hood Canal and moves through **Union**, a small community rising from the shore. When lumberjacks began sawing through the surrounding forests, the Wilson and Anderson trading post opened here in 1858 to cater to the logging camps pitched in the area. The Rush House, a two-story hotel and bar, opened a year later, reflecting the growing number of saw-swinging settlers.

Steamers were used to carry the timber to mills on the Puget Sound, but logging company owners deemed the process too slow and tried to garner the services of the railroad. Their request was granted in 1889 when the Union Pacific Railroad announced plans to build a major terminal here, and the town was platted almost immediately. Word of the approaching tracks brought speculators scurrying, and one acre lots were sold for up to $1,000, an amazing price for land at that time. Construction on the railway began and abruptly ended in 1893 when the financial crash brought growth to a grinding halt. The small village has been quiet ever since.

Leaving Union, the highway winds north along the shoreline to **Twanoh State Park**. The forest surrounding the waterfront park was logged in the 1890s, but a century worth of growth has returned the area to its natural state. The buildings and rest rooms near the sandy beach were built by the Civilian Conservation Corps in 1937.

From the park, Highway 106 continues seven miles north to a connection with Highway 3 at the end of Hood Canal. ℭ

State Highway 107 from a junction with U.S. Highway 101 northeast to a junction with U.S. Highway 12 in Montesano. Route length: eight miles.

Highway 107 bypasses Aberdeen and provides a shortcut between Highways 101 and 12. The road crosses **Preacher's Slough**, a tidal stream in the Chehalis River drainage area. In the mid-1800s, Methodist Episcopal minister Rev. J.S. Douglass took his boat up the slough mistaking it for the Chehalis River, and becoming thoroughly lost in the process. Along the way, the road passes the Weyerhaeuser Tree Farm, the nation's first tree farm. ℭ

State Highway 108 from a junction with State Highway 8 in McCleary northeast to a junction with U.S. Highway 101 in Kamilche. Route length: 12 miles.

Logging trucks still barrel down Highway 108, though with considerably less frequency. The road heads towards Shelton and the southwest extremity of Skookum Inlet by way of the Kamilche Valley. Kamilche is an alteration of the Twana Indian word Ka-bel-chi, meaning "valley," so in essence you are driving the "valley valley." ℭ

State Highway 109 from a junction with U.S. Highway 101 in Hoquiam west to North Beach then north through Moclips to Taholah. Route length: 40 miles.

Running west along the northern reaches of North Bay, an extension of Grays Harbor, the highway pushes towards the coastline of the Pacific Ocean. At the junction with Highway 115, Highway 109 turns north to explore the seaboard stretch collectively known as North Beach. The small unincorporated communities strung along North

Beach support an abundance of beach houses, motels, bed-and-breakfasts and gift shops and are as equally packed in the summer months as they are desolate during the off-season. Three state parks — **Ocean City**, **Griffiths-Priday** and **Pacific Beach** — provide ample room to walk the beach, climb sand dunes or dig for the tasty razor clam. The scenic drive weaves from thick patches of forest to high, jagged bluffs overlooking sandy beaches. The beach is accessible in several locations, and by virtue of a 1901 law, it is legal to drive on the sand. (All beaches north of Moclips are controlled by the Quinault Indians. Permission to access these areas must be obtained from the tribal headquarters in Taholah.)

This is a place to walk and think and reflect for an hour, a day, or a month.

At the end of this line of small towns is **Moclips** (MOH-klips), once a promising resort destination. By the turn-of-the-century, Moclips had secured two elements crucial to a coastal town's success: a sawmill and a railroad connection. A terminal, the last stop on North Beach, was built by the Northern Pacific in 1903, and carried cedar planks and shingles destined for Grays Harbor. The line helped support an already expanding tourist trade by making the town easier to reach. To take full advantage of the seascape, the 270-room Moclips Hotel was built just 12 feet from the hard-packed beach. Advertising a "perfect view of the Pacific," the hotel earned a reputation as one of the finer accommodations on the coast, elevating Moclips to a popular, though short-lived, vacation spot.

The waterfront location, the hotel's major selling point, eventually proved its downfall. In the winter of 1913, huge waves propelled by gale-force winds pounded the coast, destroying much of the hotel

109 and many other buildings in town. What remained of the establishment wobbled on unstable pilings before finally collapsing into the sea. Cedar planks that once served as ceilings, walls and floors were collected by the tides and smashed and scattered along the rocky coastline.

The highway continues north to its conclusion at the mouth of the Quinault River in **Taholah**, the headquarters of the **Quinault Indian Reservation**. A mosaic of deep, hidden rivers and partially-ravaged rain forest, the 190,000-acre reservation was created in 1855 after the Quinaults surrendered much of their land in exchange for promises of education, medical care and exclusive rights to traditional fishing areas and methods. The reservation was enlarged in 1873 to accommodate members of other tribes who either refused to sign the original treaty or were so scattered or isolated that they slipped between the authoritative cracks.

A sovereign Quinault Indian Nation now exists, giving the people the power of self-governance. The idea of a separate Indian nation was the result of encroachment by settlers and timber-mongers into the rain forest. Logging companies purchased the rights to the timber on large sections of Quinault land, then clear-cut until the land was unfit for farming or future tree cultivation. Protests came to a head in 1971 when members of the tribe blocked logging roads, thrusting the issue of land management into the national spotlight. Many of these conservation programs are stifled since timber companies still own portions of the reservation, but now that the old-growth is depleted the companies want to sell. The Quinaults are currently making efforts to buy back their land, and with it, part of their heritage. ∞

110 **S**tate Highway 110 from a junction with U.S. Highway 101 in Forks, west to La Push. Route length: 14 miles.

Follow the **Bogachiel River** west through thick, damp forest until it drains into the **Quiluete River**. Here the highway branches; the north fork follows the Quileute (Kwil-uh-yoot) to the ocean and **Rialto Beach**. This is an ideal spot for hiking and exploring the rugged coastline, riddled with sand dunes, wind-bent trees and tide pools galore. At low tide, walk a sandy mile north to the **Hole in the Wall**, a spectacular rockbridge carved by the surf.

The southern branch of the highway ends at **La Push**, the westernmost town in the continental U.S. In addition to a U.S. Coast Guard station, the town is occupied by the **Quileute Indian Reservation**. A series of staggered sea-stacks (massive rock monoliths) rise from the ocean floor just off the coast. The largest, **James Island**, is an ancient Quileute burial ground that once served as a safe haven for women and children during slave raids from neighboring tribes.

Quileute (Kwil-uh-yoot) Indians were adept hunters of the sea in their hand-crafted canoes.

Migrating whales can be seen in the area of these sea-stacks from March to May.

According to an 1856 treaty, the Quileutes were to forfeit their land and join the Quinault Indians on a reservation 40 miles to the south. Despite the treaty, the small Quileute tribe never left their home; a fact that failed to attract immediate attention due to their isolated location. After a series of territorial disputes with white settlers, a one-square-mile reservation was established here in 1889.

Skilled hunters of the sea, the Quileute people crafted cedar canoes, some up to 60 feet in length and others capable of carrying three tons of cargo, to intercept whales and seals on their migratory paths. When a harpoon found its mark, the whale's mouth was sewn shut to create air pockets in the stomach and ensure flotation. Several days were often required to drag the massive creatures to shore. Nets and fish traps were used to catch salmon, smelt and steelhead on the Quileute River.

Social hierarchy and prestige were determined by the potlatch, an elaborate ceremony in which possessions were exchanged or even carelessly destroyed in a grandiose display of riches. The highest honor was then bestowed on those who gave the most away. If a clan could not afford the presentation of goods — blankets, skins, animals, slaves, etc. — it would decline in status. In this way, wealth and power were periodically redistributed. This practice was common to most tribes along the Northwest coast, with each having their own variations.

The approximately 350 remaining tribal members are currently reviving ancient customs and traditions, some of which are known by only a few elders. A school has been established to teach children and older members the nearly-forgotten and isolated Quileute language. Unrelated to any other known Indian dialect and unique in terms of grammar and phonetics, it is only one of five languages on earth that uses no nasal sounds. Pronounced with a series of clicks

![110 WASHINGTON] and guttural explosions, several suffixes can be added to a single word to create a highly descriptive sound that would be the English equivalent of several sentences worth of information or ideas. While not all young people attend this school, enough are doing so to ensure the language's survival into the next generation. ca

![112 WASHINGTON] State Highway 112 from a junction with U.S. Highway 101 west via Clallam Bay and Sekiu to Neah Bay. Route length: 62 miles. Four miles west of Port Angeles, Highway 112 branches from U.S. 101, crosses the Elwha River and meanders among the damp forest as a lonely two-laner. After passing several tiny communities the road breaks for the coastline, providing glimpses of the wide **Strait of Juan de Fuca**. For centuries the waterway was rumored to be the mythical "Strait of Anian," a navigable route often called the

Northwest Passage which was believed to cut across North America and link the Pacific and Atlantic oceans. The strait is the namesake of a Greek mariner named Apostolos Valerianos, who sailed for Spain for over 40 years under the alias of Juan de Fuca and allegedly made the discovery in 1592.

Strait of Juan de Fuca, once rumored to be the mythical "Strait of Anian."

According to de Fuca's version of events, he sailed north from Acapulco, Mexico to a strait between the 47th and 48th parallels which he followed for nearly three weeks before reaching the Atlantic and returning to Acapulco. Word of his travels caused a stir among seamen eager for a short-cut to the Orient for trading purposes, and theories surfaced regarding the route's location. One popular belief was that the strait joined the Mississippi River, providing access to the Gulf of Mexico.

Since no written log of his journeys was ever found, the authenticity of Juan de Fuca's voyage was, and continues to be, debated, though he did provide some convincing verbal descriptions of geographic features and Indian tribes. Despite the doubts and lack of verification, books and maps of his travels were printed in England and Spain, enticing sailors to search out the mysterious passage. It was not until 1788 that British Captain John Meares charted the entrance to the strait and named it in honor of the Greek captain who first brought the legend of the passage to life. Four years later Captain George Vancouver made a thorough exploration of the strait on his way to Puget Sound, and the myth of the Northwest Passage was firmly laid to rest.

The road moves inland again to a connection with State Highway 113 before heading back to the coastline at the town of **Clallam Bay**. Settled on the shores of a bay of the same name, the quiet town operates as moorage for a small fleet of charter and commercial fishing vessels. For centuries the sheltered cove served as a safe haven for trading and exploring vessels threatened by storms along the Strait of Juan de Fuca.

Tucked at the western end of Clallam Bay is **Sekiu** (SEE-Kyoo), a collection of homes and motels scattered over a steep hillside overlooking the water. Summers find the town packed with sport fishermen and countless charter and pleasure boats tied to the long docks; in winter most of the businesses lock their doors, leaving a few people and the lonely sound of the crashing tide. Fishing became a way of life here over a century ago when a cannery opened to receive the bounty from numerous vessels working the strait. As wharves were built along the waterfront, logging took root and rail lines stretched from the thick forest to a mill and barges waiting to haul timber into Puget Sound. Both activities ceased due to resource depletion.

From Sekiu the highway winds west, offering clear views of the strait and of Vancouver Island before ending in **Neah Bay** (Nee-uh), the headquarters of the **Makah Indian Reservation**. The Makah — "cape people" — are the southernmost branch of the Nootka and more closely identified with tribes of southeastern Alaska than with other tribes on the Washington coast. As their location would indicate, they are heavily reliant upon the ocean for survival, and are historically known for their canoe building and whale hunting prowess. The 28,000-acre reservation was created by a treaty with Territorial Governor Isaac I. Stevens on January 31, 1855 and enlarged in 1873.

For a look at the history and art of the Makah people, visit the **Makah Museum** located along the highway at the eastern edge of town. On display are the remains of a 500-year-old Makah village once buried in a mud slide and uncovered by tidal erosion. The site was discovered in 1969 about 15 miles south of Neah Bay on the Ozette Indian Reservation. The excavation took 11 years and recovered entire structures and over 50,000 artifacts in unusually good condition; some wooden tools and weapons were so well preserved that they appeared almost new. Ozette is believed to have been the largest of the Makah villages on the Northwest Coast.

In 1792 a ship arrived at Neah Bay from a Spanish outpost in San Blas, Mexico to become the first European settlement in the state.

112 Under the leadership of Lieutenant Salvador Fidalgo, Spanish colonists settled near Fort Nunez Gaona, built two years earlier by Manuel Quimper, with instructions "to establish a small battery on the mainland, respectable fortifications, provisional barracks for the sick, a bakery and oven, a blacksmith shop, and to cut down all trees within musket shot." Most of these objectives were carried out, but the settlement was abandoned after only five months and moved to Nootka on Vancouver Island where talks were being held with the British concerning claims to the Northwest Coast.

Though ships stopped periodically to trade with the Makahs, a permanent settlement did not exist until 1851 when Samuel Hancock established a trading post and a warehouse for Indians to store their whale oil. Hancock's post attracted vessels from all along the West Coast, and eventually this contact brought white diseases. By 1854 hundreds of natives had perished from smallpox, causing their population to plummet.

From Neah Bay an unpaved road leads to **Cape Flattery**, the "Northwestern Tip of the Continental United States." This high, rocky bluff was named by British Captain James Cook in March of 1778, who after discovering it to be false wrote in his journal: "there appeared to be a small opening that flattered us with hopes of finding a harbour there." One mile offshore sits rocky **Tatoosh Island**, home to a lighthouse (built in 1857), weather and naval station, and once the site of a school and post office. The best way to view the island is from one of several hiking trails exploring the cape. ∽

113 S tate **Highway 113** from a junction with U.S. Highway 101 in Sappho north to a connection with State Highway 112. Route length: 10 miles.

Also listed as Burnt Mountain Road, this connector is most often employed by logging trucks, as the surrounding hillsides can attest, and folks headed to Neah Bay. Though there are no towns to speak of, there is plenty of isolation to be found along this wooded route. ∽

115 S tate **Highway 115** from junction with State Highway 109 south to Oyhut and continuing as Ocean Shores Boulevard to Ocean Shores. Route length: six miles.

From the small community of Oyhut, continue along the beachfront to **Ocean Shores** (Elevation 14, Population 2,620), the largest resort and vacation community on Washington's coast. A continuous row of hotels, motels and restaurants line the sandy beach, punctuated by go-cart tracks, bumper-boats, miniature golf, horseback riding, an aquarium and other family-oriented amusement. Clam digging is the local sport of choice; hordes flock the hard-packed sand with buckets and shovels all summer long.

Ocean Shores sits on a flat, two-mile-wide peninsula that features a surprisingly diverse landscape. The peninsula, really more of a giant sand spit, is enclosed by a circle of sand dunes created by the moving surf. Small lakes and ponds peppered with pine trees, and connected by streams where salt and freshwater mingle, stretch north to south up the interior. Marshes covering the southern tip are part of the **Oyhut Wildlife Area**, where ducks, snowy plovers, sandpipers and a large variety of other aquatic birds live and breed.

Once sparsely populated by cattle-ranchers and squatters, the present city of Ocean Shores was conceived and raised by real-estate developers. A barrage of civic improvements were made during the 1960s. Streets were paved, neighborhoods laid out, and commercial and retail zones developed. Celebrities and famous Hollywood types were heavily targeted in an attempt to bring some high-class ritz (and money) to the coast, leading to a short-lived claim as the "Richest Little City in the U.S." But early demand for such an ambitious resort community fell short of the supply, resulting in accommodation over-kill. Within a decade construction projects sat in mid-completion; neon signs advertised hotel vacancies; and nervous investors scrambled to evacuate.

Meanwhile, a sizable population of permanent residents took advantage of reduced land prices and quietly trickled in, securing steady business for grocery stores and other ventures less reliant on tourism. This diversity brought more stability and afforded the town some necessary time to be discovered by vacationers and urban escapists. As a result, Ocean Shores has recently experienced a surge in growth, making it one of the busiest destination cities in the state.

S **tate Highway 116** from a junction with State Highway 19 east via Indian Island to Marrowstone Island then north to Fort Flagler State Park. Route length: 11 miles.

Highway 116 starts just north of Chimacum at Nesses Corner. **Indian Island**, a short bridge crossing away, shows evidence of over 3,000 years of Native American habitation. The island is a U.S. Navy Reservation and closed to the public except on Fourth of July, when the gates open for Independence Day celebrations and a fireworks display. Naval ships entering

Flotsam for an evening driftwood fire.

289~

Puget Sound for repairs are required to unload their ordnance here, sort of like taking off your shoes before entering the house.

Filling the gap between Indian and Marrowstone islands is Kilisut Harbor (KIL-i-suht), a Clallam Indian term meaning "protected water." The harbor was used as a hideout in Prohibition Days by booze-smuggling bandits on the lam from the Coast Guard.

Cross another mini-bridge to **Marrowstone Island**, a seven-mile-long island discovered by George Vancouver on May 8, 1792. The English navigator gleaned the name from the north point cliffs that were comprised of marrowstone, a white clay-like substance.

At the end of the road is **Fort Flagler**, now a state park but once the southern corner of Puget Sound's "Triangle of Fire." Together with the heavy batteries of Fort Worden on Point Wilson and Fort Casey on Admiralty Head, Fort Flagler formed a coastal fortification system designed to prevent hostile fleets from breaching Admiralty Inlet and reaching such targets as the Bremerton Navy Shipyard and the cities of Seattle, Tacoma, Olympia and Everett.

Coastal forts such as Fort Flagler, effective at the turn of the century with their six inch disappearing guns, became obsolete with the arrival of World War I and new ships armed to the teeth with larger, more accurate 14-, 15-, and 16-inch guns. During both World Wars,

Fort Flagler barracks. The fort once protected Admiralty Inlet.

Fort Flagler gun battery. Part of the "triangle of fire".

Fort Flagler served as a training facility for wet-behind-the-ears inductees as well as engineers and other troops involved in amphibious military maneuvers. It was shut down permanently in 1953 and purchased as a state park in 1955.

Fort Flagler State Park is bordered by a driftwood-covered shoreline on three sides and wide views of the Puget Sound. An expansive campground overlooks Kilisut Harbor and Port Townsend Bay. The park also contains a youth hostel and a forest interpretive trail, detailing the "inner workings of the land as an organism."

Spread throughout the park are nine gun batteries and mortar emplacements with fixed, deactivated armament. Most are open to the public and may be found by picking up a brochure at the park entrance or by following well-marked road signs. ɕ

S tate **Highway 117** from a junction with U.S. Highway 101 north via Port Angeles to Port Angeles Harbor. Route length: two miles.

Trucks loaded down with timber use Highway 117, a connector between the mill and harbor area to U.S. 101, to avoid Port Angeles' downtown (U.S. 101) and its string of stoplights. ɕ

119 **S** tate Highway 119 from a junction with U.S. Highway 101 northwest to Lake Cushman. Route length: 11 miles.
Branching from U.S. 101 at Hoodsport, the highway (Lake
Cushman Road) cuts through the woods and to the banks of **Lake
Cushman**, a man-made lake surrounded by the Olympic Mountains.
Prior to 1926, the lake was just over one mile long and home to
several resilient farming families and two resort hotels. Though
secluded and relatively difficult to reach, the lake and surrounding
area was a favorite destination for hunters and fishermen.

Then technology arrived. Two dams were constructed across the
North Fork of the Skokomish River, submerging the resorts and transforming the once-small lake into a ten-mile long reservoir. Tacoma
City Light set up one power plant at the southern end of the lake, and
another along Hood Canal to harness the energy. A model of efficiency,
for nearly two decades the electric rates in Tacoma were among the
lowest in the nation due to the productive capacity of the dams.

New resorts, summer homes and **Lake Cushman State Park** have
since replaced the facilities lost to flooding, making the lake a haven
for water-sport enthusiasts. The road ends at the public campground
in Staircase, one half mile north of the lake and within the boundaries
of the Olympic National Forest. ∞

121 **S** tate Highway 121 from a junction with U.S. Highway 12 in
Rochester northwest to Littlerock, east to Deep Lake then
north to a junction with Interstate 5. Route length: 16 miles.
Highway 121 is the route to the **Mima Mounds Natural Area
Preserve** and Millersylvania State Park. Texturing the prairie lands of
southwest Thurston County, hundreds of thousands of the mounds
exist, stretching up to 30 feet across and rising two to ten feet high.

There are almost as many theories for how the mounds were
formed as there are mounds themselves. Lieutenant Charles Wilkes,
during his expedition of 1841, dug into a number of them, thinking
they might be Indian burial mounds, but found only gravel and dirt.
He determined that "... They are evidently of old formation by a
bygone race... as they have the marks of savage labour... such a labour
as a whole nation had entered into."

Nineteenth-century naturalist Louis Agassiz believed that the piles
were constructed by spawning fish when the area was underwater.
Victor Scheffer, a prominent twentieth-century zoologist, argued that
gophers created the mounds. Another scientist expanded on the
gopher theory, claiming the mounds were the work of giant gophers
who no longer lived on earth. Still more explanations circulate,
ranging from Indian-built buffalo decoys to earth pockets created by
gas and oil pressure. The most probable account is that passing
glaciers dropped sediment as they melted.

To reach the mounds take Littlerock Road (Highway 121) from Rochester six miles north to the town of Littlerock and turn left on 128th Avenue. Continue a half mile to the top of the hill and turn right on Waddell Creek Road. One mile further watch for a small, easily-missed Mima Mounds sign on the left.

From Littlerock, Highway 121 bolts east, crossing under I-5 and turning north on Tilley Road. In 1881, having been exiled from their homeland for an unapproved marriage, Johann Meuller, a general in the Austrian army, and his banished wife, the daughter of Emperor Franz Josef I, settled among the towering stands of Douglas fir that shelter today's **Millersylvania Memorial State Park.**

Salmon, giant gophers, gas, buffalo or Indian mounds?

In the 1930s, after the property was donated to the state, President Roosevelt's Depression-era Civilian Conservation Corps went to work breaking trails and clearing land for campsites. They were careful to leave most of the old-growth timber that remains amidst a proliferation of trails, including a one-and-a-half-mile fitness trail, and nearly 200 campsites.

The highway leaves the park, runs north to 93rd Avenue and completes its zigzag journey by merging with I-5 to the east. ᘒ

State **Highway 122** from a junction with U.S. Highway 12, north to Mayfield Lake then south to a junction with U.S. 12 in Mossyrock. Route length: eight miles.

Highway 122 provides access to **Ike Kinswa State Park**. From the intersection of Interstate 5 and U.S. 12, drive east 14 miles and head north on Silver Creek Road (Highway 122). At two miles turn right on Harmony Road and continue another mile to the park.

The park extends from the banks of Mayfield Lake and follows the shorelines of the Tilton and Cowlitz rivers, covering 450 acres. For years the Cowlitz Indians fished and camped along the two rivers. When the Tilton River was dammed to form the reservoir, most of the Indian burial grounds were swamped. The name of the park was changed from Mayfield to Ike Kinswa to honor a member of the tribe. ∞

State **Highway 123** from a junction with U.S. Highway 12 north to a junction with State Highway 410 at Cayuse Pass. Route length: 16 miles.

Highway 123 approaches Mt. Rainier from its eastern side at the Ohanapecosh Entrance. The road is closed in the winter. ∞

State **Highway 124** from a junction with U.S. Highway 12 in Burbank, east via Harsha and Prescott, rejoining U.S. 12 in Waitsburg. Route length: 45 miles.

Highway 124 begins below the Snake River and precisely follows its course first east and then northeast six miles to Ice Harbor Drive. Turn north two miles to reach the **Ice Harbor Lock and Dam**. Completed in 1962, the hydroelectric dam was named for a nearby ice-free cove used for winter shelter by early stern-wheel riverboat operators making hazardous trips to Idaho goldfields in the 1860s and 1870s. There is a fish viewing room, fish ladders, and an Indian Memorial. Ice Harbor Lock is the second largest navigation lock in the world.

Ice Harbor Dam separates Lake Wallula and **Lake Sacajawea**, which stretches 32 miles northeast to Lower Monumental Dam. Like most of the Columbia River, the Snake no longer flows freely; it is also obstructed by the Little Goose and Lower Granite dams.

Highway 124 will satisfy one seeking sparsely populated terrain or those who appreciate a farmer quietly tending his crops and live-stock. If, for some reason, the road is too congested (unlikely), several back roads, including Touchet Road at Eureka and Harvey Shaw Road at Harsha, connect 124 and U.S. 12 near Walla Walla.

Follow the Touchet River from Eureka 12 miles to **Prescott** (Elevation 1,025, Population 280), established in 1882 by the Oregon

Improvement Company, then nine miles to a reunion with U.S. 12 at Waitsburg. Ⓒ

State Highway 125 from the Washington-Oregon border through Walla Walla and north to a junction with State Highway 124. Route length: 24 miles.
From the border the highway passes through Walla Walla and by the State Penitentiary and accompanies Union Pacific's lines north through crop and graze land. The railroad's influence in eastern Washington is best seen on a two-laner such as Highway 125. The railroad created tiny communities like Hadley, Berryman and Ennis: laying tracks, leaving settlers, and returning later to transport the products of labor. The highway now aids in the shipping process as well as connecting U.S. Highway 12 and Highway 124. Ⓒ

Gentle, hypnotic curves of wheat.

State Highway 127 from a junction with U.S. Highway 12 in Dodge, north across the Snake River at Central Ferry to a junction with State Highway 26 in Dusty. Route length: 28 miles.
This short road serves as a link between U.S. 12 and Highway 26. From Dodge (U.S. 12) drive 10 miles to the Snake River crossing at **Central Ferry**. Ferries once launched from the south bank of the Snake. For a brief period in 1881, a post office was established and its employees affectionately named the area *Reform*. Hard to imagine getting away with much in those days! After postal operations ceased, the name reverted back to Central Ferry. Today the area is an active state park and recreation area amidst high bluffs and wheat fields.

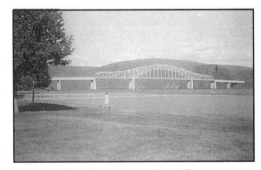

Snake River crossing at Central Ferry.

The highway climbs out of the river ravine and travels 17 miles through rolling wheat fields to an intersection with Highway 26. Ⓒ

State **Highway 128** from a junction with U.S. Highway 12 in Pomeroy, south through Benjamin Gulch into the Umatilla National Forest, then east to rejoin U.S. 12 in Clarkston. Route length: 40 miles.

Highway 128 appears as an unidentified wavy, black line on most maps. The highway/road heads south out of Pomeroy, rising and climbing, bumping and bouncing past spectacular scenes, making it an adventurous but slow-paced alternative to U.S. 12. The lightly-used route can be considered a back road in the truest sense, right down to the mid-section where asphalt turns to loose gravel. Passing from golden wheat fields into the foothills and ridges of the Blue Mountains, the drive presents a variety of terrain. In parts, the landscape is as barren as the road itself. After leaving the trees on the edge of the Umatilla National Forest, steep cliffs devoid of vegetation lead to a level plateau. The final few miles descend into the Snake River Valley before arriving in Clarkston where it again finds U.S. 12. ⌀

State **Highway 129** from the Washington-Oregon border, northeast across the Grande Ronde River through Anatone and Asotin to Clarkston and a junction with U.S. Highway 12. Route length: 42 miles.

The highway originates high in the Blue Mountains, a rugged and scenic range with elevations up to 6,250 feet. Shared by southeast Washington and northeast Oregon, the mountains were named by pioneer David Thompson for the blue or azure appearance of the peaks from a distance.

A likely assumption is that whoever designed the first stretch of Highway 129 used the Grande Ronde River as a model. Both feature more twists and turns than a runaway roller coaster. Four miles from the Washington-Oregon border the highway crosses the Grande Ronde or "great round," which natives claim was formed by a frantic beaver who had stolen fire from the pine trees.

This extremely winding road descends 11 miles and enters **Fields Spring State Park**. Its main attraction is **Puffer Butte** (4,450 feet), named for settler A.J. Puffer, whose arrival coincided with the Bannock-Paiute War. The Puffers took advantage of the sweeping vista as a means of detecting intruders on their farmland below. A look from the butte will reveal the Puffers' forethought, as well as views into parts of Idaho, the Wallowa Mountains in Oregon, Washington's Blue Mountains, and the Grande Ronde and Snake River basins.

From the park the road finally straightens and leads four miles to **Anatone** at the edge of the Blue Mountains. It is common for a small town to have multiple versions explaining why it carries the name it does. There is usually one probable, sometimes bland explanation and another apocryphal but more flavorful version. Anatone is no different. The Nez Perce name for Tenmile Creek, two miles east, is Anatone. But rumor persists that an attractive, local Nez Pierce woman admired by many was named Anatone. Others believe that her name was Tony Ann, which was reversed to create Anatone.

As early as 1787, Anatone was established as a stopping point between Asotin to the north and the gold fields of Florence and Elk City in the Salmon River area of Idaho Territory. In 1862 a sawmill was raised to provide lumber for the construction of Lewiston, Idaho. A general store was built and workers and immigrants en route to growing Lewiston once again stopped in Anatone. In the late seventies, rumors of impending trouble with the Indians sent the settlers of the region scurrying to a stockade a half-mile from Anatone, 100-feet square and stocked with provisions and arms. No hostilities occurred, but the fort served to hold settlers in the region until fear subsided. By 1900, the town had added a sawmill, expanded its store and grown in population to 100.

Heading north from Anatone to **Asotin** (Uh-SOH-tin, Elevation 580, Population 1,046) a distance of a little over 19 miles, you find yourself nestled in a deep gorge beside the Snake River. Few settlers came to the fertile land along Asotin Creek until the close of the Nez Perce War in 1878 stimulated rapid homesteading. In 1881, ferries began transporting passengers across the river between Washington and Idaho. Except for a few rough mountain trails, the only means of transportation was the river.

The town contains mostly brick buildings from the early 1900s and large, unpretentious homes. On the riverfront, an 1899 church with an impressive steeple reveals the proud craftsmanship of the time. The county historical museum on Third and Filmore contains restored pioneer buildings and a pole barn with branding irons and old horse carriages.

Asotin County: Asotin is the county seat of Asotin County, which was organized in 1883 and was once part of Garfield County. It is located in the far southeast corner of the state and borders Oregon on the south and Idaho on the east. The word Asotin is Indian for Eel Creek. In 1805-1806, Lewis and Clark passed through the county as well as Captain Bonneville in 1834. A ferry was established on the Snake River in 1855 to accommodate thousands of miners rushing to the goldfields. In 1881, a ferry was established at Asotin. Today, the county's economy is primarily agricultural, based on food and livestock raising and processing, fruit growing, and wheat and barley production.

Courthouse: 135 Second Street, Asotin 99402, FAX 509-243-4978 or 509-243-2087. Area: 633.4 square miles. State Ranking: 34th. 1993 Population: 18,300. Unincorporated: 10,529. Incorporated: 7,771.

Density: 28.9 persons per square mile. **Cities and Towns**: Asotin, Clarkston. **Principal Economic Activities**: Agriculture, lumbering. **Points of Interest**: Snake River, Blue Mountains.

Climate: (Clarkston Heights - elevation 1,186)

	Jan	Apr	Jul	Oct
Max Temp. F°	38.2	64.5	90.5	62.8
Min Temp.	23.9	38.2	53.8	38.7
Mean Temp.	31.7	51.4	72.2	50.7
Precipitation	1.07"	1.16"	.51"	1.14"

Average Annual Maximum Temperature: 63.8
Average Annual Minimum Temperature: 38.9
Annual Mean Temperature: 51.4
Average Annual Precipitation: 13.15" ◌

State Highway 131 from Randle south to the Cowlitz River. Route length: two miles.

Highway 131 leaves Randle (U.S. Highway 12) and merges with a series of forest roads leading to scenic areas around Mt. St. Helens. ◌

State Highway 140 from a junction with State Highway 14 in Washougal, north then east to rejoin Highway 14. Route length: 13 miles.

Heading north from the center of Washougal (waw-SHOO-guhl), Highway 140 joins the Washougal River and turns east. This quiet byway, which only appears on some maps, eventually climbs onto the high rolling farmland that borders the Columbia River. At its apex there are wonderful views south into Oregon. The highway eventually becomes Salmon Falls Road, winding back down to join Highway 14 at the west portal of the Columbia Gorge. An enjoyable pastoral back road when driven in either direction. ◌

State Highway 141 from a junction with State Highway 14 north through Trout Lake to the Indian Heaven Wilderness. Route length: 27 miles.

This highly scenic road winds along the White Salmon River beneath timbered ridges and through farmland, various types of fruit orchards, and some small wineries. Near the end of the highway is the little community of Trout Lake consisting of a few houses, a general store and a public campground with magnificent views of Mount Adams, nine miles to the north.

Named for the second president, **Mt. Adams** (Elevation 12,307) is one of five volcanoes and the second-highest peak in the Cascade

Range. The mountain sports four summits and a centrally-located dome, giving it a different look from every angle. Eight glaciers and deep scars on the mountain's sides are testimony to thousands of years of glacial activity. The abundant glaciation has led geologists to estimate that the last volcanic occurrence on Mt. Adams probably took place just before the last ice age, 10,000 years ago. Of all the Cascade volcanoes, Mt. Adams is closest to being all scenery and no danger.

The **Mt. Adams Wilderness** is spread over 46,800 acres along the mountain's west slope. Trails cover a variety of terrain, including glaciers, lava flows, alpine forest, wildflowers and rimrocks. From mid-July to late September, thousands come here to pick from the state's largest huckleberry and blackberry fields. Native Americans have made berry-picking pilgrimages for 14,000 years. Although picking is free and there is plenty of available land, some berry fields are set aside exclusively for Indian use.

The Country Inn at Trout Lake.

There are several access points from Trout Lake to the wilderness area. This region is a jumble of forest roads. If you have a good map or don't mind driving aimlessly, random roads will provide unexpected and incredible views of Mt. Adams, lush forest (and clear-cut land), and thousands of acres of huckleberries.

Numerous ice caves also lie in the vicinity of Trout Lake. The caves formed as air pockets that intruded lava flows during periods of heavy volcanic activity. After a volcano erupts, the resulting lava beds cool and then solidify, trapping liquid lava that leaves open tubes, or caves, when it breaks through and flows to the surface. Usually subterranean and cold, the caves were used by the white settlers in the 1880s to preserve meats and butter. Five miles east of Trout Lake, a 400-foot-long cave coated with thousands of stalactites and stalagmites is open to the public. ⌘

State Highway 142 from a junction with State Highway 14 in Lyle northeast through Klickitat to a junction with U.S. Highway 97 in Goldendale. Route length: 35 miles.

If you are on Highway 14 en route to Goldendale and wish to bypass Maryhill, take Highway 142. (From Goldendale, U.S. 97 travels north to Yakima or south to Maryhill.) The road follows a deep gorge carved by the Klickitat River 15 miles to **Klickitat** (KLIK-i-tat), a quiet and tidy lumber town nestled in a narrow canyon. The Klickitat Indians were the area's first occupants. The high, tree-covered canyon walls buffeted winter storms and the river, well-stocked with salmon, provided sustenance. Although salmon numbers are

A roadside view of the Klickitat River, beautiful even in black and white.

significantly lower, Native Americans continue to fish the river using traditional methods. Standing on a platform that extends from the riverbank, the fisherman uses a dipnet, a net about four feet in diameter fastened to a long pole, to scoop up the salmon.

In 1903, the Columbia River and Northern Railroad established a station here, a stop and pick-up point for Klickitat cattle and lumber between Goldendale and Lyle. The train continued to Lyle's waterfront and goods were then transferred to steamboats and shipped to larger, West Coast markets.

The discovery of natural carbon dioxide wells near the Klickitat River at the Klickitat Mineral Springs in the 1930s led to the production of dry ice, an effective and much-needed material for refrigeration in long-distance hauling. The Gas-Ice Corporation shipped three tons of the product per day.

From Klickitat the road climbs out of the canyon and away from the river, reaching a wheat-covered plateau with larger-than-life views of Mt. Hood and Mt. Adams. Continue across the pastoral Klickitat Valley into Goldendale. ❧

State **Highway 150** from Chelan west along Lake Chelan's north shore to Manson. Route length: eight miles.

Highway 150 winds through apple orchards and then tight along the water, past a string of time-share condominiums overlooking the lake. At the end of the road is **Manson,** "The Village on the Bay," a slowed-down rural community with fewer tourist amenities than found in Chelan. At the turn of the century the town was a timber company whose sawmills were fed by logs floated down the lake. The area now plants trees; thousands of acres of apples are harvested each year.

North of Manson are a trio of small lakes — Roses, Wapato and Dry — known for top-notch winter fishing and ample rainbow trout. The lakes are stocked and notoriously productive. Dry Lake is home to a unique variety of fish including pumpkinseed, bluegill, yellow perch and bass. Though popular, the heavy overgrowth and marshlands surrounding the lakes create a feeling of isolation that is a welcome break from Lake Chelan's crowds. ∽

Riverside dry ice house. The ice came from natural carbon dioxide wells.

State Highway 153 from a junction with U.S. Highway 97 in Pateros, north through Methow and Carlton to a junction with State Highway 20. Route length: 31 miles.

Leaving U.S. 97, the road up the Methow Valley passes through a narrow defile alongside the Methow River. Coming from the south, this is the most scenic access to the upper valley town of Winthrop and Highway 20, also called the North Cascades Highway.

About 11 miles north of the Columbia River is the tiny village of **Methow** (Met' how). It was described in the 1930s as "one short street

301∼

bordered by twin rows of lofty shade trees," as accurate now as it was then. Little changes in these parts; farming, fruit growing and small-scale logging are still a way of life here. A few miles upriver you pass the mouth of Gold Creek, once the site of a major Civilian Conservation Corps camp.

The road then twines with the river on into **Carlton,** where it breaks from its narrow confines into a broader valley of rolling hayfields and orchards, opening wider views to the west and the Cascade Range. You can drive leisurely through this pastoral setting a few miles beyond Carlton to the end of Highway 153 at a junction with Highway 20, just south of Twisp. ‿

The Belle of Chelan, 1892, was once the main mode of transportation on Lake Chelan.

tate Highway 155 from a junction with U.S. Highway 2, northeast along Banks Lake through Electric City, Grand Coulee and Coulee Dam, then northwest via Nespelem to a junction with U.S. Highway 97 in Omak. Route length: 80 miles.

Highway 155 explores some of the most historically important and geographically stunning terrain in the state. This is coulee country, punctuated by the **Grand Coulee**, which stretches from Grand Coulee Dam 50 miles southwest to Ephrata. ("Coulee" is a French word for canyon or deep gully; introduced in early Washington by French-Canadian fur trappers.) Ten to 15 million years ago a prolific period of volcanic activity produced many layers of basalt, forming

Banks Lake, Upper Grand Coulee, Columbia River.

the Columbia Plateau. A glacier dammed the Columbia River, and as the river was diverted, it carved a deep channel into the basalt; ice-age flooding further defined the Grand Coulee. After the glacier melted, the river returned to its former route, leaving the old streambed and floodway dry.

The coulee floor has since been filled with the waters of **Banks Lake**, a man-made reservoir 27 miles long and contained by two earthen dams (North and Dry Falls). Highway 155 follows its eastern shore. The Grand Coulee Dam, mostly known for its incredible power-producing capabilities, works with Banks Lake to create the world's largest irrigation system. Water raised 280 feet from the backwaters (Franklin D. Roosevelt Lake) of the dam is pumped into the lake and from there transported through canals as long as 100 miles to the arid but rich volcanic soil of the Columbia Basin, a region described by one reclamation official as "one of the most fertile bodies of irrigable land in this or any other country." The reservoir takes its name from the dam's construction supervisor, Frank Banks.

With Banks Lake to the west, Highway 155 passes beneath multi-level canyon walls with small springs and much evidence of dry waterfalls. Exposed lava formations rise in colonnade form. Trails that threaded along the base of cliffs where the road now runs were first used by nomadic Indian tribes and later by pioneers traveling west. The American Trail followed the east side of the coulee and was heavily used by soldiers commuting between Old Camp Chelan and Fort Walla Walla.

Long before reaching **Steamboat Rock**, the massive basaltic formation appears, rising 700 feet out of the northwest waters of Banks Lake. The rock was originally an island in the ancient Columbia River bed. When the Columbia changed course, the rock remained and was used as a point of reference for travelers. A list of those who passed the rock reads like a "Who's Who" in Washington state history: fur trader Alexander Ross, famous botanist David Douglas, Lieutenant Johnson of the Wilkes Expedition and numerous members of the Hudson's Bay Company all recorded the landmark in their journals. More recently the butte is sometimes used to guide pilots on training flights. Steep trails lead to its broad, flat summit. The rock covers 900 acres and is a state park with camping and access to some of the best fishing in the state.

Grand Coulee Dam. "Coulee" is a French word for canyon or deep gully.

A gravel road across from the park's launch leads up **Northrup Canyon**, a rocky passage cut by a tributary glacial drainage. Grant County's only forest fills the canyon, which is probably what attracted the area's first settlers. Dilapidated remnants of early homesteads remain as do sections of an old stagecoach and freight wagon road that once connected Almira and Bridgeport. A trail follows this road and leads to a vista point at the top of the canyon.

In 1943 Joe Hodgen, a wool grower, leads his flock of sheep across the dam crest.

Return to Highway 155 and continue past large columnar buttes to the upper end of Banks Lake. Once work began on the Grand Coulee Dam, several "mushroom communities" sprang up to accommodate the sudden influx of construction workers. **Electric City** (Elevation 1,500, Population 915), four miles southwest of the dam, was inspired by the dam's potential energy output, and envisioned a model all-electric (heating and cooking) community. The concept never materialized but the name remained.

Three temporary construction communities — Grand Coulee, Coulee Heights, and Coulee Center — merged to form **Grand Coulee** (Elevation 1,702, Population 1,018), now spread along the upper slopes of the Columbia River. Although not born until the 1930s, Grand Coulee imitated a typical Western frontier town. As the laboring hordes poured in, they were greeted with wide-open gambling and alcohol sold outside the state liquor store. In defense of Grand Coulee, the burgeoning town had no major robberies and only one killing in its first five years.

The incorporation of **Coulee Dam** (Elevation 1,100, Population 1,106) required a special act by the state legislature because its borders extended into three counties: Grant, Douglas and Okanogan. The town occupies both ends of the dam. Originally its west end was called "Engineers Town" and the east side "Mason City."

The **Grand Coulee Dam** exceeds all expectations of massiveness. Located in the middle of the semi-desert climate of northeastern

Washington, it is the largest all-concrete structure on earth — nearly a mile long — a scale so huge that actual size is difficult to grasp. The 12 million cubic yards of concrete contained in the dam could build a six-foot wide sidewalk around the world at the equator. As high as a 46-story building and as long as 12 city blocks at the spillway, the dam was labeled "the greatest thing yet built by the hands of man" when completed in 1940. More lumber was used in its construction than has gone into any other known structure. Today only the Guri Dam in Venezuela, built 47 years later, is capable of greater power generation. The third powerhouse alone (added in the 1970s) runs more water through its turbines than the average flow of the Colorado River through the Grand Canyon.

It took nine years to build the dam, but even more years of battling and political maneuvering were necessary before construction began. While it was recognized early in the century that the Columbia Basin's rich farmland needed only water to flourish, the method for providing the water was intensely debated. A Spokane group insisted upon construction of a 134-mile gravity flow canal stretching from a storage dam on the Pend Oreille River at Albeni Falls to the basin. A Wenatchee coalition favored a large dam on the Columbia River at Grand Coulee. The battle raged for 13 years.

The idea for a Columbia River dam was conceived by an average, run-of-the-mill lawyer from Ephrata, a "short, chunky and amiable fellow" named Billy Clapp. While discussing Coulee area mineral deposits over coffee and doughnuts with a friend, Clapp wondered aloud: "If ice could dam the Columbia and fill the Coulee with water, why couldn't we do the same? Then we could irrigate the whole big bend country!" Editor of the *Wenatchee Daily World,* Rufus Woods, overheard the talk, dashed off in his Model T Ford equipped with a built-in typewriter, and published Clapp's theory. Within days a headline sprawled across the front page of the July 18, 1918 edition of the *World:* FORMULATE BRAND NEW IDEA FOR IRRIGATION GRANT, ADAMS, FRANKLIN COUNTIES, COVERING MILLION ACRES OR MORE.

At first, the proposal was not well-received; most believed that attempting to dam such an immense body of water was absurd. A year later, Woods' credibility improved when he obtained support from contractor Jim O'Sullivan, who believed a dam was not only possible but "perfectly feasible," and that a dam would "yield untold electric energy, as great as a number of Niagras."

Woods and O'Sullivan convinced the state legislature to back the Grand Coulee project and by 1930, funding was approved by the Public Works Administration. After a long struggle to gain Congress' approval, all efforts appeared to be in vain: President Hoover refused to request funds for construction due to the serious deficit problem. His successor though, Franklin D. Roosevelt, looked beyond fiscal concerns and foresaw the unlimited possibilities of the dam. As early as

1908, Roosevelt had appointed an Inlaid Waterways Commission and stated in his report to Congress that:

> It is poor business to develop a river for navigation in such a way as to prevent its use for power... We cannot afford needlessly to sacrifice power to navigation or navigation to domestic water supply, when by taking thought we could have all three. Every stream should be used to its utmost.

The president understood the irrigation and power potential of the dam, but it was the more immediate and urgent need for jobs that prompted him to initiate the project.

In 1933, thousands came to the Grand Coulee looking for work, transforming the once unknown and barren land into prosperous towns overnight. The Bureau of Reclamation provided housing for project managers and engineers. Contractors and workmen lived in group housing and ate their meals at government-run cafeterias.

Before construction could began, the massive granite rock that was to serve as a foundation had to be uncovered. Shovel operators scooped up to 5,000 yards (20,000 wheelbarrows-full) of sand, gravel, and boulders in seven-hour

An aerial view of the dam and surrounding "Coulee Country."

shifts and fed the material onto conveyor belts. This conveyor belt system, the largest in the world, became known as the "river of dirt." It traveled a mile and climbed 500 feet to Rattlesnake Canyon, and was discharged at a ton per second.

The Columbia River, flowing as fast as 14 miles an hour, had to be rerouted. Coffer dams (temporary dams) were used to direct the flow of the river. In December of 1935 the first concrete was poured, and by 1938 the foundation, or so called "lower dam," was in place.

Since damming a river so large had never been attempted, the engineers had to innovate on the spot, and certain inevitable mishaps occurred. They handled the problem of a mud-oozing hillside by bringing in a massive refrigeration unit to freeze it in place. When a coffer dam sprang a leak, they stuffed the gap with any material they could get their hands on, including random items like Christmas trees and mattresses, and then added bentonite clay (which expands when wet).

There were numerous accidents during the years of construction. During one pouring of concrete, two men were trapped and sank deeper and deeper into the quicksand-like concrete with every move. Although false rumors circulated of their entombment, especially when a single, concrete-covered glove mysteriously appeared days later, the men survived and had no major injuries. However, 77 deaths occurred during original construction from falls, drowning, blasting and vehicle accidents. Four more died during the addition of the third power plant.

The main dam and first turbogenerating units were completed in 1941, and three months later America entered World War II. At the time of construction in the 1930s, the demand for power was minimal. *Colliers* magazine wondered: "What are they going to do with the power?" The dam soon proved essential to the sudden demand for massive amounts of electricity needed in the manufacture of aluminum for airplanes. By the middle of the war, half the nation's aluminum came from Northwest plants. The dam also powered the atomic bomb fuel plant at Hanford. Even after peace was established in 1945, Hanford nuclear reactors continued a high demand for power.

The Grand Coulee Dam has three primary functions: power production, irrigation, and flood control. Electricity is generated by unseen torrents of water rushing through the turbines within the dam's hydroelectric plants. The three powerhouses at Grand Coulee (the third added in 1976) have a capacity of 6,494,000 kilowatts. Each of the six pumps can lift 1,600 cubic feet of water per second (over a billion gallons of water per day) up over the canyon wall into the feeder canal, and into Banks Lake, the equalizing reservoir. This enormous flow is currently supplying over 500,000 acres with irrigation, tremendously altering Washington desert into productive farmland. Each spring the water level of Lake Roosevelt, behind Grand Coulee Dam, is lowered to make space for enormous amounts of water that flow down the Columbia when the snow in the Rocky Mountains begins to melt. The water is captured in the lake to prevent flooding downstream.

The highway continues through **Elmer City** (Elevation 1,200, Population 310), named for a Columbia River ferry operator, to **Nespelem** (nez-PEE-luhm, Elevation 1,900, Population 225), about 20 miles from the dam. Nestled in the southern section of the Colville Reservation, Nespelem is the headquarters of the Colville Confederated Tribes. It was also the home-in-exile and the final resting grounds for two important Indian chiefs.

In 1884, **Chief Joseph** was sent here with 150 of his band of Nez Perce Indians. Joseph is best remembered for his people's heroic retreat in the late 1800s, the result of their effort to resist the gradual take-over of Indian land. Terms of their treaty stated that the natives were to inhabit a reservation at Lapwai, Idaho. The Indians were

"If I cannot go to my own home, let me have a home in some country where my people will not die so fast..."- Chief Joseph

ordered by the United States government to be on the new reservation by the middle of June. This meant rounding up their huge herds of cattle and horses and moving them and all of their possessions across the flooded Snake and Salmon rivers within a month. During the move some of the young men were involved in the revenge killing of a white man that sparked the Nez Perce War. The tribe, running with their women and children, outfought the best the U.S. Army could assemble, until, sick and freezing, they surrendered just south of the Canadian border — and freedom.

The Nez Perce were sent to a reservation in Oklahoma (indefinite exile was not in their terms of surrender). After Joseph went to Washington D.C. to defend his people and speak of his plight (431 captives had been sent east; 130 had died and most of the surviving were ill), he and his people received national attention and gained support from philanthropic and missionary organizations. Joseph pleaded to the United States Congress to let his people move to Lapwai:

> ... I only ask... to be treated as all other men are treated. If I cannot go to my own home, let me have a home in some country where my people will not die so fast...
>
> Whenever the white man treats the Indian as they treat each other, then we shall have no more wars. We shall be all alike — brothers of one father and one mother with one sky above us and one country around us, and one government for all. Then the Great Spirit Chief who rules above will smile upon this land, and send rain to wash out the bloody spots made by brothers' hands upon the face of the earth. For this time the Indians are waiting and praying.

155 The government finally listened to Joseph and worked to return the Indians to the Northwest. In 1883, the Nez Perce went home — almost. The tribe was split according to their religion; the 118 Christian natives were sent to Lapwai; Joseph and the remaining 149 of his followers were sent to Nespelem. The chief who counseled peace his entire life was considered too dangerous an influence to be allowed to inhabit the Nez Perce Reservation at Lapwai. In Nespelem, he met Chief Moses, the other figure of resistance to the government's removal policy, also forced to relocate to the designated reservation. Moses was piqued by the presence of his new neighbors, but the two tribes traded and worked together, learning to share the land. Eventually, eleven separate groups came to form the modern-day Colville Confederation. As an interesting side note, Chief Skolaskin of the Sanpoil and Nespelem tribes was displeased with the presence of both Moses *and* Joseph, considering them outsiders. Skolaskin also refused money or farm equipment from the government, believing it to be a form of coercion. For this, he was punished as a dangerous influence and sent to Alcatraz without trial until he softened his position.

A simple marble tombstone near the Indian Agency, two miles south of town, records the 70 years of Chief Moses' life (1829-1899). The Nez Perce leader, Chief Joseph, died in 1904 and is buried on a knoll at the northeast edge of town. His Indian name, *Hin-Mah-Too-Yah-Lat-Keht*, meaning "thunder rolling in the mountains" is engraved on the headstone along with his portrait.

North of Nespelem, the quiet, winding highway passes through Coyote Canyon and over Disautel Pass (Elevation 3,252) through conifer forests before opening up into French Valley and continuing into Omak and a junction with U.S. 97. ✆

160 State Highway 160 from a junction with State Highway 16 east to Southworth. Route length: eight miles.

Highway 160 commences south of Port Orchard, rolls along eight miles of steep hills and descends and ends at Southworth and its ferry terminal. Midway on the 30-minute voyage to West Seattle, the majestic green and white ferry makes a pit stop on **Vashon Island**. Tucked away in the south end of Puget Sound and not accessible by car, the 14-mile-long island reposes in semi-rural privacy amidst blackberry brambles, patches of dark, green forest and healthy gardens and orchards. The Vashon name, attached to several communities on the island, the island itself, and its northern point, was given by explorer George Vancouver for Captain James Vashon, whom Vancouver served under in the West Indies.

A hoard of buried treasure is supposedly stashed away along the banks of **Judd Creek**, which drains eastward into Quartermaster

Harbor. When logger Lars Hanson gave his new Indian bride $800 in gold with instructions to find a suitable hiding place, he assumed she would live a long, healthy life. Unfortunately for Lars, his short-lived confidant passed away unexpectantly, before revealing where the cache was located. With a little luck, Lars' loss will someday be a Vashonite's gain.

Settlement on Vashon began in the 1870s, and for the next 25 years the island enjoyed its status as one of the leading fruit, berry, and poultry-raising districts on the Puget Sound. The island's importance was augmented in 1892 when a co-educational preparatory school, the **Vashon College**, was founded in Burton, at the southeast edge of the island, attracting boatloads of young students from Tacoma. The school burned to the ground in 1912 and was never rebuilt.

East of Burton a slender sand spit connects to **Maury Island**, a five-mile long peninsula that parallels Vashon. In **Dockton**, on the east shore of Quartermaster Harbor, are several old homes once occupied by employees of the Puget Sound Dry Dock Company. The massive dry dock that was their workplace — 125 feet wide and 325 feet long — built new ships and serviced aging ocean-going vessels in need of repair. The dock was eventually moved to Seattle.

In addition to the Southworth ferry, Vashon is also accessed from West Seattle (Fauntleroy) or Tacoma (Point Defiance). The Vashon Island Highway and 99th Avenue run the length of the island. ൠ

State Highway 161 from a junction with State Highway 7 north through Eatonville and Puyallup to a junction with State Highway 99. (Overlaps State Highway 512.) Route length: 22 miles.
Highway 161 goose-necks out from Highway 7 near La Grande and moves north to **Eatonville** (Elevation 800, Population 1,545) on the Mashel River. Founded as a trading post in 1880 by Thomas Van Eaton, it eventually became an important lumber-producing area, aided by the arrival of the Tacoma Eastern Railway in 1904. Factories generated cedar shingles, railroad ties and milled lumber at a steady clip until the resource was depleted in the mid-1950s. North and west of town lies the Ohop Valley, a moist region dotted with small lakes and several creeks. The valley runs east to west and holds the **Pioneer Farm Museum**, located about two miles west of town on Ohop Valley Road. The hands-on living history museum is of special interest to children, allowing them to churn butter, work in a blacksmith's shop and bail hay like true turn-of-the-century pioneers.

Six miles north of Eatonville off Highway 161 sits **Northwest Trek Wildlife Park**, a native species park run by the Tacoma Zoo, where a five-mile tram ride affords a close-up view of the inhabitants of the forest. The highway continues north straight as an arrow through several small communities before joining Highway 512 in Puyallup, crossing I-5, and concluding south of Federal Way at a junction with Highway 99. ○ʒ

State Highway 162 from a junction with State Highway 410 in Sumner south to Orting then east via South Prairie to a junction with State Highway 165. Route length: 20 miles.

Looping south out of Sumner, Highway 162 rolls into **Orting** (Elevation 286, Population 2,240), an Indian word for "town on the prairie." Sandwiched between the Puyallup and Carbon rivers, Orting has historically supported a wide range of products; everything from hops to bulbs to berries and evergreens has been grown here. Of the 54 million daffodil bulbs produced annually in the 1930s, half were harvested on just 500 acres of rich Orting soil. Several stately, turn-of-the-century homes are sprinkled on the outskirts of town, proof of Orting's prosperity.

From Orting, Highway 162 makes a U-turn and heads seven miles northeast to **South Prairie** (Elevation 430, Population 345) and the large, adjoining R.V. park resting in a beautiful area of sun-dappled drives and dairy farms.

The highway concludes at an intersection with Highway 165 on the edge of Buckley. ○ʒ

State Highway 163 from Tacoma north to Point Defiance. Route length: four miles.

While sailing the Puget Sound, Commander Charles Wilkes spotted the narrow finger of land dividing the Narrows and the Dalco Passage and proclaimed that if properly fortified it would "bid defiance to any attack." **Point Defiance**, comprising the northwest tip of the Tacoma Peninsula, has never found it necessary to "bid defiance," but in 1866 the area was reserved for the military just in case. By 1905, the land was deeded to the city of Tacoma who, in turn, made plans to convert the 640 acres into a park.

Point Defiance Park is only a short distance from downtown Tacoma but its wooded trails and bike paths, scenic drives, sandy beaches and views of the Puget Sound and the Narrows Bridge make it seem worlds away. In addition to its natural features, the park contains several interesting historical sites. **Fort Nisqually Historic Site** contains a restored version of Hudson's Bay Company Fort Nisqually, the oldest trading post on the Puget Sound. The original fort was built just north of the Nisqually River, close to the shores of the Puget Sound but moved in the 1840s one mile inland. The historic site is a re-creation of this second more expansive post.

~312

You will likely find everything you ever wanted to know about steam logging at the **Western Forest Industrial Museum**. The museum depicts the history of steam logging from the Dolbeer Donkey to the Lidgerwood Skidder. A crew bunkhouse, a 90-ton Shay steam locomotive and other antique logging railroad equipment are displayed.

Considered one of the finest small zoos in world, **Point Defiance Zoo and Aquarium** concentrates on animals representing countries along the Pacific Rim, such as White beluga whales, sea lions and puffins, and their habitats. It also houses a wide variety of endangered species including: the golden lion tamarin, the red wolf, and African elephants.

From the Point Defiance beachfront you may catch the Point Defiance-Tahlequah Ferry to Vashon Island (State Highway 160), a 15-minute ride, or turn southwest on Ruston Way and follow the waterfront to Tacoma's Old Town District. ❧

State **Highway 164** northwest from Enumclaw to a junction with State Highway 18 in Auburn. Route length: 15 miles.
Roughly following the course of the White River through a mix of semi-rural and suburban dwellings, the majority of Highway 164 (Auburn-Enumclaw Road) passes through the **Muckleshoot Indian Reservation**, established on December 26th, 1854 by the Medicine Creek Treaty. The disparate boundaries of the reservation — diagonally-shaped sections of land touching only at the corners — has long been a source of tension between the Muckleshoots and their neighbors. Originally intended to be relocated on the Nisqually Reservation, Muckleshoot Indians from the White and Green river valleys, a fragment of the Duwamish people, were instead located here.
The highway ceases as it blends into Auburn's outskirts. ❧

State **Highway 165** from a junction with State Highway 410 in Buckley south through Wilkeson and Carbonado to Mount Rainier National Park. Route length: 25 miles.
Wilkeson (Elevation 805, Population 370), more interesting than its diminutive size would suggest, is found nine miles south of Buckley. The discovery of large coal deposits and the subsequent arrival of the Northern Pacific in 1876 prompted the cutting of coal. When the Wilkeson Coal and Coke Company took over operations in the early 1890s, hundreds of coke ovens were erected. The cokers refined the raw coal into a fuel source that could withstand the high temperatures necessary to make steel. A handful of the dome-shaped coking ovens are visible west of the highway.
In the center of town is the old Holy Trinity Orthodox Church (built

in 1910); further east the elementary school (1913) is a fine example of sandstone masonry. Both structures are listed on the National Registry of Historic Places. Sandstone from the quarry here was used commercially all over Washington, most notably in the Capitol Dome at Olympiaî

Down the win-dy road **Carbonado** (Kahr-buhn-AY-doh, Elevation 1,000, Pop-ulation 505), where "coal was king," retains some classic examples of "company town" homes. The town was own-ed by the Pacific Coast Coal Company, which paved streets, built drainage systems, and rented $14 a month homes.

From here the highway moves 14 miles to its end at the park boundaries. Mowich Lake, and some of the state's most beautiful hiking terrain, is found four miles further at the end of a gravel road. ☙

State Highway 166 from a junction with State Highway 16 north-east to Port Orchard. Route length: three miles.

Port Orchard (Elevation 15, Population 5,610), as acces-sible by water as it is by land, occupies the eastern shoreline of Sinclair Inlet, a southern extension of Port Orchard Bay. Fed by a passenger-only ferry across the cove in Bremerton, and fronted by a lengthy moorage strip and several marinas, the flow of traffic between Port Orchard's waterfront and downtown is steady. A two-story board-walk, painted sky-blue and trampled by laid-back locals and slowly-getting-the-hang-of-easy-living-tourists, embroiders both sides of Main Street and its tributaries.

The town's first business venture was a small sawmill erected in 1854 and operated by William Renton and Daniel Howard. Attracted to the sheltered bay and lumber cut to order, shipbuilders came in droves. Within a year Kitsap County's first vessel, the *I. I. Stevens*, was launched.

The community that grew up around the sawmill was named Sydney for developer Sydney Stevens. In 1903, the community borrowed the name from the adjacent bay, which, in turn, was adopted way back on May 24, 1792 by Captain George Vancouver for H.M. Orchard, a clerk who spotted the inlet from Vancouver's ship *Discovery*.

Kitsap County: Port Orchard is the county seat of Kitsap County, founded in 1857 and once part of King and Jefferson coun-ties. Kitsap means "brave chief" and is located on the west side of Puget Sound. Many geographical features of the county were named by the early explorers of Puget Sound. Captain George Vancouver named the Hood Canal, Foulweather Bluff, Admiralty Inlet and Port Orchard. In the 1850s, the county's lumber mills provided lumber to build San Francisco. In 1891 the U.S. Navy established the Puget Sound Navy Shipyard at Bremerton. Today, the county's economy is based on naval installations, wood products and agriculture.

Courthouse: 614 Division Street, Port Orchard 98366, SCAN 262-7146 (Commissioners), FAX 206-895-3932. Area: 392.7 square miles. State Ranking: 36th. 1993 Population: 210,000. Unincorporated: 145,460. Incorporated: 64,540. Density: 534.8 persons per square mile. **Cities and Towns**: Bainbridge Island, Bremerton, Port Orchard, Poulsbo. **Principal Economic Activities**: Agriculture, fishing, forest products, U.S. Government. **Points of Interest**: Hood Canal, Hood Canal Floating Bridge.

Climate: (Bremerton - elevation 30)

	Jan	Apr	Jul	Oct
Max Temp. F°	44.3	58.8	76.3	61.0
Min Temp.	33.4	40.8	53.2	44.6
Mean Temp.	38.9	49.8	64.7	52.8
Precipitation	8.46"	3.10"	.50"	4.48"

Average Annual Maximum Temperature: 59.8
Average Annual Minimum Temperature: 42.9
Annual Mean Temperature: 51.4
Average Annual Precipitation: 49.36" ∽

State Highway 167 from a junction with Interstate 5 in Tacoma, east to Puyallup then north via Auburn and Kent to a junction with Interstate 405. Route length: 28 miles.

Following the Puyallup River upstream, the highway (also called the Valley Freeway) rolls into **Puyallup** (pyoo-AL-uhp, Elevation 48, Population 26,140), once declared the "Hop Capital of the World." Farming is still a way of life for many here, though hops have given way to rhubarb, tulip and daffodil bulbs, Christmas trees and a variety of berries. Named for the resident Indian tribe, the name means "generous people," a reflection of the natives who reportedly were kind in their dealings with settlers. Puyallup is now a large residential area, collecting the overflow of urban expansion from neighboring Tacoma.

Ezra Meeker laid the first townsite in this green valley in 1862 after journeying with his wife and child from Huntsville, Ohio by covered wagon 10 years previous. Following considerable exploration of the Puget Sound and a variety of business ventures, he eventually settled here to harvest hops. One of the first to plant the crop in the state, the innovative drying techniques he used soon brought him fame and a substantial fortune. Known as the "Hop King of the World," Meeker spread his farm over 500 acres and regularly sent large shipments to England. By the 1880s he had cultivated a $20 million industry.

But in the early 1890s business was far from hopping. A plague of insects and the financial panic of 1893 spelled disaster for the industry and Meeker's millions. Rather than retire and bemoan his lost riches, the energetic pioneer decided to devote the remainder of his years to preserving the legacy of the Oregon Trail, educating the public on its significant role in American history. While urging Congress to make the route a national highway, Meeker retraced the trail at age 76 by ox team and wagon to raise preservation funds and to erect markers along the way. Subsequent trips by wagon, rail, automobile and airplane (at the ripe age of 94) were for the same cause. Unfortunately, Meeker died in 1928 without seeing his goal realized, but his efforts endured; President Herbert Hoover declared the Oregon Trail a National Historic Highway in 1931.

Ezra Meeker ready to retrace the Oregon Trail.

A prolific writer, Meeker penned several books in his zestful lifetime, the last being *Seventy Years of Progress in Washington*, which was published on his 91st birthday, weaving his own personal history with that of the state he helped to improve.

Tours are available of the three-story **Ezra Meeker Mansion** (321 East Pioneer). Built in 1890, the restored structure features stained glass windows, ceiling artwork and some of the original furniture.

Each September the town buzzes with activity as tens of thousands gather to "Do the Puyallup!" The Western Washington Fair, or Puyallup Fair as it's better known, is the largest fair in the state and runs for three weeks each September. Food and crafts booths, Ferris wheels, roller coasters, concerts and 4-H sponsored petting zoos are a sampling of the fun.

Though the Puyallup Fair Grounds is a happy place during the annual festival, the grounds played a part in a dark chapter in U.S. history. On February 19, 1942, President Franklin D. Roosevelt signed Executive Order 9066, which, citing military necessity in the wake of the attack on Pearl Harbor, called for the detention of anyone considered a threat to national security. This declaration was interpreted to include almost exclusively those of Japanese descent. In Washington state, hundreds of Japanese-Americans were temporarily held at barracks on the fair grounds before being shipped off to larger camps in Idaho and California. Other camps existed in Wyoming, Colorado, Utah, Arizona and Arkansas. Though no evidence was produced, they were accused of being spies and traitors, and imprisoned without any formal charges being filed. Ironically, the assembly center in Puyallup was called "Camp Harmony."

Those who did not come to the camp voluntarily were forced by soldiers. Those who refused were arrested, and when legal action was taken, the policy was declared legal by the Supreme Court. Though officially labeled "relocation centers," they were, in reality, concentration camps. The Japanese were denied the freedom to come and go, families were often broken up, private property was confiscated and civil rights were suspended. Not until December of 1944 were they allowed to return to their homes.

Most of the Japanese held were either naturalized citizens or born in this country, yet the Constitution failed to include them under its protective wing of democracy and freedom for all. Some came back to find that businesses or land they had owned prior to the war had since been sold to white citizens. But perhaps the most painful result of their forced ostracism was the hostility and prejudice they were met with following their return to society. In 1988, the federal government took a step towards rectification when Congress drafted an official statement of apology, and money was appropriated to recompense those who were interned.

Crossing the Puyallup River and heading north, Highway 167 rolls through a heavy commercial zone and past Auburn (State Highway 18) on its way to **Kent** (Elevation 232, Population 41,090). The arrival of a massive Boeing plant in the mid-1960s started a landslide of industrialization in Kent that steadily continues to pick up speed. Once a prolific agricultural center, Kent is now covered with carbon-copy business parks, warehouses and shopping centers.

Since there is no noticeable city center or downtown area, Kent's large population is masked by its scattered layout. City planning, largely determined by oncoming suburban sprawl from Seattle and Tacoma, has caused residential areas to spider web across the valley in an evenly distributed pattern. Reflecting this growth and the influx of commuter families, the Kent area holds some of the largest high schools in the state.

Ezra Meeker's famous hop fields spread from Puyallup to Kent, and he is credited with naming the town in 1888 after the Kentish region in England, another hop producing hotbed. Two years of bumper crops helped get the town on its feet, and when the hop industry crashed new products quickly took its place, notably lettuce, berries and dairy goods.

The Carnation Milk Company got its start here in 1889, taking advantage of a local rail line that connected them to Seattle to deliver fresh milk daily. Lettuce later became such an important item that an annual Lettuce Day was created to commemorate the leafy green.

On this day, a huge bowl was set up on main street where specially-chosen young ladies mixed a gigantic salad using pitch-forks for tossing utensils.

Highway 167 continues north to a connection with I-405 south of Renton. ଔ

 State Highway 169 from a junction with State Highway 410 in Enumclaw north through Black Diamond and west to Renton and a junction with Interstate 405. Route length: 25 miles.

Leaving the small farms and horse-breeding operations of Enumclaw behind, the highway travels north through the long shadows of the Cascade foothills. About four miles out of town turn right on the Franklin-Enumclaw Road and continue a few miles to the road crossing of the Green River Gorge, a deep chasm filled with shale and sandstone and the sparkling Green River. The road (now the Green River Gorge Road) loops past the tailings of the coal mines (there is still an open pit mine operating) into the community of **Black Diamond** (Elevation 600, Population 1,575), a hodgepodge of former miners' houses and the beginnings of new residential development. The town's historical museum, formerly the railroad depot, contains a blacksmith and a barber shop, automotive and railroad displays, and a detailed look at the area's mining past. A few doors from the museum, bread may be purchased from a bakery that has been operating for over 90 years (baked in a wood fired oven, it was delivered by horse-drawn wagon). The local meat market has been making kielbasa and other sausages and smoked meats for over half a century.

Further north Highway 169 passes several subdivisions that are springing up in the foothills, crosses under State Highway 18, and follows the Cedar River to a connection with I-405 in Renton. ଔ

Black Diamond's historical museum.

State Highway 170 from an intersection with Highway 17 east to Warden. Route length: four miles.
At the end of this lonely road sits **Warden** (Elevation 1,030, Population 1,710). Once dusty and barren and a nightmare to farm, the town has the Columbia Basin Project to thank for its green existence. Goodbye sagebrush, hello potatoes, corn, strawberries, grapes, hay and alfalfa. After the Grand Coulee water arrived, Warden's seams nearly split with opportunistic settlers, notably a large Hispanic community that now accounts for roughly half the population.

The Lind-Warden Road continues east across the Lind Coulee. The next 18 miles showcase irrigation canals, king-size sprinkler systems and wide open spaces before meeting State Highway 21 near Lind. ⚬3

State Highway 171 from a junction with Interstate 90 northeast to a junction with State Highway 17 in Moses Lake. Route length: four miles.
From I-90, Highway 171 extends across the small peninsula jutting into Moses Lake (the lake) and straight into downtown Moses Lake (the city), where it connects with Highway 17. A proposal to extend the road northeast 25 miles to a junction with State Highway 28 near Odessa is under consideration. ⚬3

State Highway 172 from a junction with U.S. Highway 2, north through Withrow, then east via Mansfield to a junction with State Highway 17. Route length: 35 miles.
Thirteen miles east of Waterville, Highway 172 leaves U.S. 2 and heads due north. The turnoff is designated on maps as *Farmer* but there is nothing here but a dilapidated, two-story, false-fronted building.

The highway crosses the Waterville Plateau through rich wheat fields filled with scattered haystack boulders. The rocks are basaltic debris picked up by ice-age glaciers and then randomly deposited as the glaciers passed by and melted. Farmers work around the large boulders as they plant and plow.

An old barn at the edge of the wide open Waterville Plateau.

319~

Six miles from the Farmer junction, **Withrow** is marked by a grove of evergreen and locust trees, a striking contrast to the miles of surrounding wheat. The small settlement was named for pioneer wheat rancher J.J. Withrow.

The road makes a 90° turn to the east, passing **Lone Butte**, four miles west of Mansfield. This hill is a drumlin, an oval mound of glacial till pushed together and streamlined by advancing glaciers. Once enough material collected, the glaciers were no longer able to push the rocks and the ice had to flow around the sides.

Mansfield (Elevation 2,280, Population 365) is a small wheat farming community at the north end of the Moses Coulee. The town, without rail transportation, struggled until Waterville financiers threatened to build their own lines between local wheat fields and Portland markets. This prompted the Great Northern Railway Company to extend a branch line to Mansfield, arriving there October, 1909. The area now depends upon irrigation water from Rufus Woods Lake behind Chief Joseph Dam, about 12 miles north.

Yeager Rock, the most prominent haystack boulder in the area, dominates the landscape four miles east of Mansfield. The rock was carried many miles from the Foster Creek area south of Bridgeport. The highway joins 17 at a place called Sims Corner. ભ

State Highway 173 from a junction with State Highway 17 in Bridgeport northwest across the Columbia River to a junction with U.S. Highway 97 in Brewster. Route length: 12 miles.

Passing through the apple-growing communities of Downing and Rocky Butte, this two-laner offers a shortcut between Bridgeport and Brewster. The last three miles of road pass along a wide stretch of the Columbia River. ભ

State Highway 174 from a junction with U.S. Highway 2 and State Highway 21 northwest through Grand Coulee, then west to a junction with State Highway 17. Route length: 41 miles.

Highway 174 is a contemplative stretch of asphalt that gives you that "where-on-earth-am-I?" kind of feeling. There are no towns to speak of for the first 18 miles, only endless sagebrush and rolling dusty hills, which make for vague landmarks. After leveling off above small coulees and canyons, the road dips between the Grand Coulee Dam and the Columbia River. Once past this brief but massive glimpse of civilization, the highway gradually ascends through small patches of dryland wheat fields and pastures before breaking out on top of a high plateau. On a clear day, Canada can be seen from this platform. ભ

S tate Highway 181 from a junction with State Highway 516 north to a junction with Interstate 405. Route length: 11 miles. The road provides access to Kent before winding briefly along the Green River and ending near Tukwila (Interstate 405). ☙

I nterstate 182 from a junction with U.S. Highway 12 and Interstate 82 east across the Columbia River to Pasco and a junction with U.S. Highway 395. (Overlaps Highways I-82, U.S. 12 and U.S. 395.) Route length: 14 miles.

I-182 connects U.S. 12 with U.S. 395 and offers exits to Richland, Pasco and Kennewick. ☙

S tate Highway 193 from Clarkston west across the Snake River to the Wawawai River Road. Route length: two miles. Highway 193 is a good starting point for the challenging Pullman-Snake River Bicycle Loop (the round trip covers 79 miles). On two wheels, you may be rendered breathless not only from the steep grade, but from the rugged serenity of the landscape. On four wheels it is more relaxing and equally as impressive. Beginning west of Clarkston, the highway quickly turns into Wawawai River Road and runs directly along the eastern shoreline of the Snake River. Staggered shelves of rocky cliffs rise dramatically from both sides of the wide river. Tamed by dams, the water flows lazy as a lullaby.

From Wawawai (Wah-wah-we, Indian for "council ground"), once an Indian winter campsite and later a ferry landing for riverbank orchards, the road rises, weaves and curves up the canyon where multi-colored layers of rock paint a geological masterpiece in brown, deep adobe red and tan.

At the top of the canyon, stay right and follow the Wawawai-Pullman Road (State Highway 194) to its connection with U.S. Highway 195. The road levels out for a stretch before a brief jaunt into Idaho along U.S. Highway 95. Prepare to ride the brake on the steep and windy descent towards Lewiston, Idaho. From Lewiston, cross the river into neighboring Clarkston to complete the loop. ☙

S tate Highway 194 from a junction with U.S. Highway 195 west to the Snake River at Almota. Route length: 21 miles. Starting two miles east of Pullman, Highway 194 is a popular road trip for students at Washington State University. The road crosses the wheat-covered plateau and drops steeply down a windy, narrow canyon to the Snake River. The Snake is a major tributary of the Columbia River, pumping in 50,000 cubic feet of water every second, roughly one-fifth of the Columbia's total flow. Early settlers believed the Snake and Columbia rivers were actually north and south branches of the same river. On its own, the Snake River is one of the country's largest rivers, beginning in a lake region of Yellowstone National Park, and stretching 1,056 miles through Wyoming, Idaho and northeastern Oregon before its collision with the Columbia in Pasco, Washington. Captain William Clark named it the Lewis River in 1805 for his traveling partner, Captain Meriwether

The Snake River rolling towards a collision with the Columbia.

Lewis, but it was changed to honor the Snake Indians who resided along its banks. Lewis and Clark used the waterway extensively during their journey west, discovering many spots where fierce rapids made navigation impossible.

Four dams along the Snake have tamed its once wild current, and recently generated debate regarding the effect the structures have on dwindling salmon runs. Diverted flows have transformed rapids into reservoirs, providing miles of recreational opportunities as well as irrigation for farmers and a power source for the Northwest. Dozens of hatcheries and fish ladders are in operation to encourage further salmon runs but fish numbers continue to plummet.

The road meets the river at Almota, historically an important wheat-shipping point on the Snake River. Farmers once descended these canyons with full wagon loads of grain. Tree trunks were attached and used as brakes. A more efficient and less taxing method of transport were chutes and tramways, which used gravity to deliver grain to waiting barges. Some cuts are still visible in the hillside.

Almota lies on a prehistoric Indian site which the Nez Perce called *Allamotin*, meaning "torchlight" or "moonlight fishing."

~322

From Almota the road leads southeast along the river. Recreation opportunities abound on this stretch of the Snake. Hot, Indian Summer days lure students from Pullman to cliff-dive into the cool waters below. On early fog-shrouded mornings, crew teams in training share the river with fisherman, both intent on their task. Within site of Almota, **Boyer Park** is crowded with picnickers and boat docks. Until the school administration clamped down in the late 1980s, the park was the site of Waterbust, an annual back-to-school blowout for W.S.U. students that supposedly was the largest party west of the Mississippi.

The Snake River is slack water now, due to the **Lower Granite Lock and Dam**, a half mile from Almota at the end of Highway 194. The dam takes its name from Granite Point, a granite rock formation six miles upstream and notable for its presence in an otherwise basalt-rich region. When it was completed in 1975 it flooded lower river terraces and formed Lake Bryan. ෨

US **Highway 195** from the Washington-Idaho border, northwest through Uniontown, Colton and Colfax, north past Steptoe, Rosalia, Plaza and Spangle to a junction with Interstate 90 and U.S. Highway 395 in Spokane. Route length: 93 miles.

Prominent on U.S. 195 are the gently rolling fields which define the **Palouse Empire**. To understand their formation, imagine the land as a desert. Over time, wind-blown, mineral-rich dust has settled in the form of sand dunes. This sediment, known as "loess," lies up to 200 feet deep, and is the main reason for the area's agricultural success. Along with the rich soil, an elevation that averages around 2,000 feet and a decent amount of precipitation combine to make the Palouse (puh-LOOS) the best wheat-growing land

John Deere tilling the fertile Palouse soil.

in the nation, a region that has never known a crop failure due to drought. Its boundaries are fuzzy, but generally stretch north-south between Spokane Valley and the Snake River, west to the Channeled Scablands and east to Idaho's pine forests.

The Palouse wears many colors. In the spring the fields are a deep green. Yellow grain stretches endlessly during the summer. By mid-fall, when the harvest is nearly over, hills are black with their rich, bare soil. Winter snow creates a white, moon-like landscape. One feature of the Palouse, like most of eastern Washington, is that even during the cold winter months, the sun often shines.

The highway begins at the summit of Lewiston Hill, overlooking a deep canyon, the confluence of the Snake and Clearwater rivers, and Washington-Idaho border towns, Lewiston and Clarkston. A short detour, one mile south into Idaho on U.S. Highway 95, improves the view.

From the border, travel five miles to **Uniontown** (Elevation 2,575, Population 295). Drive one block west of Main Street to **Saint Boniface**

Catholic Church. Completed in 1905, Saint Boniface was the result of years of effort by a large contingency of German-Catholic farmers who had immigrated from Minnesota in 1875. Two towers top the building. Uniontown had initially erected a small frame church which served the parish until Saint Boniface was

Church and grain steeples pierce the horizon. Pray in one to fill the other.

finished. This small church, and the convent of the Benedictine Sisters, who arrived in 1884, remain adjacent to Saint Boniface.

Uniontown enjoyed a brief economic boom when Northern Pacific's tracks reached the town in 1889. The event made Uniontown a popular destination for those forced to leave the train and travel on to Lewiston by stagecoach. When the railway line was continued to Lewiston, Uniontown returned to its crops.

Only three miles separate Uniontown and **Colton** (Elevation 2,550, Population 335), but residents from the past may have wished the distance was further. Trouble began in 1870 when a coalition of Uniontown businessmen, unhappy with the townsite owner, formed a new community. The Northern Pacific Railway Company reached Colton in 1888, one year before Uniontown, and the subsequent accessibility and population surge guaranteed Colton's success.

Despite the demographics of the two towns — both were filled with German-Catholics — tensions remained, and when Uniontown requested assistance with the construction of their new church, Saint Boniface, Colton refused. Instead, they built their own chapel, **Saint**

~324

Gall's. The church's high steeple graces the skyline. Colton even had the gall to open a catholic school run by nuns stolen from Uniontown. The town's name is a combination of two early settlers, Cole and Worthington.

U.S. 195 passes through Colton, skirts Pullman (State Highway 270) and descends into **Colfax** (Elevation 1,965, Population 2,790), 26 miles from Colton.

Divided by the Palouse River, basalt cliffs on the east side of Colfax and gentler hills on the west side lead to soft, white wheat fields that are considered among the richest in the world.

One-stop service, a benefit of small town living.

Colfax's success in the wheat industry is only surpassed by its legume productivity; Colfax is the "Lentil Capital of the World." The majority of the 25 million pounds of lentils produced annually are shipped to Egypt, Colombia, Italy, Spain and Venezuela. Every fall the week-long Lentil Festival occurs in neighboring Pullman.

The peaceful downtown district seems an unlikely setting for the daily gunfights and occasional lynchings which were a part of Colfax's early history as a cattle center. The town turned to wheat in the 1880s, cleaned up its image, and built a business district in a vintage, late-nineteenth century style. The downtown is punctuated by the **Whitman County Courthouse** and is similar to business districts found in western Washington's Port Townsend and Bellingham's Fairhaven, parts of Spokane, and Pomeroy, another rural county seat.

On a tree-shaded lot stands the 1884 Victorian home of Colfax's first permanent resident, **James A. Perkins**. The home has been refurbished and is open to the public. The first Republican convention in the county was held in the adjacent log cabin built by Perkins in 1870. (To

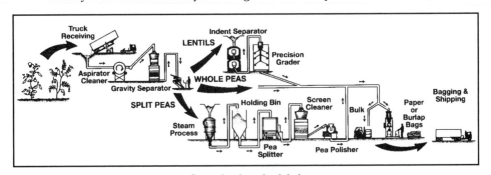

Steamed, split and polished.

325~

reach Perkins' dwellings, turn west off of Main onto Last Street, then right onto Perkins Avenue.)

Whitman County: Colfax is the county seat of Whitman County which was formed in 1871 from part of Stevens County and was named after the missionary, Dr. Marcus Whitman. It is situated in the southeastern corner of the state in the heart of the rich Palouse wheat growing region. Its early economic development was dependent on transportation. In the 1850s and 1860s the Oregon Steam Navigation Company and the Northwestern Stage Company acted as a lifeline for its residents. By the latter part of the century, four railroads were located in the county. Today, Whitman County is one of the most productive wheat growing counties in the nation. The city of Pullman is the site of Washington State University, a nationally and internationally known comprehensive university, featuring quality undergraduate training and strong research programs.

Courthouse: 404 North Main Street, Colfax 99111, FAX 509-397-3546. Area: 2,165.5 square miles. State Ranking: 10th. 1993 Population: 39,400. Unincorporated: 6,782. Incorporated: 32,618. Density: 18.2 persons per square mile. **Cities and Towns**: Albion, Colfax, Colton, Endicott, Farmington, Garfield, La Crosse, Lamont, Malden, Oakesdale, Palouse, Pullman, Rosalia, St. John, Tekoa, Uniontown. **Principal Economic Activities**: Agriculture, wood products, mining, manufacturing. **Points of Interest**: Steptoe Battlefield, Lower Granite Dam, Palouse Wheat Fields.

Climate: (Pullman - elevation 2,345)

	Jan	Apr	Jul	Oct
Max Temp. F°	33.6	56.5	82.5	60.2
Min Temp.	21.1	36.0	49.5	38.3
Mean Temp.	27.3	46.3	66.0	49.3
Precipitation	2.67"	1.49"	.39"	1.91"

Average Annual Maximum Temperature: 57.4
Average Annual Minimum Temperature: 36.3
Annual Mean Temperature: 44.0
Average Annual Precipitation: 20.49"

Eleven miles north of Colfax, take Shahan Road four miles to **Steptoe Butte**, an area of geological and historical significance.

Steptoe Butte is a mountain consisting of ancient Precambrian granite and basalt. It was once part of a chain of mountains that have since been covered in lava and loess. Internationally, geologists now use the term "steptoe" to describe a formation where there is a protrusion by an older form above a younger substance.

Steptoe is the highest point in the Palouse (Elevation 3,612). From its summit, Idaho's Bitterroot Mountains, southeastern Washington's Blue Mountains, and the expansive Palouse Empire are visible. During the Indian wars, it was used as a lookout by both the native people and their white opponents.

The Cashup Davis Hotel at 110% occupancy.

Englishman **James "Cashup" Davis** manned a roadhouse near the base of the mountain. Cashup, so named because he extended credit to no one, depended on stagecoach traffic for business. By 1888, the railroad's presence had diminished the use of stagecoaches and Cashup built a hotel and a solar observatory at the butte's summit, expecting railroad traffic to come his way. Unfortunately for Cashup, a man who craved companionship, the hotel never prospered. In 1911, 15 years after Cashup's lonely death, two boys accidentally burned the dilapidated hotel to the ground.

Today, Steptoe Butte is a state park, thanks to Colfax pharmacist, **Virgil T. McCroskey.** When the town of Colfax failed to raise enough money to buy the road leading to the summit of Steptoe Butte, McCroskey stepped forward and bought the land Colfax could not afford and an additional 80 acres now used as a picnic area. His old pharmacy, the Elk Drug Store, is open for business on Colfax's Main Street.

Return to U.S. 195 at **Steptoe**. Steptoe Butte and this small settlement were both named for U.S. Army Lieut. Col. **Edward J. Steptoe's** defeat to Palouse Indian forces on May 17, 1858.

Outgunned and outmanned, Steptoe spent a night on a hill near what is now Rosalia, and realizing that his defeat was imminent, prepared his retreat. First he sent scouts to search for a path through the surrounding Indian lines. When an escape route was discovered, the soldiers on the hill buried their dead and the bulky field howitzers that had proved useless in battle. Then they converted pack horses into mounts, replacing those that had been killed, and camouflaged their white horses in blankets. Within two hours they had made ready their flight and, under the cover of darkness, began their long journey to the Snake River.

The weary troops reached their destination after 25 hours of riding with no rest and little water. A group of friendly Nez Perce Indians camped nearby helped them cross the river. Later that day, reinforcements from Fort Walla Walla arrived, indicating that a scout had successfully made a 100-mile journey in a day and a half. The site of the battle, one mile south of Rosalia, is commemorated by **Steptoe Memorial Park**.

Lying in the narrow valley of Pine Creek, **Rosalia** (roh-ZAH-leeuh, Elevation 3,237, Population 613) is usually associated with the arched, concrete railroad trestle visible from the highway. Prosperous Victorian homes, prominent churches and brick buildings line Whitman Street, named after John M. Whitman, who platted the site in 1886. The town's name honors Rosalia Favorite, the first postmaster's wife.

U.S. 195 continues its roller-coaster tour of the Palouse seven miles to **Plaza**, Spanish for "open valley," and eight miles further to **Spangle** (Elevation 2,432, Population 245). One of the oldest settlements in the Palouse, land here was purchased and developed in 1862. Civil War veteran, William Spangle, settled in 1872 and the town was platted on June 18, 1879.

At some undefined point, the Palouse ends as scattered trees grow into thick forest, a result of the increase in precipitation, and U.S. 195 enters the outskirts of Spokane. The road drops into Hangman Valley and an intersection with U.S. 395 and I-90, 17 miles from Spangle. ∝

Highway 197 from a junction with State Highway 14 in Murdock south to the Columbia River and the Washington-Oregon border. Route length: three miles.

If "collecting" Columbia River dams is your thing, or if you'd like to better understand how fishways are supposed to help the endangered salmon, then the side trip south to **The Dalles Dam** would be well worth your time. The word *Dalles* (mispronounced "dals" by Americans) is French in origin and means "paving stones." The French (proper) pronunciation is "dahl." It refers to the tilted, basalt rock slabs found just beneath the surface of this stretch of the Columbia River.

U.S. 197 continues across the river into The Dalles, Oregon. ∝

State Highway 202 from a junction with Interstate 90 in North Bend northwest through Snoqualmie, Fall City and Redmond, then north to Woodinville. Route length: 30 miles.

The highway takes off from North Bend (I-90) and as Mt. Si fades to the north, rolls into **Snoqualmie** (snoh-KWAHL-mee, Elevation 422, Population 1,545). The town's relationship to the railroad is obvious; a siding jam-packed with historic passenger and freight cars and assorted railway accessories crowd one end of Main Street. Next door the steam-operated Puget Sound and Snoqualmie Valley Railroad operates out of a quaint 1890 train depot, carrying sightseers to and from North Bend and Snoqualmie.

The town's greatest boost was the arrival of the Seattle, Lake Shore and Eastern Railroad in the 1890s, which allowed area residents to transport farm and lumber products to western markets in hours rather than the days it took by horse and wagon.

Salish Lodge and the top of Snoqualmie Falls.

Today's Snoqualmie is a slow-paced town that is interrupted occasionally by train buffs and those on their way to see the thundering **Snoqualmie Falls**, where up to 60,000 gallons of water per minute drops 268 feet to an eroded, oval-shaped pool below. Since 1899 the falls have generated power for western Washington. The falls and the 5-star **Salish Lodge**, perched precariously close to the cliff's edge, are both visible from an observation deck. A half-mile trail descends to another vantage point at the river's floor.

Long before modern conveniences made their appearance, the falls were an attraction based on the merit of

Snoqualmie Falls, well worth the short walk to a viewpoint.

their spiritual significance. In 1916 a Snoqualmie Indian named Sia'txted spoke of the falls' creation:

> Moon came to the place where Snoqulamie falls now are, near the place where he was stolen as a child. It was then a fish wier of wood, closed so that salmon could not go up this stream. Most of the people who owned the trap lived on the prairie above. Moon turned the fish wier into a waterfall.

Moon addressed the waterfall thus:

You, waterfall, shall be a lofty cataract. Birds flying over you shall fall and people shall gather them up and eat them. Deer coming down to the stream will perish and the people will have them for food. Game of every kind shall be found by the people for their subsistence.

Down the road the riverside community of **Fall City** spreads out from the confluence of the Snoqualmie and Raging rivers. Originally called "The Landing," Fall City takes its name from its position downriver from Snoqualmie Falls.

Highway 202 (Redmond-Fall City Road) continues northwest through semi-rural land dotted with spacious homesteads and acreage for sale or rent, an indication of the population creep towards the Cascades. Blackberry bushes fill in spaces between properties.

Contrast between old and new.

From Redmond (Interstate 405) the road turns north and heads into the fertile Sammamish Valley and **Woodinville** (Elevation 50, Population 9,407), named for the pioneer family Woodin. On the outskirts of the town are several nurseries, a giant sod farm, and a group of wineries including **Chateau Ste. Michelle Winery**, one of the state's largest.

Similar to other communities along this highway, Woodinville grew up with the arrival of the Seattle, Lake Shore and Eastern Railroad and is currently experiencing the eastward movement trend. A pair of highways, I-405 and State Highway 522, assume the transportation role and take off to various eastside points.

State Highway 203 from a junction with State Highway 202 in Fall City north through Carnation and Duvall to a junction with U.S. Highway 2 in Monroe. Route length: 24 miles.

Highway 203 tours the bucolic Snoqualmie Valley, following the Snoqualmie River past dairy farms, grazing cattle and a collection of streams and ponds on its way to Carnation and Duvall.

Six miles north of Fall City, **Carnation** (Elevation 75, Population 1,360) was originally called Tolt (for the Tolt Indians) and then changed in

Hard work and Mother Nature.

1917 in exchange for the establishment of a milk condensing plant by the Carnation Company. Seven years prior E.A. Stuart had toured Wisconsin and hand-picked a group of Holdstein-Friesian bulls to bring back to his valley grasslands. Stuart and subsequently the **Carnation Research Farm** (Carnation Farms Road) have used breeding and nutrition to improve the milk production of cows. The farm labels itself as the "Home of the Contented Cows," and although it may be difficult to determine a cow's happiness, Carnation herds are consistently among the nation's leaders in productivity. The farm's maternity and calf barn, petting area, milking area and gardens are open for self-guided tours.

The road continues through the Snoqualmie Valley Wildlife Area nine miles to **Duvall** (Elevation 50, Population 3,200), a quaint little town with a proliferation of antique shops and a commanding position on a hillside above Cherry Valley and the river. A logger from Everett by the name of James Duvall bought land here in 1887 from the Port Blakely Mill Company and built a blacksmith shop, a shed for his 10 yoke of oxen and a split cedar home for his family. A skid road was constructed to transport logs from the hilltop below to the river and with facilities in place and a growing population, the Chicago, Milwaukee and St. Paul Railroad found the town worthy of a stop.

Highway 203 runs through the Cherry and Tualco valleys en route to a junction with U.S. 2 in Monroe. ∞

S tate **Highway 204** from a junction with U.S. Highway 2 northeast to a junction with State Highway 9. Route length: 2 miles. A shortcut from Highway 2 to Lake Stevens (Highway 9). ∞

Interstate 205 from the Washington-Oregon border northwest to a junction with Interstate 5. Route length: 11 miles.

I-205 is a freeway bypass that enters the state via a bridge over the Columbia River from Oregon. It passes through the east side of Vancouver, intersecting State Highway 14 on the north bank of the river, and junctions with State Highways 500 and 503 in Orchards before joining I-5 just north of Salmon Creek. ☞

State Highway 206 from a junction with U.S. Highway 2 north-east to Mount Spokane. Route length: 15 miles.

Shortly after escaping the busy hub of Spokane, the road is enveloped by a thick forest of ponderosa pine. The destination of Highway 206 is **Mount Spokane** (Elevation 5,851), a downhill ski area popular with Spokanites, and part of the 13,800-acre **Mount Spokane State Park**. Other winter activities include snowmobiling and Nordic skiing. During the summer the park opens to camping, hiking and horse-back riding. After 15 miles the highway becomes forest road and begins to climb the mountain, reaching the ski area at five miles and the summit at seven miles.

A fire lookout built of piled rocks tops the summit. Incredible 360° views allowed rangers to spot forest fires from Spokane west to the Columbia Basin, north into Canada, and east over Idaho's panhandle to the jagged peaks of Montana's Bitterroot Range. Erected in the 1930s, the lookout is no longer used for fire detection and is now aptly called the Vista House. ☞

State Highway 207 from a junction with U.S. Highway 2 north to Lake Wenatchee. Route length: four miles.

From Coles Corner, only a short jog is required to reach **Lake Wenatchee**. This deep blue lake and the adjoining state park are set in the open Douglas fir and ponderosa forests of the eastern Cascades. The lake, five miles long and at the toe of Wenatchee Ridge, is a favorite summer and winter visitor attraction.

At the east end of the lake, State Highway 209 (not on many maps) is an alternate return route to U.S. 2. The road wanders across the Wenatchee River near **Plain**, a dot on the map settled by Dunkard Church members in 1910, who asked postal authorities for a "plain" name. The road then follows Little Chumstick and Chumstick creeks, respectively, across uneven terrain into Leavenworth. This is also a popular but difficult bicycle loop when coupled with a pass through Tumwater Canyon in either direction. ☞

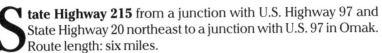

S tate **Highway 211** from a junction with U.S. Highway 2 to a junction with State Highway 20 in Usk. Route length: 15 miles.
   If you are traveling on U.S. 2 and wish to bypass Newport, which straddles the Washington-Idaho border 13 miles east, Highway 211 takes off just before Diamond Lake and heads north past Sacheen and Davis lakes to Highway 20. That highway continues north then journeys west on a cross-state venture. ☙

S tate **Highway 215** from a junction with U.S. Highway 97 and State Highway 20 northeast to a junction with U.S. 97 in Omak. Route length: six miles.
   Highway 215 passes through orchards and follows the west side of the Okanogan River. This short road bridges the gap between Okanogan and Omak, whose boundaries nearly overlap. ☙

S tate **Highway 220** from a junction with U.S. Highway 97 at Toppenish west to Fort Simcoe. Route length: 27 miles.
   This dead-end road heads west past hop vines dangling from a canopy of wire and acres of grape fields that cover the earth like a spider's web. These crops will eventually be shipped to breweries and wineries across the nation. The leafy green hop plants climb slender 18-foot poles and appear as never-ending wash lines from afar, leading straight into the remains of Fort Simcoe, now **Fort Simcoe State Park**.
   Before the fort was built, the natives called the area *Mool-Mool* — "bubbling water" — for the freshwater spring present. Historically a communal gathering spot, trouble started when white settlers began using the area as a stop-over for a trail leading to the Columbia River. As the Yakima Indians faced the threat of encroaching white settlers, they turned increasingly hostile and aggressive, sporadically attacking homesteaders moving across their land. Small bands of white vigilantes would often retaliate by burning Indian villages, stealing horses and committing murders of their own. The attacks, although not organized and

Part of old Fort Simcoe.

220
WASHINGTON

usually the result of sudden, flared tempers, reached a peak in 1855, deeming the construction of a military outpost necessary.

The U.S. Army arrived in 1856 and chose the site for Fort Simcoe, applying the shovel to a wagon road, and erecting barracks and officer's quarters. Part of their official purpose was to prevent squatters from settling on land promised to the Indians in a treaty made in 1855, but they also wanted to intimidate the tribes with an impressive display of military force. Troops saw little local action, but did play a supporting role in battles waged further northeast near Spokane.

When the Yakima Reservation was created in 1859, Fort Simcoe was converted into the headquarters for the Yakima Indian Agency. The barracks were used to house native children as part of a boarding school where they learned reading, writing and a variety of trades. Most of the structures are now gone, but an interpretive center and various markers detail the history of the fort and the Yakima Indians. ∞

221
WASHINGTON

State Highway 221 from a junction with State Highway 14 in Patterson, north then west to a junction with State Highway 22 in Prosser. Route length: 26 miles.

Highway 221 jumps headfirst into the **Columbia Valley**, some of Washington's most productive wine country. The Columbia Valley and France's famed Bordeaux and Burgundy regions all have something in common: they lie between 46 and 47 degrees latitude — just the right latitude for producing world-class wine. At this northern latitude, the Columbia Valley simply has more day-light during June, the month when grape cell division is most rapid.

The area receives two more hours of precious daylight per day than California's legendary Napa Valley. These in-

Washington wine country.

creased hours of light and heat have a marked effect on the grapes, primarily increasing photosynthesis, the process responsible for building sugars in the ripening fruit. The Columbia Valley enjoys cloudless sunny days and warm temperatures during the 150- to 200-day growing season.

The warm days are balanced by relatively cool nights. This day-night temperature difference, especially near harvest time, helps build a high sugar content while preserving the acids natural to grapes. Both are essential to balanced wines.

The Columbia Valley is located in the rain shadow of the Cascade Mountains, which reduces its rainfall to only 7 or 8 inches a year, making the area a semi-arid high desert. The region is generally characterized by broadly rolling hills broken by long sloping uplands of basalt running in an easterly and westerly direction. The soil type is critical to fine wine production. By thrusting its roots deep into the soil (20 to 40 feet isn't uncommon), the vine is able to establish a constant growing environment where nutrients are absorbed. If the earth is heavy with clay and lacks proper drainage, the roots can suffocate and the water that settles around them swells in the grapes, making dull, uninteresting wine. The sandy and silt loams of the Columbia Valley drain well. Often the soil is underlain with a basalt or calcious layer at a depth of 15 to 40 inches. To ensure proper root development, these layers must be ripped before the vines are planted. The result: light textured soils that allow rapid warming, as well as facilitating water penetration.

Perhaps the statistic that best proves the Columbia Valley's and the state's potential for future wine production is revealed through a comparison to California, where only 50,000 acres are suitable for vineyards. Washington, on the other hand, has over 250,000 — only 30,000 of which are currently being cultivated.

Columbia Crest Winery.

At the beginning of the route, just north of Patterson, the **Columbia Crest Winery** sits, appropriately, on the crest of a hill overlooking the Columbia River. Two thousand of the ten thousand acres under irrigation are drip-irrigated grapevines. Another 10,000 acres produce dry-land wheat crops. Fifty percent of all the white chardonnay grapes crushed in Washington are crushed at the winery (tours and wine tastings available).

From the Columbia Valley, the highway follows wheat lands to its conclusion in Prosser. ⌘

State Highway 223 from a junction with State Highway 22 in Alfalfa northeast to a junction with U.S. Highway 12 (Interstate 82) in Granger. Route length: four miles.

Highway 223 leaves the alfalfa fields of Alfalfa and travels a short but time-saving distance to the busy interstates. A small park outside Granger, filled with child-size dinosaurs, will cause even the most casual observer to look twice. ∞

State Highway 224 from a junction with U.S. Highway 12 in Benton City northeast through West Richland to Richland. Route length: 10 miles.

Highway 224 provides access to a few small wineries before rolling through **West Richland** (Elevation 380, Population 4,510), across the Yakima River and into Richland. ∞

State Highway 225 from Benton City north to a junction with State Highway 240. Route length: 10 miles.

Highway 225 proves that even in the "Evergreen State," the desert is close by. The road skirts the Yakima River and quickly deposits you in the sage and sand lands north of Benton City. Continue your desert tour by heading northwest on Highway 240 through the lower half of the United States Department of Energy Hanford Site. ∞

State Highway 231 from a junction with State Highway 23, north through Edwall, Ford, Springdale and Valley to a junction with U.S. Highway 395. (Overlaps U.S. Highway 2.) Route length: 75 miles.

Highway 231 veers from Highway 23 about a mile north of Sprague. Twisting through transitional terrain, a mixture of farmland, sagebrush and pockets of coniferous trees come and go. The road takes an 'S' turn through the sleepy community of **Edwall** as it heads north to a junction with U.S. 2, which it joins for a quick jaunt east to Reardan. From here, it again points north to the mountains of the upper Columbia River.

Dropping down to cross the Spokane River just below Long Lake Dam, the road climbs back into highlands, across the eastern edge of the Spokane Indian Reservation, and through alternating thick forest and open parkland to **Ford**. Now a gathering of small but prosperous farms, the land around nearby Chamokane Creek — "plain of many springs" — was once the site of the Protestant **Tshimakain Mission** (chim-uh-ken). Cushing Eells and Elkanah Walker established the mission among the Spokane tribe in 1838, hoping to convert land to farms and the Indians into Christians.

Neither plan succeeded. The Indians were friendly and accommodating to the preachers, but showed little interest in the content of
their sermons. Since hunting and gathering worked well enough, they saw no need to till the soil. As far as church services were concerned, some agreed to attend regularly, but only in exchange for tobacco. A year before abandoning the effort, Eells wrote: "We have been here almost nine years and have not yet been permitted to hear the cry of one penitent, or the song of one redeemed soul." When a measles epidemic afflicted the tribe in 1847, tolerance for the white visitors began to wane. To make matter worse, fellow missionaries Marcus and Narcissa Whitman were murdered by Cayuse Indians in Walla Walla a few months later, arousing fear and further distancing the reverends from their would-be flock. In the spring of 1848, the mission was abandoned for good.

Continue to weave north through wooded hills to **Springdale** (Elevation 2,070, Population 256) where the road intersects State Highway 292 as it heads east. Incorporated in 1903, most of the buildings and homes burned down in 1908, and the town never fully recovered. Now a collection of small houses surround a few old brick storefronts, mostly boarded up, along with a saloon or two where farmers and gyppo loggers quench their thirsts. (A gyppo is an independent logger who usually works on a contract basis.) A handful of trailer homes beside the tracks shake and rattle each time the Burlington Northern rolls through.

The highway then swings out of Springdale, skirting between forested ridges along the eastern edge of the broad Colville Valley and past the whistle-stops of **Grays** and **Kulzers**. A varied and unusual assortment of animals can be seen from the road, as peacocks, emus, llamas and alpacas graze alongside more traditional livestock. An abandoned and dismantled lumber mill rusts around the aptly entitled hamlet of **Valley**, along with a few empty buildings and a store. The larg-est objects in town appear to be huge chip-mill sawdust mounds. From here, a side road heads west to access Waitts Lake for camping, boating and fishing. This road also leads to the Huckleberry Mountains, pockmarked with mineral mines and marble quarries. From Valley, it's a short wriggle to the end of 231 where it joins U.S. 395 south of Chewelah. ⌀

S tate Highway 240 from a junction with U.S. Highway 395 in Kennewick, across the Yakima River through Richland to a junction with State Highway 24. Route length: 40 miles.

Known as the "Atomic City" for its role in nuclear development, **Richland** (Elevation 360, Population 34,080), was named after local land owner Nelson Rich, although some claim the area's rich farming soil had something to do with it.

The city was founded in 1900 by Benjamin Rosencrance, an eclectic entrepreneur who bought large plots of land from the Northern Pacific Railway Company. One of Rosencrance's first business ventures was to raise horses and rent them out for railroad work. He later established a stage station with hopes of attracting people to the area. Seeing a need for expanded irrigation, Rosencrance built a waterwheel that transported water to his land from the Columbia River via a flume. Eventually, fruits and vegetables prove prosperous.

Old Hanford town site on the Columbia River.

Prior to World War II, Richland was a farming community of about 200 people. In 1942, the Atomic Energy Commission chose the desert surrounding Richland as the locale to conduct atomic research and the population skyrocketed to 17,000. The **Hanford Site**, 25 miles north of Richland, was remote, yet near railroads, had abundant water (the Columbia River) for reactor cooling and plentiful electricity from hydroelectric dams. All full-time employees on the project were required to live in Richland. Likewise, if you were not a permanent Hanford employee, you were not allowed to live within city limits.

To house the influx of people, the government evacuated some 2,000 people from the communities of Hanford, White Bluffs, Richland and the surrounding area, a total of 640 square miles. Rows of government-owned "alphabet houses" were built. The name was given because the homes were alphabetized according to their layout and location. A and B houses were two-story duplexes; E and F were single family cottages; and Q and R models were fashionable homes located near the river.

As Richland overflowed, people moved to outlying communities such as Kennewick, Pasco and Benton City. In Hanford, massive trailer parks were erected, and kit homes, built of parts sent by mail, lay in endless, uniform lines. Hanford's temporary housing development instantly became the fourth largest city in Washington with a population of 51,000.

The research conducted at the Hanford site was a branch of the Manhattan Project, a top-secret wartime effort to design and build the first nuclear weapons. Hanford was responsible for collecting sufficient amounts of plutonium-239. A similar operation in Oakridge, Tennessee produced uranium-235. An atomic bomb is detonated when fissionable material (isotopes uranium-235 and plutonium-239) undergo a chain reaction. When the mass of the fissionable material exceeds the critical mass, the chain reaction multiplies rapidly into an uncontrollable release of energy.

Soon, the world's first three plutonium production reactors were raised along the banks of the Columbia River. Few involved in the construction project knew what they were building. Secrecy reigned. Designs were compartmentalized, with only a few top engineers knowing the overall structure that a building would assume. Visiting scientists were given code names to veil their purpose and intent.

Hanford reactor construction circa 1944-'45.

Uranium was called "base metal" and plutonium "product." Potential employees were told only that they would be "working out West, doing important war work." State and local officials were not informed about the purposes of the huge structures being erected in the desert, and even Vice President Harry S. Truman was in the dark until after Roosevelt had died.

On August 6, 1945, Hiroshima, Japan was annihilated by a uranium bomb. Three days later, the Hanford-produced plutonium bomb was dropped on Nagasaki. A Richland newspaper headline read: "PEACE. Our Bomb Clinched It." The Hanford site continued to function in a production capacity following World War II, but the need for nuclear weapons diminished at the end of the Cold War in the late 1980s, and Hanford shifted its focus towards nuclear energy and waste management. The last reactor was shut down in 1990.

Hanford currently has a cleanup contract with the Department of Energy, an agreement originally scheduled to last 30 years, but extended indefinitely because nuclear waste continues to arrive from other national facilities. For years, the site has caused controversy statewide, but regardless of its political ramifications, Hanford's environmental restoration program is considered the model for the rest of the country. The **Hanford Science Center** (825 Jadwin Ave, Richland) provides a look at the history of the atomic movement.

After leaving Richland, Highway 240 is immediately enveloped by desert. The first 10 or so miles pass through **Horn Rapids ORV Park**, which hosts motorcycle, sand drag, jeep, go-cart and motorcross races. Dune buggies and other off-road vehicles ride the sand dunes that line both sides of the road. The Yakima River briefly joins the highway here. Tract homes, a few small farms and a golf course's verdant fairways provide unusual contrasts to the surrounding sage and sand drabness.

The barren ridgeline of the Rattlesnake Hills, a 16-mile-long range, blocks the horizon to the southwest. The range was named by early settlers for the abundance of rattlers in its lower foothills. **Rattlesnake Mountain** (Elevation 3,629), on the eastern end of the range, is the tallest treeless mountain in the world.

The road continues through desolate sageflats, entering the United States Department of Energy Hanford Site. The emptiness of the region's terrain is striking and a good indication of why the government selected this area for its research. A considerable distance to the north are scattered buildings, which are inactive atomic reactors or cleanup facilities. Hanford's B-reactor, notorious for its role in the World War II Nagasaki bomb, is a National Historic Mechanical Engineering Landmark. Up the road, Highway 24 offers a closer look at these facilities. ᦉ

S tate **Highway 241** from a junction with State Highway 22 in Mabton, north through Sunnyside to a junction with State Highway 24. Route length: 24 miles.
Highway 241 offers an opportunity to get off the beaten path and explore a true rural area. After a straight shot between Mabton and Sunnyside, the road enters a high-walled canyon that runs through the Rattlesnake Hills. Refreshingly devoid of traffic, the valley is a horn of plenty; the numerous farms that dot the green prairie produce a variety of fruits and vegetables, from asparagus to okra to zucchini. Twisting and winding, the road meets Highway 24 in Black Rock Canyon. ∞

S tate **Highway 243** from a junction with State Highway 24 west then north along the Columbia River through Mattawa and Beverly to a junction with State Highway 26. Route length: 28 miles.
This road follows the east bank of Priest Rapids Lake, a calm, 15-mile stretch of the Columbia River impounded by the Priest Rapid and Wanapum dams. For centuries, the Wanapum Indians — the "river people" — lived along the shoreline, thriving off the river's prolific salmon population. In 1811, pioneer Alexander Ross named the rapids for Haqui-laugh, a friendly Wanapum priest who greeted the incoming explorers with a peace pipe and inclusion in his tribe's religious ceremonies.

Nez Perce Dreamers near Smohalla.

Considerably less hospitable was the Wanapum prophet **Smohalla**, a vocal opponent of the federal Native American reservation policy. Smohalla claimed to have received visions and instructions on a sacred mountain, making him a *twuteewit*, or "Indian doctor." Thus blessed, he started the Dreamer religion, a combination of ancient Indian rituals and communal Christian ethics. His followers would gather to sing, chant and pray, and many participants, including Smohalla, would fall into trances. Smohalla established a regimen to strengthen fading traditions that included a ceremonial calendar, flags and drums decorated with images of the sun, moon and North Star, and offerings of thanks to the salmon and roots of the prairie for giving life to the people.

The wide, relentless Columbia.

The cornerstone of the Dreamer faith was the complete and outright rejection of land ownership and the white concept of "progress." Since outsiders had moved in on their land, Smohalla reasoned, *they* should have to make concessions, not the Indians. He condemned the "unholy" reservation and believed that if traditions were kept alive, the trespassers would eventually be forced to leave. In 1855, at a time when most Indian leaders were surrendering to terms of government treaties, Smohalla warned: "Those who cut the land or sign papers for land will be defrauded of their rights and will be punished by God."

Though respected by government agents for his shrewdness and resolve, he also inspired fear and contempt for his brazen tongue and ability to stir up trouble. The influence of Smohalla's Dreamer sect spread to other tribes, most notably the Nez Perce and the Yakima, further incensing the military. When army engineers arrived at Priest Rapids in 1885 to survey the river for possible steamboat navigation, they hoped to hire local Indians to work on the project for low wages, but discovered that no one was interested. What the white man called improvement, the Wanapums considered destruction. Since the tribe refused to enter into a treaty with the U.S. they were never granted a reservation. Once 3,000 strong, a few remaining full-blooded members reside at the west end of Priest Rapids Dam.

The road passes the Desert Aire Golf Course and a few miles further, the exit to **Mattawa** (Elevation 775, Population 1,310). Mattawa's population swelled when the Priest Rapids and Wanapum dams were under construction, but when the water stopped flowing most workers moved on. Irrigation from those projects have brought people back to work the fruit orchards and vineyards which thrive in the desert climate. Mattawa is a Wanapum word for "where is it?"—which seems like an perceptive and appropriate question.

Rising above the highway, the **Saddle Mountains** extend from both sides of the road, stretching 26 miles eastward across Grant County, and 13 miles into Kittitas County, close to the Yakima River. The low-lying mountain range (Wahatis Peak is the highest at 2,696 feet) is an example of an anticline, or a fold in the basaltic lava flows. As the West Coast has moved northward in the last 10 million years, pressure has caused ancient rock to either rise, like the Saddle Mountains, or collapse in the form of valleys or canyons, such as the narrow gorges south of Wenatchee along the Columbia River. The range was named for its rolling ridge line, which appears as a saddle in many areas.

Crab Creek releases into the Columbia River about a mile south of Beverly. During the creek's run from Spokane through the heart of the Columbia Basin, mineral-rich runoff from irrigated fields and seep lakes drains into the water, making fishing along the route and where the creek empties into the Columbia some of the best in the state.

Continue north, meandering along the Columbia River until you reach the one-street settlement of **Beverly**, a site dramatically carved out by the river with the bluffs of the Saddle Mountains guarding both shores. In the height of navigation days, this was a busy shipping point; today it is a distribution point for dairy and poultry ranches. H.R. Williams, vice president of the Chicago, Milwaukee & St. Paul Railway, took the name from Beverly, Massachusetts and gave it to the town, along with its first and only economic boom.

The town itself is barely noticeable compared to the spectacular setting and impressive, albeit idle, railroad bridge built by Williams' railway company. As the state's third transcontinental line (behind the Great Northern and Northern Pacific) it was not new, but it did offer a catch: electric rail travel. Excitement peaked in 1907 when both bridge construction and work on a Columbia River irrigation system were started. Workers for both projects flooded into town, kicking up dust and bringing the town to life. Stores and saloons anxiously rose, willing to take their cut of future paychecks. The plan failed. When costs began to soar, investors quickly pulled out, leaving the pipes to rust. The bridge was finished about the same time, but that alone did not convince many to stay. The railroad ran a modern electric line from Montana to Puget Sound only until the 1960s, leaving the bridge as a lengthy reminder.

Located roughly in the middle of the state, the **Wanapum Dam** delivers power to as far west as Seattle and east to Spokane; even Oregon takes some of the juice. Built in 1965, the 7,800-foot structure sits three miles north of Beverly. A tour center offers a history of the tribe and the area, as well as a view of the fish ladder where salmon can be seen battling current and cement to continue their migration. ଔ

Tour the Wanapum Dam and watch the amazing ladder-climbing fish.

S tate Highway 260 from a junction with State Highway 17 east via Connell and Kahlotus, northeast through McAdam to a junction with State Highway 26 in Washtucna. (Overlaps State Highway 261.) Route length: 39 miles.

About 13,000 years ago, during one of the ice ages near present-day Missoula, Montana, melting glaciers fed rapidly growing Glacial Lake Missoula in an immense valley dammed by dirt and ice. When the dam finally broke, one of the largest floods in the history of the world exploded northwestward, thundering across Northern Idaho to Spokane and then south to the Washington-Oregon border.

The flow of water from the "Spokane Flood" was 10 times that of all the world's rivers combined. The estimated 2,000-foot-high wall of water created tremendous force, reaching speeds of up to 65 miles per hour and draining the entire lake in approximately two weeks. If not for the Cascade Mountain Range, the floods would have rushed straight to the Pacific Ocean.

In its wake, the flooding, which geologists believe happened numerous times, created the **Channeled Scablands**. The water washed away soil and exposed the underlying basalt. It carved steep canyons, coulees and buttes, changed the courses of streams and rivers and left behind numerous lakes and debris of broken rock. The Washtucna Coulee and former course of the Palouse River are now the path of Highway 260.

Seventeen miles separate Connell (U.S. Highway 395) and **Kahlotus** (kuh-LOT-tuhs, Elevation 500, Population 200). The Indian translation for Kahlotus is "hole in the ground," a reference to deep springs nearby. The town was originally called Hardersburg for settler Jon Harder but the post office objected to the length of the name and changed it to Kahlotus, saving all of three letters.

Highway 260 continues past spring-fed Lake Kahlotus alongside Burlington Northern's tracks and joins Highway 261 at McAdam, eight miles northeast of Kahlotus. The highway then travels through the wide, shallow floor of the Washtucna Coulee to its conclusion in Washtucna. ❧

S tate Highway 261 from a junction with U.S. Highway 12 in Delaney, northwest via Starbuck and Tucannon, across the Palouse and Snake rivers at Lyons Ferry to McAdam, northeast to Washtucna, then north through Ralston to a junction with U.S. Highway 395 and Interstate 90 in Ritzville. (Overlaps State Highway 260.) Route length: 63 miles.

From Delaney drive along the Tucannon River past irrigated alfalfa fields and graze land, eight miles to Starbuck.

In return for his name's immortality, railroad investor W.H.

261
WASHINGTON

Starbuck donated an 1893 church bell to the tiny town of **Starbuck** (Elevation 645, Population 165). The bell serves as a memorial to Starbuck, and is found in a park (Front and Baxter) next door to a restored building that once held Zink's Grocery. The original store's proprietors were named Hammer, Nail and Wood, (there were actually three stores side-by-side until someone married a Zink and consolidated them), but instead of Zink's being limited to hardware goods, Starbuck's oldest store "sold everything under the sun."

Starbuck's sleepy appearance masks its onetime status as a booming railroad town. In 1905, the Oregon Railroad and Navigation Company had a monthly payroll of over $20,000. Starbuck declined with the introduction of Mallet locomotives, which eliminated the need to add "helper engines" at this point.

Highway 261 continues two miles to **Tucannon**, a variation of the Nez Pierce word *tukanin*, meaning "bread root," an important Indian food source. One unsubstantiated legend contends that two cannons buried along the Tucannon River are the true source of the area's name. Also, the two canyons that collide at the river are a possibility.

Lyons Ferry, now a state park situated at the confluence of the Palouse and Snake rivers, is eight miles north of Starbuck. Lyons Ferry was and still is an important crossing point both historically and commercially. It has been a route and encampment used for centuries as evidenced by the discovery of the oldest documented human bones in the Western Hemisphere, carbon-dated at 10,000 years old. These were discovered by a Washington State University professor at the **Marmes Rock Shelter** just up from the confluence. Despite efforts by the Army Corps of Engineers, the rock shelter was flooded when Lower Monumental Dam was constructed across the Snake River.

The vehicular bridge that now spans the Palouse River was recycled from the crossing at Vantage on the Columbia River. It was built in 1927 and moved here in 1968. Also crossing here is the **Joso Bridge**. Constructed between 1910 and 1914, it was a vital link in the early Pacific Northwest transportation network. For years the bridge was the longest (3,920 feet) and highest (280 feet) of its kind anywhere. It is now a local historical engineering landmark. To watch and hear the clickity-clack of a freight crossing the bridge at sunset is a stirring sight.

The Palouse River was originally named Drewyers River by Lewis and Clark for George Drouillard, a civilian member of the corps of exploration who became a boon companion to Lewis — and as a tracker, scout, hunter and interpreter — one of the most valuable men on the expedition. A few years later he returned west with a company of fur traders and was killed in a fight with Indians at Three Forks, Montana.

~346

Just above Lyons Ferry is an overlook offerring spectacular views of the Palouse Canyon and Marmes Rock Shelter, which is partially submerged but still visible, along with the dike system meant to prevent its flooding.

Lyon's Ferry and Joso Bridge.

The bluff also contains the last remains of 251 members of the extinct Palouse tribe, moved to escape the floodwaters behind the dam, and 135 individuals recovered from a desecrated Indian cemetery at the mouth of the Tucannon River. If that's not enough buryin' for you there's an odd little monument carved with pansies that states, "Chief Old Bones, died Oct. 20, 1916 age 89 years," — no other information.

Lyon's Ferry's last running ferry is still afloat in a little cove near the day-use section of the park. The wooden ferry was current driven with a cable and windless (wheeled cable tightener) attachment. It was in more or less continuous operation from 1859, as part of the Mullan Road, until 1968.

Although remote, Lyons Ferry is still a busy crossing point. With campers, a marina, cars, freight trains and barges passing on the river, little has changed but the culture of the people using it.

After the crossing, the highway climbs out of the canyon and is intersected by a dirt road leading two miles into **Palouse Falls State Park**, a well-kept campground; shady and cozy with a few vehicle and tent sites.

The overlook at the park is breathtaking. There is a sheer drop to the Palouse River, which emerges from

Palouse Falls falls a breathtaking 198 feet.

347~

behind a blind corner, and then free-falls 198 feet into a large pool before meandering out of sight down the canyon. Placed in a setting that could be an artist's rendition of the open range, mesas and buttes interrupt the stark, dry, empty landscape. Behind the park is a railroad right-of-way cut so deep into the rock it looks like an open-top tunnel. The highway continues north, twisting and turning to a junction with 260 at McAdam, a lonely grain elevator.

There is little in this wild landscape but a few scattered ranches. One, the H Bar U stock ranch, has been in operation since 1887. This is "get down and come in" country where the folks like their lonesome in large chunks!

From the McAdam junction drive six miles north to Washtucna and north 19 miles through a transitional landscape mixture of wheat fields and channeled scablands across Rattlesnake Flat to Ralston, named for the Ralston-Purina company. Follow the roaming cats and grain elevators out of Ralston nine miles to its conclusion at Ritzville and the junction of U.S. 395 and I-90 on the edge of the Columbia Plateau. ॐ

State Highway 262 from a junction with State Highway 26 north then east past the Potholes Reservoir to a junction with State Highway 17. Route length: 24 miles.

Like an ocean in a desert, **Potholes Reservoir** makes a surreal appearance about 10 miles from the highway's beginning. The reservoir lies in an extremely arid region, what is essentially a desert. Sand dunes litter the area. The majority of these dunes are what geologists call "barchans," recognizable by their crescent shape and formed when winds strong enough to transport sand constantly blow in the same direction. The horns of the crescent-shaped dunes point eastward, revealing the wind's direction and the course of the migrating dune.

The reservoir, 12 miles long with an average width of three miles, is impounded by **O'Sullivan Dam**, completed in 1949 as part of the Columbia Basin Irrigation Project and the largest earthen dam in the United States. The reservoir contains 23,000 surface acres of water, most of which is irrigation runoff from northern fields that eventually will be redistributed to irrigate a quarter-million acres to the southwest. Water is reused by pumping it from drains and wasteways, and returning it to the distribution system. Though the annual diversion from the Columbia River to the project is about two million acre-feet, re-use of some of the water allows more than three million acre-feet to be delivered to project farms.

The reservoir was named for the numerous water-filled depressions scattered throughout the area. Extensive irrigation projects have caused the water table to rise and seepage to refill shallow holes formed from glacial pressure on basaltic rock. If planning on camping or fishing at the reservoir — usually hot, crowded and not so scenic — go to the potholes instead. Intertwined by basaltic outcrops, sand dunes, cattails, marshes and streams, each pothole is unique. Trails connect countless lakes which vary in size, shape, fishing conditions, and amount of traffic.

Columbia National Wildlife Refuge self-guided trails are open from March through September.

South of the reservoir, the **Columbia National Wildlife Refuge** is a scenic landscape of rugged cliffs, canyons, lakes, and arid sagebrush grasslands. Seepage from the Columbia Irrigation Project has created waterways that provide habitat for migrating and wintering waterfowl and many other species of wildlife. Almost 280 species of wildlife have been observed on the refuge. Self-guided trails are open from March through September: bring binoculars.

The road continues to a junction with Highway 17. ⚘

State Highway 263 from a junction with State Highway 260 in Kahlotus south to Lower Monumental Dam, then southwest along the Snake River. Route length: nine miles.

Highway 263 (Devil's Canyon Road) leads through Devil's Canyon seven miles to **Lower Monumental Dam**. The project is named for Monument Rock (also called Devil's Monument), a massive dome of lava found in the canyon and described by William Clark as "a remarkable rock verry large and resembling the hill of a Ship [sic]." After evaluation of several sites along the Snake River, it was decided to place the dam downstream from the formation, and the name "Lower Monumental" was chosen.

The 28-mile-long lake contained by the dam was named for Herbert G. West, a former executive vice president of the Inland Empire Waterways Association and long-time advocate of slack-water navigation on the Snake River.

Highway 263 continues along the Snake's (Lake Sacajawea) north shore, traveling close to the river's serene waters just beneath rugged basalt cliffs. The highway ends two miles further. For a round trip continue on Burr Canyon Road to Pasco-Kahlotus Road. A quiet farm-service road leads back to Kahlotus. ✿

State Highway 270 from a junction with U.S. Highway 195 east through Pullman to the Washington-Idaho border. Route length: nine miles.

Students at **Washington State University** in Pullman and from nearby University of Idaho in Moscow will always have fond, if not somewhat diluted, memories of this short piece of road that connects the two schools. Until 1987, when the drinking age in Idaho was raised

Washington State University is surrounded by rolling Palouse wheatfields.

from 19 to 21, the highway was a weekly, and for some, daily route (and rite) of passage for Pullman students looking for legal means to imbibe. The well-deserved partying reputation (this writer is an alumnus) of Pullman has always been a draw for Idaho's finest scholars. Wooden crosses planted roadside are a grim reminder of the dangers of drinking and driving.

The convergence of the south fork of the Palouse River and a pair of streams flowing besides downtown's brick-lined streets prompted

Pullman's (Elevation 2,347, Population 23,480) original name, *Three Forks*. Depending on which of Pullman's five steep hills one chooses to explore, expect diversity: a bohemian student dive; a professor's Victorian home fronted by a well-maintained garden; or a ranch home overlooking spacious farmland; all coexist in a level of peace that depends on perspective.

Settled by cattlemen in 1877, and platted in 1882, the town was renamed Pullman in 1884 to honor George M. Pullman, the wealthy president of the Pullman Car Company and inventor of the Pullman Car. A large endowment was expected from Pullman but instead he sent the town a meager $50 and a letter declaring that naming the town after him was the greatest compliment he ever received. Pullman's citizens used the money to buy Fourth of July fireworks.

The Pullman was a passenger car with comfortable, parlor-like furnishings used for night travel or long trips. A Pullman and caboose left behind by the Great Northern Pacific are found at North 330 Grand. The original train station at this location is now a commercial building but also serves as a mini-museum to Pullman's train-crazed heyday.

Initially Pullman's fertile wheat fields — 1,000,000 bushels of wheat were shipped by rail in 1890 — were the area's major industry. But that same year, when Pullman was being considered as the site for the state's land-grant school, the town put forth an effort that would make any public relations firm proud. On the day of the commissioners' visit, Pullman's small populace crowded the streets with as many humans, animals and vehicles as could be found — cattlemen rode in horseback, farmers in their buckboards, and pedestrians filled the sidewalks and stores. As intended, the visitors found Pullman to be a bustling, vibrant town. In 1892, a small but determined student body of 60 and faculty of five christened Washington Agricultural College Experimental Station and School of Science. This evolved into Washington State College, and due to the college's growing prestige and the curriculum's developing diversity, it became Washington State University in 1960.

W.S.U., or "Wazzu" is located on 600 acres, plus an additional 4,200 acres in service area and farm - land. Exploring its campus, known as "the hill," may cause a shortness of breath, but it will also reveal many old, brick buildings uniform in design. **Bryan Auditorium**, a red-brick, three-story structure, was constructed in 1908. Rising two

Bryan Auditorium and Thompson Hall at Wazzu.

stories above the main facade, chimes from the square, terraced bell tower are heard throughout Pullman and inform students they are late for class.

The oldest building on campus is **Thompson Hall**, built in 1894. Once the campus administration building, a turret pointing skyward signifies the importance of this national historic place.

Twelve-stories tall, the **Owen Science Library** is the highest point in Pullman and offers expansive views of the Palouse.

Washington State College President Ernest Holland considered the "hearty hello" between faculty and students to be "one of the school's finest traditions." Thus, a common pathway where such pleasantries were often exchanged was designated the "hello walk." Two small bronze plaques are planted in sidewalks near Bryan Auditorium; one in front of the Edward R. Murrow School of Communications and the other across from the student book store.

It's a safe bet that when a five-year-old kid with the nerdish name of Egbert Roscoe Murrow (later changed to **Edward R. Murrow**) moved to Washington from North Carolina, not a single person could have imagined that this youngest son of a lumber company employee would grow up to be one of the most talented, influential, and recognizable personalities in the history of broadcast journalism. And perhaps equally unbelievable is that Murrow's mentor during his formative years at Washington State College was a 4'6," hump-backed speech and elocution teacher by the name of Ida Lou Anderson, or "Miss Anderson" to her students.

Egbert Roscoe Murrow using the skills learned at Wazzu from Miss Ida Lou Anderson.

In his four years at Washington State College, Murrow took 15 courses from Miss Anderson, who stressed to her students that insincerity was the ultimate sin, and that "a voice . . . is only a fine instrument of something far greater than itself, which is the whole man."

In his senior year (1930), Murrow, by then student body president, and his mentor were often seen walking together across campus, engrossed in conversation — the six-foot Murrow bending over slightly and Miss Anderson (a polio victim who limped and was forced to wear dark glasses as a result of her childhood disease) looking up to facilitate their discussion.

After graduation, Edward headed to New York City, where several years later, in 1935, he took a low-level administrative job with

CBS radio. Before long Murrow's incisive intellect and professional delivery had earned him the position of chief of European correspondents, at a time when the political tensions on the continent were heating up rapidly.

When sides were finally drawn and the pitched battles of World War II begun in earnest, Murrow learned that declining health had forced his beloved Miss Anderson to give up teaching. Her most famous pupil responded to this news by having a new radio delivered to her and asking that she critique his broadcasts. On her suggestion that a brief pause in his opening dateline would add gravity to what followed, Murrow began all his subsequent commentary with what became his signature: "This . . . is London."

Several years before Ida Lou Anderson succumbed to the ravages of polio at the age of 41, Murrow had written to a friend about the influence the tiny woman had had on him:

> She taught me to love good books, good music, gave me the only sense of values I have. . . . That part of me that is decent, wants to do something, be something, is a part she created. She taught me to speak. She taught me one must have more than a good bluff to really live. ⋄

S tate **Highway 271** from State Highway 27 in Oakesdale northwest to a junction with U.S. Highway 195. Route length: 10 miles.

Highway 271 is a serene, country road that follows railroads tracks through Palouse farmland and bridges the gap between U.S. 195 and Highway 27. Photographers will appreciate the highway's lack of traffic and unspoiled rural settings. ⋄

S tate **Route 272** from a junction with U.S. Highway 195 in Colfax east through Palouse to the Washington-Idaho border. Route length: 19 miles.

There are no towns along this short highway, only farms, wheat, wheat and more wheat. The **Tour of the Palouse** bicycle route covers a portion of the highway giving the cyclist a firsthand look and feel for the Palouse's rolling hills, farmlands, creeks and country roads. From Palouse take State Highway 27 south and turn right on Clear Creek Road. Turn right again on 272 and continue east back to Palouse. The road is lightly traveled and in decent condition but keep an eye out for slow-moving farm vehicles.

The former town of **Elberton**, voted by its 20 citizens to disincorporate in 1966, is accessible from the highway. Seven miles from Colfax follow Brown Road north about three miles. Sylvester M. Wait, also the founder of Waitsburg, bought the existing sawmill and platted Elberton in 1886. He named the town for Elbert Wait, his recently deceased son. The town based its economy on the saw-mill and a newly built flour mill, but after a devastating crop failure in 1893 and having exhausted the pine and fir tree supply, Elberton decided to diversify. They planted orchards — especially prune trees. Elberton was the unlikely site of the world's largest prune dryer, 100 feet long and capable of drying 66,000 pounds of fruit daily. Unfortu-

nately, the prune market was not lucrative enough to sustain the town and slowly it disintegrated.

Visit Elberton for its ghost town feel. Efforts by students at Washington State University to preserve Elberton as a lived-in country park have failed. Buildings are boarded up and people are scarce. Despite these failures, Elberton retains a pris-

Averill Mill - architect and building contractor unknown.

tine quality; pine trees once depleted by the sawmill have grown back in abundance creating a forest amid miles of treeless fields. Given it's history though, don't look for a new sawmill anytime soon. ଔ

State Highway 274 from a junction with State Highway 27 in Tekoa northeast to the Washington-Idaho border. Route length: two miles.

Though short, the road is scenic. The golden waves of wheat covering the Palouse show little regard for state boundaries as they continue rolling into Idaho. A peek over the border reveals a blanket of light brown extending for miles. ଔ

State Highway 278 from Rockford east to the Washington-Idaho border. Route length: six miles.

Following the North Fork of the Rock Creek River, patches of forest rise alongside the water, overlooking interchangeable sections of wheat and rich, brown soil. Approaching the border, the landscape begins to change gradually, as high wooded hills come into view and welcome you to Idaho via U.S. Highway 95. ଔ

S tate **Highway 281** from a junction with Interstate-90 in George north to a junction with State Highway 28 in Quincy. Route length:10 miles.

Straight as an arrow, the highway shoots through green, irrigated fields with access to a few farm roads. The variety of crops that grow here — sweet corn, beans, grapes, alfalfa, fuji apples, etc. — are marked by signs, a sort of beginner botany class. ⊗

S tate **Highway 282** from a junction with State Highway 28 in Ephrata southeast to a junction with State Highway 17. Route length: four miles.

Think of it as an abnormally long on-ramp to Highway 17. ⊗

S tate **Highway 283** from a junction with State Highway 281 and Interstate 90 northeast to a junction with State Highway 28. Route length: 15 miles.

Beginning two miles northeast of George, Highway 283 offers a more direct route to Ephrata by bypassing Quincy. The handful of homes that exist on this stretch of road repose in privacy, occupied by farmers or possibly members of the Witness Protection Program. Wasteways and aqueducts crisscross the highway, and giant, pinwheel sprinklers feed the crops, but any land outside of their spray is dominated by sagebrush. ⊗

S tate **Highway 285** from a junction with U.S. Highway 2 south-east through Wenatchee, then east across the Columbia River to East Wenatchee. Route length: seven miles.

Highway 285 travels the length of Wenatchee's (U.S. 2) strip mall, passes through its downtown district, and crosses the Columbia to East Wenatchee (State Highway 28). ⊗

S tate **Highway 290** from a junction with Interstate 90 in Spo-kane northeast through Trentwood to the Washington-Idaho border. Route length: 18 miles.

Leaving the heart of downtown Spokane, Highway 290 follows the old Great Northern Railroad route (now the Burlington Northern) through the Spokane Valley. After crossing the Spokane River and pass-ing the outskirts community of **Trentwood**, the highway is shadowed by wooded ridges to the north that continue clear to the border. South of the road, small farms and orchards coexist with scattered indus-trial and housing developments. From mini **Moab**, a road leads three miles north to fishing, boating and camping at **Newman Lake**. The state line is one mile further. ⊗

S tate **Highway 291** from a junction with U.S. Highways 2 and 395 in Spokane northwest to a junction with State Highway 231. Route length: 33 miles.

Riverside State Park (not to be confused with Riverfront Park in downtown Spokane) begins three miles outside the city's border. The park covers nine miles of shoreline along the Spokane River and is filled with recreational opportunities. There are over 200 camping and picnic sites, challenging rapids for rafting and kayaking, equestrian, hiking and snowmobile trails and a motorcycle and ORV area.

The park is spread out and confusing to navigate but a good starting point is the **Bowl and Pitcher Area**, whose name comes from a collection of oddly-shaped basaltic formations that rise from the water and dot the river's north bank. The park's administrative headquarters are located here and offer directions to the region. (Travel one mile on Highway 291 and turn left onto Rifle Club Road. Continue a half mile and turn left again on A.L. White Parkway. Drive two miles to the park entrance.)

Return to the highway and drive five miles to the **Spokane House Interpretive Center**, situated on the former site of the Spokane House. Bracketed by the Spokane and Little Spokane rivers, the post was established in 1810 under orders of surveyor David Thompson. For nearly 16 years traders bartered for the furs of the wilderness and shipped their pelts to market. These "Nor'Wester's" were also the first to explore, map and chart the area. In 1812, the Pacific Fur Company opened shop only a half mile away and called it Fort Spokane. The close proximity was not so much for competitive reasons as it was for protection in case of trouble with Indians.

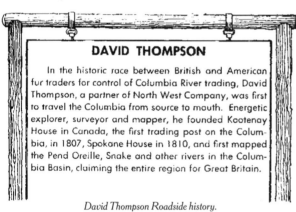

DAVID THOMPSON

In the historic race between British and American fur traders for control of Columbia River trading, David Thompson, a partner of North West Company, was first to travel the Columbia from source to mouth. Energetic explorer, surveyor and mapper, he founded Kootenay House in Canada, the first trading post on the Columbia, in 1807, Spokane House in 1810, and first mapped the Pend Oreille, Snake and other rivers in the Columbia Basin, claiming the entire region for Great Britain.

David Thompson Roadside history.

The next year the Pacific Fur Company left and the North West Company moved into their more spacious quarters. In 1821, the North West Company united with the Hudson's Bay Company, and in 1826 the business of the post was transferred to Fort Colvile at Kettle Falls, where a thoroughfare was facilitated by the Columbia River.

The highway continues through mixed pine forest along the northern ridge of Long Lake, a 20-mile-long, dam-contained stretch of the Spokane River. Near the end of the highway's run, there is a pullout that offers a spectacular overlook of the narrow canyon and Long

Lake Dam below. When the dam was completed by the Washington Water Power Company in 1910, it featured the world's highest spillway — 208 feet.

The highway winds and descends to meet Highway 231 one mile further. ∞

S tate Highway 292 from a junction with State Highway 231 in Springdale east to a junction with U.S. Highway 395 at Loon Lake. Route length: six miles.

This road roughly follows the route of a Burlington Northern spur line and Sheep Creek, named for the flocks of woollies raised here in pioneer days. The creek heads at Loon Lake and joins the Colville River north of Springdale. Orchards fill the lush valley, making for a scenic, albeit short drive. ∞

S tate Highway 300 from a junction with State Highway 3 in Belfair southwest to Belfair State Park. Route length: three miles.

Located at the southern "hook" of Hood Canal, **Belfair State Park** occupies the former campgrounds of the Skokomish Indians. Following in their footsteps, hordes of recreational vehicles and family-sized tents annually fill campsites which overlook the canal and are sheltered by an evergreen forest. Though periodically subject to contamination, the tideflats here offer an abundance of crabs, clams and oysters. ∞

S tate Highway 302 from a junction with State Highway 3 south then east via Elgin, Wauna and Purdy to a junction with State Highway 16. Route length: 15 miles.

Highway 302 dissects the north end of Key Peninsula, a 14-mile-long land mass bracketed by the Case and Carr inlets and defined by its sheltered coves and secluded waterfront dwellings. The numerous waterways here were primarily explored by Charles Wilkes in 1841, and named for members of his expedition party. With a little imagination the peninsula appears as a jagged "key," but arguably, it looks more like a giant finger pointing southward.

From the northern tip of North Bay and the Coulter Creek Fish Hatchery, the road slashes east. To drive the length of the peninsula, take Key Peninsula Highway (just west of the Minter Creek Fish Hatchery), a scenic wooded road with sporadic views of Carr Inlet. **Penrose Point State Park** lies 10 miles south. Tucked away in Mayo Cove, the park is divided by a lengthy shoreline and a thick evergreen forest.

En route to Penrose, the road buzzes **Home**, a quiet coastal settlement with a provocative past. Organized in 1896 as the Mutual Home Association, this politically-eclectic community extended an invitation to all open-minded individuals interested in experimental living. Several hundred free spirits answered the call and soon topics as varied as nudity, free-love and anarchy were discussed and practiced.

Clam digging in the tide flats of Henderson Bay.

It was the anarchy topic that first attracted trouble to Home. When President William McKinely was assassinated in 1901 by a self-proclaimed "anarchist," conservative politicians and newspapers from Tacoma attacked Home as a haven for anarchy. The postal authorities closed the Home post office on the grounds that literature originating from Home was corruptive. Later, while defending nude bathing in an article entitled "The Nude and the Prudes," Jay Fox, the editor for the local rag the *Agitator*, was arrested and sentenced to two months in jail for showing "disrespect for the law." He eventually received a full pardon from the state's governor.

Back on Highway 302, continue by the tiny hamlets of Elgin and Wauna and cross the quaint **Purdy Bridge** over Henderson Bay, tying Key and Gig Harbor peninsulas together. Pull-outs along the bridge access a half-mile-long clamming beach. On the opposite side of the bridge, the road splits north and south; both routes join Highway 16 after a short distance. ⚘

State Highway 303 from a junction with State Highway 304 in Bremerton north to a junction with State Highway 3. Route length: nine miles.

Highway 303 is a slightly longer route to Silverdale than Highway 3, but after clearing Bremerton's strip mall, less crowded.

One and a half miles after crossing the Warren Avenue Bridge, turn right on Sylvan Way and continue to **Illahee State Park**, a rugged hillside park facing Port Orchard. A pair of restored World War I navy guns guard the park's entrance. At the base of a steep wooded cliff, boat owners and scuba divers prepare to hit the water, and sun bathers soak in the nautical action.

Highway 303 meets up with Highway 3 a mile north of Silverdale. ⚘

S tate **Highway 304** from a junction with State Highway 3 east to Bremerton. Route length: two miles.
This is the exit highway to reach Bremerton (Highway 3) and the Puget Sound Naval Shipyard. ⊗

S tate **Highway 305** from Winslow northwest via Bainbridge Island to Poulsbo. Route length: 13 miles.
To reach Highway 305, some assistance from the **Washington State Ferry** system is necessary. The largest ferry fleet in the United States began in earnest in 1951 when the state purchased the Puget Sound Navigation Company. Prior to this, the waters and islands were crossed and connected by an infamous slew of independent steamers lines, dubbed the "Mosquito Fleet." The fleet was notorious for its competitive nature, each boat fighting for passengers, freight and mail.

When the state took over the role of taxiing the waters of Puget Sound, they inherited a hodgepodge of vessels; a handful of steel and wooden-hulled diesel electrics and a pair of steamers, all from San Francisco; and some diesel-powered boats native to the northwest: the *Rosario*, *Kitsap*, *Crosline*, *Leschi*, *Skansonia*, *Vashon*, and *Chippewa*. Two 70-car ferries from Maryland's Chesapeake Bay were bought, renamed the *Rhododendron* and the *Olympic* and sent to work the Lofall and Mukilteo runs.

Puget Sound. Where the buoys are.

Eventually the rapidly-growing ferry system needed to expand and so a 100-car, 1,000 passenger prototype ferry, the *Evergreen State*, was built in 1954. The *Evergreen State*-class boats would later be dwarfed by the "Superferries" of the late 1960s: the *Hyak*, the *Kaleetan*, the *Yakima* and the *Elwha*; huge vessels with the capacity for 160 cars and 2,500 passengers. Jumbo ferries, with the ability to carry about 40 more cars, have since been added.

The fleet currently numbers 25 vessels, three of which are passenger-only ferries. Twenty terminals grace harbors throughout the Puget Sound, the San Juan Islands and as far north as Sidney, British Columbia. Considered the state's leading tourist attraction, over 20 million passengers ride the ferries annually. During tourist season (all summer, or any weekend with the faintest glimmer of sunshine), expect lengthy waits at the ferry terminal, an inconvenience offset by great waterfront views, and a generally festive atmosphere.

Washington's ferries are the easiest way to see the **Puget Sound** (PYOO-juht), a saltwater network of channels, bays, passages, inlets, coves and harbors that push some 80 miles inland into western Washington. The Sound was first charted way back in May of 1792 by George Vancouver and his second lieutenant, Peter Puget. Anchoring the large sloop *Discovery* at Restoration Point off Bainbridge Island, Vancouver and Lieutenant Joseph Baker took out the ship's yawl and explored the waterway west of Vashon Island (Colvos Passage). Puget continued southward past today's Tacoma and presumably as far as Olympia. In his log Vancouver recorded: "Thus by our joint effort, we have completely explored every turning of this extensive inlet; and to commemorate Mr. Puget's exertions, the southern extremity of it I named Puget's Sound."

Carved by ice-age glaciers running from north to south, the Puget Sound contains 500 square miles of water area and now includes the northern inland waters, starting from Point Wilson near Port Townsend and running south to Budd Inlet near Olympia. The San Juans, Hood Canal, Port Susan and Bellingham Bay are not included in the territory. Some Puget Sound facts for the trivia minded: the average water temperature is a cool 50 degrees Fahrenheit; the average depth is 205 feet and the maximum depth is 930 feet; there are over 300 islands; and 1,400 miles of shoreline.

Having digressed far enough, return to Pier 52 in downtown Seattle and board the ferry to Winslow and Bainbridge Island — a 35-minute voyage.

Before **Winslow** became the western terminus of the busiest ferry route in the state, its harbor was crowded with ocean steamers and high-masted schooners either in the process of being built or seeking repairs from the Hall Brothers Marine Railway and Shipbuilding Company. Winslow Hall and his two brothers ran the company from 1902 until 1916, but shipyards remained through both World Wars and even crafted minesweepers for the U.S. Navy.

From Winslow, Highway 305 slashes northwest across **Bainbridge Island**, which at first glance does not appear as an island but as a bulging extension of the Kitsap Peninsula. The extremely narrow, easily-missed Agate Passage was overlooked by George Vancouver and later discovered by Charles Wilkes. He named the 11-mile-long landmass for William Bainbridge, hero of the U.S.S. *Constitution* (Old Ironsides) from the War of 1812.

The windy, shady roads on Bainbridge are a haven for touring cyclists and one-day vacationers who have stuffed the car with family, friends and a picnic basket. For years the affluent have built their second homes or cottage getaways on the island, but recently the population has grown to include common folk from the mainland who want to try their hand at small-town living. Professionals linked by computers to careers in the outside world, solitude-seeking artists, and retirees add to the mix.

The Walla Walla Bainbridge bound.

305 Follow Blakely Avenue from Winslow to the south end of the island and **Fort Ward State Park**. Along with an outpost across Rich Passage in Manchester, the fort served as a coastal fortification in the early 1900s, protecting the entrance to Bremerton's Naval Shipyard. Most remnants of its military past have been removed, so some imagination is necessary to visualize the three-, five- and eight-inch gun batteries which formerly peppered the property. Submarine nets stretched across the waterway further bolstered the defense. The state park offers waterfront picnic and recreation sites.

North of Fort Ward, **Port Blakely's** calm setting will challenge even the most imaginative person to recreate the bustling scene that took place on the waters of Blakely Harbor. During the late 1800s, 1,200 able-bodied men toiled in the world's largest sawmill, cutting 400,000 feet of lumber per day. The harbor was so crowded with ships being built and lumber schooners loading up for world markets that one could nearly cross the harbor by hopping from deck to deck.

At the northeast tip of the island, the presence of **Port Madison**, which actually began cutting wood long before the Blakely mill, added to the island's status as a giant in the Northwest lumber market. The mill was established in 1854 by George Meigs, a businessman from San Francisco who encouraged clean living and hard work. Aided by a great demand for lumber and prices that reached from $200 to $500 per board feet, the prosperous town grew rapidly, adding a foundry, machine shop and shipyard. Port Madison was nearly named the seat of Kitsap County but lost that honor to Port Orchard, an event that signaled the end of Port Madison's rise. Today, much like Port Blakely, Madison is content with its role as a quiet neighborhood for sea-loving residents.

Immediately after Highway 305 crosses Agate Pass, the narrow entrance to Bainbridge's west shoreline, turn north on Suquamish Way and follow it one mile to **Old Man House State Park**. The park is the former site of a 900-foot cedar longhouse, and home to Chief Sealth, leader of the Suquamish (soo-KWAH-mish) tribe. The roomy dwelling was separated into 40 apartments by partitions of split logs, and housed not only Chief Seattle, but his people as well. It was razed in 1870 under the pretense of being "uncivilized." A display at the waterfront park illustrates how the structure was built.

The famous leader is buried in the town of Suquamish at Memorial Cemetery, a few blocks from the park. A mini-longhouse tops his grave and the inscription on the tombstone reads: "Seattle, Chief of the Suquamish and Allied Tribes. Died June 7, 1866, the firm friend of the whites and for him the City of Seattle was named by its founders." (Sealth was pronounced *See-YAH-til*, and anglicized to its current spelling, *Seattle*.)

~362

Continue up the road a short distance to **Poulsbo** (PAWLZ-boh, Elevation 20, Population 5,350). In the late 1880s, fisherman, farmers and loggers of Norwegian descent began to settle here, likening the adjacent deepwater bays and timbered ridges to the fjord country of Norway. The population grew with the arrival of friends and relatives, and by the turn of the century, Poulsbo was over 90 percent Norwegian.

The three-mile long, picturesque Liberty Bay on which Poulsbo is located was originally called Dogfish Bay, for a type of small shark that inhabited local waters. The bay was the launching point for a large fishing boat fleet headed for salmon runs in the Sound or Straits, or the distant waters of Alaska. By far the largest operation was the Pacific Coast Codfish Company, which thrived on the great quantities of codfish found in the Puget Sound and as far away as the Bering Sea. The company employed much of Poulsbo, either on the high seas or at home in the processing plant. Upon the schooner's return the fish were cleaned, mild-cured (lightly

Velkommen to Poulsbo's sweet smells and tastes.

salted), dried in the open air, and wrapped and packed for shipment to eastern markets. Business was good until the 1950s, when the demand for dried fish tapered off.

Boats continue to moor in Liberty Bay but are now of the pleasure variety and not used for employment. The town has welcomed tourism, but unlike some theme towns in the state, Poulsbo's ethnic background gives it an air of authenticity, seen in its rosemaling (painted murals) or tasted at sidewalk bakeries, which peddle pastry delicacies. Poulsbo's rich Scandinavian heritage holds up against the flocks of picture-snapping, T-shirt buying tourists. Highway 305 ends one mile east at a junction with Highway 3. ∞

State Highway 307 from a junction with State Highway 305 northeast to a junction with State Highway 104. Route length: six miles. Beginning one mile north of Poulsbo, Highway 307 (Bond Road) follows a portion of the **Poulsbo-Port Gamble Bicycle Loop**, a favorite among touring cyclists, beer lovers, and beer-loving touring cyclists. The route passes through a thick forest of ferns, evergreens and black-

berry brambles two miles to the **Thomas Kemper Brewery**, a popular microbrewery (small-scale production of high quality beer) open for tours and tastings.

Refreshed, continue to a junction with Highway 104 and follow the Puget Sound shoreline to the historic mill and seafaring town of Port Gamble (Highway 104). To finish the round trip, pedal west one mile to State Highway 3 and travel south seven miles to rejoin Highway

It's Kemper time. Small-scale production of high quality beer.

307. The loop covers 18 miles and offers views of Hood Canal and the Olympic Mountains. ∞

State Highway 308 from a junction with State Highway 3 east to Keyport. Route length: three miles. **Keyport's** one-street downtown and small portage area is dominated by the **Naval Undersea Warfare Center**, established in 1914 as the Navy's sole depot and testing facility for torpedoes and mobile targets.

Although the Naval Reservation is closed to the public, the state-of-the-art **Naval Undersea Museum** (the large building to the right at the conclusion of Highway 308) offers an extensive look at the world undersea. Underwater habitats, vessels, salvage and rescue operations, and man's latest technological advancements are featured. ∞

State Highway 310 from a junction with State Highway 3 east to Bremerton. Route length: two miles. Highway 310 leaves and enters Bremerton (Highway 3) from its north end. ∞

US **Highway 395** from the Washington-Oregon border, the Columbia River and a junction with State Highway 14 in Plymouth, north through Kennewick and Pasco to Connell, northeast via Ritzville and Sprague to Spokane, north northwest through Deer Park and Chewelah to Colville, west past Kettle Falls across the Columbia River, then north to the Canadian boundary at Laurier. (Overlaps U.S. Highways 2 and 12, Interstates 82, 182 and 90, and State Highway 20). Route length: 286 miles.

Stretching from Mexico to Canada, U.S. 395 is a road marked with diversity. The state's southern portion ambles through fields of wheat and fruit and sparsely populated towns until reaching Spokane. North of Spokane the road enters fertile Colville Valley which dissects the Colville National Forest, meets again with the Columbia River just past Kettle Falls and travels alongside the twisting Kettle River to the international border.

The road starts from the Umatilla Bridge and passes a massive basaltic rock embedded in the north shore of the Columbia River. The shoreline area and rock are called **Plymouth**, but the circumstances surrounding this Plymouth are less pleasant than its distant eastern cousin.

Plymouth was the site of an attack by a passing government steamboat on two Columbia River fishing villages during the Bannock-Paiute War of 1878. Neither man, woman nor child were spared. In retaliation, a white couple was killed while traveling by stage to Yakima City; the couple is buried in a Union Gap cemetery.

Roughly 10 miles north of Plymouth are the low, rolling **Horse Heaven Hills**, once home to numerous roaming packs of wild horses who enjoyed the abundant, native bunchgrass. In the 1870s, the Switzler brothers claimed as many as 15,000 horses but when market prices dropped in the 1890s, the remaining herds were sold to an Oregon cannery.

Only an occasional vineyard or a scattering of cattle grazing on the lush grass interrupt the mostly barren, rolling hills as the highway descends into the open desert valley at **Kennewick** (KEN-uh-wik, Elevation 469, Population 45,110). The southernmost member of the Tri-Cities, Kennewick began as a small community in

Floating a new span into place.

when the Northern Pacific Railway Company was constructing a bridge over the Columbia River. It was a bunchgrass wasteland until 1892, when the Northern Pacific Irrigation Company stabilized the region. Their irrigation canals were fully functional by 1903, and with the help of the Yakima Irrigation and Improvement Company, which imported settlers from the Midwest and the Mississippi Valley, Kennewick boomed.

Kennewick is a Chemnapam Indian name with multiple translations including "winter paradise," "grassy place" and "dried acorns." Colorful displays at the **East Benton County Historical Museum** (205 Keewaydin Drive) in Keewaydin Park concentrate on the pioneers who followed Lewis and Clark.

Pasco (Elevation 383, Population 21,370) is a short bridge crossing away. Founded in 1884 as a Northern Pacific camp called Ainsworth, Pasco lies on the confluence of the Columbia and Snake

Downtown Pasco parade in 1913.

rivers. The name Pasco comes from *Cerro de Pasco,* a town located high in the Andes Mountains of Peru. Henry M. McCartney, a location engineer for Northern Pacific, considered the location of a railroad he had once surveyed in the Andes to be the coldest place in the world. McCartney encountered a sandstorm and excessive heat on his first day in eastern Washington and because of the contrast between the two places, he named the town Pasco. Captain John C. Ainsworth, whom the town had originally been named after, would have been glad of the change since he deemed the area a "miserable place."

Ainsworth was a wild, lusty town known more for its brawls, gunfights and hangings than for its real estate value. The site was chosen by Northern Pacific as a starting point for a developing railway that would later connect with Spokane, and after joining forces with the Oregon Railway and Navigation Company, western Washington.

The railway and the prospect of large-scale irrigation helped build the population of Pasco in the early 1900s. A second and larger population surge occurred in the early 1940s when World War II necessitated an Army supply depot and naval air station. More importantly, the Hanford Project was underway and in a few months, the population of Pasco would grow to more than 10,000 people in the city limits and 50,000 people on its outskirts.

Take Exit 13 past **Volunteer Park** where a Northern Pacific Railway car has retired to the **Franklin County Historical Museum** (305 Fourth Avenue). The museum was constructed in 1910 as part of steel magnate Andrew Carnegie's worldwide library construction program. In 1898, Carnegie gave over $40 million to build 1,679 public libraries across the country.

The Franklin County Courthouse was built in 1913.

Just down the street, the **Franklin County Courthouse** (1016 Fourth Avenue) has Corinthian columns and is topped by a gilded metal dome visible for miles. An elaborate marble design marks its interior.

Two miles east of Pasco on Highway 12 is **Sacajawea State Park**. A stone's throw from the Columbia River, the grassy park sprawls beneath a well-established maple grove and includes an interpretive center with informative exhibits on Lewis and Clark's expedition and Native American artifacts. Sacajawea was a Shoshoni Indian woman who led Lewis and Clark on their historical journey; the party arrived in Pasco in October of 1805. Clark's servant, York, was the first black man to visit the region.

Franklin County: Pasco is the county seat of Franklin County, which was created in 1883 and was formerly part of Whitman County. It was named after the American patriot, Benjamin Franklin. It is situated in the southeast part of the state and is bounded by the Columbia River on the west and the Snake River on the east. Its early history centered on transportation. The Cariboo Trail used from 1859-68 traversed the county while navigation and the establishment

Sacajawea.

of ferries on the Columbia and Snake Rivers were prominent events which were closely followed by the introduction of railroads through the county. Today Franklin County bases its economy on agriculture with wheat, barley and beans its principal crops.

Court House: 1016 North Fourth Avenue, Pasco 99301, SCAN 726-3535 (Commissioners), FAX 509-545-2130. Area: 1,259.7 square miles.

State Ranking: 27th. 1993 Population: 41,100. Unincorporated: 16,840. Incorporated: 24,260. Density: 32.6 persons per square mile. **Cities and Towns**: Connell, Kahlotus, Mesa, Pasco. **Principal Economic Activities**: Food processing, publishing, agriculture, metal fabrication. **Points of Interest**: Ice Harbor Dam, Lake Sacajawea.

Climate: (Eltopia - elevation 920)

	Jan	Apr	Jul	Oct
Max Temp. F°	36.4	65.8	89.7	64.5
Min Temp.	22.2	38.1	55.7	37.6
Mean Temp.	29.3	52.0	72.8	52.1
Precipitation	.99"	.51"	.09"	.56"

Average Annual Maximum Temperature: 63.7
Average Annual Minimum Temperature: 39.1
Annual Mean Temperature: 51.5
Average Annual Precipitation: 8.31"

Back on 395 the road ventures north 15 miles to **Eltopia** (El-toh-pee-uh). Originally a watering hole established by the Northern Pacific Railroad in 1881, Eltopia now serves as a dusty, wheat-shipping railroad stop. There are two versions as to the naming of Eltopia. One account is that after a severe storm wrecked weeks of railroad construction a cockney laborer proclaimed there would be "hell to pay." This evolved into "Eltopay," then Eltopia. A more probable, though less interesting, explanation is the Indian name for the area, El-To-Pai.

The **Juniper Dunes Wilderness**, east of Eltopia, is an unlikely setting for a desert, but the area contains the finest sand dunes in Washington. The large dunes and fragrant western juniper groves are home to a unique blend of wildlife, including coyote, mule deer and small rodents. The area is accessible for day hikes only with a permit.

The Spanish translation of **Mesa** (Mee-sah, Elevation 500, Population 315), nine miles further, is "tableland," but instead of resting on a plateau, Mesa lies in a coulee. Another in a series of towns created by the railroad, Mesa wisely turned to agriculture in the early 1900s, survived the Depression and years of drought, and was finally saved by the Columbia Basin Project in the 1950s. Today, Mesa is a healthy agricultural shipping center.

Continue eight miles through a desolate region of sagebrush, gray sand and dried water courses to **Connell** (kah-NEL, Elevation 838, Population 2,375). Intersected by State Highway 260, Connell lies in the heart of the Channeled Scablands. During the last ice age, approximately 13,000 years ago, flooding glaciers washed away topsoil leaving rugged basalt in the forms of gullies and steep canyons. Drive east on State Highway 260, the former route of the Palouse River, to sample the numerous coulees. Connell was the namesake of a former Northern Pacific station worker.

Centered in a rich wheat-growing area at the junction of I-90, 63 miles southwest of Spokane, **Ritzville's** (Elevation 1,795, Population 1,740) history of prosperity is symbolized through its founder, Philip Ritz. A former successful businessman from Walla Walla, Ritz confidently bought 8,000 acres of Northern Pacific land with the hopes of selling wheat to England and bringing settlers to the area. In return for his business, Northern Pacific gave him a contract to plant trees along the newly-laid track from Pasco to Ritzville. This would help convince prospective settlers, who often decided where to live by scanning the passing countryside through their train windows, that

This old timer is taking a long, much-needed rest.

the land was fertile. Apparently Ritz's plan worked; by 1904 Ritzville was then considered the country's busiest wheat-shipping point.

The result of Ritzville's prosperity is a firmly established brick downtown and pleasant residential area. Also interesting is **Dr. Frank R. Burrough's** home (408 West Main), now the county museum, which shows a family doctor's life in rural Washington.

Adams County: Ritzville is the county seat of Adams County, which was organized in 1883 from parts of Whitman County. It is named after President John Adams and is located in the southeastern part of the state. It was first visited by European fur traders in 1811 and early travelers first passed through the county on the Colville Road in 1826. The county was settled in 1869 and later attracted a large number of hardy Russian-German immigrants. The county's economy is primarily agricultural with wheat the most important crop. Barley, oats, beans and peas are also grown.

Court House: 210 West Broadway, Ritzville 99169, SCAN 537-1011(Information), FAX 509-659-0118. Area: 1,893.5 square miles. State Ranking: 16th. 1993 Population: 14,300. Unincorporated: 7,044. Incorporated: 7,256. Density: 7.6 persons per square mile. **Cities and Towns**: Hatton, Lind, Othello, Ritzville, Washtucna. **Principal Economic Activities**: Food processing, agriculture. **Points of Interest**: Mullan Road, Sprague Lake.

Climate: (Ritzville - elevation 1,795)

	Jan	Apr	Jul	Oct
Max Temp. F°	33.8	62.3	88.8	63.6
Min Temp.	20.2	35.2	53.2	37.5
Mean Temp.	27.0	48.8	71.1	50.6
Precipitation	1.44"	.74"	.29"	1.19"

Average Annual Maximum Temperature: 61.4
Average Annual Minimum Temperature: 36.8
Annual Mean Temperature: 49.1
Average Annual Precipitation: 11.67"

The first significant outcrop of pine trees breaks the landscape's monotony as you approach **Sprague Lake**, 17 miles north of Ritzville. This low-lying lake was formed by the same flooding glaciers that carved the outlying Channeled Scablands. Six miles long and shaped like an inverted Italy, the lake lies in a northeast direction. The orientation of the lake is common among lakes in the region, and indicates the course of the Spokane Flood.

Church of Mary Queen of Heaven in Sprague.

Local personality, "Hoodoo Billy" Burrow, gave **Sprague** (Elevation 1,980, Population 445) its first name, Hoodooville. Unfortunately for "Hoodoo," the subsequent prosperity Northern Pacific Railway brought to the community in the 1880s demanded that Hoodooville be changed to Sprague, in honor of Gen. John W. Sprague, director of the railway.

In the late 1870s, Sprague was a vibrant sheep camp whose main industry was the transport of wool to the East Coast. The railroad came in 1881 and by 1883 Sprague had won the Lincoln County seat. Fifteen years later a fire destroyed the town, Northern Pacific rerouted their tracks and Sprague lost the county seat to Davenport. Vestiges of nineteenth century architecture still remain; most notable is the Gothic Revival **Church of Mary Queen of Heaven** (East 103 North First; built in 1902).

The road continues northeast through fertile farmlands, scab and lava rock ledges and rolling pine forests to a junction with U.S. 2 on the southwest outskirts of Spokane (see I-90). There it enters the city, leaves I-90 and U.S. 2, and heads north 23 miles to **Deer Park** (Elevation

2,150, Population 2,445). An occasional deer may be spotted in this sawmill town, but not in the same abundance as during the pioneer days.

Northwest of Spokane, U.S. 395 and the curious traveler bid fare-well to the rolling wheatfields of southeastern Washington and enter the expansive **Colville National Forest**. The area covers 1,096,097 acres and is dominated with grand firs, and to a lesser extent, Douglas firs, ponderosa and lodgepole pines and the western larch.

Thirty-eight miles northwest of Spokane is two-mile-long **Loon Lake**, a clear, shallow lake that was once a popular loon nesting place. Washington's most infamous outlaw, Harry Tracy, once camped out on the lake's shore. A private resort at the north end of the lake was established by railroad builder and banker D.C. Corbin and is now a public recreation center.

Chewelah (Chuh-wee-luh, Elevation 1,680, Population 2,212) is 58 miles north of Spokane. During three major intervals, 50 to 190 million years ago, granite magma intruded the Precambrian sedimen-tary rocks in this area. This geological occurrence produced a gener-ous supply of mineral deposits that filled the hills surrounding Chewelah with magnesite, gold, silver, copper and lead. Between 1916 and 1949 and especially during World War II, magnesite, which is the primary raw material for magnesium metal and high-grade steel, was extracted to such an extent that Chewelah was the largest magnesite operation in the United States. Presently, magnesite removal almost exclusively takes place in sea water, rendering the mines of Chewelah useless.

Chewelah was the center for agriculture in the Colville Valley in the late 1800s. In 1873, the federal government established an Indian agency that taught farming methods and distributed farm machinery and seeds to the native people. The agency moved to Nespelem in 1885 but the original log-cabin building remains at 309 Third Street.

Chewelah, an Indian name meaning "small, striped snake," may have derived from the snake-like appearance of a stream that runs through the town.

If not paying attention while driving the 23 miles from Chewelah to Colville, traces of towns that were small even in their heyday will be missed. Blue Creek, Addy, Arden and Orin run north along or near the Colville and Little Pend Oreille rivers. These grist and sawmill towns utilized the rivers as a method of transport. The towns were also used as lumber shipping points and staging stations by the Spokane Falls and Northern Railway.

After nearly missing Orin, drive four miles to **Colville** (KAWL-vil, Elevation 1,609, Population 4,420). To explain the origins of Colville it

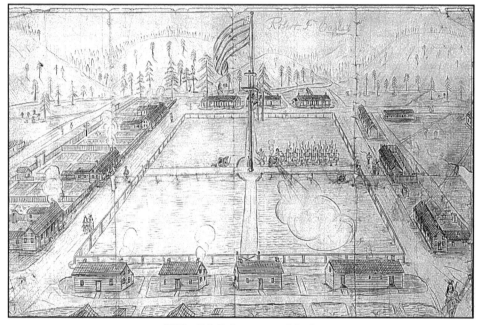 is first necessary to discuss another Colville, **Fort Colville**, and its neighboring community **Pinkney City**. Fort Colville was established after a series of violent outbreaks occurred in 1855 between native people and white prospectors and settlers. Once the site was chosen, two companies with a questionable repute arrived in the spring of 1859 under the command of Major Pinkney Lugenbeel. The troops, consisting largely of convicts from San Francisco who had the choice of prison or enlistment, spent the next 20 years mediating land disputes and enforcing restrictive government policy inflicted upon the Native Americans.

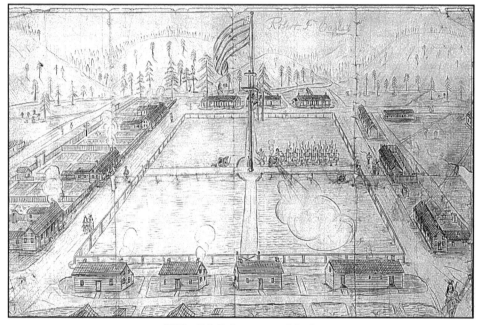

Old Fort Colville from an original sketch.

Nearby Pinkney City provided housing and supplies to off-duty soldiers, miners, settlers and Indians. It was also the county seat of a large area covering what is now northeast Washington. When the garrison was moved to Fort Spokane in 1882 because of its more convenient location, the residents of Pinkney City stripped the fort of all essential items and relocated a few miles west to what is now Colville.

Drive two miles north on the Colville-Aladdin Road to a gravel pit where a sign reads, "Here stood Fort Colville protecting the Last Frontier, 1859-1882." The minuscule remains of Fort Colville are rivaled by the emptiness at the former site of Pinkney City, now a hayfield three miles northeast of Colville.

Described by railroad magnate D. C. Corbin as "an open door to a magnificent country," Colville is situated in the beautiful Colville Valley, enclosed by the peaks of the Okanogan Highlands. Corbin's endorsement of the region helped generate a steady influx of people beginning with the first trainload of people in October of 1889. The city is littered with several turn-of-the-century homes and buildings. The **Keller Historical Park** includes the **Keller House** (built in 1910), Colville's first schoolhouse (1885) and the **Stevens County Historical Museum.**

The Keller House is on the National Register of Historic Places.

Stevens County: Colville is the county seat of Stevens County, which was created in 1863 from Walla Walla County. It was named after the first Territorial governor, Isaac Stevens. The county is located in the northeastern part of the state and is bounded on the north by Canada and on the west by the Columbia River. The Spokane Indian Reservation occupies the southern portion of the county. Europeans first entered the county in 1811 when David Thompson visited Kettle Falls. In 1826, the Hudson's Bay Company erected Fort Colvile as a fur trading center for the region. Protestant missions were established in the county in 1835 and 1837, and in 1845 Father De Smet founded St. Paul's Mission near Kettle Falls. Today, the county's economy is based on mining, agriculture, food processing and tourism.

The Keller House Rock Garden; home for ferries, nymphs, and such.

Court House: 215 South Oak Street, Colville 99114, 509-684-3751 (Information), SCAN 246-1011 (Commissioners), FAX 509-684-8310. Area: 2,481.2 square miles. State Ranking: 5th. 1993 Population: 33,400. Unincorporated: 24,633. Incorporated: 8,767. Density: 13.5 persons per square mile. **Cities and Towns**: Chewelah, Colville, Kettle Falls, Marcus, Northport, Springdale. **Principal Economic Activities**: Wood products, mining, metals processing. **Points of Interest**: Fort Colville, Roosevelt Lake, Little Pend Oreille National Wildlife Range.

Climate: (Colville - elevation 1,635)

	Jan	Apr	Jul	Oct
Max Temp. F°	30.3	64.5	86.6	59.6
Min Temp.	17.2	33.9	49.1	34.6
Mean Temp.	23.5	48.6	68.0	46.8
Precipitation	2.05"	1.07"	.71"	1.69"

Average Annual Maximum Temperature: 59.4
Average Annual Minimum Temperature: 34.0
Annual Mean Temperature: 46.5
Average Annual Precipitation: 17.36"

From Colville, drive nine miles east to **Kettle Falls** (Elevation 1,652, Population 1,382), named after the booming waterfalls that existed here before the Grand Coulee Dam was erected and the site was swamped by the rising reservoir. French-Canadian trappers called the falls *Les Chaudieres* or "the Kettles": huge, circular holes formed by the churning Columbia River. The Indian name for the place is *Schwan-ate-ku,* meaning "the place of deep-sounding water." Father Pierre Jean Desmet, a missionary who taught Christianity to the native population, describes the falls:

> ... It was indeed a most imposing spectacle all around the noble rock and the distant roar of the cataracts breaking in on the religious silence of that solitude. From the eminence over-looking the Columbia River could be seen the impetuous waters, freeing themselves from their limits and rushing in fury, dashing over piles of rocks and casting upwards a thousand jets, whose transparent columns reflect in varied colors the rays of the dazzling sun.

In the 1930s, the town of Kettle Falls was one of many cleared away by the Works Progress Administration to make way for the lake. More important than the loss of the townsite were the falls themselves. For at least 9,000 years salmon were trapped and speared, supporting generations of Native Americans of many tribes and cultures. The falls were also a summer meeting place for at least 11 commonly recognized tribes who gathered to trade, fish, and participate in religious observances and sports. The day the falls were flooded the Colville Indians held a ceremony of tears. There were no fish ladders, effectively ending salmon spawning along the upper Columbia River.

Before the Columbia was dammed, productive orchards lay on the outskirts of Kettle Falls, ferries transported prospectors to mines in Republic, and visitors from across the country came to see what newspapers were describing as "God's Country." The rising reservoir stranded the residents of Kettle Falls, but they were prepared, eyeing a new home in nearby Meyers Falls, three miles to the east. At a town meeting, in which Kettle Falls' voters held a four-to-one majority over

Meyers Falls' citizens, the displaced residents elected to consolidate with Meyers Falls and retain the name Kettle Falls.

The first grist mill on the upper Columbia River was built in 1826 near Meyers Falls (the waterfall), two miles south of Kettle Falls. The first permanent resident of Meyers Falls, Louther Walden Meyers, arrived from Bellsville, Ontario, Canada in 1862 and rebuilt the mill in 1871. Meyers died in Colville in 1909. Shortly before his death, he recalled his experience coming west:

> In June in 1862, I was with two brothers Tobias and Jacob, George B. Wonicott, a half brother, and George F. C. McCray, Frank McConnell and Adam Arnolds, school day chums; all young men met at Fort Gary now Winnipeg. Equipped with small arms, no provisions and possessed of only the clothes we stood in and with our young spirits and high hopes decided our course to the setting sun, regarding not our journey's end. For nearly four months we followed the Indian trails with an occasional Hudson's Bay post to cheer our sagging spirits. Beginning our pilgrimage on foot we gathered substance in the chase. We slept like babes on the bare grass-covered prairies and with blue skies for a blanket. The Hudson's Bay company factors gave us an occasional lift and clothing that replaced the tatters that had served their day shielding us from the searching winds that swept the broad spaces. For those we paid in labor. In the same way we procured horses and by the time we reached the Rockies we were well-mounted and made good speed. By October we were at old Fort Colville where we found ready employment, for each of us was an artisan in some line and in demand.

Finding **Fort Colvile**, not to be confused with the previously mentioned Colvilles, is challenging since it is covered by the Columbia River. Fort Colvile was created in 1825 by the Hudson's Bay Company as a trading post and supply depot for other company posts in the Columbia River basin. In conjunction with adjacent Saint Paul's Mission, it boomed with people looking for supplies and companionship. By 1840, the post was processing 18,000 furs a year. It supplied food for much of the West and shipped commodities as far away as Alaska and Hawaii. The fort was named after Andrew W. Colvile, a former governor of the Hudson's Bay Company.

Saint Paul's Mission, located upon a high plateau, survived the flooding caused by the Grand Coulee Dam. Located midway between the salmon fishery at Kettle Falls and Hudson's Bay's Fort Colvile, the chapel is the second oldest in the state. During a period when the native people were seeking Christianity, Father Pierre Jean DeSmet picked the site for a mission in 1845. Missionaries believed that

 cultural changes by the Colville Indians would result in a "spiritual improvement." Conversion was facilitated by the Colville's inherent belief in the guardian spirit faith, which bears some resemblance to Christian beliefs, and a creator they called "Great Man." The hand-hewn log church is an historical site.

After crossing the Columbia River at the south end of Roosevelt Lake, the highway heads due north into the Kettle River Valley. Follow the scenic, twisting road to **Boyds**, 10 miles past Kettle Falls. The rising waters of Roosevelt Lake and white man's treaties forced the natives from idyllic Boyds. Farming was once successful, but the most fruitful farm lands are now covered by water. Besides some logging operations and small farms, all that remains today is scenic views and abundant wildlife.

Continue through thick forests to **Orient**, a former mining town 10 miles south of Canada. At the Orient weather station a rock hanging from a cross piece says "Observe the rock. If it is swinging, the wind is blowing. If it is white, it is snow-

For many, a view like this stirs a long, deep yearning.

ing. If it is wet, it is raining. If you can't see the rock, it is foggy." Primitive, but it seems to work. A brick schoolhouse built in 1910 and registered as a historic place remains. U.S. 395 ceases at **Laurier**, another former mining town that is now the location of the U.S. Customs and Immigration Station. ☙

 State **Highway 397** from Kennewick southeast along the Columbia River. Route length: 10 miles.
Highway 397 ventures into an industrial area between Kennewick and the river. ☙

 State **Highway 401** from a junction with U.S. Highway 101 at the Columbia River northeast then north through Naselle to a junction with State Highway 4. Route length: 15 miles.
Departing U.S. 101 at the Astoria-Megler bridge, the first few miles are highlighted by a view of the Columbia River as the highway

follows its bank northeast. A procession of fishing boats, tugs and barges are dwarfed by the wide river — over four miles across at this point — including the rusting remains of one unfortunate vessel that is beached not far from shore. Due east, the altered crater of Mt. St. Helens is visible on clear days. Regardless of weather or wind, a handful of pick-up truck fisherman stand on the rock dikes along the road with a hopeful line in the water.

Pilings rise from the river's surface as a reminder of ferry landings, canneries and hard-luck fishing towns that long ago slipped beneath the waves and into obscurity. One of the larger wooden skeletons lies offshore of **Knappton**, where rotting logs in neat rows of varying height are all that remain of a sawmill built around 1870.

Leaving the river behind, the road moves north for eight miles past unnamed creeks and overgrown thicket, clear cuts and tree farms into a marshy valley and the town of **Naselle**. Five creeks meet the Naselle River here on their way to Willapa Bay, creating a system of waterways that served as both transportation and livelihood for native tribes and settlers alike. The Nasal Indians, a branch of the Chinook tribe, plucked fish from these waters for centuries, relying almost solely on canoes for transportation. *Na-sil* is their word for "sheltered," "protected" or "hidden."

The first documented white face in the area was a roaming Belgian missionary who traveled through the valley in 1808. After planting an apple orchard beside one of the creeks and delivering a few sermons that fell on mostly disinterested ears, he went on his way. But though his stay was brief, this clerical Johnny Appleseed left his mark, as the apples eventually worked as a beacon for later homesteaders. Attracted to the full-grown orchard, Phillip Pierre and his Cree Indian wife arrived in the mid-1850s to become the first permanent settlers in the area. In addition to a bit of amateur missionary work, Pierre taught the Indians how to plant vegetables and bake bread in exchange for first-hand lessons on the ways of the river. He also acted as an interpreter, helping the Indians to receive fair prices for their furs at the Astoria trading post. (The apple orchard was eventually lost to river erosion.)

Finnish immigrants arrived in Naselle in the 1880s, and as letters went home calling for family and friends, the population began to grow. Lured by the promise of fertile soil, plenty of space and thick salmon runs, ambitious Finns journeyed to America to make their fortune. After towering timber was cleared, most started dairy farms, supplemented by fishing in the summer months. Schools and community centers were erected and students used rowboats to get to class. This ethnic heritage is celebrated each year with a Finnish-American Folk Festival. Adding to the international feel, a sizable Irish and Nova Scotian population settled in Naselle when timber

401
WASHINGTON

companies began buying tracts of surrounding land and hiring out for loggers.

To access the 42-mile **Naselle-Seaview Bicycle Route**, follow Parpala Road northwest along the Naselle River to a junction with U.S. 101, then southwest past the Willapa National Wildlife Refuge and on to the town of Seaview.

Highway 401 leaves Naselle and merges with Highway 4 a half mile north. ∽

INTERSTATE 405

Interstate 405 from a junction with Interstate 5 in Tukwila east to Renton, north via Bellevue and Kirkland to Woodinville, then northwest to rejoin I-5. Route length: 31 miles.

A true commuter pipeline, I-405 threads together the dense mass of residential and business space blanketing the east side of Lake Washington. From a connection with I-5 near the giant Southcenter Mall, the highway moves east, skirting the industrial parks of **Tukwila** (Elevation 100, Population 14,660) before moving north into Renton on the south end of the lake.

The most industrialized city on Lake Washington, **Renton** (Elevation 40, Population 43,470) began as a coal mine in 1853 when Dr. R. H. Bigelow discovered large deposits while working on his homestead. The lode was rich, but early transportation problems hampered development and kept profits low. Reaching Seattle with the ore was a tedious process that required several days. Heavy barges had to first negotiate the shallow Black River (now dried up), then the Duwamish River, before reaching the Puget Sound.

The inefficiency continued until 1873 when Captain William Renton purchased the mine. As owner of the Port Blakely sawmill, at one time considered the largest in the world, Renton knew how to run a major operation. By modernizing methods and equipment and building ample housing for employees, he created a full-scale company town. The money started rolling in when a local railroad connected Renton to Seattle in 1877.

When oil became the fuel of choice around the turn of the century, the coal industry collapsed like an abandoned mine shaft. Clay-product mills, foundries and poultry farms held Renton over until the 1950s when Boeing opened a huge plant near the lake. This employment brought a renewed spark to the town, luring new residents to the housing developments springing up along the hillsides, and turning Renton into a bedroom community of Seattle.

The **Boeing** story began way back in 1910, only seven short years after the Wright brothers' famous flight, when a 28-year old Seattle timberman named William E. Boeing decided to learn how to fly. On his way home from Glenn Martin's aviation school in Los Angeles —

flying a Martin Hydroplane he had purchased — William misjudged his water landing on Puget Sound and sheared off the plane's pontoons. Although admitting that he had hit too hard, Boeing deflected some of the blame for the accident on the poor construction of the aircraft. When told that it would take over six months to get replacement parts, he chose to rebuild the pontoons himself. The birth of America's aviation industry was at hand.

With the help of a friend, Naval engineer Conrad Westervelt, Boeing attempted to improve on the fragile planes of the time and designed a twin-float seaplane, the B&W, which an unusual team of shipwrights, carpenters, cabinet makers, and a seamstress then proceeded to assemble in a two-story wooden boathouse affectionately called the "Red Barn." Boeing had purchased that first assembly plant in 1916 for "$10 and other considerations."

The lowest paid of his 24 employees earned 14 cents an hour, while the company's top test pilots made $200-300 a month. Backup pilots made $1 an hour. Since the B&W was not a commercial success, Boeing paid all of these wages out of his own pocket. Fortunately, his residual timber interests were still profitable.

In July of that same year, Boeing incorporated his airplane manufacturing business, creating the Pacific Aero Products Company. Two years later its name was changed to the Boeing Airplane Company. At this stage in the company's infancy, William made the following timeless statement to his capable, if underpaid, cohorts: "We are embarked as pioneers upon a new science and industry in which our problems are so new and unusual that it behooves no one to dismiss any novel idea. . . . Our job is to keep everlastingly at research and development."

Boeing's next effort, and its first commercial success, was a seaplane called the Model C, the first all-Boeing-designed aircraft. Although the U.S. Navy bought 50 of the planes to use as trainers, William was worried that this country's civilian population was derelict in its preparation for America's entry into the Great War. To make his point, Boeing flew over Seattle dropping missile-shaped leaflets advocating increased vigilance.

A flood of surplus airplanes on the market after the war hurt the company's sales, again forcing Boeing to dip into his own wallet to keep the enterprise solvent. His solution to the problem? Airmail. On March 2, 1919, Boeing and pilot Eddie Hubbard took off from Lake Union, heading north at 65 miles per hour. The next day — and one forced landing later — the duo returned from British Columbia with a pouch of Canadian mail, thereby completing the first international airmail flight to the United States.

Unfortunately, airmail deliveries did not solve the company's financial woes. Boeing was forced to drastically cut his staff, and even resorted to building boats and furniture just to keep the doors open.

It wasn't until the company began to produce the Model 40A in late 1927 that it pulled out of its fiscal nose-dive. After learning that the U.S. Post Office planned to turn over all transcontinental airmail routes to private carriers, Boeing engineers designed a plane that could carry passengers as well as 1,000 pounds of mail. Soon it had landed two reasonably lucrative routes: San Francisco — Chicago, and Seattle — Los Angeles.

After Lindbergh's attention-grabbing solo flight across the Atlantic, the future of aviation looked boundless. To finance expansion, William took the company public, issuing shares on the New York Stock Exchange. With 800 employees, Boeing was by then one of the

It's hard to believe these mammoths can fly.

largest manufacturers in the country. And true to his early pep-talk, William continued to "keep everlastingly at research and development."

In 1928, Boeing introduced the Model 80, America's first airliner designed specifically for passenger comfort and convenience. It offered its 12 passengers leather upholstery, reading lamps, forced-air ventilation, and hot and cold running water. The pilot and co-pilot operated the plane from an enclosed cabin in front of the passengers. When the plane was enlarged to hold 18, registered nurses were hired — the industry's first stewardesses.

Two years later, the Monomail (and its military counterpart the B-9 bomber) made traditional biplane construction obsolete. The all-metal plane had retractable landing gear and a streamlined fuselage. The B-9 had a top speed of 186 mph, which enabled it to outrun even the fighter planes of the day.

A legacy of the Monomail, the Model 247, was able to carry passengers from New York to Los Angeles at 155 mph, completing the trip in an amazing 20 hours — almost 8 hours faster than the best previous airliner time. The trip did necessitate seven stops, however.

In the heart of the Great Depression, Boeing responded to Pan American's need for a long-range, four-engine flying boat by designing the Model 314. Dubbed the "Clipper," the 106-foot-long and 82,000-pound behemoth had a 4,900-mile range, which enabled it to cross oceans and open new routes.

With the advent of World War II, the Allied demand for huge quantities of advanced bombers fueled a rapid increase in production and personnel at Boeing. Soon thousands of workers (including many women who went by the collective nickname "Rosie the Riveter") began cranking out B-1 Flying Fortresses and B-29 Superfortresses. By March 1944 the Seattle plant was turning out 360-some planes a month. The record for one 24-hour period was 16 planes!

In a repeat of the slump that occurred after World War I, the end of World War II meant another economic crash for Boeing. The workforce plummeted from a high of 78,000 to 8,000 in one year. It wasn't until the advent of the jet age in 1949 — with the creation of the speedy B-47 and B-52 bombers — that things turned around for the company. The immensely versatile 707 (introduced in '52), followed by the 727, 737, and jumbo 747 would lead Boeing, healthy and profitable, into the present.

The only dip in the ever-ascending earning curve occurred in 1973 when market projections overestimated increases in air travel. This resulted in a financial crisis for the company, which was forced to lay off a whopping 65,000 employees — two-thirds of its workforce. Obviously, such massive downsizing caused a severe recession in the Seattle area, but the region was forced to consider the wisdom of depending so much on one industry. The upside of the recession was that many of Boeing's talented former employees took their skills into the area's burgeoning electronics and software industries.

Without a visible break in housing and commercial development (or traffic), I-405 continues north along the lake to the city of **Bellevue** (Elevation 148, Population 89,710). Since the end of World War II, Bellevue has redefined the concept of suburban sprawl, exploding from a slowly awakening suburb into the fourth largest city in the state. Incorporated in 1953 with less than 6,000 residents, the population has catapulted to nearly 90,000.

The first trickle of movement to the east side started in 1940 when Bellevue was connected to Seattle by the Interstate 90 floating bridge. The new route cut the commute to downtown by more than half, enticing young, white-collar families to head across the lake in search of quiet neighborhoods with modern homes and big backyards. Slowly

 but steadily the trend continued until the need for a second bridge arose. By the time the Evergreen Point floating bridge (State Highway 520) was completed in 1963, the floodgates had opened wide. The march to the suburbs was underway.

Reflecting decades of rapid growth, modern-day Bellevue is a hodgepodge of development. Some areas are consumer paradise; streets lined with countless shops and contrived strip malls butt up against long rows of car dealer-ships. Looming large in the center of town is Bellevue Square Mall, a large shopping mecca where department stores, restaurants and dozens of specialty and retail outlets fill an enclosed city block. Adjacent to the mall are glass high-rises with reflective windows that resemble massive upright mirrors, surrounded by business parks, hotels, condominiums and apartment buildings.

Entrance to Bellevue's giant mall.

Before the soil was buried beneath concrete, thick forest covered much of what is now the center of Bellevue. After trees were cut and fed to a sawmill that worked the area in the 1890s, farmers claimed the cleared land and strawberries became the crop of choice. Steam-powered ferries carried produce to markets in Seattle, and in time the boats began shuttling people over to Bellevue for day excursions and leisure. By the 1920s, city folk had become enchanted with the pristine area, and many who could afford it bought land along the shoreline and built summer cabins. The site of these early waterfront homes now represent some of the only areas in Bellevue where development has not laid its heavy, mechanized hand. Manicured estates with private beach access sit among thick trees far from the asphalt overkill in high-end neighborhoods such as Medina and Hunts Point.

Follow the flow of vehicles to **Kirkland** (Elevation 500, Population 41,700). The city's roots run back to the 1880s, but most of its growth occurred in the 1980s when the population more than doubled. Business parks and apartment complexes overlooking the lake rose seemingly overnight, as quiet neighborhoods spread to the borders of Bellevue and Redmond. The quaint shops and ritzy restaurants in the center of town have a modern look to them that hints of its recent development. Several small parks provide prime views of the water and docks lined with pleasure vessels.

From its outset, Kirkland had all the trappings of success, including burgeoning industry and financial backing, but timing was not on its side. In 1886, a millionaire named Peter Kirk immigrated from England to start a steel mill, purchasing what he believed to be promising coal and iron mines on the Snoqualmie River. Placing the proverbial cart before the horse, he first focused on selling plots and constructing ornate buildings before the mill had generated even one thin dime. The structures housed personnel Kirk hired to oversee operations, but business was over before it began.

When the economy went belly up in 1893, investors scrambled to cover their own losses and withdrew support for the project. With money running low, the lode was too much to bear; excavating the mines became expensive beyond practicality; and the advancing railroad was stopped in its tracks, ending Kirk's attempt to build a boom town on the lake. In the wake of the panic, the town sported an impressive facade, but the buildings, along with most of the town, were empty. Three of these original structures still stand along Market Street as reminders of that optimistic era.

Puddle jumpers statue in Kirkland.

Snaking northward from Kirkland, you will pass connections with State Highways 522 and 202 near Woodinville. I-405 runs through high population centers at the northern end of Lake Washington and blossoming suburbia east of the highway. Patches of forest can be seen from the freeway, but the typically heavy traffic indicates that the region is not as rural as it appears. The highway ends at a connection with I-5 north of Lynnwood. ∞

S tate **Highway 409** from a junction with State Highway 4 in Cathlamet south via the Columbia River to Puget Island. Route length: three miles.

From Cathlamet, cross a high, arching bridge to Little Island, and continue over a low, short bridge to **Puget Island**, the only

383~

409 populated island on the Columbia River. Five miles long and about one mile wide, the island is crisscrossed by dikes and irrigation ditches that cover more ground than roads do. Grazing sheep, cattle and llamas are a constant on this trapezoid-shaped patch of floating farmland, along with a variety of birds that drift over

The ferry Wahkiakum *running from Puget Island to Westport, Oregon.*

from the wildlife refuges to the north and west. Numerous small fishing boats flying Scandinavian flags are moored just offshore. The highway ends at a dock where the *Wahkiakum*, the only active ferry left on the lower Columbia, makes daily 15-minute runs to Westport, Oregon. ∞

410 **S** **tate Highway 410** from a junction with State Highway 167 at Sumner, east through Bonney Lake to Buckley, northeast to Enumclaw, east to Greenwater, south to Chinook Pass, then east to a junction with U.S. Highway 12. Route length: 109 miles.

Regardless of the questionable association between the WCTU (Women's Christian Temperance Union) and the profits they reaped

The Sumner train clickity-clackin' along.

from the production of hops (they flavor beer), the town of **Sumner** (Elevation 60, Population 7,550) prospered, adding berries, vegetables, rhubarb and flower bulbs to its agricultural base. The town, still heavily involved with farming, was named to honor Senator Charles S. Sumner, a staunch slavery opponent from Boston.

Highway 410 curves east out of town past the Manfred Vierenthaler Winery. A side trip though **Bonney Lake** (Elevation 585, Population 8,500) on the Sumner-Buckley Highway will bring you to Connell's Prairie, the site

of the final engagement of the Puget Sound Indian War. Skirmishes throughout the year of 1855 ended with a bloody battle on March 10 after which hostilities west of the Cascades ceased.

Move eastward to **Buckley** (Elevation 720, Population 3,720), once a prosperous lumbering community, now quietly centered amidst fertile farmlands and plateaus.

Consider a stop at Bill's before calling on the loan officer next door.

Joining Highway 165 for a few miles, the highway passes north into **Enumclaw** (EE-nuhm-klaw, Elevation 750, Population 9,205). Despite its birth name "place of the evil spirits," Enumclaw has grown into a clean and lively community that serves as a gateway to the Chinook and Naches Passes and to the skiing and recreation areas around Mt. Rainier. Much of the town's original prosperity is attributable to the early Danish and Norwegian settlers who brought the practice of cooperatives from their respective homelands. They formed a cooperative creamery, an egg and poultry association, and even a cooperative department store with grocery, hardware, furniture and clothing departments, and a hay, sand and grain warehouse. Unfortunately, like many of the small towns at the foot of the Cascades, Enumclaw is starting to feel the presence of the subdivisions and the subsequent commuters from the Seattle-Tacoma metropolitan corridor to the west. Yet some things change slowly; the Danish Hall on Myrtle and Porter Streets is still a center for social events in the town as it has been since the early days.

From Enumclaw the road shoots east, gently climbing beside the mostly-hidden White River 17 miles to **Federation Forest State Park**. The park is situated at an elevation between the Coast Forest and Mountain Forest zones and shows tree species from both. Over 10 miles of trail explore the park's 600-acres of virgin timber, and a wide variety of flora and fauna. Inside the park, the **Catherine Montgomery Interpretive Center** details the state's seven biotic zones and the subsequent diverse collection of plants and animal life.

The road continues to the one-stop village of Greenwater at the confluence of the White and Greenwater rivers and continues its climb towards the southern Cascade crest, offering occasional but stunning views of Mt. Rainier.

If you are drawn by the beauty of the mountain and decide to change your travel plans, turn south on State Highway 123, which approaches the mountain from its eastern side at the Ohanapecosh Entrance. When the weather permits, incredible views of Mt. Rainier develop as Highway 410 summits at **Chinook Pass** (Elevation 5,430). The pass (and the town, creek and Indian tribe) are named for the warm moist winds that hail from the southwest, known to melt depths of snow in a few hours and cause flooding. Local Indians named the wind because it came from the direction of the Chinook tribe, who lived near the mouth of the Columbia River.

Summit Lake near the White River.

Pullouts on the east side of the pass overlook sharp broken peaks, the deep, pine-covered valley of the **American River** and Bumping Lake. The river that heads here follows the highway a short but powerful distance to a confluence with the Naches River at Sawmill Flat, which then takes its turn to accompany the road.

The highway gradually descends past several campgrounds and tiny resort communities. The heavy cover of fir and larch trees limits visibility but guarantees that every turn of the road is a new visual experience. The larch is the only tree in the western United States that loses its needles in winter.

About thirty miles from the summit, take a right at Camp Roagunada to the **Boulder Cave.** Formed by the erosive action of Devils Creek, the 400-foot-long cavern is open for exploration. Follow the trail that leads from the picnic area to the cave entrance.

Gradually the thick cover of Ponderosa pine begins to thin, exposing the underlying lava flows that define the arid slopes of the east side. An occasional pine juts out of a rock crack like some lost bonsai tree. A notice to the unobservant one: you are in eastern Washington now. A cluster of orchards and a junction with U.S. 12 greet the highway's conclusion in the Upper Naches Valley. ⌘

State Highway 411 from Kelso north to a junction with Interstate 5 in Castle Rock. Route length: 11 miles.
From West Kelso, this rolling highway, though not spectacular, is a relaxing alternative to busy I-5 across the Cowlitz River. Between Kelso and Castle Rock dredged piles of ash that filled the river from the Mt. St. Helens eruption are visible. Though ostensibly ending in Castle Rock, a road continues north as the West Side Highway to Vader (State Highway 506), and then as the Winlock-Vader Road to Winlock (State Highway 505), all the while a short distance from the Cowlitz River. For quiet, scenic driving, it's a route worth taking. ⌘

State Highway 432 from a junction with State Highway 4 east through Longview to a junction with Interstate 5. Route length: nine miles.
When the plans for the city of Longview were laid out in 1922, the industrial district was segregated from residential and commercial areas. A good idea in theory, but it makes for odd juxtapositions. The quick transition from bucolic backwoods to industrial overkill along Highway 432 is a case in point. The first two miles pass swampy sloughs before winding around the base of **Mt. Solo**, a healthy chunk of nature overlooking the city and the Columbia River. Next door to the natural wooded park are pulp and paper mills, warehouses, factories and immense electrical substations surrounded by barbed wire fences and warning signs; forklifts and 18-wheelers race along the riverfront in an attempt to keep up with the progress. Running south of downtown, the highway is the dividing line between neighborhoods and the bustling port system, moving east across the Cowlitz River to a meeting with I-5 south of Kelso. ⌘

State Highway 433 from the Washington-Oregon border and the Columbia River north to Longview. Route length: two miles.
From Oregon take the towering **Lewis and Clark Bridge** across the Columbia River where you get a bird's-eye view of the bustling **Port of Longview** below. The port is the third largest in the state (behind Seattle and Tacoma) and characterized by a flurry of activity and transition, as a parade of freighters carve a collective wake

433
WASHINGTON

66 miles to the ocean and access to the Pacific Rim. The waterlines of ships and barges rise and fall as cranes transfer cargo from dock to boat and vice versa. The port's transportation hub is aided by major railroad lines from both the U.S. and Canada and Interstates 5 and 84 just minutes away. For a closer look at the port, tours are avail-

Logs in repose in Longview's lumber yards.

able with a one-day advance notice (10 Port Way). From the port, the road jumps into downtown Longview. ⊘

500
WASHINGTON

State Highway 500 from a junction with State Highway 14 in Camas as Everett Road, north then west through Orchards to a junction with Interstate 5. Route length: 19 miles.

Winding through hill and dale this short route is fed by many small farm roads before reaching Orchards, a northern suburb of Vancouver. The road joins I-5 a few miles west. While not a particularly spectacular drive, it is an easy paced way to avoid Vancouver traffic and get a feel for the countryside that the first settlers in Washington encountered as they expanded out from Fort Vancouver. ⊘

501
WASHINGTON

State Highway 501 is broken into two segments. The first, northwest from Vancouver to Vancouver Lake. Route length: 12 miles. The second, from a junction with Interstate 5 west to Ridgefield. Route length: three miles.

The southern stretch of Highway 501 hooks out of downtown Vancouver around Vancouver Lake and dead ends on the Columbia River flood plain at the Shillapoo-Vancouver State Wildlife Refuge.

Drive north 13 miles on I-5 to the northern Highway 501 (Exit 14) and continue three miles to **Ridgefield** (Elevation 35, Population 1,445). Fate or predestination may have led Judge Columbia Lancaster to this place. Born in

Judge Columbia Lancaster's House.

Connecticut in 1803 and named Thomas, he was renamed "Columbia" after Lewis and Clark returned from their exploration with tales of the "Great River" to the west. Forty-four years after the explorers passed through this area Judge Lancaster (Washington Territory's first delegate to congress) built a home in Ridgefield.

While here look for the **Arndt Prune Dryer** two miles west of town. The dryer is the only remaining example of the nearly 200 of its type that once existed in Clark County, whose farmers shipped prunes worldwide until the 1930s. Also west of town is the **Ridgefield National Wildlife Refuge**, home to an old basalt quarry and over 250,000 wintering waterfowl each year. ⌘

S tate Highway 502 from a junction with Interstate 5 east to a junction with State Highway 503. Route length: eight miles. Highway 502 glances off I-5 at 179th Street a couple of miles north of the I-5/205 interchange. It basically follows section lines through farmlands into Battleground. ⌘

S tate Highway 503 from a junction with State Highway 500 northeast via Battle Ground to the Mt. St. Helens National Monument, then southwest to a junction with Interstate 5. Route length: 63 miles.

Highway 503 is not the most direct route north up the I-5 corridor, but with some back-tracking, this lightly-used road is a pleasant side trip out of mainstream traffic. From the northern suburbs of Vancouver,

Single-lane bridge. First come, first served.

Highway 503 branches east then north through a rapidly urbanizing rural area to **Battle Ground** (Elevation 284, Population 4,244). The town's ominous namesake was drawn from an incident in the Indian wars of 1855 when a Klickitat Chief was mistakenly shot and killed nearby.

The area was first settled by Hudson's Bay employees and then by a mix of Irish, Italian, Swedish and Finnish immigrants who were lured by the promise of rich and fertile farmland, a condition most had to create after their arrival, though by the 1930s it was described as a "brisk little trading center, with one of the largest cheese factories in the state."

By driving north on Highway 503, and then east on Worthington Road you will reach **Yacolt** (YA-kawlt, Elevation 700, Population 715); an excursion train from Battle Ground also spans the gap during the summer. Yacolt was the site of a tragic forest fire in 1902 that killed 38 people and burned a quarter of a million acres of timber.

Away from the madding crowd.

Continuing northeast, the highway wraps around the shores of Yale Lake and Swift Creek Reservoir (both dam-created bodies of water on the Lewis River) and runs into forest roads south of the Mt. St. Helens National Volcanic Monument.

From its eastern terminus near Swift Dam, the highway returns to Yale Lake and then doglegs west along the north shore of 12-mile-long Lake Merwin (also a dammed portion of the Lewis River) before reaching I-5 at Woodland. ଔ

State Highway 504 from a junction with Interstate 5 in Castle Rock east to Mt. St. Helens. Route length: 45 miles.

The road to Mt. St. Helens is remarkably diverse. The drive starts through a canopied path of fir, hemlock and Western cedar,

then, after crossing the Toutle River, mud flats and lava beds gradually appear like a displaced lunar landscape. Stretches of the gray, ash-laden wasteland that have occupied the area since the 1980 eruption are striking, but slowly disappearing; the regenerative process continues to return the land to its natural state.

Lava flats on the Toutle River.

Drive four miles east to the **Mt. St. Helens National Volcanic Interpretive Center**, which presents a thorough study on the inner-workings of a volcanic eruption. Telescopes set up outside the building are aimed at the distant rim of the volcano. Inside, exhibits trace the recorded history of St. Helens, ranging from Indian accounts to its recent geological activity. An intricate 20-foot model of the volcano presents a crater-lip view of the forces at work during an eruption. Take the flight of stairs deep into the interior to get the full geological effect and a simulated peek into the center of the earth.

The interpretive center rests on the western end of the shallow, four-pronged **Silver Lake**. Six miles long and one and a half miles wide, the lake has three islands and a maximum depth of just 15 feet. Water lilies dot the surface, their white and yellow blossoms floating among clusters of cool green pads. Grasses and reeds grow up from the bottom, creating a marshland around the perimeter and hiding spots for bass and crappies.

Once past Silver Lake, the road bends and curves with the muddy North Fork of the Toutle River. From here the scenery begins its trans-formation as if following a trail of destruction. Crossing the river, notice the debris dams where fallen trees have rerouted the water and built up the banks with a thick ooze. Patches of green on hillsides, contrasted with the brown of the mud flats around the river, emphasize the before-and-after theme at work here. As the mountain approaches, the vegetation grows noticeably thinner, and saplings rise from the ashes where full-size trees once stood.

Highway 504 ends at the **Coldwater Ridge Visitor Center**, six miles north of the crater. Coldwater Lake — the "newest lake in the state" — was created at the time of the eruption when mud and debris sealed off a creek, stranding the water in a deep depression caused by the explosion. The view is unforgettable; the lava dome and tops of several smaller glaciers can be seen to the south, along with a pumice plain that spreads across the side of the mountain.

Prior to May 18, 1980, **Mt. St. Helens'** (Elevation 8,364) smooth, rounded summit was often referred to by locals as "the ice-cream cone in the sky" for its near perfect slopes and symmetry. Since its creation, the mountain had experienced no catastrophe significant enough to alter its appearance, and a lack of erosion made it look the same from almost any angle. A mere toddler in geological terms at about 2,500 years old, its youth also made it the most active volcano in the state. Captain George Vancouver is credited with naming the mountain in 1792 in honor of the British ambassador to Spain. The Indian name, *Low-We-Not-Thlat*, though certainly more difficult to pronounce, is also a more accurate description of the setting. It means "throwing up smoke" or "the smoking mountain." Both the Klickitat and Cowlitz tribes called it the "mountain of fire."

As a precursor of things to come, Dr. Meredith Gairdner of Fort Vancouver recorded the first eyewitness account of a Mt. St. Helens' eruption in 1836. Just six years later, when only a few pioneers inhab-ited the area, the mountain erupted on a greater scale, shooting clouds of black smoke and ashes into the air. Pumice was reported falling from the sky as far away as The Dalles, over 60 miles southeast. Less turbulent belches of smoke and light debris were common, and minor activity was steady until 1857. Pressure then quietly built for the next 123 years.

During March and April of 1980, a string of small earthquakes below the volcano were registered, rattling windows and tilting wall-hangings in homes in the immediate vicinity. Steam explosions quickly followed and cracks and bulges began to show on the north face. Dangerous signs to be sure. Few citizens outside the epicenter seemed to notice, but geologists intently monitored the signs and attempted to predict the unpredictable, poised for what could be the Big One.

At 8:23 a.m. on May 18, accompanied by 20 seconds worth of a 5.1 magnitude earthquake, the entire north flank of the mountain slipped away in a colossal landslide, the largest in recorded history. Moving down the slope at 200 miles per hour, it devoured everything

in its path before pounding into the North Fork of the Toutle River. Centuries of forest growth were uprooted in an instant. Mt. St. Helens blew away almost a cubic mile of its summit, lowering in elevation from 9,677 feet to 8,364 feet and creating a 2,100-foot-deep crater. Within 10 minutes, pumice and ash were vaulted over 13

Mt. St. Helens - before....

miles straight up, and would continue to spew at this rate for nine hours. Easterly winds carried 520 million tons of ash across the country, bringing complete darkness in the middle of the day to much of eastern Washington. People as far away as Spokane were advised to stay in their homes, while police donned gas masks to rescue blinded motorists.

Statistics are often dry and misleading, but in this case they prove not only to be astounding, but necessary to comprehend the magnitude of nature's power: 59 people lost their lives; four million board feet of timber were blown down by the lateral blast, enough lumber to build 77,100 three-bedroom homes (half of the timber was later salvaged); 0.3 cubic miles of uncompacted ash, enough to bury a football field to a depth of 150 miles, swept across the U.S. in three days; the steam explosion released energy equivalent to 21,000 atomic bombs; mudflows destroyed 27 bridges, 185 miles of road, and over

200 homes; temperatures at the sinking summit reached 750 degrees centigrade; and the Toutle River was buried by an average of 150 feet of steaming mud and debris, backing up tributaries and stranding 31 ships on the Columbia River. Three years later ash still covered the ground.

For all the fury, there was a mysterious lack of sound in the immediate vicinity of the mountain during the eruption. This phenomena is attributed to the tremendous heat and volume of material that smothered the noise and carried it upward with the ash cloud. The only real sound close to the base was the snapping and crunching of falling trees. An eyewitness of the 1980 explosion, ham operator James L. Lanterman, describes the moment:

...and after.

> ... we felt no explosion, sound or vibration. Our neighbors drove up, honked and yelled, 'Helen has blown her top.' Eventually, black clouds were all across the sky. It started raining pea to grape-size mud balls... We were in total darkness for the next two hours. Light wouldn't penetrate the falling ash the way it penetrates the fog or smoke... Other ham operators called wanting to know what was going on... I reported to stations all across the U.S., Alaska and Canada. This information was picked up and relayed to newspaper, television and radio stations... I didn't know it at the time, but this was probably the first news out of this area.

Gordon E. Glockner of the U.S. Forest Service summed up the aftermath with his cleverly apt forecast: "Mostly ashy with partial afternoon breathing."

Of all those who lost their lives to the eruption, perhaps the most well-known is **Harry R. Truman**, now buried beneath a wall of ash, mud and stone. Truman, 84, inherited legendary status when a landslide from the exploding Mt. St. Helens swallowed his home, a short five miles from the summit and now marked by a white wooden cross. The wise but stubborn man received national attention when he refused to evacuate his home of over 50 years, despite repeated warnings and personal attempts by scientists to warn him of the possible danger. Dismissing the threat, he often joked of having a secret cavern stocked with bourbon where he could retreat and wait out an eruption. Perhaps he is there now.

Spirit Lake is four miles northeast of the Mt. St. Helens summit and near the home of the late Harry Truman. The lake was created, and nearly destroyed by, volcanic activity. In the 1840s, a smaller eruption buried a section of forest and plugged a stream with timber, thus creating the lake. The 1,300-foot-deep lake was popular among fishermen and hikers, but was drastically altered when the eruption forced a 200-foot wall of water over the northern ridge. White pumice and forest debris then filled the bottom, causing the water to spread out as the depth was reduced.

The native history of Spirit Lake reads like a ghost story. Indians believed that unexplainable, often eerie, sounds of nature were the haunting voices of departed spirits. One myth speaks of an Indian brave who, while hunting, trailed a giant bull elk a great distance to the shore of the lake, only to discover he had been following an illusion. Before he could escape, a phantom led him into the water where he drowned. Legend claims that the Indian's ghost can be seen tracking the elusive elk over the surface of the lake on a certain night each year.

Spirit Lake is also the home of supernatural beings called *Siatcos*, the spirits of departed Indian chiefs. Enraged with the Indians for permitting the white man to encroach upon their land, the Siatcos forbade the people from hunting, fishing or gathering berries around Spirit Lake or Mt. St. Helens. Fearful warnings and dire tales of maidens and warriors being seized and dragged to the depths of the lake discouraged Indians from collecting the bounty of the mountain.

Life continues around Mt. St. Helens since nature's housecleaning. Erosion broke down most deposits of overlying ash

A storeback in Toledo - look closely.

~394

in the first winter after the May explosion, stimulating the regeneration process and nourishing the soil. The Forest Service has planted trees on over 10,000 acres to help jump-start reforestation. Starting from scratch, small buds and seedlings sprout in the midst of what appear from afar to be lifeless-looking fields. As vegetation returns, so does an array of wildlife, as elk, deer, bears, mountain lions and other species begin reclaiming their homes among the volcanic desert. ☙

S tate Highway 505 from a junction with State Highway 504 northwest via Toledo to Winlock. Route length: 15 miles.
This is a scenic and uncrowded alternative for sightseers returning from Mt. St. Helens and Highway 504. The road passes through a thick tunnel of evergreen trees and emerges in the flats of Layton Prairie, textured by its old square barns and neatly-rowed tree farms.

The road jumps briefly back into forest and holy! **Toledo** (Elevation 142, Population 625), crosses the important Cowlitz River. Two miles downstream at Cowlitz Landing, early settlers beached their canoes, freshened up, and continued northward by whatever mode of transportation they could find, be it steed, stage or foot. The town takes its name from the side-wheel steamer *Toledo*, which provided transportation for passengers and farmers' goods to distant cities.

Toledo remains a peaceful backwater, a mood accentuated by the placid Cowlitz River. Some residents work on outlying corn farms and many commute to mill jobs in Chehalis, Longview or Portland.

From Toledo you may either hook up with Interstate 5 or venture three miles further to the highway's end in **Winlock** (Elevation 308, Population 1,090). The abnormally large, man-made egg on the

A Winlock church.

corner of Fir and Kerron is not your typical "largest ball of twine" attraction; it reveals the importance of Winlock's egg- and poultry-producing industry. Energy is now primarily directed toward fryer production.

When General Winlock Miller stumbled across a handful of yokels breaking ground for a new settlement, and discovered that they had not yet chosen its name, he promised the burgeoning community a school bell if they would use Winlock. Apparently the general's end of

505 the bargain slipped his mind before he died and the bell was never sent. Upon learning of her son's absentmindedness via a letter, Mrs. Miller provided the school bell they had been promised. ∞

506 **S**tate Highway 506 from a junction with Interstate 5 west via Vader to Ryderwood. Route length: 12 miles.

Five miles west of I-5, on the banks of Olequa Creek, you will encounter **Vader** (VAY-der, Elevation 139, Population 425) and have a hard time believing that it once boasted a population of over 5,000. (This figure does not include early settler Herr Vader, who upon hearing that state legislature had named the town for him, moved to Florida in an outrage.) The intersection of four railroads, a millworks, brick and clayworks, and of course logging, caused the town to boom in the late 1800s. These industries now mostly serve as ghosts to the quiet community that exists today.

The Ryderwood Post Office - the good ol' days are now.

Continue for another seven miles to the end of the highway and **Ryderwood**. Now a retirement community, it was built as a model company logging town by the Long-Bell Lumber Company to provide a stable living situation for its workers and to preempt the labor strife that was prevalent in the industry at that time. Near here on acreage now reforested, the company harvested trees that were considered to be the largest in the world. ∞

507 **S**tate Highway 507 from a junction with Interstate 5 in Centralia northeast via Bucoda, Tenino, Rainier, Yelm and Roy to a junction with State Highway 7. Route length: 37 miles.

From downtown Centralia northward, Highway 507 pauses briefly at Schaefer County Park before passing **Bucoda** (Elevation 254, Population 545), set on the banks of the Skookumchuck River. In contrast to the town's present peaceful disposition, Bucoda was once the site of the state's first territorial prison from 1874 until 1887. Convicts spent their hard-time working in the surrounding mines, logging camps and farms until the institution was moved to Walla Walla.

Continue north across Frost Prairie to **Tenino** (ti-NEYE-noh, Elevation 286, Population 1,330), which began as a construction camp for railroad workers in the early 1870s. The probable origin of the name derives from an Indian word meaning "fork or crossing," but local folklore cites the arrival of the Northern Pacific Engine 1090 (ten-nine-o) as the source of inspiration. When the depot was moved from the center of town to a rail junction one half mile away in 1890, a hotel followed on rollers to the new location, along with several businesses and most of the population. Fearing Tenino's demise, the founding fathers drew residents back by enticing them with free land; thus persuaded, the hotel and other structures rolled back to their original sites.

Tenino's solid store fronts.

Tenino received national attention in 1932 when wooden money was issued to prevent the local bank from going under. This clever move not only saved the bank, but turned a profit as well when $11,000 worth of "lumber jacks" were snapped up by collectors nationwide.

Further north you find the small communities of **Rainier** (Elevation 453, Population 1,290) whose fortunes rose and fell with the lumber industry and **Yelm** (Elevation 310, Population 1,510), located on a prairie of the same name. Yelm derives from *chelm*, an Indian word meaning "heat rays rising from the sun" that was used to indicate fertility.

From Yelm cross the Nisqually River near the former milltown of McKenna and continue north to the farms and pastures of **Roy** (Elevation 315, Population 345). At one time a bustling trading center, the town has since settled into the quiet life.

North of Roy, Highway 507 passes through the eastern boundaries of the **Fort Lewis Military Reservation**. The fort began as a gift from the citizens of Pierce County to the U.S. army, a 70,000-acre parcel of land purchased for $2 million. This gift of land from civilians to the government for the purpose of building a military installation was the first of its kind.

In 1917, construction on the fort began. Within 90 days, 10,000 men had completed 1,750 buildings, as well as 422 other structures, all fully plumbed and wired, prompting the job foreman, Colonel D. L. Stone, to boast, "We completed those barracks at a rate of one every forty minutes . . . twelve each eight-hour day." The job used 73,000 board feet of lumber.

At the end of World War I, money set aside for the upkeep of Fort Lewis decreased significantly and the fort fell into deep neglect. Along with the decline in maintenance, the fort also lost a major portion of

507
WASHINGTON

its military populous, prompting one local newspaper to warn, "Give us a payroll or give the land back to the county."

In 1926, a 10-year building plan was passed in Congress. The plan was designed to refurbish several Army bases across the country, Fort Lewis being one of them. One year later, the reconstruction was finished and Fort Lewis was up and running again with an increased workload and population.

As World War II grew increasingly near, the population at Fort Lewis skyrocketed. Between the years of 1939 and 1941, the population went from 5,000 to 37,000. To house the influx of new troops, a new 2,000-acre North Fort Lewis complex was built.

In 1943, the fort underwent another size increase. Over 18,000 acres south of the Nisqually River was converted into a training installation, the Rainier Training Area. The new area allowed for the training of large numbers of troops, a luxury the fort previously did not have. The 2nd Infantry Division was seasoned at Rainier and was the first American division to leave the country for the war in Korea.

During the Vietnam conflict, Fort Lewis trained over 300,000 men and processed over 2.5 million soldiers going to and from the Pacific. The fort has also trained National Guard units from all over the country and is home to the highly-decorated I-Corps.

For more detail on the military history of the Pacific Northwest visit the Fort Lewis Military Museum (I-5, Exit 120). Exhibits range from Lewis and Clark's early adventures through both world wars. Military vehicles and armaments are also featured.

Highway 507 continues through the reservation to a conclusion with Highway 7 just south of Spanaway. ෆ

508
WASHINGTON

State **Highway 508** from a junction with Interstate 5 east through Onalaska to a junction with State Highway 7 in Morton. Route length: 33 miles.

Jutting east from I-5, Highway 508 skirts the South Fork of the Newaukum River and passes through what's left of **Onalaska**, a former milltown that once held a population of 1,200 and cut up to 150,000 board feet of timber per day. Created by the Carlisle Lumber Company of Wisconsin in 1914, the town became the scene of bitter labor disputes in 1935 which led to clashes between striking union workers and the Washington State Patrol. The strike dragged on until 1938 when the union men got their jobs back, but the mill closed four years later. Today, Onalaska claims little more than a 225-foot smokestack to mark its past lumbering glory.

Rolling east, the highway winds along logged-off hillsides and over Bremer Mountain before meeting the Tilton River and terminating at a junction with U.S. 12 and the beginning of northbound Highway 7 at Morton. ෆ

S tate **Highway 509** from a junction with Interstate 705 in Tacoma north via Brown's Point, Dash Point, Des Moines and Burien to a junction with State Highway 99. (Overlaps Highway 99.) Route length: 30 miles.

From I-705 in Tacoma, Highway 509 (11th Street) passes through Tacoma's industrial port, where ships bound for the Pacific Rim dock at freight forwarding yards and pulp and paper mills to load up with grain, wood products and other northwest commodities. The port is North America's sixth largest container port.

Take a leisurely walk along Dash Point...

Turn left on Marine View Drive and climb to **Brown's Point**, a former gathering spot for Salish Indian tribes. At the edge of the cliff-top community, a lighthouse erected in the 1930s guards the east entrance to Commencement Bay.

The scenic coastline route — a treat for passengers but frustrating for the driver who can't afford to take his eyes from the road — continues a short distance to **Dash Point State Park**. The park's campgrounds are located on the east side of the highway. To reach the saltwater swimming area turn left (west) and either drive down a steep hill to a parking area below, or park immediately and hike through a dense forest peppered with trails. Below are picnic facilities and a wide sand beach. An additional six miles of hiking trails are found south of the campgrounds.

From Dash Point, the road doglegs right and is absorbed by Highway 99, which continues north four miles to State Highway 516. To rejoin Highway 509, you must take Highway 516 to **Des Moines** (duh-

...or on Des Moines Pier.

MOIN, Elevation 30, Population 19,460), out of the way but a littoral diversion from the stoplight muck of Highway 99.

In exchange for the financial support necessary to start a town, F.A. Blasher promised his friends back in Des Moines, Iowa to bring his hometown's name with him. Thus began Des Moines, but little more than a sawmill existed here until the turn of the century when summer homes with views of the Puget Sound began to line the shores.

399~

509 Present-day Des Moines continues to focus on the Sound. An extended pier, crowded with fishermen, juts out from the water's edge. Next door, a marina runs the length of beachfront.

Highway 509 continues past Seattle-Tacoma International Airport and busy **Burien** (Elevation NA, Population 27,800), incorporated in 1993, joining Highway 99 just south of the Duwamish Waterway. ଓ

510 State Highway 510 from a junction with Interstate 5 southeast to a junction with State Highway 507 in Yelm. Route length: 13 miles.

Highway 510 begins just south of Lacey, and within a short distance the headaches of the interstate are replaced by a canopy of evergreen. The route works its way through the **Nisqually Indian Reservation**, established by the Medicine Creek Treaty of 1854. Originally granted 1,280 acres, the Nisquallies were given an additional 3,420 acres at the conclusion of the Indian Wars of 1855-56. Then, in 1917, Pierce County condemned the land north of the Nisqually River and incorporated the property into the Fort Lewis Military Reservation. Transactions such as these most likely gave birth to the term "Indian-givers," defined in Websters as "one who gives something to another and then takes it back." At present, the Nisqually Reservation totals 2,500 acres.

The road passes some privately-owned farms and rolls into Yelm, the "Pride of the Prairie," and a junction with Highway 507. ଓ

512 State Highway 512 from a junction with Interstate 5 east to a junction with State Highway 167 in Puyallup. Route length: 12 miles.

Highway 512 is the route to Puyallup from south Tacoma. Immediately after crossing the Puyallup River, the road joins Highway 167.ଓ

513 State Highway 513 from a junction with Interstate 405 northeast to Sandpoint then northwest to a junction with Interstate 5. Route length: nine miles.

Highway 513 is one possible route to the University of Washington campus but it is more commonly used to reach the school's athletic facilities, including Husky Stadium and Hec Edmundson Pavilion.

Although this route is officially listed as State Highway 513, it is unlikely you will see any signs indicating such. After leaving the busy interstate, Montlake Boulevard (Highway 513) crosses the **Montlake Cut**. Completed in 1917, the channel links the waters of Lake Washington, Lake Union and the Puget Sound. Today, commercial and recreational boaters travel the busy water highway to points east and west.

· MONTLAKE · BRIDGE ·

SEATTLE   **ERECTED 1925**   **WASHINGTON**

West Elevation

Scale: 1/16" = 1'-0", 1:192

On the first Saturday of every May, amateur crew teams from around the world compete for the **Windemere Cup**, a race through the Cut that marks Opening Day of boating season. Thousands of supporters line the banks to root on the perennially-strong U.W. team.

You will cross the channel on the 1925 **Montlake Bridge**. Guarded by two Gothic columns, the drawbridge frequently stops traffic to allow large vessels to pass. In Seattle, where drawbridges are as common as grey skies, commuters appear unphased by the delay; using the time to finish dressing for work or daydream of being at the helm instead of stuck behind the wheel.

Montlake Drawbridge is guarded by Gothic columns.

The road continues past the football and basketball facilities, merges right onto 45th Street, and passes Graves baseball field, a golf driving range, and Children's Hospital and Medical Center before joining Sand Point Way.

Follow Sand Point to Naval Station Puget Sound, an abandoned U.S. Navy base now partially occupied by **Magnuson Park**. Spread out along the western shores of Lake Washington across the water from Kirkland, the park is a popular swimming area and boat launch point. The 14-mile-long **Burke-Gilman Trail** also runs through the park. The bike and pedestrian path stretches from Fremont northeast to Kenmore and is heavily used by Seattle recreationists. The trail was named for Judge Thomas Burke and Daniel Gilman, who in 1885 provided the impetus and cash to start the Seattle, Lake Shore and Eastern Railroad, a major regional line serving Puget Sound logging areas. The trail now follows the old right-of-way.

Sand Point Way visits the shoreline briefly before turning northwest to join I-5. ∞

State **Highway 515** from a junction with State Highway 516 north to Renton. Route length: eight miles.
A south King County suburban highway that runs parallel to State Highway 167. ∝

 State **Highway 516** from Des Moines east via Kent to a junction with State Highway 169 in Four Corners. Route length: 17 miles.
Rising from the harbor in Des Moines (State Highway 509), Highway 516 pushes through Kent proper (State Highway 167) and then its suburbs before merging with Highway 169. ∝

 State **Highway 518** from a junction with State Highway 509 east to a junction with Interstate 5 in Tukwila. Route length: three miles.
Beware of frantic drivers on Highway 518, the exit highway to **Seattle-Tacoma International Airport**, known locally as SeaTac (See-Tack). Proposed by the Seattle Port Commission in 1942, the airport was christened in 1944 when a United Airlines mainliner DC-3 made the first official landing. SeaTac is the closest West Coast gateway to both Asia and Europe, a nine hour flight to Tokyo and London. ∝

 State **Highway 519** from a junction with Interstates 90 and 5 in Seattle, west then north to the Washington State Ferry Terminal. Route length: two miles.
Highway 519 (Royal Brougham Way) starts south of the Kingdome, and leads to a junction with Alaskan Way. From there,

follow the waterfront past Pier 48 and Alaska Square Park to the ferry terminals on Piers 50 (Bremerton and Vashon Island) and 52 (Bainbridge Island and Bremerton). Due to sporting events at the Kingdome and commuters or tourists en route to Puget Sound destinations, this is one of the busiest routes in downtown Seattle (I-5). ∝

The Kingdome is one-upped by the Olympic Mountains.

S tate Highway 520 from a junction with Interstate 5 east across Lake Washington via Bellevue to Redmond. Route length: 13 miles.

Branching east from I-5, the highway passes over a small bay overlooking the backside of Husky Stadium and the Seattle Yacht Club. Behind the stadium, the **Waterfront Activities Center** rents canoes and rowboats for exploring the marshland and wildlife area beneath the highway. As these small crafts negotiate the pilings below, you will glide over Lake Washington on the **Governor Albert D. Rosellini-Evergreen Point Floating Bridge**, named in honor of the governor who served from 1957 to 1965. Supported by concrete pontoons and stretching 1.4 miles, it's the longest floating bridge in the world, eclipsing the Interstate 90 bridge built to Mercer Island 23 years earlier.

The first procession of cars crossed the lake on August 28, 1963. As the populations of Bellevue and Kirkland have grown, so has usage of the highway. The bridge is now synonymous with traffic; morning commuters pour from the east side to work in downtown Seattle and return in the evening. Rush hour looks like a

At 1.4 miles this is the longest floating bridge in the world.

buoyant parking lot, but at least the congestion comes with a waterfront view. Freer forms of transport such as sailboats, sculls and water-skiing can be seen from the bridge, arousing feelings of mild envy in motorists stuck in the bumper-to-bumper grind. Mt. Rainier rises on the southern horizon, adding to the already spectacular view.

Just under 20 miles long, **Lake Washington** is the state's second-largest natural lake behind Lake Chelan. The Duwamish Indians called it *It-kow-chug*, appropriately translated as "large body of fresh water." With the exception of some industry at the southern end near Renton, the lakeshore is surrounded by primarily affluent neighborhoods with large homes and lake access.

Before the advent of floating bridges, a fleet of steamers provided a shuttle service to dozens of communities edging the lake. Launched in 1906 as the Lake Washington Steamboat Company, 14 vessels ran passengers, supplies and produce several times a day. Business on the lake increased in 1916 when canals were dug connecting Lake Washington, Lake Union and Puget Sound. The ambitious project, which lowered the water level over nine feet, allowed greater commercial access for farmers and loggers plying their wares along

403~

communities on the Sound, and more mobility for fishermen. Pleasure boats now represent much of the traffic through the channel.

Summer brings a daily flotilla of recreational vessels; each August the week-long **Seafair Festival** culminates with the much-anticipated hydroplane races on the south end of the lake. Adding to the fanfare, the Navy's famed Blue Angels perform their aerial acrobatics high above the water, thrilling thousands of onlookers crowding the shoreline and floating logbooms.

Since Seattle receives its fair share of grey skies throughout the year, summer sunshine is a cause for jubilation, as evidenced by the throngs of pale bodies that hit the beaches at the first sign of cloud break, eager to soak up some rays. But for a spell in the mid- to late 1950s, water sports seemed destined for a permanent washout due to pollution. The rapid growth and development along on the shoreline sent so much raw sewage into the water that most swimming areas were declared closed and fishing was considered risky. To combat the problem, a new regulatory commission was formed in 1959 comprised of members from communities bordering Lake Washington. Part of the cleanup plan included the construction of new sewer lines that diverted waste away from the lake and towards modern treatment plants. The results were remarkably effective. Before long, the only things floating on the surface were beach balls and air mattresses.

Moving past a pair of exits leading to the city of Bellevue and a connection with Interstate 405, Highway 520 reaches into wooded edges and descends to its conclusion in **Redmond** (Elevation 30, Population 40,095). Originally settled in 1871, the town was a model of quiet rural living for over a century, with dairy, poultry and fruit farms providing most residents a livelihood. The biggest boost in technology came in 1888 when the Seattle, Lake Shore and Eastern Railroad connected the town with the more populated areas around Lake Washington.

Much of this rustic feel faded in a flash of construction when the population more than doubled in the 1970s. Collecting the overflow from Seattle's rapid growth, Redmond went from an outskirts community to a center for suburban growth. Large computer and bio-technology companies helped to lure new residents by providing employment and eliminating a long commute to Seattle. To accommodate the flow, housing developments sprang up as fast as land developers could lay them out.

A haven for bicycling enthusiasts, Redmond has a well-organized path system that runs throughout the city, and a velodrome located in **Marymoor Park** (Lake Sammamish Parkway). The racetrack, one of just a handful in the country, was the site of the 1990 Goodwill Games cycling events. Marymoor Park offers access to the **Sammamish**

River Trail, a paved walking and biking path that stretches 14 miles north to Bothell. The park also contains an exhibit on local history at the Marymoor Museum. ∞

S tate Highway 522 from a junction with Interstate 5 northeast via Bothell, Woodinville and Maltby to a junction with U.S. Highway 2. Route length: 25 miles.

Highway 522 proceeds first as Lake City Way and then Bothell Way, rounding the northernmost tip of Lake Washington and entering **Bothell** (BAH-thuhl, Elevation 317, Population 24,530), 23 miles north of Seattle. Founded by David C. Bothell and his family in 1886, Bothell's proximity to the lake and the Sammamish River determined its early role as a shingle mill and logging camp. Until 1916, when canals linked Lake Washington to the Puget Sound and made commerce between the lake and the river impossible, steamboats loaded with timber chugged downriver and across the lake to markets in Seattle.

From Bothell the highway skirts Woodinville (State Highway 202), shoots northeast via Maltby, once an important lumber center, and crosses a wide section of the **Snohomish River**

This is the Snohomish, not the Snoqualmie or the Skykomish.

(snoh-HOH-mish). The Snohomish originates a stone's throw east of the overpass at the confluence of the Snoqualmie and Skykomish rivers, and flows 24 miles west to Everett's Port Gardner Bay.

The highway passes the Washington State Reformatory and terminates one mile west of Monroe at a junction with U.S. 2. ∞

S tate Highway 523 from a junction with State Highway 99 east to a junction with State Highway 522. Route length: three miles.

Highway 523 (NE 145th Street) ventures across teeming Interstate 5 via an overpass and ambles through the suburban community of Kenwood to Highway 522 (Lake City Way, Bothell Way). ∞

S tate Highway 524 from Edmonds east through Lynnwood, Thrashers Corner and Turner Corner to a junction with State Highway 522 in Maltby. Route length: 16 miles.

Highway 524 starts as a hilly, south Snohomish County suburban road (196th Street) that accesses Lynnwood and the massive retail area around Alderwood Mall. East of Interstate 5, the road adopts a more rural characteristic, passes the supermarket and filling station intersections of Thrashers Corner and Turner Corner, and slides into Maltby as Maltby Road. ⌘

State Highway 525 from a junction with Interstate 5 in Lynnwood northwest to Mukilteo and across Possession Sound via ferry to Clinton, east to Freeland then north through Greenbank to a junction with State Highway 20 in Keystone. Route length: 31 miles.

The highway starts as an interurban route in Lynnwood and proceeds to **Mukilteo** (MUHK-il-TEE-oh, Elevation 0 to 580, Population 14,035), a coastal suburb overlooking Possession Sound. Territorial Governor Isaac Stevens signed a treaty with the leaders of 22 area Indian tribes here in 1855, relieving the natives of all their lands from Point Pully north to the Canadian border and ceding them to the whites. Confused by the language used in the treaty, the chiefs were shocked when they realized the amount of land they had lost. Mukilteo's beachfront contains a fine lighthouse and a small but popular state park.

There seem to be more people at the ferry terminal than in all of Mukilteo when lines swell with those waiting for the 20-minute ride to **Clinton** on Whidbey Island. From Clinton, little more than a ferry dock, a small marina and a handful of houses, drive a few miles on Highway 525 and turn onto a loop road that takes you through **Langley** (Elevation 20, Population 935). Built above a smooth stretch of beach overlooking Saratoga Passage, the small community has long been a major trading center for the islands' south-enders, and is enhanced by a tidy downtown area with gift shops and galleries.

Heading north up the southern half of Whidbey Island, Highway 525 passes through **Freeland**, named for the Free Land Association, a socialist group that folded in the early 1900s. The town is a quiet residential area on a low shore at the end of Holmes Harbor. Further north a winery, gift shop and loganberry farm mark **Greenbank** and the end of Highway 525. ⌘

State Highway 526 from a junction with Interstate 5 in Everett west to a junction with State Highway 525. Route length: five miles.

This short highway accesses Boeing's Everett plant (tours are available). Inside the world's largest manufacturing building a fleet of commercial airplanes rest in various stages of assemblance.

The road also passes Paine Field, the largest airport in Snohomish County. In addition to small private planes, the occasional jumbo jet, recently purchased from Boeing, will ascend from the tarmac (without passengers, of course). The road junctions with Highway 525 two miles south of Mukilteo. ∝

Appropriately, an aerial view of the Boeing Aircraft plant.

S **tate Highway 527** from a junction with State Highway 522 in Bothell north to a junction with Interstate 5. Route length: 12 miles.

In the quest for some elbow room, residents from the state's heavily populated regions continue to migrate to the woods enclosing Highway 527 (Bothell Highway), a reasonable commute to Seattle. Development in communities such as Thrashers Corner, Mill Creek and Murphys Corner is rapid and changing the face of the once-rural landscape. ∝

S **tate Highway 528** from a junction with Interstate 5 in Marysville east to a junction with State Highway 9. Route length: three miles.

A quick country road connection covering the green fields between I-5 and Highway 9. ∝

529 S tate Highway 529 from a junction with Interstate 5 in Everett, west then north to rejoin I-5. Route length: six miles.

Highway 529 breaks off from the interstate and tours Everett (I-5) via West Marine View Drive, a vibrant waterfront stretch that peruses the Port of Everett. The port contains a pleasant mix of old and new; retired lumber mills and venerable fishing boats are interspersed with yachts and modern shipyards and dwarfed by cruisers from the naval base. The road continues beneath a ridgeline dotted with substantial homes built for turn-of-the-century lumber barons, and crosses the Snohomish River and Steamboat Slough on its return to I-5. ∞

530 S tate Highway 530 from a junction with Interstate 5 east through Arlington and Darrington, then north to a junction with State Highway 20 in Rockport. Route length: 51 miles.

Highway 530 moves east through Arlington (State Highway 9), and then past the blink-and-miss communities of Oso, Halterman, Rowan and Hazel. Oso, the largest of these rural communities, is announced by a combination post office and store and a small fistful of homes.

The highway meanders alongside the Stillaguamish River, famed for its steelhead fishing, east then north towards the Cascades and the logging community of **Darrington** (Elevation 527, Population 1,085), planted beneath the rugged peaks of Whitehorse, Three Fingers and Whitechuck mountains. The town was an early meeting and berry-gathering place for many Indian tribes. Today it is a major access point to the Glacier Peaks Wilderness Area and the Mountain Loop Highway that runs through Darrington and the Sauk River Valley. It takes little imagination to conjure up the scenes of long ago where at the King Tut Hall "husky loggers and their woman-folk view movies, dance to mountain music and hold their social affairs."

Highway 530 leaves Darrington and follows the Sauk River north for about 20 miles to join Highway 20 at Rockport. ∞

Lake Goodwin, Wenberg State Park on Highway 531.

S tate **Highway 531** from an intersection with Interstate 5, west to Lake Goodwin and east through Edgecomb to a junction with State Highway 9. Route length: 10 miles.

Heading west from I-5, Highway 531 (172nd Street NW) moves into a sparsely populated area due north of the Tulalip Indian Reservation, past Lake Ki and scattered farmhouses. Bending south onto East Lake Goodwin Road, travel the length of **Lake Goodwin** to **Wenberg State Park**. Tucked among the trees at the southern end of the lake, the family-oriented park and campground is generally packed during the summer. The lake is especially popular for water-skiing and trout fishing.

The eastern segment of 531 leads through **Edgecomb**, once an active logging community with the arrival of the Seattle, Lake Shore & Eastern Railroad in 1889, and continues three miles to a connection with Highway 9, just south of Arlington. ⌇

S tate **Highway 532** from a junction with Interstate 5 west via Stanwood to Camano Island. Route length: 10 miles.

Moving west from I-5, the briny smell of the sea leads to East Stanwood and a bluff overlooking the tideflats and farmlands of **Stanwood** (Elevation 101, Population 2,250). Now incorporated as one city, these communities were once separate entities split by the whim of the railroad. Begun as a trading post in 1866 by Robert Fulton, Stanwood, despite its stability, did not secure a rail link that arrived at the turn of the century. Instead, a train depot was built outside of the existing town, and East Stanwood sprang up around it to greet the locomotives and take advantage of the trade and transit opportunities. Not to be outdone by the new kid on the bluff, Stanwood created the

Pastoral Stanwood by the sea.

unofficial "world's shortest railroad," an independent line less than one mile long that connected them to the new community, and more importantly, the new line. Led by a "dinky," an old, run-down engine that sputtered and coughed through the center of town, the mini-railroad operated until 1938.

Two miles south of Stanwood, the **Stillaguamish River** drains into Port Susan, spawning a maze of sloughs and waterways that feed the surrounding farms. Bordering the farmland along the banks are swampy sections of tall reeds, grasses and cattails that provide habitat for aquatic birds that drift down from the **Skagit Wildlife Area** north of Stanwood. Stillaguamish means "river people," a reference to the tribe that inhabited the area.

Sediment left by thousands of years of consistent flooding by the Stillaguamish has translated into rich, fertile soil along the flats, but preparing the land for cultivation was no easy task. Early white settlers, mainly of Norwegian stock, found the region blanketed by salty marshlands, willow trees and an overwhelming frog population. Undaunted by the intensive labor needed to ready the land and encouraged by an unusually long growing season, the homesteaders filled in the tideflats, dug irrigation ditches and removed trees to make room for pea patches and dairy farms in the 1870s and 1880s. The back-breaking process required years and plenty of patience, but settlers survived by selling the removed timber to mills until tilling could begin. Logging continues to a lesser extent today; forest edges are trimmed to accommodate growing farms and to stretch grazing space for sheep, cattle and llamas. A large food processing plant towers over the other buildings in town, providing an economic boost to farming.

Three miles west of Stanwood, cross the General Mark W. Clark Bridge over Davis Slough to reach **Camano Island** (Kuh-MAY-noh). This slim waterway separates the island from the mainland by only a quarter-mile, but once aboard the crescent-shaped isle the distance seems greater. Isolated, sparsely populated and devoid of anything resembling a tourist trap, Camano Island attracts boaters, clam-diggers and beach combers in the summer, but manages to preserve the solitude treasured by locals.

On the southwestern tip, **Camano Island State Park** faces Whidbey Island to the west and the jagged Olympic Mountains. On the island's east side, Cavalero Park and boat launch confront the Cascades and the foothills of the mainland. Highway 532 ends at the intersection of East Camano Drive and North Camano Drive. ⌘

An old abandoned dream on Highway 534.

S **tate Highway 534** from a junction with Interstate 5 east to a junction with State Highway 9 at Lake McMurray. Route length: five miles.

Though it does not venture far from I-5, the highway quickly leaves the traffic behind and assumes the feel of a country road as it

heads east towards the foothills of the Cascade Mountains. After passing a rural elementary school and sportsman access to fishing and boating at Sixteen Lake, the winding road dives into the forest. Farm houses and weathered barns are tucked in among the timber, surrounded by acres of tilled soil and groves of fruit trees. The recent construction of townhome development proves that suburban sprawl can reach even the most remote areas.

The highway ends at the shore of Lake McMurray and a connection with Highway 9. ભ

A calm day at Lake McMurray.

S **tate Highway 536** from a junction with Interstate 5 in Mount Vernon northwest to a junction with State Highway 20 in Fredonia. Route length: four miles.

A light traffic shortcut from Mount Vernon to Highway 20 that presents views of green fields and farmsteads while bypassing the I-5 connection. ભ

S **tate Highway 538** from a junction with Interstate 5 north of Mount Vernon east to a junction with State Highway 9. Route length: three miles.

The shortest and easiest route from Mount Vernon to Highway 9, with vivid farmland scenery to boot. ભ

S **tate Highway 539** from a junction with Interstate 5 north via Lynden to the Canadian boundary. Route length: 15 miles.

Driving due north from Bellingham, the highway rolls into the wide Nooksack Valley past hayfields, farmsteads and isolated sideroads leading to small, unincorporated communities. Two miles north of Wiser Lake, follow Trump Road east to reach the dairying community of **Lynden** (Elevation 95, Population 6,480). When Holden and Phoebe Judson journeyed to this flat, largely unsettled valley in

1869, they discovered a muddy woodland overrun with thicket and a large river choked with downed timber and debris. These were not the easiest of living conditions, but the raw materials for cultivation were available, so the couple made the rustic setting home. Phoebe was impressed enough to name the fledgling town after her favorite poem, "Hohenlinden" by Thomas Campbell, which begins:

Lynden is a major red-raspberry producer.

"On Linden, when the sun was low . . ." The "y" was substituted to enhance the poetic appearance of the spelling.

The Campbells were not alone in the wilderness for long. Over the next decade, settlers trickled north to claim land and make a living off of the rich resources. Sawmills cut a profit on the downed trees and transportation along the Nooksack River was secured when a long-standing logjam was cleared south of town. Previously, no vessel larger than a canoe was able to negotiate around the wooden deadlock. As fruitful farmland replaced the thick stands of Douglar fir and cedar, word of available land spread like wildfire. Many Northwest inhabitants answered the call, but the greatest response came from across the Atlantic in Holland.

Windmills reflect Lynden's Dutch influence.

Beginning at the turn of the century, teams of Dutch immigrants rode the Nooksack River from Bellingham Bay or caravaned overland from Seattle to claim sites and till the earth in the cool, moist clime reminiscent of their homeland. A barrage of letters mailed home to Holland inspired others to come to Washington and take advantage of land opportunities. Soon after the influx of new residents arrived, fields of tulips, high-arched barns and four churches turned a small corner of the Nooksack Valley into a genuine Dutch village. A large windmill has since been built downtown to complete the feel. To celebrate this heritage, the **Holland Days** festival is held each May. The **Lynden Pioneer Museum** (Third and Front Street) also highlights the area's Dutch influence and houses a variety of antique tools, buggies, restored vehicles and photographs.

In addition to logging, dairy and poultry farms and tulip bulb cultivation became the principle money-makers of early Lynden. The same is true today with the exception of the tulips; the Skagit Valley managed to corner this colorful market, but they are still a favorite in the yards around town. Lynden is a major contributor to the state's red-raspberry production, an industry in which Washington ranks first in the nation. Potatoes and other berries are also among the current cash-crops.

Back on Highway 539, a four-mile stretch leads to a customs house on the U.S.-Canadian border. ☙

A breathtaking view of Mt. Baker - except, perhaps, to cattle.

State **Highway 542** from Bellingham northeast to Mt. Baker. Route length: 62 miles.

Southeast of Bellingham, **Mt. Baker** rises prominently above the wooded foothills of the North Cascades. Winding through a tight forest, past mud flats and wildflowers and along the North Fork of the Nooksack River, Highway 542 (Mt. Baker Scenic Byway) climbs steadily eastward towards the dormant volcano. Turnouts along the route, especially one at milepost 41 that leads to the 100-foot Nooksack Falls, provide spectacular viewpoints. The Nooksack Indians call Mt. Baker *Koma-Kulshan*, meaning "white, shining mountain," for the sparkling effect the sunlight has on the 12 glaciers and 44 square miles of ice fields that surround the peak. The present name was coined by Captain George Vancouver for Lieutenant Joseph Baker, who spied the summit from the deck of the *Discovery*.

Mt. Baker commonly belches up clouds of steam from its crater, but when plumes of ash and smoke blew skyward in March of 1975, local residents eyed the mountain nervously. Not since 1880 had any significant activity been recorded, and these sudden rumblings brought geologists scurrying. After numerous tests and assessments ranging from the apocalyptic to the conservative, the mountain cooled off and returned to its old steaming self. Though only a false alarm, the brief display of power served as a reminder that the mountain is still a volcano, even if declared dormant.

The land surrounding the mountain remained remarkably free of human exploitation until a rich gold lode was discovered around the glaciers in 1897. Soon after, logging companies moved in to cut trees in preparation for a railroad to carry the deposits out. The trails cleared by the railroad became the foundation for what would later become the highway.

In an attempt to halt the logging and mining operations, a group of local conservationists created the Mt. Baker Club around 1910. Working to place the forest under the protective wing of national park status, the club organized the Mt. Baker Marathon in 1911 as a publicity stunt to get the attention of the federal government. The race they created was a grueling 118-mile event that makes modern triathlons look like a walk in the park.

Starting in Bellingham, participants had the choice to travel either by train or car to a designated spot where they would begin the trek to the summit. From there, they would dash up the wooded, snow-packed slopes, check in with race officials at the top, then slip, slide and tumble their way back down the precarious incline like drunken mountain goats. The train left as soon as the first athlete boarded, giving a distinct advantage to the leader. The rest were left to hitch a ride by car, horse or any other method available in order to get back to Bellingham and the finish line. The winner received nothing more than wide recognition for his daring exploit and athletic ability. The standing record for the marathon is 9 hours and 34 minutes, set by Paul Westerlund in 1913. The race was canceled the same year when one participant fell into a crevasse and nearly died.

The spirit, though not the severity, of the race was reincarnated in 1973 as the annual **Ski to Sea Race**. This tamer version, now a relay, has grown into a local institution designed to highlight the various outdoor activities offered in the area. The Ski to Sea Race is 82 miles long and has seven different legs: cross-country skiing, downhill skiing, running, road biking, canoeing, mountain biking and sea kayaking. Parades and festivals are held before and after the race, attracting people from all over the Puget Sound.

The final 10 miles of the highway cut along a series of switchbacks and access the Mt. Baker Ski Area before opening up to reveal Heather Meadows and spectacular views of the glaciers, Mt. Baker and the jagged peaks of Mt. Shukan to the east. Heather Meadows was a popular vacation spot in the 1920s when a first-rate lodge was erected that contained over 100 rooms and plush accommodations. A fire burned much of the lodge in 1931, ending a luxurious era.

During the late 1930s, Civilian Conservation Corps and Forest Service crews saved what remained of the resort and turned it into the **Heather Meadows Visitor Center**. They also constructed the original trail system and several campgrounds in the area. Open only in the summer, the visitor center highlights the natural and cultural history of the Mt. Baker Wilderness Area.

Highway 542 ends at Artist Point, a 5,140-foot viewpoint with access to hiking trails leading into the Mt. Baker Wilderness. ⌀

S **tate Highway 544** from a junction with Highway 539 east then northeast through Everson to a junction with State Highway 9. Route length: nine miles.

Swinging east through the hayfields and berry farms that cover much of the Nooksack Valley, the road then veers northeast through the old sawmill town of Strandell and across the Nooksack River to **Everson** (Elevation 85, Population 1,685). This quiet hamlet was first settled in 1871 after serving as a thoroughfare for miners heading to the Fraser River during the gold boom of 1858. The town takes its name from Ever Everson who was believed to be the first white homesteader north of the Nooksack River.

The road ends at a connection with Highway 9. ⌀

S **tate Highway 546** from a junction with State Highway 539 east to a junction with State Highway 9. Route length: nine miles.

With Mount Baker looming large to the southeast, the bucolic highway shoots across the Nooksack Valley towards the foothills of the Cascade Mountains. Farmsteads, barns, supply stores and grazing livestock are indications of what most folks do for a living around these parts. Patches of trees provide contrast to the otherwise flat landscape, growing thicker with each mile until the road connects with Highway 9 south of Sumas. ⌀

Mt. Baker looming large.

415~

S tate **Highway 548** from a junction with Interstate 5 west to Birch Bay, north to rejoin I-5. Route length: 14 miles.

Heading due west from I-5, Highway 548 leads to **Birch Bay** and a small resort community overlooking the water. Captain George Vancouver anchored in this calm bay for five days in June of 1792 while conducting exploratory missions of the coastline. The ample birch trees along the bluffs gave him the inspiration for the name. Advertised as "the warmest, safest, saltwater beach on the Northwest Pacific Coast," the area is a popular family vacation and summer home spot. Easily accessible from the highway is **Birch Bay State Park**, located on the southern end of the bay (go west on Bay Road and follow the signs). Sandy beaches, hiking trails and a marshland bird sanctuary are among the attractions.

After the highway bends north, it crosses the mouth of California Creek where it drains into Drayton Harbor. Past the bridge, follow the scenic Drayton Harbor Road west along the water to reach **Semiahmoo Spit** (Seh-mee-ah-moo). This thin finger of land was once the location of a cannery where boats from Alaska unloaded their hauls of sockeye and king salmon. What began as a small operation turned mighty when the Alaska Packers Association bought the cannery, modernized it, and made the safe, enclosed harbor a stopover for their fleet. The old buildings have since been converted into a museum featuring a history on the fishing industry, and a gallery that highlights local artists. A golf course and resort occupy the tip of the spit.

Highway 548 connects with I-5 south of Blaine. ⌘

S tate **Highway 702** from a junction with State Highway 507 in McKenna east to a junction with State Highway 7. Route length: nine miles.

Mt. Rainier.

If the hordes of cattle found along both sides of Highway 702 weren't so preoccupied with the rich prairie grass beneath them, they would enjoy the large view of Mt. Rainier that looms ahead. For a closer look at the mountain turn south onto Highway 7 to State Highway 706, the road to Mt. Rainier. Another option is to continue straight through the stoplight on 352nd Avenue to State Highway 161, a short, scenic wooded drive. North on Highway 7 will transport you to Tacoma. ⌘

Interstate 705 from a junction with Interstate 5 north to a junction with State Highway 509 in Tacoma. Route length: one mile.

This short highway is designated as an interstate but should be called Intercity 705. Starting from I-5 just west of the Tacoma Dome, I-705 approaches Tacoma (I-5) from the waterfront, passing the federal courthouse along the way. ෙ

Erector-set-like-dinosaurs guarding Tacoma Harbor.

State Highway 706 from a junction with State Highway 7 east to Mt. Rainier National Park. Route length: 14 miles.

You can be near **Mt. Rainier** (Elevation 14,411) for weeks at a time and never catch a glimpse of it, but when clouds clear and the sun breaks, the sight of the massive snow-covered mountain against a bright blue sky is incredible. This highway's proximity to the

Reflection Lakes south of Mt. Rainier's Mazama Ridge.

417~

mountain provides stunning views but unfortunately the road is usually packed with sight seekers. Try spring or late fall to avoid the crowds.

As the face of the mountain constantly changes, depending on weather, season, and time of day, so does the mountain's interior. Its inner rumblings remind us it is a mountain whose story is still being told.

Mt. Rainier — originally called *Tahoma* (White Mountain) by the Nisqually Indians — is a dormant volcano, part of the so-called "Ring of Fire" of volcanic ranges that dot the Pacific Ocean. The 1980 eruption of Mt. St. Helens, located about 50 miles southwest of Mt. Rainier, and the 1991 eruption of Mt. Pinatubo in the Philippines demonstrate the volatile nature of the Ring of Fire.

Mt. Rainier is the fourth highest peak in the United States — behind Mt. McKinley in Alaska (Elevation 20,320), Mt. Whitney in California (Elevation 14,494) and Mt. Elbert in Colorado (Elevation 14,433) — and the highest volcanic peak in the Cascades, a range that stretches from Mt. Garibaldi in British Columbia to Lassen Peak in northern California. The mountain wasn't formed in a single, cataclysmic event, but rather as a result of years of volcanic activity. It is a composite volcano, or stratovolcano, made from sluggish, intermittent lava flows and explosive eruptions of ash and rock.

Beginning about 122 million years ago, magma from the earth's core built layers of rock below the surface. About one million years ago, fiery forces thrust molten lava through a weak split in the earth's crust. Rock and pumice spewed out violently, building a volcanic cone. Mt. Rainier grew to an estimated 16,000 feet above sea level.

Then about 5,800 years ago, the smoldering fires inside Mt. Rainier erupted, and the mountain literally blew its top. Gone was 2,000 feet of the summit, leaving an east-facing depression nearly two miles in diameter. Tons of rock, mud, and debris rolled down the peak's northeast flank. A wall of mud 100 feet high cascaded like a river of wet cement across 125 square miles, ending in the waters of Puget Sound.

This mud slide created the Osceloa Mudflow. The towns of Kent, Sumner, Auburn, and Puyallup are built on top of the flow. The remains of the older, higher cone are seen in Liberty Cap and Point Success. The two craters overlap at Columbia Crest, the mountain's summit.

A small eruption occurred about 150 years ago and the mountain may continue to spew ash and steam intermittently during the next century, causing small floods and mudflows. But only time will tell if Mt. Rainier will erupt again or be eroded away by the actions of ice, water, and wind.

For thousands of years, the Taidnapam, Upper Cowlitz, Yakima, Nisqually, and Puyallup tribes lived in the foothills of this majestic mountain they called Tahoma. They fished, hunted, and gathered

Mt. Rainier, Nisqually Glacier.

berries and herbs on its lower slopes. But because of the great reverence and awe the indigenous peoples felt for the mountain — or perhaps as a function of their sensible fear of the unpredictable and dangerous weather that occurs at its upper altitudes — they never ventured near the summit.

The first white man to explore what is now **Mt. Rainier National Park** was a young Scotsman named William Fraser Tolmie. He and five Indian guides mounted an expedition in 1833 in order to gather some needed medicinal herbs. Twenty-four years later, Army Lieutenant August Valentia Kautz, with the help of a Nisqually guide named Wahpowety, had to turn back only 400 feet from the summit, but nevertheless proved that such an ascent would be possible.

The first well-documented attempt to reach the top of Mt. Rainier was made in 1870 by General Hazard Stevens (Civil War hero) and Philemon Van Trump (the private secretary to the territorial governor). They were guided to the lower slopes by James Longmire who, in the late 1850s, had established the rough-hewn Packwood Trail from the Pacific coast to Mt. Rainier. A Yakima tribesman named Sluiskin agreed to take the two adventurers to the timberline, but not before issuing them a sober and poetic warning: "Your plan to climb Tahoma is all foolishness. At first the way is easy . . . but if you reach the great snowy dome, then a bitterly cold and furious tempest will sweep you off into space like a withered leaf." After barely surviving a freezing, stormy night on the summit, the adventurers made it back to their base camp, where Sluiskin — joyous that they were still alive —

embraced them and cried, "Skookum tillicum! Skookum Tantum!" ("Strong men! Brave hearts!")

Thirteen years later (1883), Von Trump returned to the summit, this time with the 63-year-old trailblazer and guide, Longmire. On the trip, Longmire's horse wandered away from camp, eventually holing up at a mineral spring on Mt. Rainier's south side. When Longmire finally found his horse, he decided then and there to return to the idyllic spot one day. In 1884, he and his wife did just that, eventually building Mt. Rainier's first hotel, the Mineral Springs Resort, on the site.

In 1890, Fay Fuller, a teacher from a small town near Olympia, became the first woman to reach Rainier's summit. The accomplishment is all the more impressive when one considers her climbing apparel: She was wearing a sun hat, a long woolen skirt, and shoes with nails driven through the soles for traction!

The largest climbing party to ever tackle Mt. Rainier set out from Portland in 1897. With over 200 participants, 45 tents, 4 tons of supplies, 2 head of beef, 7 milk cows, and many horses, it's amazing any of them ever reached the mountain itself. Fifty-eight of the party eventually made it to the top, where a celebratory fireworks display was greatly enjoyed in Tacoma, 55 miles to the northwest.

The first climbing fatality was recorded that same year. Since that time, there have been over 50 lives lost. But the thousands of climbers who have made it to the summit (in 1990 alone there were 4,534!) — as well as the many thousands of others who simply enjoy the views, vegetation, animal life, and 300 miles of hiking trails — would probably agree with John Muir's assessment: "Of all the fire mountains which, like beacons, once blazed along the Pacific coast, Mt. Rainier is the noblest." ∝

US Highway 730 from a junction with U.S. Highway 12 south to the Washington-Idaho border. Route length: six miles. The road starts at Wallula Gap (U.S. Highway 12) and follows the Columbia River a short distance before entering Oregon. ∝

State Route 821 from a junction with U.S. Highway 97 and Interstate 82 north along the Yakima River to a junction with Interstate 90. Route length: 27 miles.

Highway 821 (Canyon Road) is a beautiful alternative to U.S. 97 and I-82. If your itinerary requires traveling between Yakima and Ellensburg, consider taking this twisting canyon route along the Yakima River. Steep, multi-colored cliffs of sage and exposed basalt lead to green cottonwoods and aspen sustained by the river. Drive the road early in the day or late in the evening when the element of shadow varies the scenery.

The road begins just north of Yakima and Selah at a railroad station called **Pomona**. Pomona's name, for the Roman patroness of gardens and fruits, is justified by an occasional orchard. Farms succumb to rolling sagebrush hills leading to the steep Umtanum and Manastash ridges.

Stop for lunch at the **Squaw Creek Recreation Area** and then investigate the **Roza Dam**. The **Roza Irrigation Project** began in 1918 when extensive research was conducted by a board of engineers. In 1935, President Franklin D. Roosevelt, renowned for his support of Washington projects, allocated $5,000,000 to develop a system that would irrigate 72,000 acres of desert land in the Yakima Valley. The water flows southwest through 90 miles of canals, ditches, flumes and tunnels mostly built in 1941.

Roosevelt is not the only politician associated with the Yakima River Canyon. In

Twenty-inch rainbow and cutthroat trout watch construction of a new railroad bridge across the placid Yakima River.

the 1960s, a local group of concerned citizens invited Supreme Court Justice William O. Douglas to float the river. Douglas, a Yakima native known for being an outdoorsman and environmental activist, did not need much prodding to secure the area as a recreation preserve and scenic route.

Activities abound on the placid Yakima River. Rafters find relief from the summertime heat (there are a number of start and take-out points including those at Roza Dam, and the Squaw Creek and Umtanum access areas). Twenty-inch rainbow and cutthroat trout draw fly fisherman from west of the Cascades who consider the river some of the finest trout waters in the state. Numerous pullouts make for great picnic sites or photo opportunities. Eagles are not an uncommon site, and the hills attract hunters in search of bird and deer.

After leaving the canyon near Thrall, it is possible to join U.S. 97 and I-82 or stay on Highway 821 which connects with I-90 west of Ellensburg. ❧

State Highway 823 from a junction with U.S. Highway 97 and Interstate 82 northwest through Selah to a junction with U.S. 97. Route length: five miles.

Selah (SEE-luh, Elevation 1,108, Population 5,110), is an Indian word for calm and peaceful, and descriptive of the stretch of the Yakima River flowing through this agricultural community. Credit for the name has been given to Paudosy, a missionary who considered the Indian meaning close to the biblical use of the word — pause and meditate.

Fruit-packing and cold-storage plants, acres of productive orchards, and the **Tree Top Company**, the largest apple juice producer in the world, are Selah's main interests. ⌘

State Highway 900 from a junction with Interstate 5 east through Renton, then north to a junction with Interstate 90 in Issaquah. (Overlaps Interstate 405.) Route length: 16 miles.

At present, this sylvan stretch of road passes through a region whose inhabitants hope to incorporate as Cedar County, indicative of a common tree found here. Once the domain of coal miners, the land is dotted with small-scale farms and logging operations. Shortly after

Morning shift at the Coal Creek mines.

leaving Renton, Highway 900 climbs into the Cascade foothills, flanked by Squak Mountain to the east, and providing a shortcut for those headed to Issaquah, I-90 and destinations east. ∞

S tate Highway 902 from a junction with U.S. Highway 395 northwest through Medical Lake to rejoin U.S. 395. Route length:12 miles.

The road accesses several lakes and travels through the town of **Medical Lake** (Elevation 2,420, Population 3,705) before returning to the main highway.

Medical Lake sprawls north and south besides a mile-long lake bearing the same name. The lake's salty waters, a sodium bicarbonate solution, have historically been thought to possess medicinal properties. Indians believed swimming in the lake would cure rheumatism. In 1856, Andrew LeFevre was hauling supplies to Fort Colville and when searching for some lost ponies stumbled upon the lake. He homesteaded there in 1872 and called it "lac de medicine," after finding that bathing in the water greatly relieved his rheumatism. More white settlers discovered the lake's healing powers in the 1870s and by 1889, informal health facilities blossomed. Allen's Sanatorium advertised: "We can cure you of rheumatism, skin diseases, stomach and kidney trouble by the use of Medical Lake Mud and Water Baths, each mud bath consists of steam bath, hot fresh mud bath, shower, blanket pack and massage." Health seekers rode the 15-mile Washington Water Power electric train to bathe in the water and wallow in the mud.

To compliment the lake's therapeutical attractions, two dance halls and resorts (Coney Island Pavilion and Boathouse, Camp Comfort and Stanley Park) were established and soon Medical Lake was one of the state's premier resorts. Camp Comfort was the only resort in the state licensed to have dances on Saturday night. On one hot summer day so many people came on horseback that there were not enough trees to tie the horses to.

Englishman Lord Stanley Hallett, Medical Lake's first mayor, developed Stanley Park. His daughter took the electric train to school in Spokane and on Friday nights would bring home about 20 of her female classmates. The next day the boys would come for dances in the third floor ballroom. Hallett's house (on Lake and Stanley), called "the Castle," is said to resemble the English crown. The unique, baronial house has been converted to apartments.

Hallet also helped create the Eastern Washington Hospital for the Insane, located on the east shore of the lake. The hospital was later moved and called the "School for the Feeble Minded." At that time mental illness was considered incurable and subsequently patients, committed involuntarily, were treated like inmates. ∞

State Highway 903 from a junction with Interstate 90 at Cle Elum northwest through Roslyn and Ronald to Cle Elum Lake. Route length: 10 miles.

Roslyn (Elevation 2,222, Population 885) was named by the general manager of the Northern Pacific Coal Company for his girlfriend's hometown — Roslyn, New York. The town has recently gained popularity as the outdoor set for the fictional town of Cicely, Alaska on television's *Northern Exposure*. Fans will recognize Dr. Fleischman's office, Chris' radio station, the Roslyn Cafe mural of the camel and palm tree, the local drug store which doubles as Ruth Anne's general store, and Cicely's main watering hole, the Brick.

Roslyn Cafe mural of camel and palm trees.

Vast coal fields underlie what was once the most productive coal mining town in the state. After the Northern Pacific Railroad discovered the quality and abundance of the area's coal, they proceeded to purchase most of the land, built lines connecting to major routes, and platted a town. In 1892, Roslyn produced 1,039,870 tons of coal, more than any mine in the state. The next year, at the Chicago World's Fair, a 25-ton block of Roslyn coal was displayed, the largest ever cut at that time.

After the railroad began mining in 1886, with approximately 500 laborers, life in Roslyn was disturbed periodically by industrial strife and tragic disasters. Forty-five men were killed in a mine explosion in May 1892; in a second explosion in October 1909, ten miners were killed. By the late 1800s, Washington had the dubious distinction of leading the country in mining fatalities.

In 1888, poor working conditions prompted the Knights of Labor to organize a strike. Northern Pacific responded by recruiting a Black work force; the first significant immigration of blacks into the state. Initially, labor and racial tensions were high, but they eventually mellowed, and for a while the town observed Emancipation Day every August 4th and Seven Hour Day on the first of April each year.

In addition to the large influx of Blacks, a melting pot of immigrants from places like Italy, China, Austria, Norway, Germany, Russia, Hungary, Scotland and Syria came to work the mines. Evidence of Roslyn's ethnic diversity is scattered over the pine-covered hillside cemeteries off Fifth Street along Memorial Way. The cemeteries are divided by nationality, religion or fraternal orders into 26 separate plots.

The immigrants brought with them Old-World traditions. A courtship custom among the Croats and Slavs decreed that when a man wished to propose, he would take a group of friends to the woman's house and there, on bended knees, make his proposal. If rejected, he bought a keg of beer for the crew to drink away their sorrows; if accepted, his friends would pay the wedding fees.

Drinking was common recreation among the thirsty, mostly-bachelor miners; at one time Roslyn accommodated 23 saloons. Built of lo-

Pizza and ice cream Roslyn style.

cal sandstone in 1889, the **Brick Tavern** (Pennsylvania and First) features a 20-foot long running water trough which is used as a giant spittoon. One block north of the Brick is the **Office Tavern** (Washington and First), formerly the site of the Ben Snipes Bank, Roslyn's first bank. In 1892, the bank was allegedly robbed by Butch Cassidy and the Sundance Kid Gang.

Head west on Highway 903 two miles to **Ronald**, once a mining camp at the site of the old Number Three mine. The mine furnished coal to trains crossing the Cascades and was operated by a 400-man Italian crew.

Just past Ronald, the highway ends at eight-mile-long **Cle Elum Lake**, which provides local irrigation. The dam at the south end of the lake was built in 1933.

According to Indian legend, Cle Elum Lake was the habitat of Wishpoosh, an important figure in the state's mythical history. Wishpoosh was an enormous beaver who roamed the earth destroy-

Cicely, Alaska or Roslyn, Washington?

ing lesser creatures. Speelyia, the Coyote-god, challenged Wishpoosh to combat, and during the struggle that followed, Wishpoosh tore out the banks of the Keechelus, sending most of the water rushing down the canyon, creating many lakes in the Yakima Valley. The greatest lake of all, backed up by the Umatilla Highlands and the Cascades, finally broke through the mountains and created the Columbia River. Wishpoosh was washed into the ocean, where he devoured whales and fish, until Speelyia, transforming himself into a floating branch, drifted down the river and into Wishpoosh's mouth. Once inside, Speelyia resumed his former shape and size and with his knife-edged teeth slew the belligerent beaver. He then divided the carcass of Wishpoosh and from it formed Indian tribes.

Salmon La Sac Road continues along the lake's eastern edge three miles north to **Salmon La Sac**, a giant pothole in the Cle Elum River. The hole was an historic Indian fishing spot named by early French-Canadian fur traders who observed Indians using sack-like baskets woven of cedar bark to catch salmon. *Sac* is the French word for "bag" or "sack."

By the 1890s, French investors had become interested in the Cle Elum Mining District. Hoping to make a profit by transporting a variety of valuable ores, they built a train depot at Salmon La Sac but abandoned it when war threatened in Europe. The log structure is empty now, but served as a ranger station for most of this century. ᢗ

State Highway 904 from a junction with U.S. Highway 395 north through Cheney to rejoin U.S. 395. Route length: 17 miles. **Cheney** (CHEE-nee, Elevation 2,340, Population 7,870) began as "Section 13," a plot of land open for settlement. Later the name was changed to *Willow Springs* and then *Depot Springs* with the arrival of the railway. When Depot Springs lost out to Spokane Falls as the seat of Spokane County, citizens decided to concentrate their efforts in attaining an academy and appealed to a wealthy director of the Northern Pacific for help. Benjamin P. Cheney of Boston donated $10,000 for the budding school and the town was renamed, once again, in his honor.

Benjamin P. Cheney Academy opened its doors in 1882 to 200 students. In 1890, it became the State Normal School at Cheney with "the purpose of instruction of persons, both male and female on the art of teaching the various branches that pertain to a good common school." It was designated Eastern Washington College of Education in 1937, Eastern Washington State College in 1961, and in 1977, **Eastern Washington University**.

Cheney is surrounded by quiet residential neighborhoods; terraced streets climb softly scalloped hillsides leading to the university. Besides education, agriculture is Cheney's mainstay. A large flour mill (First Street) owned by Clarence Martin, Washington's governor in 1932, was once the most productive in the state. Also of interest is the 1907 **Washington Water Power Company** railroad depot (Second and College). For years an electric interurban line connected Cheney with Medical Lake and Spokane and served as a popular mode of travel until the automobile cut into its business.

EWU students on campus. Perusing a copy of Washington for the Curious, *no doubt.*

South of Cheney is the **Turnbull National Wildlife Refuge** spreading over 15,500 acres of small lakes, ponds and sloughs. The refuge is home for white-tailed deer, coyotes, beaver, raccoons, muskrats and mink, and nesting grounds for redheads and other diving ducks. Up to 50,000 ducks, geese and various migratory birds visit in the fall. The refuge is accessible via Cheney-Spangle Road or Cheney-Plaza Road. ∽

S tate **Highway 906** from a junction with Interstate 90 at Snoqualmie Pass southeast to rejoin I-90. Route length: two miles.

Highway 906 accesses four downhill ski resorts, miles of Nordic ski terrain and the **Alpine Lakes Wilderness**, an area covering 306,000 acres and filled with trails, wildlife, lakes and streams. Its proximity to Seattle and number of recreational opportunities makes Snoqualmie Pass (I-90) a popular destination. To alleviate overcrowding, permits are required to hike in the wilderness area. ☙

A wild white roar bursts from the tranquil green of the Alpine Lakes Wilderness.

S tate **Highway 908** from Kirkland east to a junction with State Highway 520 in Redmond. Route length: three miles.

Highway 908 climbs and descends the hillock between sister cities Kirkland (Interstate 405) and Redmond (Highway 520). ☙

S tate **Highway 970** from Cle Elum east to a junction with U.S. Highway 97. Route length: seven miles.

Highway 970 connects Cle Elum to U.S. 97, which leads north to U.S. Highway 2, Leavenworth and Wenatchee. ☙

S tate **Highway 971** from a junction with U.S. Highway 97A in Winesap north to Lake Chelan then east to rejoin U.S. 97A. Route length: 13 miles.

Highway 971 follows the Navarre Coulee seven miles to Lake Chelan State Park. The road then covers Lake Chelan's (U.S. 97A) south shore and arrives in the town of Chelan six miles further. ☙

Index

PHOTO CREDITS

RECOMMENDED READING

————ed. *Year By Year: 75 Years of Boeing History, 1916-1991*. Seattle: Boeing Historical Archives, 1991.

Alt, David D., and Donald W. Hyndman. *Roadside Geology of Washington*. Missoula: Mountain Press Publishing Company, 1984.

Andrews, Ralph W. *This Was Logging*. West Chester: Schiffer Publishing, Ltd., 1984.

Brewster, David, and David M. Buerge, eds. *Washingtonians: A Biographical Portrait of the State*. Seattle: Sasquatch Books, 1988.

Callander-Hedtke, Patricia, and John V. Hedtke. *Washington Trivia*. Nashville: Rutledge Hill Press, 1991.

Clements, John. *Washington Facts: A Comprehensive Look at Washington Today*. Dallas: Clements Research II, Inc., 1989.

DeVoto, Bernard, ed. *The Journals of Lewis and Clark*. Boston: Houghton Mifflin Company, 1953.

Ficken, Robert E., and Charles P. LeWarne. *Washington: A Centennial History*. Seattle: University of Washington Press, 1988.

Hitchman, Robert. *Place Names of Washington*. Tacoma: Washington State Historical Society, 1985.

Kirk, Ruth, and Carmela Alexander. *Exploring Washington's Past: A Road Guide to History*. Seattle: University of Washington Press, 1990.

McLean, Duse. *The Pocket Guide to Seattle*. Bellevue: Thistle Press, 1994.

Mueller, Marge. *The San Juan Islands: Afoot & Afloat*. Seattle: The Mountaineers, 1979.

Mueller, Marge, and Mueller, Ted. *Washington State Parks: A Complete Recreation Guide*. Seattle: The Mountaineers, 1993.

National Geographic Society Book Division. *National Geographic's Guide to Scenic Highways and Byways*. Washington D.C.: National Geographic Society, 1995.

Phillips, James W. *Washington State Place Names*. Seattle: University of Washington Press, 1971.

Powell, Jay, and Vickie Jensen. *Quileute: An Introduction to the Indians of La Push*. Seattle: University of Washington Press, 1976.

Satterfield, Archie. *Country Roads of Washington*. Issaquah: Sammamish Press, 1989.

Schwantes, Carlos Arnaldo. *Hard Traveling: A Portrait of Work Life in the New Northwest*. Lincoln: University of Nebraska Press, 1994.

Scott, James W. and Roland L. DeLorme. *Historical Atlas of Washington*. Norman: University of Oklahoma Press, 1988.

Strickland, Ron. *Whistlepunks & Geoducks: Oral Histories from the Pacific Northwest*. New York: Paragon House, 1990.

Thollander, Earl. *Back Roads of Washington*. Seattle: Sasquatch Books, 1992.

Tuhy, John E. *Sam Hill: The Prince of Castle Nowhere*. Goldendale: Maryhill Museum of Art, 1991.

White, Sid, and S.E. Solberg, eds. *Peoples of Washington: Perspectives on Cultural Diversity*. Pullman: Washington State University Press, 1989.

Woodbridge, Sally B., and Roger Montgomery. *A Guide to Architecture in Washington State*. Seattle: University of Washington Press, 1980.

Yates, Charity, and Yates, Richard, eds. *1994 Washington State Yearbook*. Eugene: Public Sector Information, Inc., 1994.